WORKS ISSUED BY
THE HAKLUYT SOCIETY

VOYAGES TO HUDSON BAY
IN SEARCH OF A NORTHWEST PASSAGE
VOLUME I

SECOND SERIES
NO. 177

PLATE I.   Inscription on rocks at Sloop Cove, Churchill, the wintering place of
Captain Middleton's discovery vessels, 1741–2
(Photograph Provincial Archives of Manitoba)

Voyages to Hudson Bay
in Search of a Northwest Passage
1741–1747

VOLUME I

THE VOYAGE OF
CHRISTOPHER MIDDLETON 1741–1742

Edited by

WILLIAM BARR

and

GLYNDWR WILLIAMS

THE HAKLUYT SOCIETY
LONDON
1994

ISBN 0 904180 36 0
ISSN 0072 9396

Typeset by Waveney Typesetters, Norwich
Printed in Great Britain at
the University Press, Cambridge

Published by the Hakluyt Society
c/o The Map Library
British Library, Great Russell Street
London WC1B 3DG

CONTENTS

VOLUME I

Maps and Illustrations

PREFACE

The first European discovery of Hudson Bay remains veiled in obscurity. If the shadowy evidence of early maps can be trusted, Portuguese navigators may have sighted the entrance of Hudson Strait at the beginning of the sixteenth century, and it is just possible that Sebastian Cabot led an expedition through the ice-choked waters of the Strait and into Hudson Bay itself in 1508 or 1509. Cabot was searching for a navigable sea-route to Asia – the Northwest Passage of later generations – and for long the area was of interest to explorers only because it was thought to conceal the entrance to a way through to the Pacific. Support for the ventures came from government, merchants and nobles; for all were aware of the advantages which the discovery of a shorter trade route to the East would bring. From China, Japan and the East Indies would come goods by a quicker and cheaper route than the long haul around the Cape or overland to the Levant, and direct trade with those remote regions would open new markets to English manufactures.

After a vain search by English seamen in the reign of Elizabeth I for a passage farther north, Henry Hudson in 1610 crossed the 'furious overfall' at the entrance of Hudson Strait and sailed hundreds of miles westward into the great bay that has since borne his name. Whatever the reality or otherwise of earlier voyages into Hudson Bay, it was Hudson's voyage which established the fact and not merely the rumour of a great inland sea in the northern parts of the American continent. Reports from the survivors that they had encountered a strong flood tide from the west raised hopes that a route to the Pacific was there for the finding, and the next twenty years saw explorations of the Bay by Thomas Button (1612–13), William Baffin (1615), Jens Munk (1619), Luke Foxe (1631) and Thomas James (1631–2). As their surveys sketched and then closed the icebound western shores of the Bay, so enthusiasm dwindled and died.

Foxe, it is true, maintained that there were indications of a strait in the far northwest corner of Hudson Bay, but the years of costly failure had brought disillusionment to promoters at home.

Not until 1668 did another English vessel enter Hudson Bay, and although the captain of the *Nonsuch* was ordered 'to have in yor thoughts the discovery of the Passage into the South sea and to attempt it as occasion shall offer', the main purpose of the venture was to trade for furs. In 1670 the promoters were granted a charter, and the energies of the young Hudson's Bay Company were devoted almost entirely to developing the fur trade. To the Governor and Committee in London the matters of most concern were the supply of furs, the risks of the yearly voyages by the Company ships between England and Hudson Bay, and the danger of French competition and raids. Posts or 'factories' were established along the southern shores of Hudson Bay, but there was little exploration either inland or along the coast to the north-west. No attempt was made to renew the search for a Northwest Passage until the disastrous voyage of James Knight in 1719, fitted out by a reluctant Hudson's Bay Company. The loss of Knight and his crews, and the failure of trading voyages by Company sloops along the west coast of the Bay, put an end to this brief flurry of exploration. The North-west Passage seemed once again to have been consigned to the realms of nostalgic fantasy, but among those in the Company's employ at this time was one man at least, Christopher Middleton, who remained hopeful that a passage might yet be found. By a coincidence of events involving the Irish MP and promoter, Arthur Dobbs, Middleton twenty years later was to command an expedition in search of a passage, not in the service of the Hudson's Bay Company indeed, but in the name of the Crown.

Middleton's voyage of 1741–2 forms the centrepiece of Volume I of this work. Volume II, to be published separately, will deal with the subsequent voyage of William Moor in 1746–7. Together, the Middleton and Moor expeditions provide a story remarkable for its mixture of achievement and disappointment, ambition and intrigue. Their surveys resulted in the first reliable maps of the west coast of Hudson Bay, but the implications of the two expeditions went much further than this. The publicity surrounding the voyages opened to view a vast but little-known region of North America, threatened the very existence of the Hudson's Bay Company, and almost – but not quite – closed the door on all hopes that a navigable passage would be found through Hudson Bay.

We are grateful to various archives and libraries for permission to publish documents and maps in their possession: the Public Record Office, Kew (whose material is Crown Copyright, and is reproduced here with the permission of Her Majesty's Stationery Office); the Deputy Keeper of Records, the Public Record Office of Northern Ireland, and the National Trust Northern Ireland Committee (the Ward Papers); the Provincial Archives of Manitoba, Winnipeg (the Hudson's Bay Company Archives); the Trustees of the National Maritime Museum, Greenwich; the Ministry of Defence, Whitehall; the British Library. We are also glad to take this opportunity to thank various individuals for their help. Judith Beattie, Keeper of the Hudson's Bay Company Archives, and her predecessor Shirlee A. Smith, have greatly assisted the editors on their visits to Winnipeg. Ann Savours, then with the National Maritime Museum, generously made available a microfilm copy of Lieutenant John Rankin's log (ADM L/F/109). Derek Howse and Patricia Fara supplied expert knowledge on navigational matters and instruments, as did David Lyon on the plans of the *Furnace*. Andrew David drew our attention to the previously unknown manuscript map by Middleton in the Library of the Ministry of Defence. We are greatly indebted to Keith Bigelow and Derek Thompson of the Department of Geography at the University of Saskatchewan for drawing the maps. At Churchill in the summer of 1992 our trips to various locations, including Sloop Cove and the site of the 'Old Factory', were much helped by the boatmanship of Dave Rolston. Our visit to Churchill was made possible by the good offices of Bob Coutts (Parks Canada), and by a generous grant from the President's Social Sciences and Humanities Research Fund, University of Saskatchewan.

WILLIAM BARR
Department of Geography, University of Saskatchewan

GLYNDWR WILLIAMS
Department of History, Queen Mary and Westfield College, London

ABBREVIATIONS

Adm	Admiralty Records, Public Record Office
ADM	Admiralty Records, National Maritime Museum
HBC	Hudson's Bay Company Archives (Provincial Archives of Manitoba)
SP	State Papers, Public Record Office
Ward Papers	Papers of the Ward Family (Viscounts Bangor), Public Record Office of Northern Ireland

EDITORIAL NOTE

Dates prior to 1 January 1752 are given in Old Style (OS), with the year beginning on 25 March. For example, 10 February 1741 (OS) would be 10 February 1742 on a modern calendar.

Until 1805 nautical time differed from civil time in that the twenty-four hour day extended from noon to noon, not midnight to midnight. Thus, entries for 12 May in a seaman's log would cover the afternoon and evening of 11 May (civil time) and the morning of 12 May (civil time).

I

GENESIS OF THE VOYAGE

INTRODUCTION

The expedition of Christopher Middleton in 1741–2 to Hudson Bay in search of the Northwest Passage was ten years in the making. It represented, above all, the hopes and ambitions of Arthur Dobbs, an Ulster landowner, member of the Irish House of Commons, and (from 1733) Surveyor-General of Ireland. By 1730, when Dobbs was introduced to the prime minister, Sir Robert Walpole, with the commendation, 'He has for some time applied his thoughts...to the making of our colonies in America of more advantage than they have hitherto been',[1] he had extended his interest in Irish trade to that of the British colonies in North America. There he was disturbed by the growing threat of French encroachment and encirclement. It was in this context that his reading of the journals of the explorers of the continent convinced Dobbs that despite earlier failures the entrance of the Northwest Passage might yet be found in Hudson Bay. Its discovery and exploitation, he argued, would bring massive benefits to Britain's position in America and to her overseas trade generally. In 1731 he drafted a seventy-page memorial[2] expounding both the feasibility and commercial significance of a passage, and began to send copies to those persons of rank and influence who might support a venture to Hudson Bay.

The first section of the memorial contained an examination of the Arctic voyages of Elizabethan and early Stuart explorers in which Dobbs eliminated those regions where he considered that

---

[1] Desmond Clarke, *Arthur Dobbs Esquire 1689–1765 Surveyor-General of Ireland Prospector and Governor of North Carolina*, London, 1958, p. 32.
[2] Document 1 below, pp. 9–36.

there was no possibility of a passage. The route by way of Davis Strait and Baffin Bay (where in the nineteenth century the eastern entrance of the passage was finally located) was ruled out because the west coast of Baffin Bay was choked by ice, and also because Baffin in 1616 had not observed there any sign of a tide from the west. The voyages of Button (1612–13), Bylot (1615), Foxe (1631) and James (1631–2) seemed to show that there could be no passage either by way of Foxe Channel or along the west coast of Hudson Bay south of latitude 64°N. The only remaining possibility was the large opening in the northwest of the Bay – the depressing Ne Ultra of Button, the more buoyant Roe's Welcome of Foxe. There in about latitude 64°N some of Foxe's men had made a number of rather sketchy observations of the tide, which when taken together might be construed (though Foxe himself did not do so) as a tidal range of eighteen feet at neaps. In contrast, the general run of observations showed that from Hudson Strait westward to Cary's Swan's Nest at the southeast tip of Coats Island the tide fell away, as the distance from the ocean increased, to a mere six feet. Foxe's tide could only be explained, Dobbs argued, 'if we suppose a Western Ocean flowing in at a Streight nigh Ne Ultra into the Bay'.[1] Other evidence used by Dobbs to support his case was the location of whale sightings in Hudson Bay and the apparent anomaly of an open sea near Ne Ultra while that to the south was frozen; but tidal observations were the crux of the matter. Dobbs's explanations in the memorial are convoluted and relentlessly academic, and it is a relief to turn to the simpler elucidation of the significance of tides in a book written by one of his associates some years later.

'We may consider Hudson's-Bay, as a kind of Labyrinth, into which we enter on one side through Hudson's-Straits, and what we aim at, is to get out on the other side ... the Tide is a Kind of Clue, which seems to lead us by the Hand through all the Windings and Turnings of this Labyrinth, and if studiously and steadily followed must certainly lead us out.'[2]

---

[1] P. 24 below.

[2] Henry Ellis, *A Voyage to Hudson's Bay by the Dobbs Galley and California. In the Years 1746 and 1747, For Discovering a NorthWest Passage*, London, 1748, pp. 330–31.

Dobbs's reliance on tides followed established precedents, but his information came to him second-hand from published journals whose entries were sometimes garbled, and whose observations were often scattered and few. Dobbs had no personal knowledge of conditions in Hudson Bay, nor did he have a seaman's experience which would have revealed the problems of gauging tides and currents from the deck of a ship, or even from hurried boat trips ashore. Foxe's flood tide on which Dobbs set such store was an altogether less certain matter than the memorial supposed.[1] Basing his arguments on a rigid application of general rules of tidal behaviour, Dobbs failed to appreciate the point put to him by Middleton after his own discovery voyage to Hudson Bay – that 'It is not possible to account for all the Anomalies and Peculiarities of Tides, without an accurate Knowledge of the almost infinite Causes and Circumstances to which they may be owing'.[2] Difficulties in taking precise measurements account for some of the high tides reported by explorers on the west coast of Hudson Bay; but added to them was the crucial factor that the weak tide reaching that coast past Cary's Swan's Nest is reinforced by the flow running through two channels unknown to Dobbs: Frozen Strait (discovered by Middleton in 1742) and Fisher Strait (not discovered until 1868).

The final section of the memorial was devoted to the advantages which the discovery of a passage would bring, and here Dobbs broke clear of the strait-jacket of technical observations to lay before his readers a glittering prospect. He appealed to anti-Spanish sentiments, to the expectation of exclusive privileges, to the hope of finding new markets for English woollens, as he joined the mercantilist doctrines of his day to those old beliefs in the existence of rich countries somewhere in the unknown expanses of ocean between America and Asia. It was an appeal to national pride, to commercial acquisitiveness, to old fantasies of the wealth of the South Seas. It was Dobbs's hope that the influential politicians and merchants to whom his memorial was addressed could not fail to mark the contrast between the gains to the nation which the discovery of a navigable passage would

---

[1] See p. 21 n.1 below.
[2] P. 285 below.

bring, and the small effort which would either reveal or disprove its existence.

Dobbs first sought support for a discovery expedition on visits to England in 1731 and 1733, when he showed the memorial to Colonel Bladen, one of the Lords Commissioners of Trade and Plantations, and Sir Charles Wager, First Lord of the Admiralty. On his second visit Dobbs met Samuel Jones, Deputy Governor of the Hudson's Bay Company, whose annual supply ships to its Bayside posts, Dobbs had remarked rather airily in the memorial, might take a detour north to look for the passage. Jones's attitude towards the project was not encouraging, and for the first time Dobbs heard about a relatively recent voyage in search of the Northwest Passage, that by the veteran Company servant, James Knight, in 1719.[1] The expedition of two vessels, fitted out at Knight's insistence, and probably against the inclinations of the Company's directors, left London for Hudson Bay to search for a passage in the same area, north of latitude 64°N, to which Dobbs was pointing. The ships were lost with all hands, and although Dobbs insisted that this had no bearing on the question of whether or not a passage existed, the revelation of the expedition and its fate did not make an auspicious beginning to his negotiations with the Hudson's Bay Company. It was his first encounter with the cautious, secretive men who ruled the Company at this time, and evidently it gave him food for thought. On his next visit to London in 1735 Dobbs obtained permission from Bladen to inspect the charter of the Hudson's Bay Company in the Plantation Office, and was clearly surprised by the extent of the Company's grant.[2] By their very nature monopolistic companies were wedded to secrecy as a defence against the

[1] See the recent account of the Knight expedition by John Geiger and Owen Beattie, *Dead Silence: The Greatest Mystery in Arctic Discovery*, London, 1993; also Glyndwr Williams, *The British Search for the Northwest Passage in the Eighteenth Century*, London, 1962, ch. I.

[2] The Charter of 1670 granted the Company 'the whole Trade and Commerce of all those Seas, Streights, and Bays, Rivers, Lakes, Creeks, and Sounds, in whatsoever Latitude they shall be, that lie within the Entrance of the Streights commonly called Hudson's Streights, together with all the Lands, Countries, and Territories upon the Coasts and Confines of the Seas, Streights, Bays, Lakes, Rivers, Creeks, and Sounds aforesaid'. *Report from the Committee Appointed to Inquire into the State and Conditions of the Countries Adjoining to Hudson's Bay, and of the Trade carried on there*, London, 1749, Appendix I, pp. i–ii. This will be referred to hereafter as *Parliamentary Report*, 1749.

PLATE II. Section of World Map by John Senex, 1725
(British Library)

twin threats of foreign rivals and domestic interlopers, and under their long-serving governor (1712–43) Sir Bibye Lake the Hudson's Bay Company pursued this policy with obsessive intent. Details of the difficult passage through Hudson Strait, the position of harbours in the Bay, the trade in furs with the Indians, were kept from outsiders. Instructions from the Company's London Committee to the Bay insisted that 'no person send any Intelligence to, or carry on any Correspondence, relating to the Company's affairs, with any Person whatsoever.'[1] Committee members themselves were warned against letting copies of the charter out of their possession. The Company's shares never came onto the open market, and their last public quotation had been in 1700.

In his memorial Dobbs had outlined the advantages which the discovery of a Northwest Passage would bring to the nation; he now realised that the benefits might well be confined to the anonymous shareholders of the Hudson's Bay Company. With this in mind he obtained an interview in 1735 with Lake, and argued that as the Company alone, by virtue of its monopoly, stood to profit from the discovery of a passage through Hudson Bay, then it was reasonable that it should undertake the search. Like his deputy two years earlier, Lake was unenthusiastic, but finally agreed that Company sloops stationed at Churchill, farthest north of the Company's posts, should be sent north along the coast the following year. For Dobbs the purpose of the slooping expedition was to reach Ne Ultra, test the tides, and find the passage.[2] For the Company, although the sloops were to be 'very particular' in taking tidal observations, the main object of the expedition was to open up the northern trade, especially in whale products, and to search for minerals.[3] Clearly, Dobbs's jubilant claim that 'I have got the Hudsons bay Company to undertake once more the Northwest Passage'[4] was premature.

During 1735 and 1736 Dobbs worked independently of the Company to obtain more information about the northern reaches of Hudson Bay. He took the sensible if (as it was to prove) fateful step of approaching one of the Company's ship-

---

[1] HBC A 1/122, p. 26.
[2] See p. 39 below.
[3] See p. 40–41 below.
[4] P. 36 below.

6

captains, Christopher Middleton, to seek his views on the passage. Middleton's name was known to Dobbs only because the captain's observations on the variation of the magnetic needle had been published in the *Philosophical Transactions* of the Royal Society. This chance encounter had far-reaching results, for Dobbs found that Middleton had originally joined the Company's service in 1721 and wintered at Churchill in the hope of sailing north the next summer on a Company discovery expedition, commanded by John Scroggs.[1] Middleton had been turned away by Scroggs, a rebuff which was the more vexing since Scroggs not only reached further north in the Welcome than any navigator since Foxe, but also came across wreckage from Knight's lost ships. Middleton showed a ready interest in Dobbs's plans, and promised – unknown to his employers – to seek further information at the Bay posts about the existence of a passage.

In the event, there was no northern voyage from Churchill in 1736, and that of 1737 was a fiasco. The sloops reached only as far as Whale Cove in lat. 62°15′N, two hundred miles short of the Welcome, and returned home with no discoveries to report and only a 'trifling' trade.[2] Neither the objectives of the Company nor of Dobbs had been realised. Lake made the most of a feeble venture, stressing the cost and danger of such northern voyages, for even 'old Northwesters', he told Dobbs, 'have so terrible an Opinion of going to the Northward'. The Company, he felt, had done enough.[3] The reply from an unimpressed Dobbs was forthright and threatening; he would apply 'to others who I believe will undertake it chearfully'.[4] This proved easier to state than to implement. At the Admiralty Sir Charles Wager was interested but pessimistic, and suggested that the venture was for private enterprise rather than for public support.[5] Dobbs and Middleton kept in touch, and it was agreed that if an expedition was fitted out, Middleton should command it.[6] One of the problems confronting Dobbs in his attempts to enlist mercantile support was the knowledge that any advantages

[1] HBC B 239/a/6, 4 Sep 1721; B 42/a/2, 25 Jun 1722.
[2] P. 42 below.
[3] See p. 45 below.
[4] P. 47 below.
[5] See p. 50 below.
[6] See p. 51 below.

accruing from the discovery of a passage would probably be confined to the Hudson's Bay Company. Only when the search for a passage became linked with an attack on the Company's monopoly could Dobbs look to significant private investment for an expedition to the Bay.

In the autumn of 1739 Middleton returned from his yearly voyage to the Bay to find that with war against Spain imminent there seemed less chance than ever of attracting government support for a discovery expedition. The setback was the more frustrating because at Churchill that summer the factor Richard Norton, who as a young man had sailed north with Scroggs in 1722, told Middleton that he had observed the tide to rise no less than five fathoms in the Welcome. When he went ashore Norton saw the land falling away 'to the Southward of the West', and thought there was 'a clear passage' in that direction.[1] The Company had given Middleton a copy of Scroggs's journal to examine, and he sent extracts from it to Dobbs which confirmed Norton's memory of a five-fathom tide in the Welcome.[2] This news spurred Dobbs into activity with letters to Wager and Walpole stressing the advantages the discovery of a passage would bring to British warships attacking Spain's Pacific possessions.[3] That was no doubt correct, but with such a short-cut yet to be found, and with the Admiralty committed to sending ships to the Caribbean with Vernon and round the world with Anson, it was understandably reluctant to involve itself in a minor expedition to Hudson Bay. In London Middleton, who was by now being eyed with increasing suspicion by the Company, lingered at Court and the great houses in the hope of a change of mood. In May 1740 he was ready to sail for the Bay once more when a last-minute occurrence transformed the situation. Wager had spoken to George II about the matter, and the king had given his approval.[4] Wager at last had the higher authority without which he had refused to act. Royal patronage, however casually bestowed, had cleared away the obstacles; and in December 1740 Wager confirmed that there would be an expedition the following spring.[5]

[1] See p. 55 below.
[2] See p. 59 below.
[3] See pp. 63–5 below.
[4] See p. 66 below.
[5] See p. 68 below.

GENESIS OF THE VOYAGE

DOCUMENTS

1. Arthur Dobbs: Memorial on the Northwest Passage, 1731[1]

Sir,

You may be Surpriz'd that I should at this time endeavour to revive an attempt to discover the Northwest passage to the great Southern & Western Ocean of America, which has in a Manner been Exploded since the Year 1631, A Century ago, when Captain James & Captain Fox both attempted it in the same year, Captain Fox in the Charles Pinnace from London, & James in the Mary from Bristol, both commissiond by King Charles the first. Since that time it has been reviv'd but once, by Zachariah Gillam Commander of the Nonsuch Ketch in the year 1667, who pass'd Hudsons Straits, went into Baffins Bay to the Latitude of 75°, and from thence returnd to the Bottom of Hudsons Bay to the Latitude of 51° or thereabouts, where he found a River by him calld Prince Ruperts, where the Hudsons Bay Company have since carryd on an advantagious Trade for Furs except when they were dispossess'd by the French.[2] By All the Journals

---

[1] There are several manuscript copies extant of the Memorial: one among the Dobbs Papers in the Public Record Office of Northern Ireland (D.O.D. 162/25); one addressed to Frederick, Prince of Wales, in the Library of the Hunterian Museum, Glasgow (MS Hunter 434); a slightly shorter and apparently earlier version in the John Carter Brown Library (Codex Eng 15); and two in the Archives of the Hudson's Bay Company (Provincial Archives of Manitoba) (HBC E 18/1). The copy in the Hunterian Museum has attached to it 'A New and Correct Chart of the North Part of America from New Found Land to Hudsons Bay by [John] Thornton Hydrographer'; the copy in the John Carter Brown Library has bound into it 'Map of the North Pole' by Herman Moll. The copy of the Memorial printed here is one of those in the Hudson's Bay Company Archives, E 18/1, ff. 71–105, in Dobbs's own handwriting.

[2] This is a garbled reference to the voyage of the *Nonsuch*. It occurred in 1668–9, not 1667, and once he passed through Hudson Strait in August 1668 Gillam sailed south to James Bay and Rupert River, where he wintered. There was no northern detour to Baffin Bay and latitude 75°N.

I have read, of those who made any considerable progress towards that Discovery, there Seems to be strong Reasons to believe there is a Passage to Northwestwards of Hudsons Bay, and that Passage no way Difficult by being pester'd with Ice, Except in Hudsons Strait, before they go into the Bay; which Strait & the Season of passing it is now very well known to our Mariners, and no way so dangerous as at first when it was little known; and that part of the Bay, where the probability of the Passage appears from the facts and observations laid down in their Journals, is the only place which has never yet been thoroughly search'd; I therefore think it may be of Service to the Publick to revive the Reasons that appear for it in their Journals, and make further observations upon them; and at one view Shew what steps have been taken towards that Discovery; By which it will appear, if We can depend upon the observations and facts they have laid down and related in their Journals, that there is one place Northwestward of Hudsons Bay, where there is the highest Probability of a Passage, no farther North than the Latitude of Sixty-five Degrees, and Consequently neither very difficult nor dangerous after Entring the Bay, and that now an opportunity offers to ascertain whether it is so or not, with little or no Expense to his Majesty or the Publick. In order to do this I shall first take some Short Extracts from the Journals of those who have any way Remarkably attempted that passage, & make some General observations as I go along, in order to make out from Reason the probability of a Passage from the Facts and observations they have laid down in them...[1]

... Having thus finish'd the Extracts I have taken from the Journals of those who have attempted it, I shall now beg leave to make some General observations, and afterwards apply them where necessary to shew the probability of a Passage from the facts laid down in their own Journals who have formerly attempted it.

The first I would make is this that in Northern Latitudes ceteris paribus, The Cold is more intense on the Eastern Shores of Continents & Islands, & the Coasts more incumberd with Ice

---

[1] Now follows a summary of the voyages in search of the Northwest Passage from Martin Frobisher's in 1576–8 to those of Foxe and James in 1631–2. This section (ff. 71d–87) has been omitted here.

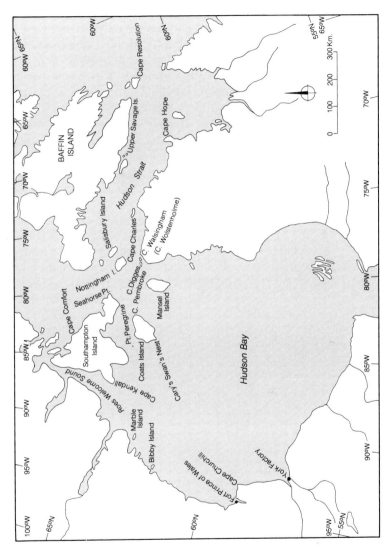

PLATE III. Hudson Bay
(Drawn Keith Bigelow and Derek Thompson)

than the Western Coasts. To begin with Nova Zembla,[1] we find there from Barents that the East Coast was all incumberd with Ice & the West Coast tolerably free,[2] so in Waygate Streight the East Side fill'd with Ice & the West Coast free; At Spitzberg the West side free of Ice beyond the Lat. of 80° & the East side so pester'd with it That no good discovery has yet been made of it.[3] The East Coast of Greenland from Spitzberg to Cape Farewell so full of Ice as scarce to be approach'd, The West side up Davis Streights as high as 78° Lat. in Baffins Bay, is free from Ice[4] when the West side of that Bay which is an East Coast is full of Ice, so it is likewise in Hudson's Streight.

The East End at Resolution Isle is more fill'd with Ice than at Mill & Nottingham Islands. It is so upon the West Coast of the Land[5] that ly's North of Nottingham Isle & Mill Isle, as high as Lord Westons Portland in 66°:47', that Coast being clear of Ice, when upon the East Coast opposite to it,[6] near Cape Comfort, the Ice ly's in great quantity. There is also some between Sea horse point & Point Peregrine, towards Carys Swans Nest, which is an East Coast.[7]

It is also so in Hudsons Bay, the East side which Hudson coasted & by which his Men return'd was free from Ice, when at the West side of the Bay, both by him & Capt. James, it was filld

[1] Novaia Zemlia.

[2] This is a direct result of the moderating influence of the North Atlantic Drift which, passing between Iceland and Scotland flows northeastwards along the Norwegian coast into the Barents Sea, thus making the west coast of Novaia Zemlia substantially less ice-encumbered than the east (or Kara Sea) side.

[3] The North Atlantic Drift is again responsible for this difference between the east and west sides of Svalbard or Spitzbergen.

[4] The east coast of Greenland is indeed more ice-infested than the west coast, largely due to the East Greenland Current which, flowing out of the Arctic Basin, carries vast amounts of ice with it; indeed this is the major exit-route for ice from the Arctic Basin. Along the West Greenland coast, by contrast, the currents tend to be southerly and hence the coast of Southwest Greenland is largely ice-free year-round.

[5] Foxe Peninsula on Baffin Island.

[6] Southampton Island.

[7] For these various locations see Map III, p. 11. Cape Comfort and Sea-horse Point had been named by Bylot in 1615 (Miller Christy, ed., *The Voyages of Captain Luke Foxe of Hull, and Captain Thomas James of Bristol, in Search of a North-West Passage in 1631-32*, London, 1894, I, pp. 216-17), and Point Peregrine by Foxe in 1631 (ibid., II, p. 376). Christy would argue that Foxe's Point Peregrine and Cape Pembroke, i.e. the northeastern tip of Coats Island, are one and the same (ibid., II, p. 376n).

with Ice. So it is in General upon the European Coast & American. The Coast of Norway and German Shore are free from Islands of Ice when the Coast of America, North of Newfound Land is with Difficulty approachd for Ice, & Many Islands of Ice are met with on the East Coast of America as Low as the Banks of Newfound Land in Lat. 46° & 47°, opposite to part of the Bay of Biscay & Brittish Channel.[1]

There is no place where it is observ'd Contrary to this come to my knowledge, Except at the Mouth of the White Sea and in the North West of Button's Bay from Port Nelson to Ne Ultra & Carys Swans Nest, where was no Ice tho' at the same time the Bottom & middle of the Bay was full of Ice as may be observ'd by Button's Fox's and James's Journals.

I would further observe that Ice is sooner form'd & in greater quantity in fresh water than in Salt, that it is also form'd in greater quantity where Continents are large than where there is little Land. That it is also form'd more in Shallow Seas than in Deep & much more where there are small Tides than where there are high Tides. These are Evident from the first General Observation & from the Extracts of the Journals I have already given & from Most other Journals; it is the fresh Water in the River Oby that occasions the great quantity of Ice to the Eastwards of the Strait of Nassaw or Waygate, where upon Tryal the Water was found fresh. The quantity of Ice in the White Sea is pretty much occasion'd by the fresh Waters of the Divina & the small Tide there. The Ice in the Baltick is owing to the freshness of the Water there, from the great Rivers running into it, & the small Tide which is scarce sensible. Thus we find the Rivers Elbe, Weser Rhine and Maase in Germany and the Low Countries, and St. Lawrence Hudson & Delawere in America, with the Large inland Lakes there all frozen over, which is occasion'd by the Waters being fresh, & indeed it is presumable that Salt Water wont freeze without the Most intense Cold, the Saline particles dissolving with the least Moisture & warmth.

---

[1] In this reference to the contrasts between the opposing sides of the North Atlantic as a whole, the main contributing agents at work are the North Atlantic Drift, keeping the coasts of Europe free of 'islands of ice', i.e. icebergs, and the Labrador Current which carries a constant stream of icebergs from Baffin Bay and Davis Strait south along the Labrador coast.

We find the Seas in Baffins Bay in the Bottom of Hudsons Bay, and at the Northwest End of Hudsons Strait, above Cape Comfort are frozen, which is occasiond by the small Tides & from the Shallowness of the Waters there. This also generally happens in other Bays that are Shallow and have Small Tides or in Seas surrounded by Great Continents, whilst on the Contrary in the Ocean where are Bluff Steep Shores, Strong Tides & Currents, & Deep Water, there is no Ice, Except what is drove from such Shallow Inlets & Rivers.

It may be presumd that it requires a great Degree of Cold to freeze Water impregnated with the least Salt, because Salt attracts moisture with the least heat & will dissolve, and when Salt Water freezes with intense Cold it will thaw much sooner than fresh water Ice from its Attractive quality.[1] Another Reason why Rivers and Shallow Bays freeze sooner than Deep Seas is from their being less Disturb'd. The Snow also which falls being colder than the Water and bearing a greater proportion to Shallow Water than to Deep, from the quantity of Water's being less in proportion to its Surface upon which the Snow falls, it Cools it faster, & so brings it soone to the freezing point. This is demonstrated by James in Hudson's Bay where the Land winds were coldest and the Snow was thick on land before it froze the Sea,[2] it afterwards freezing on the Sands, which were dry at Low Water, on the Return of the Tide made a kind of thick water, being in part frozen. After it had brought the Water near to its own Degree of Coldness, then the flakes

[1] Dobbs's observation (that salt water freezes and thaws at a lower temperature than fresh water) is, of course, correct, but his explanation is a little wide of the mark. Freezing point is the temperature at which the vapour pressure of the solid and liquid phases are the same and in the case of a solution, e.g. salt water, the lowering of the vapour pressure (and hence of the freezing point) is proportional to the molality of the solution, a 1 molal solution being one which contains 1 mole of solute per 1000 gm of the solvent. Thus, for example, due to the lowering of the vapour pressure a 1 molal solution will freeze at $-1.86°C$. Hence the higher the salinity of sea water, the lower the temperature at which it will freeze.

[2] On 29 November 1631 James wrote from his wintering place on Charlton Island: '...till within this fortnight, the Southerly winde was the coldest. The reason I conceive to be, for that it did blow from the Maine land, which was all covered with snow, and for that the North winds came out of the great Bay which hitherto was open.' Christy, *Voyages of Foxe and James*, II, p. 521.

of Snow lay upon the Water as they fell without dissolving & so froze. This was the Reason why the Bottom of Hudsons Bay was frozen over, when it was probable there was no Ice in Hudsons Streight, from the Strong Tide and deep water there, tho' it is 8 or 9 Degrees more Northerly than the Bottom of Hudsons Bay.

The Reason why Continents are colder in Winter and warmer in Summer than Islands seems to be from Waters being in a Medium between what we Call Heat & Cold & is longer in being brought to partake of either quality.

The Great Islands of Ice are formd mostly of Flakes of Snow and not of water froze into Solid Ice, Such as we See upon Standing Pools of water, which seldom or never freezes deeper than Six foot, for in James's Ship the Water was not froze in the Bottom of the Hold the whole winter, but the Sea Water had a free Communication with the Water in the Hold, by the hole they had made to Sink the Ship. Thus the Islands being form'd by the Ice's breaking & being forc'd upon one another by the violence of the Waves & afterwards being increas'd by the Snow which freezes upon the Top, We must not Conclude when we see Islands of Ice above 100 feet higher than the Water, by computing the Specifick Gravity of Solid Ice to Water, that therefore they must be 8 or 9 times as Deep in the Water and consequently aground in 100 or 150 fathom. For since they are only froze along the Edges into Solid Ice where the Wind & water touches them and are Seldom above or in the Middle any More than frozen Snow, which is above Nine Tenths made up of Vacuity and Air, The presumption is that they are not a ground at ½ the Depth of their own height, and when they generally seem to be aground they are only wedg'd in by one another near the Shore or are in Shallow Water, or upon Rocks where there is an uneven Bottom, and this is plain in Hudsons Streight where Islands of Ice setting upon Rocks at Ebb Water, The Tide falling much, they would Split and Tumble over with a terrible Noise, which had they been form'd of Solid Ice they would not have done, nor would a Storm in open Sea and Deep Water be able to break them into Small pieces were it not from their Little Continuity within, that they were easy to be Broke and dispers'd. I think it must also be so from the Vast quantity of Ice in Hudsons Strait in May and June when little or none of it was to be seen when the Ships return'd in September or October.[1]

The next observation I would make is in Relation to the Tides since the Great Sr. Isaac Newton has demonstrated that our Tides are occasion'd by the Mutual Attraction of the Sun, Moon & Earth, according to the quantity of Matter and distance of Each, We can reason more fully upon them and Shew that All Great Tides are occasion'd by the quantity of Water Attracted & Consequently put in Motion by it. From hence follows That Great Tides are only to be found where there are Great Oceans or Seas, & in Inlets bordering upon the Ocean & within its influence.

He has also demonstrated that the Sun & Moon in Conjunction or opposition, by a meeting together or at opposite sides, in Case the Whole Globe was coverd with a fluid, would form it into an Ellipsis, The longest Diameter passing thro' their Centers, and would then raise the Greatest Tides which We call Spring Tides. These Tides are at the highest Two or three days after Each Conjunction or opposition since upon their coming together or being at opposite points, their power is upon the increase, & Continues increasing until the Moon by her quicker Motion in her Orbit gets at a distance from the Sun & then their influence or Attraction being divided, they draw different Ways or upon a Different direction; & that is the Cause of the Neap Tides, or smallest Tides. The Moon being then 90 Degrees from the Sun, They attract at right Angles from Each other, & consequently obstruct one another. This is also true in relation to heat and Cold, our Weather is Warmer a Month or more after the Solstice than when the Sun is nighest our Pole & our Weather is colder in Winter some time after the Solstice than when the Sun is at the greatest Distance from our Northern Hemisphere.

We also from the Same principle find that the Sun and Moon in Conjunction or opposition at the Equinoxes occasion the highest Spring Tides in the Year or at least the Next after the Equinoxes, for the foregoing Reason, which happens from their moving round our Globe at that time in a great Circle occasion'd by our

---

[1] This appears to be a reference to the annual supply voyage of the Hudson's Bay Company ships to and from the Bayside posts. They normally passed through Hudson Strait, often with great difficulty due to ice, in July and August; and after as short a stay as possible at the posts, returned through the Strait in September or October.

Diurnal Rotation round our Axis, which is not so when they Approach the Tropicks, they moving then in a Small Circle, & Consequently our Tides are then lessen'd, for were the Suns & Moons Motion in their Orbits at right Angles to our Equinox or Diurnal Rotation, when they would come to our Pole there would be no Diurnal Tides at All, but would occasion a Deluge there by their Attraction and it would continue so until they again receded from it.

Hence it follows that the greatest Tides All other Circumstances being Equal are under and near the Equinox & they are less & less as they recede from it, and Supposing our Globe was All fluid under the Pole there would be no Tide at All. What is now at or near the Pole is occasion'd by the Different disposition and quantity of Water among the Inlets near it.

Hence also follows that the greatest Attraction being where the Moon is on the Meridian (for the Moon being so near us influences our Tides vastly more than the Sun) the Greatest Current is then there, which is always at half Tide; for at full Sea & Low Water there is no Current but a Stagnation for Some time; Consequently a S.W. & N.E. Moon in the Ocean makes full Sea, it being then three hours after the Moon has been upon the Meridian, when there was the greatest Current and Attraction. This we Also find agrees pretty Exactly at All Headlands in the Ocean.

Hence also follows that where Any Small Seas have not a free Communication with the Ocean, there must be Little or No Tide. This holds in the Caspian, the Euxine, the Mediterranean and Baltick, where are Little or No Tides.

Hence also follows that Tides in Seas at Some distance from the Ocean are Later and Later, according to their Distance from it, and the Breadth of the Channel thro' which it passes. This we See holds true in the Tide flowing round Britain & Ireland, & in such Like Seas, for as you go from the Ocean the Tide flows later, and if You go towards the Ocean the Tide meets you & flows sooner. Thus for Instance, at the Lands End, when the Moon is at E.N.E. it is full Sea; at Plimouth Later when at E; at the Isle of Wight S.E. Easterly; at the South Foreland S.S.E.; at the North Forland a South Moon makes a full Sea; so that the Tide is 7½ hours later of flowing at the Thames than at Lands End. So likewise as you go Northwards to the Ocean, You there again begin to meet the Tide sooner; at Harwich a S.S.E. Moon makes full Sea; at Yarmouth

S.E.; at Blackny & Lyn E.; at Humber E.N.E.; at Whitby N.E.; at Berwick N.N.E.; at Buchaness N. by E.; at Orkney N; or after that Manner, insomuch as Any person May know whether he is going towards an Ocean or from it according as he meets with or follows the Tide.

Another observation I would make is that High Tides are Either occasion'd by the Ocean in a Passage or Inlet Somewhat narrow, within which there is a Sea, Gulph or Lake, in which there is a Tide which Reciprocally Ebbs and flows thro' that passage by which Means there goes a Rapid Current in the Passage, from the Oceans Tide being check'd by the Headlands near the Passage which raises the Water in the Streight higher than ordinary, in order to Supply the Inland Sea or Bay with a Sufficient quantity of Water, which after passing the Strait or Inlet is again Expended in the larger Sea within, which upon the return of the Tide is again forced out with Equal Velocity; or high Tides are otherwise occasion'd by Two Headlands between which is a Deep Bay or River, which is gradually Lessened within So that the Tide Entering between the Headlands is crowded together by the Approaching Sides & so is rais'd to a great height, and again Returns with Equal Velocity like the Vibration of a Pendulum which the higher it is forc'd on the one side, the higher it goes on the other upon the Return.

The first answers the Tide in Hudsons & Davis Streights where Each has an Inland Sea to fill; & there the Tide is very high in Each passage, & very much lessend in the Several Seas within; The other answers the Tide at Bristol, at the Soam in Picardy, & in the Bay of Fundy in Nova Scotia. The Reason Why No Such Tide is found in the Streights of Gibraltar is this, that the quantity of Vapours rais'd from the Surface of the Mediterranean Sea, and falls again upon the Adjoining Continent is greater than Can be Supply'd by All the Rivers running into it, as is plainly Shown by the ingenious Dr. Halley;[1] and the Streight being very Narrow, by which the Ocean Communicates with it occasions a Constant Indraught or Current Eastwards, to raise the Surface of the

---

[1] Edmond Halley (1656–1742), whose work on tides was represented in his chart of the English Channel (c.1702) and in his essay on 'The true theory of the tides, extracted from that admired treatise of Mr Isaac Newton, intituled, *Philosophiae naturalis principia mathematica*', *Philosophical Transactions*, XIX, London, 1697, pp. 445–57.

Mediterranean Sea to a Level with the Ocean; it being Lower than the ocean without the Streight, from the great quantity of Vapours rais'd from it by the Sun and Wind.

I would further observe, that generally in the ocean, unless near the Discharge of Some Great River, the Lands are high and Waters Deep, & in All passages from the Ocean thro' which a Strong Tide flows, the Sea is deep, for this Reason that where there is a Rapid Current the Sand and Owze cant Settle but is carry'd from thence and left in the Eddy or in Some Bay where the Tide is not Strong.

It may be further observ'd that Most fish love to be in quick Waters where there is a Brisk Tide or Current, for by means of that their food is brought to them without much trouble, whilst the Young Fry go to Shallow Water where the Tide is not so rapid, to be protected from the Larger fish which prey upon them. Thus the Great Fish follow the Smaller into the Shallows in the Summer time they being their food, & again Retreat in the Winter into the Deeps of the Ocean, where they lye Warm in Northern Climates & undisturbed, being below the Agitation of the Waves rais'd by the Winter Storms.

We find also that Water fowl that feed upon Fish always resort to Coasts that are plenty of fish, the more readily to get their food.

Having thus fixed upon Some preliminary observations, I will now return to the Matter I proposed, & Consider from these and the facts I have here taken from the Journals, whether there be a Passage which communicates with the Western Ocean of America, Northwestward from our Atlantick Ocean.

By the Journals of Davis & Baffin we find that by Davis Streights no passage is to be Expected, there being neither a Strong Tide nor any Tide meeting them from the Westward, but only a Tide flowing from the South, which in Baffins Bay flows but little, That All the West Coast there is so fill'd with Ice, that no Passage that way cou'd be found in July & August, the only Months most free from Ice, in which a Northern Voyage can be attempted with Success.[1] It is Agreed also that the Passage

---

[1] Baffin was particularly emphatic on this point. On his return in 1616 from the voyage during which he explored the bay later to bear his name, he wrote: '...There is no passage nor hope of passage in the north of Davis Streights. We having coasted all, or neere all the circumference thereof, and finde it to be no other then a great bay...' Clements R. Markham, ed., *The Voyages of William Baffin 1612–1622*, London, 1881, p. 150.

Northwestward of Mill Isle in Hudsons Streight near Cape Comfort is not to be met with, altho' Sr. Thomas Button imagind there was a Tide of Flood there which came from the Northwest[1] for the Reverse of this was prov'd by Bylot, & by him and James there was No passage there for Ice in August.[2]

By Hudson, James, Button, and Fox, it is also plain there is no passage Westwards of Hudsons Bay or Buttons Bay from the Lat. of 51° to 64°, nor is there a probability of a passage from Carys Swans Nest to Sea horse point, the Tide of flood coming all that way from E & SE. Yet Fox thought there might be an inlet there,[3] for ought he knew, having not Seen Land between Point Peregrine & Sea horse Point, but as he found Ice there & no great Tide, little can be Expected from it; & if that be allow'd to be the place where Munck winterd, as I have reason to believe from the Abstract of his Journal, Then from the great quantity of Ice, & the Tides flowing there but five hours, it may be in a Manner demonstrated that he was in a River or Head of a Bay, & Consequently that there is no passage there.[4]

The only place left then, if there be a passage, is from Carys Swan's Nest to Sr. Thomas Rowes Welcome, or the Ne Ultra of Sr. Thomas Button;[5] Since none were there by any Accounts I have seen, but Button and Fox, by their Journals the presumptions are Strong for a Passage, & that there is a Communication with the Western American Ocean in that place.

---

[1] On 20 August 1613 Button noted that near Nottingham Island 'when the tyde came, it came with such force & strength out of the N.W. and by N. as hee had much adoe to ride at [anchor], and could not have ridde it had he not steered the ship all the tyde time'. Christy, *Voyages of Foxe and James*, I, p. 198.

[2] On 13 July 1615 a hopeful Bylot named Cape Comfort on the northeast coast of Southampton Island, 'But this suddaine was soone quailed, as he saith; for, the next day, having doubled the Cape, and proceeded not above 10 or 13 Leagues, but hee saw the Land trent from the Cape to the Westward, untill it bare from him N.E. and by E. and very thick[ly] pestered with ice.' Ibid., II, p. 409.

[3] See ibid., II, p. 377 where Foxe refers to the possibility of 'a through-let'.

[4] In fact Jens Munk, the Danish explorer, wintered in 1619 farther south, at the mouth of the Churchill River, where all his crew except three died; but some maps continued to show his wintering place as an inlet in approximately 64°N on the west coast of Hudson Bay. See Map IX, pp. 246–7.

[5] In 1613 Button explored the opening which stretched along the west coast of Southampton Island and reached about 65°N before deciding that he was in a bay. For some time after this was known as Button's Ne Ultra, or simply Ne Ultra. In 1631 Foxe explored the same area, which he named Sir Thomas Roe's Welcome. The name Ne Ultra has long since disappeared from the maps, which now show the opening as Roes Welcome Sound.

The presumptions are these, a Tide of Flood there in Lat. 64°10′, which in the Neap or smallest Tide, flow'd 18 feet;[1] that it flow'd there ½ Tide, as in the Usual Ocean Tides upon Headlands, that is the Tide of flood in the offing or Channel run until it was half Ebb on Shore, and then the Ebb return'd & run until it was half flood on Shore. He observ'd there also that a W.S.W. Moon made full Sea; so far Fox. Sr. Thomas Button observ'd, July the 27th 1612 at Six at night Slack Water, that is, Either high or Low Water, near the Same place; & at 8 a Strong Current Setting from N. by E. which he did not know whether it was flood or Ebb. The next Day about one he observ'd it was again Slack Water, his Boat being on Shore. This answerd to the observation the Day before since the Tide should be 48 Minutes Later. Now in order to know which was flood & which Ebb I find the Moon chang'd that Year the 17th of July at 12, so then the 27th that he observ'd was the tenth Day and Neap Tide. The Moon coming South that day at 8 Minutes after 8, it being Slack Water at 6 a S.E. by S. Moon made Low Water, and a S.W. by W. Moon made full Sea; which answerd to Fox's observation, and thus the Tide of flood came from N. by E. agreable to Fox.

I also find that on July the 10th, 1631 at Six in the Morning, the Moon chang'd which was a Day sooner than Fox supposd it. He observ'd that it was full Sea the 21st at ½ an hour after 2, which being 3 days & 8 hours after New Moon, it was then near the height of the Spring Tides, & Consequently a South Moon made a full Sea, which flow'd but 6 foot & 4 hours. He observ'd it was full Sea at 11 on the 27th at Ne Ultra; which being nine days after the Change & a Neap Tide, a S.W. by W. Moon Made full Sea, a point more Southerly than he observ'd it, by mistaking the Day of the Change; which is directly agreable to Sr. Thomas Button's observation 19 Years before; Sir Thomas Button having

---

[1] For Dobbs this was to be a crucial observation; indeed it is really the linchpin of his entire argument for a Northwest Passage through Hudson Bay; but Foxe's journal entry has a more tentative feel to it than the Memorial's assertion implies. Foxe's entry for 27 July 1631 in Roes Welcome ran: 'The boat went on land at clocke 6, and stayed 3 glasses, or one hour and ½, in which time it flowed neere six foot. It was flood before they went; for, while they were rowing to shore, I did observe it had flowed at least 3 foot, by certain rocks that were dry at our first approach. They say that it had about 9 foot to flow. At clocke 8, the tide returned, and set to S.W.-ward, which sheweth that it runs halfe-tide, or else the Main beyond it is an Island about which the tyde may have an uncontrary course...' Ibid., II, p. 318.

had an Observation the 26th found he was in Lat. 62°42'; from that time to the 29th when he Sent his Boat on Shore among the Breakers to observe the Tide, by protracting his Course I find he was got North about 26 Leagues, & was in Lat. 64° or thereabouts, so that Seems to be very near the place Fox was at, but rather a Little to the Southward; Fox having been in Lat. 64°10',[1] which also agrees with Fox, who says it was broken Land & that there were Many Islands 2 Leagues into the Sea below the High Land on the Main. Fox had fine clear Weather & Saw to the Northeastward at least 10 Leagues without seeing any Land towards the East or S. E. Fox by his Instructions being oblig'd to Sail to the Southward, could make no further discovery there,[2] and Sr. Thomas Button in a Storm standing E.N.E. & E. at least 20 Leages in the night, & seeing Land next Morning East from him about Two Leagues, & then Standing West four Leagues finding Land West of him, when computing that he was 7 Leagues from the East Land, & above 12 Leagues from the West Land he parted with the night before, he thought himself Embay'd,[3] & the Wind coming N.N.E. & blowing a Storm he stood along the East Coast S.S.W., & Coasted until he came into 62° 57' by observation; & from that time never Saw Land until near Carys Swans Nest; so that it is plain he could not know whether it was a Bay or not,[4] & by his Depth off that West Land from 73 to 44 fathom in which time he judg'd himself near the Shore, the presumption is it was not a Bay, but the Land he Saw next Day West of him was an Island in the passage; & this Seems the more probable by the Setting of the Tide & the height of it.

I shall next Consider, how so high Tides cou'd be there & whether that is agreeable to a Bay there or a Passage, it being 18 foot there at Neap Tide; the presumption is that at Spring Tide

---

[1] Foxe must have been slightly to the south of his stated latitude of 64°10'N, and the island on which his men landed would have been one of those off Cape Fullerton (lat. 64°00'N).

[2] Foxe was already farther north than his instructions allowed, 'for I was directed by the letter of my instruction to set the course from Carie Swanns Nest N.W. by N., so as I might fall with the West side in 63d., and from thence, southward, to search the passage diligently,' ibid., II, pp. 321–2.

[3] See ibid., I, pp. 181–2.

[4] This was Foxe's gloss on Button's discovery: 'I cannot find that it is proved a Bay, nor is it one by any thing herein written, and, for other things knowne, is none.' Ibid., I, p. 182.

it must be at least 4 fathom; and Since it was by Fox fine, clear, Easy Weather with West & Northwest Winds when he made the Shore, & in Summer, No Storm could occasion it; so it must be from Some Regular Ocean Tide. Now as I observ'd before, that Great Tides were either occasion'd by Headlands leading to a Bay or River from the Ocean, which contracting by Degrees rais'd the Tide as at Bristol, or were otherwise occasion'd by a Narrow passage from the Ocean into an Inland Sea or Bay, which by the Violence of the Current inwards and outwards, raises the Tide high in the passage; & this is verify'd by the Tide in Hudsons and Davis Streights, where it flows 3 or 4 fathom tho' in Baffins Bay it flows but Six foot.

Now if we Suppose this Ne Ultra to be a Bay, then it being already prov'd that there is No other Communication with the Ocean but by Hudsons Streight, we will See how Any Tide from thence could occasion it. I have already observ'd from the Journals the Tide following them thro' it from the S.E. until they came to Diggs Isle and Cape Wolstenholm on the South side of the Entrance of the Bay: & to Sea horse Point, and so on to Carys Swans Nest on the North side, in which time & distance the Tide is diminish'd from upwards of 4 fathoms to Six foot, & to flow but 4 hours; from thence it Expands itself into the Great Bay, & by the Scituation of those Lands should direct its Motion towards Port Nelson and the Bottom of Hudsons Bay, or more directly against Cape Henrietta Maria. Now as both Buttons & Hudsons Bays are great indraughts, and have the advantage of being nearer the Equinox they ought have greater Tides than Ne Ultra, that being more Northerly than 64° Lat.

But it so happens that in Hudsons Bay by Captn. James's Journal it does not flow above 3 foot, Except occasion'd by a Storm at North, nor is there any Difference between Spring and Neap Tides. We find also by Fox, that at Port Nelson it flows but nine foot at Neap Tides, and 14 foot at Spring Tides, but at Ne Ultra it flows 18 foot at Neap Tide, and this place is so far in the Eddy of the Current that instead of flowing on directly Southwestwardly, it must by Carys Swan's Nest return Eight points and flow Northwestwardly; and that from a Tide that flows there but four hours & rises but Six foot; so that it can never be occasion'd by that Tide, and if it be from any Tide in the Bay, which can't be without Communication with the Ocean, it ought, according to the General observation I made of the Tide, to flow Most at the South End of the Bay, being nearer the Equinox. But on the Contrary, if we Suppose a Western Ocean flowing in at a Streight nigh Ne Ultra into the Bay, then there is the Same reason for a high Tide's flowing There as at Resolution Isle in Hudsons Streight, & also in Davis Streight.

The next presumption of there being a Passage there is from the floods coming from the N.N.E. & the Ebb from S.W. Here it is plain it could never come from Carys Swans Nest which is in 62° to Ne Ultra which is in 64°, & come at the same time from N.N.E. but ought rather to Set in directly upon the Shore or rather flow along it towards the N.N.E., since the Lands bear from one another S.S.E. & N.N.W. Leagues asunder, & the Land at Ne Ultra lying from the N.N.E. to W. by S., a Tide flowing from S.E. would flow almost directly against it.

Another presumption of a Passage is from the time of the flood at Ne Ultra, and the Tides flowing Later as it went to the Southward towards Port Nelson, for a W.S.W. Moon (or when corrected) a S.W. by W. Moon made full Sea at Ne Ultra, & from thence to Port Nelson it flow'd later still. That is a W. & further on, a W.N.W. Moon made full Sea, as they proceeded on to the Southward, until at Port Nelson a N.W. Moon made full Sea. If it flow'd from the Tide in Hudsons Streight by Carys Swans Nest, where a South Moon made full Sea,then Port Nelson being in a Manner the direct Way of the Tide, and Ne Ultra the Eddy, it ought to be full Sea at Port Nelson as soon as at Ne Ultra, but we find it is Six points, or at least 4½ hours later than at Ne Ultra. But if we Suppose a passage from a Large Ocean Westward or Northwestward of the point near Ne Ultra, then it is Easy to Account for it; for on the Ocean a S.W. Moon makes high Water, and if we Suppose a Headland within 60 Leagues of that opening to the Western Sea or Ocean, then it Naturally follows that a S.W. by W. or S.W. by W. ½W. Moon should make a full Sea there & so flow Later untill it arrive at Port Nelson, where a N.W. Moon would make full Sea. This wou'd also fully answer the other observation of its being so high there, and lessening as it Expands itself towards the Bottom of the Bay.

Another Strong presumption is from the Temperateness of the Weather, and the Seas being free from Ice, from Carys Swans Nest & so down the Bay to Port Nelson; when more

Southwardly in the Bay it was all Ice by Captn. James's Acct. at the Same time; and also to the Eastward of Carys Swans Nest by Cape Comfort in the Same Latitude there was Ice there in All Seasons, as observd by Bylot & James, Even in the Latter End of August when it is Most dissolv'd. Tho' if they were both Bays, there would be more reason for there being Ice at Ne Ultra than at Cape Comfort, the Last being in the direct Current of the Tide from Resolution Isle, and the other in the Eddy at the Head of the Bay where there cou'd be Little Tide rationally Expected. This temperate Weather & freedom from Ice is therefore a Strong presumption of a Passage & open Sea to the West & Northwestward of Ne Ultra, for tho' it may be objected, why then so much Ice in Hudsons Streight, which is a passage to the Ocean, Even until the Latter End of July. The Answer is obvious, for Notwithstanding the Strong Tide there, which prevents the Ice's being continuous, Yet for other Reasons there Must be much Ice there, for there are Many Bays on Each side of it where are no great Tide which are frozen over, and upon breaking up of the Ice it is thrown in there, as also the Ice from Hudsons Bay near Mansels Isle, & the Ice near Cape Comfort, and a Vast quantity of Ice from Baffins Bay & Cumberlands Inlet thro' Davis's Streight, which as Baffin observes, by the melting of the Snow & Ice there, occasions a Strong Tide of Ebb to Set to the Southward, which coming off the Entrance of Hudsons Streight, by a Strong Tide of flood there, which is afterwards expanded & Lost in Hudsons Bay, is forced into that passage & Choaks it up & is stop'd afterwards by the Many Islands in the Inlet. This is the Reason why so much Ice is in the Southeast End of Hudsons Streight the Beginning of July, and We find there alone is the greatest Difficulty, for as they advance further towards Hudsons Bay They have still less Ice, Yet Notwithstanding the quantity of Ice in the Month of August it is almost dissolved, for Ships returning Even as late as October were in no Danger of being stopd by Ice in it.

If We further Consider from the General observation that East Coasts are more pester'd with Ice than Western, and No Ice being on this East Coast, tho' vastly crowded with it to the Southward in the Bay; it must give us reason to believe it is occasion'd by the Strong Tide there & a Great open Sea to the Northward and Northwestward of it; and this I find exactly corresponds with perhaps a parallel Instance, at the Mouth of the White Sea, where Ships don't complain of Ice, altho' it be an East Coast, because a Great open Sea comes round the North Cape of Lapland & Norway, which is also a Bold & deep Coast & prevents Ice from being form'd there.

We find a great disproportion of Cold between the South part of the Bay in Lat. 52°3' in Charleton Island, & at Port Nelson in Lat. 57°10' & farther Northwards to Ne Ultra by James's, Button's & Fox's observations; for in Charleton Island the Cold set in in October, and the Sea was hard frozen in November, and it did not break up by the Shore until the 24th of May, and the Bay was firmly frozen till the Middle of June, when by Button's Account the River at Port Nelson, tho' not above a Mile over, and which by being fresh ought to have been sooner frozen, was not froze over until the 16th of February, and they had many Warm thawing days before that time, and it broke up again the 21st of April, from which time they caught many fish in it, and in All Fox's passage, from Carey's Swans Nest to Port Nelson, he had nothing but Warm Weather, Except when it blew hard from N.W. In the Lat. of 59° he Saw fine Green fields like Meadows, and thick Rows of Trees about them as at Barn Elms near London, and in All his passage from Ne Ultra to Port Nelson he coud observe but one River,[1] and that within a Degree of Port Nelson, which is Another presumption that No great Continent is to the Westward, otherwise Some great River might have been observ'd along the Coast which Extended at least 120 Leagues.

Another presumption of a Passage is from the height of the Land & Depth of the Water near Ne Ultra & from the quantity of Tangle and Rock weed floating there, which has very much the Appearance of being near the Ocean.

But over and above All these presumptions, the Number of Whales, Seals & other fish, and fowl feeding on Fish near that place, as also SpermaCeti Whales as far down as Port Nelson on the West Side of the Bay, is a great Confirmation of a Great Sea's being to the Westward of Ne Ultra, for by the Several Accounts of those who have passd Hudsons Streights, outwards & homewards, No Fish were to be found there. Fox indeed Saw Some Sea Unicorns about Nottingham & Salisbury Isles, and Sea

---

[1] Churchill River.

horses were Seen at Sea horse point, Diggs Isle and Carys Swans Nest, but as these last ly upon the Ice they may be Suppos'd to have come thro' Hudsons Streight; but neither Whales, Seals nor other Fish were Seen until near Ne Ultra and down the West side of the Bay. Now if it be Difficult for them to come thro' Hudsons Streight, from what other place can they come free from Ice, Except there be a Communication there with an open Sea to the Westward where they can retire to in the Winter. For if that be a Bay & not a passage they would be clos'd in Hudsons Bay all the Winter, whereas it is to be presum'd they go into the Deeps of the Ocean in Winter to be preserv'd from the Coldness of the Ice & from being disturb'd by the Agitation of the Sea from the Winter Storms, and in Summer Return to the Banks & Shoal Water to Spawn and get their food within the Influence of the Sun's warmth.

Another presumption is from the observation of a Burial place at Ne Ultra, and from the Darts found there headed with Iron & Copper. Hence it is plain people Resort there, and since We Don't find Europeans head their Darts with Copper, & much Copper being found towards Japan and Northwestward of Mexico, if We may believe Lahontan among the Tahuglaucks, a Civilized Nation above California,[1] We May reasonably Suppose those people who bury'd there had an intercourse with Some Nations to the Westward, from whom they had that Copper, & the Most probable intercourse at Such a Distance may be pre-sum'd to be by Sea, So that also Confirms the other observations.[2]

---

[1] This is a reference to the vastly popular *New Voyages to North-America*, Lon-don, 1703, of Baron Lahontan, which included a description of sizeable cities and towns along a 'Long River' west of the Mississippi, and (imaginary) nations which included the Tahuglahuks.

[2] The 'Burial place at Ne Ultra' was the island in about 64°N where Foxe's men landed to test the tides. It was, Foxe wrote, 'a Sepulchre' with about 500 graves, with corpses and grave goods. 'Their Darts were many of them headed with Iron (and nailes), the heads beaten broad wayes. In one of their Darts was a head of Copper, artificially made, wch I take to be the work of some Christian, and that they have come by it by the way of Canada, from those that Trade with the English and French.' Christy, *Voyages of Foxe and James*, II, p. 320. In his note to this passage Christy points out that the area between Hudson Bay and Lake Superior was rich in copper; and that the iron and nails could have come from the wreck of Button's ship at Port Nelson, or from the French traders far to the south.

If We may, after these Several presumptions taken from the observations of our Sailors, give Credit to the Account given to Mr. Michael Lock at Venice in 1596, by Valerianus[1] an old Seaman, who had serv'd the Spaniards 40 Years as Pilot in the South Sea, it will absolutely confirm there being a Passage, for he inform'd him that he had been sent out by the Vice Roy of Mexico to the then much talk'd of Streight of Anian, to find if there was a Streight there, in order to have it fortify'd to prevent the English Entering the South Sea by that Streight, the Northern passage to India being then much Sought after by them. He sail'd in a Caravel attended by a Pinnace, & sail'd about California until he came to the Lat. 47°, & there he found the Land to fall away to the North East; he sail'd into a Sea there which at the Entrance was about 30 or 40 Leagues wide, and was very much inlarg'd within, the Land falling away N.W. & N.E., where he found Several Islands & Saild 20 Days in it. He landed in Several places and found people Clad in Beast Skins, & it seem'd a Rich & pleasant Country. Upon this having no power to resist the Natives he return'd, thinking he had performd the Task allotted to him, & came to Mexico where he expected a Reward; he was well receiv'd there but was told by the Vice Roy the King would reward him in Spain, & Sent him to Europe in hopes of it; when he came to Spain he was much applauded, but the English then not pushing the Discovery he was neglected & made his Escape to Venice; & offer'd his Service to Mr. Lock to find the passage for the English, but before that coud be fix'd he Dy'd.[2]

From these Several observations & Circumstances coinciding, I think there are Strong presumptions that there is a passage Westward from Buttons Ne Ultra, and this I am persuaded We may be Assured of, that it has not been determined to the Contrary by Any whose Journals are extant.

The only objection against this passage, that Seems to have Any weight in it at first view, is this. Since a South Moon at Cary's Swans Nest makes full Sea, how can a S.W. by W. Moon make full Sea at Ne Ultra, Either, by the Tide flowing from Hudsons Streight, or by Supposing a passage there from a Western

---

[1] More often known as Juan de Fuca.

[2] The account of the Fuca voyage, still the object of debate and conjecture among scholars, was first printed by Samuel Purchas in the fourth book of the second part of *Hakluytus Posthumus or Purchas His Pilgrimes*, London, 1625.

Ocean; for if it flow'd thro' Hudsons Streight by Cary's Swans Nest, it wou'd be as long nearly in flowing 72 leagues they are distant from Each other, as it is in flowing 200 leagues from Resolution Isle to Carys Swans Nest, since it is but 6 points, viz. from E.S.E. to S., in flowing 200 Leagues, and is 5 points, viz. from S. to SW. by W. in flowing 72 Leagues from thence to Ne Ultra, and on the Contrary supposing a Tide at Ne Ultra flowing from an Ocean to the Westward, how cou'd it flow regularly down the West side of the Bay to Port Nelson, and not at the Same time flow down the East side to Carys Swans Nest, which if We Suppose it did and the two Ocean Tides met there, then it wou'd be 11 points in flowing from Ne Ultra to it, being but 72 Leagues, whilst it flows down to Port Nelson 130 Leagues in 7 points or 5¼ hours. This is I think the objection in its full weight, and from thence it would follow that the observations made have not been Exact.

To this I answer that the first part of the objection, if nothing was to be answer'd but the Different time the Tide took in running the 200 Leagues, and 72 Leagues might be solv'd thus, that the latter being an Eddy Tide, it might be longer much in flowing after being expended in the Bay, than the direct Tide in the passage from Resolution Isle to Carys Swans Nest, for in this the Current being confin'd is rapid, in the other it is Spent in the Bay, & being turn'd off into the Eddy, becomes much slower in its Motion than the other; but yet to a Demonstration it can't be that Tide, for a Tide that is Spent in that place, so as not to rise above 6 foot, and to flow but 4 hours at Spring Tide, coud never by an Eddy run 72 Leagues and raise a Tide of 18 foot at Neap Tide, to flow Six hours.

As to the other part of the Objection, that makes a Difficulty that a Tide from a Western Ocean at Ne Ultra woud run down the West side of the Bay regularly to Port Nelson 130 Leagues in 7 points or 5 hours and quarter, & not at the Same time run down the East Side, or if it did that it shou'd be 11 points or 8 hours & quarter in running 72 Leagues, I answer thus. Let us take it for granted that there are Two Tides setting into Hudsons Bay, one by a Passage at Ne Ultra, and the other by Hudsons Streight, and by comparing those with other Tides See what wou'd be the Consequence at that Island Fox stop'd at near Cary's Swans Nest as it is Scituated.

From Sir Isaac Newtons Theory of the Tides I have already shewn that at Headlands in the ocean a N.E. and S.W. Moon makes full Sea which agrees also with Most observations. Now we find at Resolution Isle an E.S.E. Moon makes full Sea, and Cape Farewell in Greenland being a Headland in the Ocean and about 200 Leagues from it, it naturally follows a N.E. Moon makes full Sea in the Ocean near that Cape; so that it has 4½ hours to flow to Resolution Isle and we find it is just so long in flowing an Equal Distance to Carys Swans Nest; so in like manner if a Headland lay near the Ocean by Ne Ultra, then a S.W. or N.E. Moon wou'd make full Sea at that Headland and a S.W. by W. Moon making a full Sea at Ne Ultra, the Ocean would not be above 40 Leagues from it; or if Valerianos's Account be true then the Streight he enter' from the Southern Ocean being in 47° about 560 Leagues from Ne Ultra, Southwest, then it wou'd be 17 points or 12¾ hours in flowing from that Entrance to Ne Ultra, Viz. from N.E. to S.W. by W. and it would answer in proportion to the Distance from Cape Farewell to Carys Swans Nest, where it flow'd 400 Leagues in 12 points or nine hours. The Tide from the Eastern Ocean being forced down by Sea horse point & Cape Pembrook alters its Direction into the Bay by Diggs Isle & Cape Wolstenholm & so is push'd down the Eastern Shore of Hudsons Bay until it is spent in the Bottom of the Bay; at the Same time the Tide from the Western Ocean being check'd by the Eastern Land Sail'd along by Button after he cross'd the Passage, or suppos'd Bay, which he Says lay from N.E. to S.W. or W.S.W., this woud naturally divert the Tide and make it flow down the West side of the Bay to Port Nelson & Cape Henrietta Maria; & the Islands near Carys Swans Nest would be in the Eddy of Both Tides, so that they woud meet & Stop Each other farther down the Bay to the Southward, and the Sea at Carys Swans Nest woud be affected according as each Tide approach'd it; for it might so happen as the Water there might not rise at all but only have a Strong Current, for were it so Scituated as to be full Sea at it by one Tide when it was Low Water by the other, the Sea there would always be at the height of ½ flood in other places without Ebbing or flowing for as one Tide woud sink at that place the other woud rise and woud only occasion a Rapid Current to Set Six hours Each Way. So in like Manner, if the Tide on one side flow'd Two hours sooner or

later than the other in that Eddy, then at Each full Sea and Low
Water it woud keep at the Same height for Two hours & rise but
four hours and fall four hours, and the height of Each Tide
woud be but ⅔ of Either Tide since at Low water it woud not fall
by ⅓ so low as it would if both Tides Ebb'd at the same time; and
this Seems to me to be the reason of the Spring Tides being So
Small there, and of the Tides flowing but four hours, and from
this Eddy's being very great, the Tide might be reasonably Suppos'd to be much longer in flowing to that place than in its direct
Course down the West side of the Bay without appearing im-
probable, which I Shall shew from a parallel Instance by comparing it with the Tide flowing round Britain and Ireland,
where We find the direct Tide thro' the British Channel running
much faster than the Tide that runs obliquely in the Irish Channel, for the Tide from the Chops of the English Channel Runs in
as Short time to Ostend, as to Dundrum Bay in Ireland, tho' one
be near twice as far as the other, for a N.E. Moon makes full Sea
without both Channels, and at Ostend a South Moon makes full
Sea, and the like Moon in Dundrum Bay. So likewise I find it is
12 hours later in coming down the East side of Britain from the
Northwestern Ocean than it is thro' the Channel, for as the
Tides from the North & West meet at the North Foreland, so at
Scarborough I find an E.N.E. Moon makes full Sea, as well as at
Lands End or the Chops of the Channel, and as that Tide comes
round Scotland from the Western Ocean where a S.W. Moon
makes full Sea the presumption is very Strong that it is 12 hours
longer in flowing round from the Western Islands of Scotland to
Scarborough, which makes 12 hours difference between it & the
Channel Tide. So likewise when we find that the Tide from
Flanders to Holland and so on to the Eems, the Weser & Elbe
flows later as you Sail along that Coast, We know it is the Chan-
nel or Southwestern Tide that flows along the German Coast.
Thus at the Flushing a S.S.W. Moon making full Sea, at the
Maase S.W., at the Texell a W.S.W., without Texel W., the West
Eems N.W., the East Eems N.N.W. & at the Weser and Elbe a
North Moon makes full Sea. This also Shews that the Channell
Tide flows faster and runs much farther in its direct Course than
in the Eddy on the English Coast, Viz. as far as Hamburgh on
the German Coast and no farther than the mouth of the Thames
on the Eddy Coast, & the Northern Tide flows down as far as the

Theames on the Coast it flows along & no farther than Hamburgh on the other Coast, and the Tides at Sea off the Coast of Holland being in the Eddy & meeting of the Two Tides have very irregular Currents & flowings as may be seen from the Pilot Books.

Now We find much the same inequality at Carys Swans Nest from the Eddy of Two Tides, and they ought to be more difficult still by being occasion'd by Tides coming from different Oceans, than if they proceeded from one Ocean round an Island such as Britain, for Tides coming from the same Ocean round an Island, the general Effect is only to stop one another at the place of meeting without any very irregular Tide; but Two Tides meeting from different Oceans where the Moons Impulse is begun under very different Meridians must have a very different Effect at meeting & may occasion Such Currents & Tides as is mention'd at Carys Swans Nest, Such as flowing but four hours, or more or less, according as one Tide is before the other as I have before observ'd.

If we compare the Tides at Carys Swans Nest and in Hudsons Bay with the Tides about England We will find much the Same method observ'd, for there the Tide from Ne Ultra may be compar'd to the Channel Tide in England, and by the direction of the Coast, it flows faster down in its direct Course after being push'd back by the Lands on the East side of the passage, to Port Nelson on the West side of the Bay and much farther than in the Eddy to Carys Swans Nest, so the other Tide by Hudsons Streight being directed after the Same Manner flows down the East side of the Bay, whilst both Tides Expending themselves in the Bay are very much lessend & the Eddy of both being at Carys Swans Nest, there are found Small Irregular Tides. Now since this fully answers the objection and I can no other way Account for the facts laid down in the Journals, but by believing a Different Tide from Ne Ultra from an Ocean there. This seems to me to Corroborate the opinion that there is a passage there.

But perhaps it may be objected, that the Tide of Flood at Ne Ultra which came from N.N.E. may have come thro' a passage Northwestward of Hudsons Streight Above Cape Comfort, or by a Passage down from Baffins Bay, Either of which passages might occasion that Current from N.N.E.

To this I answer, that if such a passage were allow'd, then thro' that passage the Ice wou'd come down in great quantitys into the

West part of the Bay, there being always great quantitys of Ice above Cape Comfort and Baffins Bay, which by that Current woud be carry'd that way. Nor by this passage could any Reason be given for the height of the Tide at Ne Ultra, for Both beyond Cape Comfort and in Baffins Bay the Tide is weak & Spent & Consequently rises but little & cou'd never raise a Tide at Ne Ultra Equal to the Tide at Resolution Isle, where the whole Strength of the Tide is, which is afterwards All Expended & lost in the Bay, and beyond Cape Comfort. Besides it would be a Much Shorter way for the Tide to flow from Carys Swans Nest, than to go Northwards and afterwards to return to Ne Ultra.

Upon the whole notwithstanding Every particular Observation has not been taken with the greatest Accuracy Requisite to form a Certainty of a passage there. Yet when we Consider, that the Several observations made in their Journals, can only be solv'd by supposing a passage there, and that All that have been made concurr in Supporting that opinion, I think it very much the Interest of Britain since it can now be attempted at little or no Expense, to try that passage & for the future convince us of the Truth or falsity of it, and of the facts laid down in their Journals, for I must beg leave to Say, if they have done justice in the facts & observations laid down in them there are the Strongest presumptions in the World if they ben't allow'd to be a Demonstration for it.

I have thus in My Judgment, made it highly probable, from the observations laid down that there is a passage to the Western Ocean of America near Ne Ultra, and that passage not further North than 65° about the Latitude of some part of Norway & Iceland; which Coasts are free from Ice most part of the Year; & from the General Observation I made that Western Coasts are free from Ice when the Eastern in the Same Latitude are incumber'd with it, We have no reason to believe that Any Ice would be seen in the Voyage from Ne Ultra to California, Yedso[1] or Japan

---

[1] Yedso, Yezo, Yesso (to give only a few of its variant spellings), present-day Hokkaido, had been the subject of rumour and speculation since Jesuit reports from Japan in the sixteenth century. Dutch explorations in the mid-seventeenth century increased the confusion, and in the 1730s Yedso was often represented on maps as a land-mass somewhere between Company Land (thought to be part of North America) and Kamchatka. One of the objects of the second Bering expedition in 1741–2 was to resolve the confusion over these various lands in the north Pacific.

or Any place towards the Great Southern Sea & Consequently no danger from it in the Voyage, but in Hudsons Streight which is now so well known that little danger is to be apprehended there if the proper Season is taken in July or August to pass it; for those Ships need not go so early as those which go to the Bottom of the Bay & return the Same Season.

I Shall be very brief in mentioning the Advantage to Trade & to the Publick by finding an Easy passage that way; The hazards run in Attempting it may convince us that the Greatest Men who countenanced it thought it very great, if it had been found. What great Advantages might be made by having a passage to California in three or four Months & so down the Western Coast of America into the South Sea where a New and beneficial Commerce might be carry'd on along the Spanish Coast & among many Islands & Countrys in the Great Southern Ocean not yet fully discover'd Such as the Islands of Solomon etc.[1] How Great would be the benefit in time of War to be able in a Short time to send Ships of War or Privateers into the South Sea to intercept the Spanish Commerce. How great would be the benefit to send Ships an Easy & short way to Japan & Even to China, & to be able to send a Squadron of Ships, Even to force Japan into a Beneficial Treaty of Commerce with Britain. How great would be the Advantage of opening a New Trade for our Woollen Manufactures in the Temperate & Cold Regions near California in America & along the Country of Yedso & other Countrys in our passage yet unknown, where there is a Strong presumption that there are Many civiliz'd Nations as well from Lahontan's Account, as from the Spaniards that push'd their discoveries Northwestward of New Mexico, into Cibola & Quivira,[2] who All affirm it, and since it is highly probable that North America at least was peopled from the Eastern Regions near Japan, there is more Reason to believe they are better

[1] Reached by Mendaña in 1568, the Solomon Islands frustrated all later efforts to rediscover and locate them until the later eighteenth century. In 1720 John Welbe petitioned the Crown to support his plan to exploit the islands which, he claimed, 'abound in gold'. See C. Jack-Hinton, *The Search for the Islands of Solomon 1567–1838*, Oxford, 1969; Glyndwr Williams and Alan Frost, eds., *Terra Australis to Australia*, Melbourne, 1988, p. 135.

[2] Half-real, half-mythical, Cibola and Quivira were will-o'-the-wisps of the western parts of North America which lured the Spaniards ever farther north in search of them and their fabled wealth.

civiliz'd in those Countrys, the nearer We approach to the Asiatick Coast. By making a few Settlements there we should ingross All their Commerce & open a New Market for our Manufactures vastly advantagious to us, Inlarge our Trade for furrs, increase our Navigation, and Employ all our Poor, & by civilizing these Countrys make Numberless Nations happy, & this advantage We already have, that both by Treaty[1] & prior possession We already have All the Country & Trade in Hudsons Bay & Streight, & by our Discovery & by making early Contracts with the Nations for Settlements upon their Coasts, His Majesty & the People of Britain wou'd have a Legal & just pretension to Settle Colonies in proper places without the other Powers of Europe having Any pretence to make any, according to the Rules laid down in making former Settlements in America.

Whilst the South Sea Company follow'd the Whale fishery in Davis Streight, this passage might have been ascertain'd without any Expense to the Publick, by prevailing with the Directors to have Sent Two or three of their Ships to have try'd the Whale fishery at Ne Ultra; where if they had found no passage they might have made a good Return in Whales, Sea horse, Seals, etc. which are there in Abundance & are undisturb'd but they having given up that fishery now that opportunity is Lost.

At present I imagine it would be no Loss to the Hudsons Bay Company to fit out a Ship for that purpose & try to get a New Trade along that Coast with the Natives for furs; nor do I think but the Ships they send to Ruperts River might spare time to go to Ne Ultra before they went into the Bay, & fix whether there be a passage there or not, and yet have time to make their passage home in the Same Season.

If this can't be done it would be but a Trifling Expense for his Majesty or for the Lords of the Admiralty to fit out Two Strong Sloops to make the Tryal which might be done in three or four Months & to promise a Reward to the Several Crews in Case they found out a passage to the Westward from that place.

Thus, Sir, I have endeavour'd to make out what I propos'd in the Beginning, that there is the greatest probability of a Passage

---

[1] The Treaty of Utrecht (1713), on which see E. E. Rich, *The History of the Hudson's Bay Company 1660–1870*, Vol. I:1670–1763, London, 1958, ch. XXXIII.

from our Atlantick Ocean into the Great Western & Southern
Sea of America, by the Northwestward of Hudsons Bay, and
wou'd fain hope that it would meet with Your Approbation.

I am with great Truth & Regard

Sir

Your Most Obedient,

Humble Servant

2. Arthur Dobbs to Judge Ward.[1] 29 April 1735.[2]

I have got the Hudsons bay Company to undertake once more
the Northwest Passage, but as they are apprehensive of a Warr
they are to be fully employd this year and the next in finishing a
stone fort at their settlement on Churchill River,[3] but when that
is finished they instruct their Governr. there to Renew the
attempt by Sloops from that Settlement.

3. Arthur Dobbs to Captain Middleton. 23 December 1735.[4]

Dublin, Dec 23, 1735.

Sir.

I hope this will meet you in London safe after your Return from

[1] Dobbs's cousin and confidant, Michael Ward, was a landowner in County
Down, and an Irish judge.

[2] Ward Papers: D 2092/1/4/123.

[3] The building of the great stone fortress at Churchill River (Fort Prince of
Wales) had begun in 1731, and was to continue – on and off – for forty years.

[4] Christopher Middleton, *A Reply to the Remarks of Arthur Dobbs*, London, 1744,
Appendix, pp. 1–2. Middleton had joined the Hudson's Bay Company's sea
service in 1721, and became one of its ship-captains in 1725. During sixteen
voyages to the Bay he visited all the Company's main factories, and in 1734 he
was given command of the Company's newest vessel, the 170-ton *Seahorse*. In
1726 the Royal Society published his observations on magnetic variation in
Hudson Bay, and in 1737 elected him a Fellow. It was his article in the *Philosophical Transactions* which first brought his name to Dobbs's attention. For short
biographies of Middleton see E. E. Rich and A. M. Johnson, *James Isham's
Observations on Hudson's Bay, 1743....*, Toronto and London, 1949, pp. 325–34,
and Glyndwr Williams in *Dictionary of Canadian Biography*, IV, Toronto, Buffalo
and London, 1979 (hereafter *DCB*, IV), pp. 446–50.

Churchill River, in Hudson's Bay. I was in hopes to have met you at the Union Coffee-House the Day you left London, but was a Quarter of an Hour too late.

I would esteem it as a particular Favour if you would let me know whether any thing Remarkable happened whilst you were in Hudson's Bay, or whether you made any farther Enquiry, about the Probability of a Passage near ne Ultra. Sir Bibye Lake[1] told me little or nothing could be done whilst a War was apprehended with France, because all their Thoughts were taken up in erecting a Stone Fort in Churchill River, but as soon as Hands could be spared, proper Instructions should be given to renew the Attempt, by Sloops from thence, early in the Season, which would be done at a small Expence, since the Apprehensions of a War are now pretty well over. I hope no Danger is to be apprehended of any Attack by the French in Hudson's Bay, so that they may have spare Hands next Season to proceed upon the Discovery from Churchill River, which I shall again apply for, if you be so good as to let me hear from you, how you found every Thing upon your Arrival there, and whether the Situation of Affairs be such as it may be proper to give Instructions next Season to prosecute the Discovery in Sloops from thence. I shall trouble you no further, but wish you Success in all your Affairs.

4. Captain Middleton to Arthur Dobbs. 16 January 1735 (OS)[2]

Captain Middleton's first letter to me

London, January 16, 1735

SIR,

I had the Honour to receive your Letter dated from Dublin the 23rd ult. the Contents whereof I communicated immediately to Sir Bibye Lake, who allows me the Liberty to inform you, that the Company did, by the Ships which sailed hence last Year, transmit your Directions to their Agent at Churchill, for preparing a Sloop, and such other Matters as should be necessary to

---

[1] Governor of the Hudson's Bay Company from 1712 to 1743, a length of office which earned him the title of 'The perpetual Governor'.

[2] Arthur Dobbs, *Remarks upon Capt. Middleton's Defence*, London, 1744, Appendix, p. 1.

prosecute the Discovery you mention; about which they design to give their farther Instructions next Season.[1]

I was not at Churchill myself last Summer, as you seem to think, but at Albany; and I could not there receive any new Information about the Probability of a Passage.

5. Arthur Dobbs to Sir Bibye Lake. April 1736.[2]

A rough Draft of my Letter to Sir Bibye Lake in April, 1736.

SIR,

By a Letter I had from Captain Middleton last Winter, which he had communicated to you, I find you were so good as to give proper Directions to your Governor of Churchill, to fit out a Sloop to attempt the Passage at Ne Ultra; and that you would continue your instructions to the same Purpose next Spring by the Ships you send into the Bay. The Hurry I have been in of late prevented my making my proper Acknowledgments to you and the Company, for your so readily promoting a farther Attempt of that Passage after your former Disappointments, upon the Reasons I laid before you, which were the Foundation of my firm Belief that there must be an easy Passage from Ne Ultra.

Since you were pleased to approve of the Reasons I offered, why a fresh Attempt should be made to discover that Passage, I shall beg leave to offer my Thoughts of the manner in which the Attempt may be made, with most Certainty and least Expence, and what Observations the Masters of the Sloops ought to make and send you, in order to your forming your Judgment, whether they have taken the proper Method and Course to find the Passage; in order to your prosecuting it, in case their Accounts be satisfactory, with Advantage to your Company, and Benefit of England.

I think two Sloops would be necessary; and they ought to be

---

[1] The Directors of the Company considered the matter further at the beginning of March, when 'several Journals and Accounts relating to the Companys proceedings in former Years on the said discovery were now Inspected and consider'd.' HBC A 1/122, 3 Mar 1735 (OS).

[2] Dobbs, *Remarks*, pp. 87–90.

no larger than is requisite to protect them from the Natives (in case any should appear) in the Creeks, into which they put from time to time, as they coast along the Shore, and they ought not to draw above four Feet Water. They ought each to keep a particular Journal of their Course, in case they at any Time separate from each other, which (if possible) they ought to avoid. The earlier in Summer they sail from Churchill the better, before the Ice breaks up in the Bay; for since they draw little Water, they may sail along the Shore within the Ice. They ought to make the best of their Way, until they come to the Latitude 64° without being inquisitive about the Harbours or Creeks from Churchill to that Latitude, unless blowing Weather or contrary Winds make them take shelter in their Passage; and then they ought to take the Soundings and Bearings of the Lands, the setting and risings of the Tides, whether they meet the Flood coming from the W. or N.W. as the Lands lie, and whether it flows half Tide in the Offing, whether it be earlier upon the southing of the Moon than at Churchill, and whether it rises higher; and also observe the Variation, and whether the Coast be bolder, or whether there be more or less Ice than farther down in the Bay; and what Fish appear, whether Whales or other Fish; and as they sail along northerly or westerly, if the Coast falls off, as it is expected, they must observe to look out for a Creek or Harbour, in case they should take Harbour, and whether any Signs of Inhabitants, and must endeavour to keep in with the Western Coast; and if they find an open Sea to Westward, after they pass 65° and the Land should fall away to Westward, and the Tide of Flood meets them, and an earlier Moon make full Sea, then the Passage is gained; and they may only sail 50 or 100 Leagues farther Westward, and look out for an Harbour for Ships, which may go next Season, and then return to Churchill for fear of any Disaster, and send over a Journal to the Company of their Observations.

By proceeding after this Manner, a Discovery may be made for a trifling Expence; and one Summer may ascertain whether there is a Passage or not....

6. Governor and Committee of the Hudson's Bay Company to Richard Norton, Factor at Prince of Wales Fort, Churchill. 6 May 1736.[1]

We do hereby order, upon the Arrival of Capt. Spurrell[2] and Capt. Coats[3] at Churchill-River this Year, which may probably be in July 1736, that you fit out the Churchill Sloop, James Napper[4] Master, and the Musquash Sloop, with all Expedition, for the Sea; the Churchill Sloop to carry Twelve Sailors, and the Musquash Six Sailors; also to take with you Three or Four Home Indians;[5] and to sail directly as far as Sir Thomas Roe's Welcome to find out a proper Bay or Harbour to lie secure in, and trade with the Indians;[6] also to pitch a Tent on the Land, and make Observations how far distant from Trees, and what the Soil is; and to endeavour to promote a Trade by persuading the Indians to kill Whales, Sea-Horses, and Seels, for Whale-fins, Ivory, Seel-Skins, and Oil, in the best manner they can, using them very civilly; and to acquaint them that the said Sloops will return the next opening of the Ice to the same Bay or Harbour, &c. We likewise order, that the said Two Sloops shall be fitted out with all proper Necessaries, and the same Number of Men, early the next Spring, as soon as the Ice is broke up (which may be the

---

[1] HBC A 6/5, ff. 108–9. Richard Norton, Chief Factor at Churchill since 1731, was home on leave during the winter of 1735–6. In March 1736 he was re-appointed to Churchill for five years, and promised a gratuity of £100 'in case he do Undertake such Voyages and Expeditions to the Nor'ward during his Stay in the Country as he shall be Ordered and directed by the Compa.' HBC A 1/144, f. 76d. For a biographical sketch see A. M. Johnson in *Dictionary of Canadian Biography*, III, 1741 to 1770, Toronto and Quebec, 1974 (hereafter *DCB*, III), pp. 489–90.

[2] George Spurrell, longest serving of the Company's ship-captains in the eighteenth century. He took a ship into Hudson Bay each year from 1722 until his retirement from the sea in 1756. See Glyndwr Williams in *DCB*, III, pp. 598–9.

[3] William Coats, a Company ship-captain from 1727 to 1751; also author of a projected description of Hudson Bay, eventually edited by John Barrow and published by the Hakluyt Society in 1852 as *The Geography of Hudson's Bay*. See Glyndwr Williams in *DCB*, III, pp. 127–8.

[4] James Napper, Second at Churchill, had served the Company on land and at sea since 1716. See L. S. Neatby in *DCB*, II, p. 493.

[5] 'Home Indians' were Cree who lived around the Company factories, hunting for the garrisons, running letters to the other factories, and generally making themselves useful to the Company.

[6] The orders which follow make it clear that these 'Indians' were in fact Eskimo (Inuit).

beginning of July 1737, or sooner); and that they be directed to sail close along the Western Shore, trading with the Indians as far as the Bay or Harbour near Sir Thomas Roe's Welcome; and pitch a Tent on said Land, and stay there trading with the Indians, and digging in several Places in the Earth in Search of Mines; and to take a particular Observation and View of the Land, &c. until the Ship shall call on you which goes out of England next Year; which we purpose to give Directions to the Commanders so to do, and may possibly arrive with you about the 24th July 1737 – And in case the said Ship shall arrive with you by that time, you are, in Company with the said Ship, to sail as far to the Northward as possible, and endeavour to make what Discoveries you can; and keep a exact and particular Account of every Transaction that shall happen: But in case the said Ship from England do not come to you before the 20th August 1737, then you are to return to Churchill-River. It is our Order, that the Masters of the Sloops appointed to go on the aforesaid Discovery be directed to be very particular and exact in sounding the Depth of the Water, taking Account of the Current of the Tide, the Rise and Fall at Ebb and High-Water, and the Distance of the time of Flood; and to enter the same in proper Journals, which are to be delivered to the Chief at the Factory, in order to be transmitted to us.

7. Richard Norton, Factor at Prince of Wales Fort, Churchill, to Governor and Committee of Hudson's Bay Company. 26 July, 23 August 1737.[1]

[26 July] Mr Napper and Mr Crow[2] Saild in the Churchill and Musquash sloops from this place to ye Northward on Discovery on the 4th of this Instant they not being able to gett the Churchill Sloop afloat Sooner on Acct of Ground Ice on the Flatts.[3]

[23 August] The Churchill sloop arrived on the 18th of this

[1] HBC A 11/13, ff. 35d, 40d.
[2] Robert Crow, who had reached Churchill the previous year as second mate on the *Mary*.
[3] The sloops attached to the factory at Churchill were normally laid up for the winter at Sloop Cove, and were dug out of the ice each spring. In 1737 the sloops were not cut free and able to float until 2 July. See HBC B 42/a/17, f. 43d.

Instant at wch time we heard that Mr. Napper dyed at Whale Cove on the 7th. of August, and Mr. Light,[1] who had the charge of the Sloop, upon Mr Nappers Death Saild from the said Cove for this river in comp with the Musquash Sloop on the 15th day of August...And from the success of their Expedition to the Northward we find noe Encouragement to Send the Sloops there next year, the coast being perrilous, No Rivers Navigable that they could meet with Nor noe woods and the Trade trifling and Inconsiderable, the Perticulers of which being as follows viz. 100 lbs of Whalebone, 20 lb of Ivory, Some Unicorns Horns[2] and 3 barrels of blubber.

8. Captain Middleton to Arthur Dobbs. 5 November 1737.[3]

In Summer (1737) I was in London, and waited upon Sir Bibye Lake, who then told me they had ordered the Sloops to try the Passage that Summer. Captain Middleton was then upon his Voyage, so I had no farther Correspondence with him, until the Ships returned in October, when I had the following Letter from him

SIR, London, Nov. 5, 1737.
I am now, thank God, safely arrived from Hudson's Bay, and thought proper to inform you that the Company sent two Sloops upon the Discovery this last Summer; but, in my Opinion, the people on board were not duly qualified for such an Undertaking. They prosecuted their Voyage no farther than Latit.62°¼ North, and returned without making any new or useful Discovery, so far as I can learn.[4] They found a great many Islands, Abundance of Black Whales, but no very great Tides, the highest about two Fathoms, the Flood coming from the Northward. If the Expedition was undertaken in good earnest, and proper

---

[1] Alexander Light, shipwright, had been at Churchill since 1733.
[2] The hollow tusk of the narwhal.
[3] Dobbs, *Remarks*, Appendix, pp. 90–91.
[4] In 1737 Middleton was at Churchill in the *Hudson's Bay* only from 20 to 25 July, and so missed both the departure and return of the sloops on their northern expedition. He presumably got his information about their explorations from Captain Coats, whose ship the *Mary* did not sail from Churchill until 23 August that year. The sloops returned from the north on 18 August (*Churchill*) and 22 August (*Musquash*). See HBC B 42/a/18, ff. 2d., 3.

Persons employed, with suitable Encouragement, it would soon determine what Success might be expected; and it seems not impossible but a Passage would be found. If you should be in London this Winter or next Spring, I shall be extremely glad of the Honour to wait upon you, and tender my Service in any Thing that may be in my Power. In the mean Time you'll be pleased to do me the Favour of signifying the Receipt of this Letter, and so good as to conceal any Intelligence I may have an Opportunity to give you from Time to Time of this Affair.

Be pleased to direct for me in London Street, near Ratcliff Cross.

9. Arthur Dobbs to Captain Middleton. 20 November 1737.[1]

This I answered in the latter End of November, of which the following is a rough Draught; and at the same time wrote to Sir Bibye Lake;

SIR,
I had the Favour of yours of the 5th Instant Yesterday, and am exceedingly obliged to you for the Information you have given me in relation to the late Attempt for the N.W.Discovery.

I must join with you that they seem not to have been duly qualified, or they would not have stop'd short at 62°¼ N. and returned before they got to 64°10′ where Fox and Button had been: However, it is so far an Encouragement, as it confirms the Tide's flowing from the North, and the Whales there must come from that Side, none coming thro' Hudson's Streight. The Tide there, tho' only two Fathom, is much higher than in the Bottom of the Bay, and consequently can't come in thro' the Streights. I am, from the Confirmation of these alone, convinced of a Passage; and nothing is wanting but a Person of Judgment and Capacity to make a thorough Discovery. I'm sorry I can't be over next Spring, having only returned from London three Months ago; but even from hence can promote its being effectually set on Foot by Sir Charles Wager,[2] in case the Company should not heartily engage in it; and you may be assured, whatever farther

---

[1] Dobbs, *Remarks*, Appendix, pp. 91–2.
[2] First Lord of the Admiralty from 1733 to 1742.

Light you can give me in it, shall not be discovered by me, but just so far as you will give me Leave, nor your Name mentioned. However I hope for a more particular Account, if you can, of their Journal.

Last Summer, when I was over, I waited upon Sir Bibye Lake, and he told me they had given Instructions to their Commander at Churchill River to fit out Sloops for the Discovery; so I shall write to him by this Post, as if I had heard nothing, but only to desire him, since I hear their Ships are returned, to let me know what Accounts they have had, and if any Thing has been done, that he would send me an Extract of their Journal for my Animadversions, that I may form a Judgment of it; and by his Answer I shall judge whether they are in earnest in prosecuting the Discovery, and can form my Measures accordingly. And if I knew your Inclinations as to your own attempting it, or any of your Friends, I would promote it, with Sir R.W.[1] in case the Company don't effectually set about it; for whoever will effect it, will certainly deserve a Reward from the Public.

10. Arthur Dobbs to Sir Bibye Lake. 20 November 1737.[2]

The following is the rough Draught of mine to Sir Bibye Lake, the same post.

SIR
Having an Account in the Public Papers that your Ships are returned from Hudson's Bay, it would be a great Pleasure to me, to know if the Sloops had made any Progress in the Discovery of the N.W.Passage by Ne Ultra, according to the Instructions that were sent them from London, of which you were pleased to inform me last Summer.

If they were sent out, and made any Progress, I should be much obliged to you for an Extract of their Journals, and the Observations they made, that I might form a Judgment of their Abilities, and how far they confirm or contradict those who went

---

[1] Sir Robert Walpole, first or prime minister of the Crown. Dobbs first met Walpole in 1730, and owed his appointment in 1733 as Surveyor-General of Ireland to his patronage. See Clarke, *Dobbs*, pp. 22, 32, 33, 35, 39, 41, 42.
[2] Dobbs, *Remarks*, Appendix, p. 93.

before them, and from thence form a Judgment of the Probability of the Passage.

I shall trouble you no more, but wish you Success in all your Undertakings....

11. Sir Bibye Lake to Arthur Dobbs. 16 December 1737.[1]

I have received your Favour of the 20th past, and should be very glad the great Care and Charge the Company have been at would have furnished me with an Answer more to your Satisfaction.

The Sloops, according to the Company's orders, set out from Churchill very early in the Spring,[2] well provided with every Thing which could be thought necessary to make all possible Discovery, and mann'd with the ablest Hands we could procure; but they could not find any Rivers or Inlets on the Western Coast to the North of Churchill, nor any the least Appearance of a Passage, altho' they remained out till the 22d of August.

I have prevailed with the Company to make this Attempt in Compliance with your pressing Importunity, which I assure you has been attended with the utmost Danger of our Vessels and Mens Lives, and in which we lost one of our Governors in Hudson's Bay;[3] and our Captains, who have been old Northwesters, have so terrible an Opinion of going to the Northward, that it was with great Difficulty we prevailed upon one of them to undertake to go and see what was become of the Sloops, and what Success they had met with.[4] In this Situation I hope you will excuse me from running the Company into any farther Danger or Expence, for I am already blamed a good deal for that I have already persuaded them to undertake in this Matter.

---

[1] Ibid., pp. 93–4.

[2] In fact, on 4 July. See p. 41 above.

[3] A reference to James Knight's expedition of 1719.

[4] This reference is far from clear. The context reads as if it is a reference to one of the expeditions sent north from Churchill in the years immediately after Knight's disappearance, except that Knight had not sailed in sloops. Alternatively, it could be a reference to the instructions given to Captain Coats in May 1737 to meet the sloops of the Napper expedition and help them in their explorations – instructions Coats was unable to follow because of his lateness in reaching the Bay that year. See HBC A 6/5, ff. 109d, 129d.

12. Arthur Dobbs to Sir Bibye Lake. [January, 1738].[1]

SIR,

I Had the Favour of yours in relation to your Attempt last Summer by two Sloops to find out the N.W.Passage, and am very much obliged to you alone, Sir, for what you have done, though without Success, but can't say the same for the Company; because I must beg Leave to say, by the Manner of communicating it to me, without their sending me a Journal of the Sloops Proceedings, and their Observations, for my animadverting upon, (which I dare say from your Goodness you would have done, had it been agreeable to the Company that I should have seen it) that they were not inclinable that a Discovery should be made, tho' the whole Tenor of their Charter shews, that the great Powers and Royalties granted to them was in order to their making the Discovery.[2]

Since then they don't think proper to let me know how far the Sloops proceeded, and what Obstacles they met with, or Observations they made, pursuant to the Instructions you gave them (for I dare say you gave those I sent you to give, or at least others more particular) you must give me leave to animadvert upon so much as you think proper to acquaint me with.

Were they mann'd by sailors capable of keeping any Journals, or in the least knowing the Art of Navigation? Was it probable, if they behaved as they ought to do, that they should have been out early in the Spring, and continue out until the 22d of August, and in that Time not be able to sail two hundred Leagues? For it is not so far from Churchill to Ne Ultra, the Difference of Latitude not being more than six Degrees; if they trifled away their Time in looking out for Inlets or a Passage to the Southward of it, they did not know their Business, nor follow their Instructions, or they were unwilling to find out whether there was a Passage or not. Had they been as far as 65°.N and had met with any Thing to obstruct their Passage, by being land-lock'd, or meeting with Ice, they would have produced their Journals,

---

[1] Dobbs, *Remarks*, Appendix, pp. 94–6.

[2] The only reference in the Charter of 1670 to this supposed obligation was in the preamble, which noted that the preliminary voyage of the *Eaglet* and *Nonsuch* to Hudson Bay in 1668 was 'for the discovery of a new Passage into the South Sea'. Rich, *History*, I, p. 56.

and acquainted the Company with it, which not having done, otherwise you would have acquainted me with it, it is plain to a Demonstration, that they have been idle or faulty, or thought it might please the Company that no Passage should be found: For to say that they were afraid to go to 66° Latit. when they have an open Sea, and no Ice in that Season to obstruct them, when the Whale Fishers, north at Spitzberg and in Baffens Bay, sail every year to 78°. and 80°. is scarce credible.[1] As to your mentioning the Loss of one of your Governors in the Attempt, which I suppose was in the former Attempt, and not this made last Summer, and also the sending out a Captain to know what was come of the Sloops, which I apprehend was also before, since the Sloops came back in good Time, it is only by way of Discouragement, to prevent any farther Attempt. However, since your Company is unwilling to make the Attempt, I shall be far from desiring them to do it. As for my own Part, I am not only convinced that it is practicable, but also that it is easy, and no way dangerous, after passing Hudson's Streights. I only apply'd to them as I thought it not only their Interest that they should find it, but that it was also expected from them by their Charter; yet since they are pleased to neglect and despise it, I shall now apply myself to others who I believe will undertake it chearfully, as they are convinced it will be a national Benefit: For, as I am willing that England should reap the Benefit of it, I shall not publish to the World the full Proof I have of a Passage, because I know other Nations would attempt it before us, that they might set up a Right to the Trade thro' it, as the first Discoverers....

13. Captain Middleton to Arthur Dobbs. 21 January 1737 (OS)[2]

Sir Bibye's Letter and this Answer I sent a Copy of to Captain Middleton; but before he received it he sent me an Answer to my former Letter in the following Words:

I Have the Honour of yours of the 20th of November, and am

---

[1] A considerable exaggeration. In 1616 Baffin sailed as far north as Smith Sound in lat. 78°N, a latitude not reached again until the expedition of John Ross in 1818. The Davis Strait whalers rarely entered Baffin Bay itself.
[2] Dobbs, *Remarks*, Appendix, pp. 97–8.

sorry it is not in my Power to answer your Request, of giving you a more particular Account from the Journals of those who were sent last Year upon the Discovery; the Company alone can give you that Satisfaction, and no doubt will transmit them to you, by which you will be able to judge of the Skill and Conduct of those who were employed in that Affair, and may also form some Judgment, whether the Company are desirous of prosecuting it in earnest.

However, it is my Opinion, that nothing will be done in it to any Purpose, unless the Government will give a sufficient Encouragement to some Persons of known Abilities to undertake it, and then I should not despair but the whole might be accomplished by passing two whole Winters at Churchill, and proceeding on the Discovery with Resolution during the Summer: For my own Part, I confess I should be ambitious of attaining the Honour of such a Discovery, and should hope very much that Success would crown the Undertaking; but as I have a certain Income from the Company, as long as I am able to go that Voyage, it would not be prudent in me to quit their Employment upon an Uncertainty; and if they should come to the Knowledge of my having any Intention of accepting such an Offer, I have too much Reason to apprehend they would immediately discard me; so that what I now write being unknown to them, I rely on your Honour will not be divulged to my Prejudice. In short, I believe the Company think it their Interest rather to prevent than forward new Discoveries in that Part of the World; and for that Reason they will not suffer any of our Journals to be made public. All the Intimation I am able to give is, that the Tides rise more with a N. and N.W. Wind at neap Tides, than ever the Spring Tides do at Churchill or Albany with a southerly or easterly Wind; and as there is little or no Tide between Mansfield and Cary's Swan's Nest, nor any in the N. or N.N.W. of Mill Isles in that Bay, it must come from the Welcome, which cannot be far from some Western Ocean. Also in Mr. John Scrogg's Journal, in 1722, he mentions that in Latit. 64°.56′. the Tide ebb'd five Fathoms, but gives no Account which Way or from whence the Flood came; and they all agree that a great many black Whales are seen in the Welcome, whereas I don't remember to have seen any in other Parts of Hudson's Bay, and I have been in all Parts of it, except the Welcome, all which are favourable Circumstances....

14. Sir Charles Wager to Arthur Dobbs. 4 March 1737 (OS)[1]

On the 20th of February I wrote Letters to Sir C. Wager, Mr W.[2] and Colonel Bladen[3] acquainting them with the Usage I had received from the Company, notwithstanding the Prospect there was of Success, had they prosecuted it in earnest, letting Sir Charles know that now I had no other Resource but to get it undertaken by the Public, and hop'd he would get it promoted, by sending out two Sloops from the Admiralty. To which he was pleased to send me the following Letter:

SIR   Admiralty-Office, March 4, 1737 (OS)
I received the Favour of your Letter of the 20th past. I believe you judge very right that the Hudson's Bay Company do not desire to have any Body interfere with them in the Fur Trade in those Parts; they seem to be content with what they have, and make (I believe) considerable Profit by it; and if it should be farther extended, which might be the Case if a farther Discovery was made: For tho' they should not find a navigable Passage thro' into the South, they might probably find Indian Nations, from whom Furs might be bought cheaper than they are bought in Hudson's Bay, and that would be a Disadvantage to their Trade.

The Probabilities of finding a Passage, as you propose, seem to be very strong; the Flood coming that Way is almost a Demonstration; what Difficulties may be in the Execution can't be foreseen. If a Passage could be found into the South Sea, it would open a very large Field, and very probably of a very profitable Commerce; but the first Projectors, let the Affair succeed never so well, have seldom if ever found their Account in it. However, that should not hinder others from exerting themselves in the discovering any Thing that may be advantageous to the Public; but a Spirit of that Kind seems to have been asleep for many Years. War may have perhaps prevented, in some Measure, and diverted Mens Thoughts from any Enterprize of that Nature. I confess I have myself had Thoughts of that kind, and especially since I read your Manuscript of a Probability of a N.W.Passage

---

[1] Ibid., pp. 100–102.
[2] Possibly Horatio Walpole; see p. 52 below.
[3] Colonel Martin Bladen, one of the Lords Commissioners of the Board of Trade and Plantations.

to the South Sea, but I have found but very few that were willing to bestow any Thoughts about it. I remember Lord Granard[1] and I have talk'd about it sometimes, but it was Talk, other Things and Business nearer Home has employed our Time and Thoughts too. I think the best Way to undertake such a Discovery, is to have, as you propose, two proper Vessels to go at a proper Time of the Year, and to winter there, if it was found necessary; and to carry with them a Cargo, not a great one, of Goods proper to trade with any Indians they may meet with; and capable and honest People to be employed in the Expedition, if such are to be found in the World, which I doubt; and ten or a dozen Persons, or more if thought proper, engaged in it, who would advance Money sufficient to carry it on, who may in Time, if it should succeed, be better intitled to the Name of the N.W. or South Sea Company, than the present South Sea Company has to that Name, who are not permitted to trade in any one Place within the Limits of their Charter, which made such an Eclat at the first establishing it.[2] If this should be once agreed on, and proper Persons be found to join in it, it may then be considered what Authority may be proper to obtain from the Crown, that the first that go and succeed, may not only beat the Bush, and others come afterwards to catch the Hare. For tho' I do not much like exclusive Companies, where it is not absolutely necessary; yet I would not have the Advantages that may be found by some, be given away to others. As to Vessels being sent at the Public Expence, tho' it would not be great, yet the Parliament may think, especially at this Time,[3] that we ought not to play with the Money they give us, for other and particular Services. However, if Sir Robert Walpole, or other proper Persons, should think that the Government should attempt it at the Public Expence, I shall not be against it.

---

[1] George Forbes, 3rd Earl of Granard, and an Admiral.

[2] A reference to the wildly optimistic hopes of commercial expansion which accompanied the establishment of the South Sea Company in 1711.

[3] By this time relations with Spain were deteriorating fast, and war followed in 1739.

15. Captain Middleton to Arthur Dobbs. 8 April 1738.[1]

I acquainted Captain Middleton with my writing to these Gentlemen, and sent him a copy of the above Answer from Sir Charles Wager, to which I had the following Advice:

SIR   London, April 8, 1738.
I am honoured with yours of the 20th Ult. and observe, that altho' the uneasy Situation of Affairs may have rendered your Application in Behalf of the Discovery fruitless at this Time, yet you intend to push the Attempt next Season, when you come to England; and then I hope you will find the Circumstances of the Times more favourable. I return you many Thanks for the kind Assurances of your Friendship and Interest in recommending me as a proper Person to be employed in so great an Undertaking, and shall, according to your Request, make all such farther Enquiries and Observations this Voyage as may lie in my Power.

I am particularly obliged to you for the Favour of your communicating to me a Copy of Sir Charles Wager's Letter; and if I can make any Judgment from the Tenor of it, he seems not to have any hearty Inclination for the Enterprize....

What you propose, that the Government should allow a sufficient Premium for the Discovery, in case of Success, and that they should think fit to allow a free Trade through it, must be thought very reasonable; especially as Companies with exclusive Privileges are generally dislik'd. Whether it would be needful to apply to Parliament for a Resumption of so much of the Grant to the Hudson's Bay Company as intitles them to the Benefit of the Trade, I am under some Doubt, because I know not whether they derive that Privilege by Act of Parliament, or only by a Grant from the Crown;[2] if it be from the latter, I apprehend there is an Act made in the Reign of James I which has abridg'd the Prerogative in their Power of granting exclusive Privileges; and if that be the Case, I believe it would not be difficult to find three or four Persons who would be at the Charge of fitting out

---

[1] Ibid., pp. 102–4.
[2] The Charter of 1670 was a royal grant. In 1690 it was confirmed by Parliament, but for seven years only, and the Company's attempt in 1698 to renew this Parliamentary confirmation failed. From then on it was 'forced to relapse into dependence on Royal prerogative only'. Rich, *History*, I, p. 364.

two Sloops to winter there, in order to prosecute the Discovery, provided they might have the Liberty of trading in the Bay, without being called to an Account for it. It is not possible to pass the Winter to Northward of Churchill, neither is there any Hopes of a gainful Trade at present with the Northern Indians;[1] so that I should be glad to know whether the Company have an Act of Parliament to confirm their Charter or not; and if you hear from H. Walpole[2] or Col. Bladen in Favour of the Attempt, I shall be much obliged to you, if you please to acquaint me of it. I reckon we shall sail about the 20th of next Month.

16. Captain Middleton to Arthur Dobbs. 15 May 1738.[3]

This I answered the 17th [April], to which I had the following Reply

SIR, London, May 15, 1738

I Have the Favour of yours dated from Lisburn, April 17, and am convinced that the Situation of our public Affairs is such at present,[4] that no Proposal could be properly made to the Ministry about the Discovery at this Time: However, I make no question but you may be able to influence Sir Charles Wager and others to give Encouragement for it, when the Circumstances of the Times alter for the better. Mean while I shall continue making all such Observations as may tend to promote the Undertaking; and before I received your last Letter, I had proposed something of that Kind to the Company, but they took no notice of it, which shews they have no Design of prosecuting that Design at all, even where it would be no Detriment or Delay to our Voyage. In four or five Days we shall sail from hence, and if it please God to grant me a safe Return, you shall hear from

---

[1] 'Northern Indians' was the term used by the Hudson's Bay Company traders to describe the Chipewyan, whose hunting grounds stretched west and northwest from Churchill to Athabasca.

[2] Probably Horatio Walpole, younger brother of Sir Robert, and ambassador at the Hague at this time.

[3] Dobbs, *Remarks*, Appendix, pp. 104–5.

[4] Another reference to the growing crisis in relations with Spain; after debate in Parliament in April 1738 the decision was taken to send British fleets to the Mediterranean and Caribbean.

me on our Arrival, and from what you wrote before I hope for the Honour of seeing you next Spring.

P.S. I am now ordered by the Company to go to the South Parts of the Bay,[1] which, in some Respect, may disappoint me of making the Observations I proposed to them.

17. Captain Middleton to Arthur Dobbs. 24 May 1739.[2]

[After a further exchange of letters] *Thus Things stood till I went over in April, 1739, when we met; but finding it not a proper Time to push it, he was only to continue to make proper Observations, and get what Accounts he could in the Bay; and upon his going out he wrote me the following Letter:*

SIR,   Yarmouth, May 24, 1739
As I am now upon my Departure from England, and had not an Opportunity, thro' the Hurry of my Business, to wait upon you in Person, I thought proper to assure you, that I have so ordered my Affairs as to be ready next Year to undertake the Discovery, in case you should find Means to have it put in Execution, when the Season comes on, tho' I am doubtful our national Concerns are not so thoroughly settled as to give our Ministry Leisure to think of it: However that be, you may depend upon the Sincerity of my Intentions, and Readiness to promote the Undertaking, (if it please God to bless me with Health) whenever Matters shall be ripe for it.

18. Captain Middleton to Arthur Dobbs. 18 October 1739.[3]

Upon his Return I had the following Letter from him:

Honoured Sir,   London, Octob. 18, 1739
I think it my Duty to embrace the first Opportunity of acquainting you with our safe Arrival, and of returning you my Thanks

---

[1] Middleton sailed to Albany and Moose in 1738.
[2] Ibid., p. 107.
[3] Ibid., pp. 108–9.

for the Respect you were pleased to shew me before my Departure. I should have been extremely glad to have seen you at London at this juncture, where I find our Preparations for War more vigorous than ever,[1] and consequently all Thoughts of Application about the former Design fruitless, till a more convenient Season: But as so great a Number of Men of War have already been fitted out, as to take almost all our old Officers into Commission, and several Twenty-Gun Ships are now building, I should not doubt but I might obtain the Command of one of them, thro' your Interest in my Behalf, if you should think me deserving of so great a Favour, and you are not under any pre-Engagements. I am very well acquainted with the Navigation on the Coasts of both New and Old Spain, having been many years in those Parts before I engaged with the Hudson's Bay Company, and was in several Letter of Marque Ships in Queen Anne's War[2] at my first setting out as a Sailor.

I am personally known to Sir Jacob Ackworth,[3] Sir John Norris,[4] and all the elder Brothers of the Trinity-House; and I believe that none of them would object to my Qualification, provided I should have any Friend of Weight that would think it proper to solicit in my Behalf; and tho' I have the Honour but of a very late Acquaintance with yourself, yet I hope you'll excuse the Freedom of this Address in an Affair which I judge to happen opportunely to my Advantage; and if I should have the good Fortune to succeed, might facilitate my being employed hereafter when it may be thought proper to undertake the Discovery. If you should think fit to do me the Honour of your Recommendation to any of the Lords of the Admiralty, or others, on this Occasion, my future Behaviour (I hope) will shew me not altogether unworthy of so high a Trust, nor ungrateful to my Benefactor.

I was this Voyage at Churchill Factory, where Mr. Norton is Governor. He was along with Scroggs in 1722, and remembers very well that when they came to an Anchor in the Welcome, near the Latitude 65°. they had twelve Fathoms at High-water, and but seven at Low-water; and he seems confident, from a

---

[1] The formal declaration of war was approved by the government the next day, 19 October.

[2] Otherwise known as the War of the Spanish Succession, 1702 to 1713.

[3] Sir Jacob Acworth, Surveyor to the Navy Board.

[4] Admiral of the Fleet.

View that he took from a Promontory ashore, that there must be a clear Passage; the Land is very high, and falls off to the Southward of the West.[1]

This Year some of the Natives, who came down to trade at Churchill, and had never been before at any of our English Settlements, informed him they frequently traded with Europeans on the West Side of America, near the Latitude of Churchill by their Account, which seems to confirm that the two Seas must unite.[2]

19. Arthur Dobbs to Sir Charles Wager. 30 October 1739.[3]

I answered this the 30th, and inclosed to him Letters of Recommendation to Sir Robert Walpole, Lord Conway,[4] and Sir Charles Wager, of which I need only give a Copy of what I wrote to Sir Charles Wager, viz.

SIR,

I find, by Captain Middleton, who is returned safe from Churchill in Hudson's Bay, that the Accounts he has had there this Year confirm there being a safe Passage at the Welcome.

Here I recited the last Paragraph of the above Letter.

Since these Facts confirm the former Accounts, and demonstrate a Passage, I am humbly of Opinion, that if we have a War with Spain, it would be highly advantageous to attempt it next Summer. If we discover it, and the War should continue the following Year, we might intercept their Acapulco Ships,[5] and

[1] Probably Chesterfield Inlet, not discovered and mapped until 1747. For details of this suggested identification see p. 59 n. 2 below.

[2] There is no specific reference to this in the Churchill factory journal; but on 25 June 1739 Richard Norton noted the arrival of six canoes of 'Western Indians' (as well as the more usual arrivals of Northern or Chipewyan Indians). HBC B 42/a/19, f.31d.

[3] Dobbs, *Remarks*, Appendix, pp. 110–11.

[4] Francis Seymour Conway, 2nd Baron Conway (later Earl of Hertford), nephew of Sir Robert Walpole. At Walpole's request, Dobbs acted as agent for the Conway estate in Ireland, and also as adviser to Conway, who was still a minor (b. 1719). See Clarke, *Dobbs*, ch. 4.

[5] The annual treasure galleon from Acapulco to Manila. Possibly unknown to Dobbs, the Admiralty was at this moment considering such a plan by way of an expedition around Cape Horn. This sailed in 1740 under the command of Commodore George Anson on a voyage which was to become celebrated as much for its disasters as for its triumph in capturing the Acapulco galleon.

make many Prizes from California to Panama, before they would suspect our being upon their Coasts; and when they should know that we had found the Passage, our being capable of attacking them in the South Sea in so easy a Manner, would soon humble them, and make them value our Friendship.

I therefore beg leave to recommend Captain Middleton to you, as a Person capable, from his Knowledge of Sea-Affairs, particularly in Hudson's Bay, of being of great Service to Great-Britain; and even if it should not be judged proper to attempt it this Season, hope you will think him worthy of a Command under his Majesty, that he may be ready to attempt it whenever it may be thought proper...I hope, Sir, you will pardon the Earnestness of my Sollicitation in his Favour; but as you know I have the Discovery much at Heart, you will the more easily forgive me. I have wrote to Sir Robert Walpole upon the same Subject, and if other more important Affairs don't take up his Thoughts, he may probably speak to you upon this Subject.

20. Captain Middleton to Arthur Dobbs. 29 November 1739.[1]

I Received the Favour of your obliging Letter of the 30th of October, with the inclosed to Sir R. Walpole, Sir Charles Wager, and Lord Conway. I did myself the Honour to wait of these Gentlemen immediately, and was received with great Civility and Respect by Sir C. Wager, not finding any Opportunity to be introduced to Sir Robert, by my Lord Conway's happening to be out of Town, for several Days after the Receipt of your Letter. Sir Charles assured me that he was very desirous of having the Discovery undertaken, and would do all that was in his Power to promote it. Accordingly he ordered me to wait upon him a second Time in an Evening with a Chart of Hudson's Bay; which I did last Monday Night, when we had a good deal of Discourse relating to the Method that might be proper to be pursued, in case it should be put into Practice next Spring; but he told me he had not then got your Manuscript from my Lord Conway,[2] who

---

[1] Dobbs, *Remarks*, Appendix, pp. 111–12.

[2] This is presumably Dobbs's memorial of 1733, a copy of which remained in the possession of the Hertford family until 1959. See *Historical Manuscripts Commission*, 4th Report, pt I, London, 1874, p. 251.

being in Town, I waited of him, and he told me it was not proper
for him at that Time to introduce me to Sir Robert, but he would
give me Notice when I should attend him, and took Directions
how to send to me. As Sir Charles has given me Liberty to wait
of him as often as I please, I make no doubt but he will discourse
Sir Robert on the Affair as soon as he can conveniently; for at
this Juncture Sir Robert is so extremely full of Business, that I
despair of the Honour of waiting of him personally: However, I
shall have the Pleasure to acquaint you from time to time what
Progress is made in it, from the free Access I have to Sir Charles,
who will not (I believe) let any Opportunity slip that may seem to
favour the Design.

21. Captain Middleton to Arthur Dobbs. 8 January 1739 (OS).[1]

*This I did not immediately answer, but had from him the following
Letter*:

SIR,   London, Jan. 8, 1739
Since my last I have not been honoured with any from you,
neither have I yet the Pleasure to inform you of any great
Progress made towards the Execution of our Project: However I
constantly wait on Sir Charles once a Fortnight, or oftener, who
receives me with great Civility and Respect. I gave him a Copy of
the inclosed Paper, which is the Substance of one I delivered to
the Company last Winter.[2] Sir Charles seem'd to be pleased in
perusing it, and said he had not yet got your Papers from my
Lord Conway. I told him I had waited upon my Lord a great
many Times, but had not found a proper Opportunity of being
introduced to him: However, Sir Charles was so good as to say,
that I might spare myself the Trouble, for it lay more immediately in his Way to forward the Affair; and I hope he will not let
slip any proper Occasion of doing it. I shall not fail, for my own
Part, to put him in Mind of it pretty frequently, as he has been
pleased to give me leave to attend him as often as I think
convenient. From time to time I shall do myself the Honour to
acquaint you what Proceedings are made in the Affair.

[1] Dobbs, *Remarks*, Appendix, pp. 112–13.
[2] That is, on the Scroggs expedition of 1722. See Document 22 below.

22. Extract from the Journal of John Scroggs, 1722.[1]

Here below is the Paper he inclosed me about Scroggs's Discovery:

An Account of Sir Thomas Row's Welcome, or Ut [Ne] Ultra, extracted from the Journal of John Scroggs, in a Voyage he made from Churchill to the said Welcome, Anno 1722.

June 22d, 1722, sailed from Churchill in 59°.North, and Longitude from the Meridian of London, 95°.West in the Latitude 62°. He traded with the Indians for Whalebone and Sea-horse Teeth.[2] Monday, July 9th in the Evening, he anchored in twelve Fathoms. The Weather for several Days before had been hazy and thick, and he drove into this Depth. When it cleared up he found himself about nine or ten Miles from the North Side of the Welcome, in Lat. by Account 64° 33′N. He saw several Islands bearing from the S.W. by W. to the S.W. by S. and a Head-land at the same Time, which bore E.N.E. about 3 Leagues distant. This he named Whalebone Point,[3] after the Name of his Sloop.

July 10, at seven in the Morning, he sent his six-oar'd Boat on Shore, with seven Hands and two Northern Indians; Mr. Norton, who is now a Governor at Churchill, was then Pateroon[4] of the Boat, and spoke the Northern Indian Tongue. The two Indians had been entertained at the Factory all the foregoing Winter, upon the Account of this Discovery. They gave us Intimation of a rich Copper Mine, that lay near the Surface of the Earth, and said they could direct the Sloop or Ship to lie by it,

---

[1] Ibid., pp. 112–18. There is no manuscript copy of Scroggs's journal extant. Extracts exist in two rather different forms: in Dobbs's *Remarks*, supplied by Middleton in 1740 and printed by Dobbs in 1744; and in the Clerk of the *California* [T.S.Drage], *An Account of a Voyage for the Discovery of a North-West Passage by Hudson's Streights*, London, 1748–9, II, pp. 174–80. Middleton was asked by the Company to look at the journal; it is less easy to explain how the clerk of the *California*, member of an expedition regarded by the Company as an interloping one, came to see it – and why the two versions differ so much.

[2] The version by the clerk of the *California* has additional detail here which, among much else, refers to wreckage from the Knight expedition: '...in the Latitude of 62 Deg. 48 Min. sent a Boat for a peice of Wood, which was a-float, and they found it to be the lower Part of the Ships Foremast, broke off about five Foot above the Deck.' Ibid., II, p. 174.

[3] Modern Whale Point.

[4] Master or officer in charge of a ship or a boat.

where she might load very soon. We had several Pieces of Copper brought down to Churchill, which made it evident there is a Mine somewhere in that Country. These Indians sketch'd out the Land with Charcoal upon a Skin of Parchment, before they left the Factory, and as far as the Sloop went, they found it agree very well.[1]

Scroggs says he saw both sides of the Welcome, from the South back to the West, being up in the very Cod of the Welcome, as he terms it.[2] The Land is as high as Hudson's Streights, as he and his Men all agreed, and that Land we can see in clear Weather very well 15 or 20 Leagues. Where he continued at Anchor, he mentions it was very good Soundings. He always continued the Variation the same as at Churchill; for he knew not how to observe it. Then it was 26° W. and is now but 20° West at Churchill, tho' we find in the same Latitude 50 or 60 Leagues to the Eastward almost 50° Variation westerly, which makes the Welcome above two Points nearer the Meridian.

Tuesday, July 10, he continued at Anchor in the same Place; and the Boat returned on Board at five o'Clock in the Afternoon. He says they saw several black and white Whales here. At four the next Morning went on Shore again with the aforesaid Indians, and came back about five in the Evening. They found none of the Natives, but Plenty of Deer, wild Geese, Ducks, &c. Some of the Deer they killed. At 10 in the Forenoon calm, he says it ebbs five Fathoms where he lay at Anchor, for they anchored in twelve Fathom at High-water, as Mr Norton this Year also confirmed to me, and they found but seven Fathom at Low-water.[3] At Noon he and his Mate observed the Latitude to

[1] This is one of several maps drawn in this period by Chipewyan Indians of the land between Churchill and the far-off Coppermine River. For a recent discussion of them see Richard I. Ruggles, *A Country So Interesting: The Hudson's Bay Company and Two Centuries of Mapping 1670–1870*, Montreal, 1991, pp. 30–31.
[2] The reference to being in 'the very Cod [or end] of the Welcome', and the earlier reference to 'the North Side of the Welcome', make little sense if read literally. Scroggs was 150 miles distant from the northern extremity of the Welcome at Repulse Bay, and in any case it is difficult to speak of anything but the western and eastern shores of the Welcome. Scroggs was probably not in the main channel of the Welcome at all, but in Daly Bay. The 'very Cod' and the 'North Side' of the Welcome on this reading would be the stretch of shoreline between Daly Bay and the entrance of Chesterfield Inlet. See Clerk of the *California, Account*, II, p. 175.
[3] According to the clerk of the *California*, this measurement 'being made not by a settled Standard ashore, but by a Line from the Ship, it was a mistake, and owing to the Ships swinging off into the Tide'. Ibid.

be 64°56′N. Here he named the southermost Island that bore S.W. by S. Cape Fullerton, after one of our Directors.[1]

Wednesday, July 11, continued in the same Place at Anchor. He observed the Latitude again, and found it as before 64°56′N. by a good Observation. His Mate, he tells us, agreed with him. He sent his Boat up to the Cod of the Bay, as he terms it, to sound, and the two Northern Indians went in her. One of them, he says, had a great Desire to go Home, which he told them was but three or four Days Journey from thence, but they detained him with fair Words and Promises.

Thursday, 12th of July, at four in the Afternoon, the Boat returned from the Shore. He gives us no Account of the Soundings, tho' they went out for that Purpose; but he asserts there was a Bar across the Welcome, and that they could go no farther.[2] All the Men agreed, when they returned,[3] that they were at least ten Leagues from what he would have to be a Bar. At five in the Afternoon he weighed from that Place, where he had laid at Anchor ever since the 9th Instant, and steered out S.E. by Compass for two Miles, and then S.W. by ditto about four or five Miles more. Here he sounded in 45 Fathom, and continued sailing to the South-west Quarter.

July 13th, observed the Latitude at Noon to be 64°39′, and

[1] John Fullartine, a Company director from 1711 until his death in 1738. See A. M. Johnson in *DCB*, II, pp. 231–3.

[2] The clerk of the *California* has an explanation of this fictitious bar. 'Two Northern Indians, whom he had brought with him, and who knew the Country very well, and had a great desire to go Home, saying they were but two or three Days Journey from their Family, told him that there was a Bar of Stones in his Way, which would prevent him from entering the Welcome. This Mr. Scroggs was determined to try, and at eight in the Morning of July the eleventh he sent away his Boat to make Trial, at four that Evening the Boat returned, and the People reported that there was a great Shoal of Stones beyond the Bar, above Water, and not water for the Boat on the Bar, so that he was positive that there was no Passage beyond the Welcome, though the contrary hath been experienced as the Sequel will show.

For the right understanding how this happened, it must be observed, that many of the People who went out with Mr. Scroggs on this Expedition, were the people who were to return to England that Year with the Hudson's Bay Ships; and they being apprehensive that the Hudson's Bay Ships might be come, and be returned before they could get back; they therefore used all Expediants they could, that Mr. Scroggs might return and not proceed further, that they might arrive in Time at the Factory, to get Home with the Ships for England; and Mr. Scroggs being a Timerous Person, and no Way fond of the Expedition, very readily consented to what they said.' *Account*, II, p. 177.

[3] To Churchill.

had 40 or 50 Fathom Water. The next Day 14th, returning Home, he found the Latitude by Observation to be 64°20′ and the Soundings 60 to 70 Fathoms. These Sounding he called the Mid-channel. In Lat. 64°13′ by Observation at Noon, on the South or rather East Side of the Welcome, the Flood came on so strong, and hove them so near the said South or East Shore, that he was obliged to come to an Anchor in ten Fathom. He does not say from whence the Flood came, nor does he ever give his Opinion of it during his whole Voyage in his Journal; but being set on the East side, it must come from the Northward, according to the Course of the Welcome.

July the 15th, he crossed the Welcome in seventy fathoms, and observed the Latitude to be 64°15′. He makes the Welcome to be 15 or 20 Leagues broad in this Lat. from Side to Side, by computing the Distance from his Log-book. He saw many Whales in Lat. 64°8′.

Governor Kelsey, in his Journal 1720, takes Notice, that in Lat. 63° on the West Side of the Welcome, the Tide comes strong from the N.E. which is near the Course of the Welcome. He calls it a soking Tide, and says it flows neap and Spring Tides from 12 to 17 Feet.[1]

Last Winter the Hudson's Bay Company sent me the Journals of Scroggs and his Mate to examine, in order to have my Opinion of the Passage. I gave them an Account much the same as the foregoing, and incurred the Displeasure of some of those Gentlemen, for declaring my Opinion so freely for a Passage. 'Tis what they are not desirous of discovering, lest any should interfere with their Trade. I offered to undertake it for them, but they cared not to come into the Proposal. I was at Churchill when Scroggs went out, and wintered there at the same Time with him, being then Mate to one of the Company's Ships.[2] It was proposed that I should go with Scroggs on the Discovery to draw

---

[1] Henry Kelsey, Governor in the Bay in succession to James Knight, sailed north from Churchill along the west coast of Hudson Bay in 1719 and 1721, but *not* in 1720, when the northern slooping voyage was commanded by John Hancock. None of the journals from these voyages survives.

[2] The crew of the *Whalebone*, sent out to the Bay in 1721, refused to winter there; and Middleton, second mate on the *Hannah*, was among those engaged by Kelsey to make up numbers for the northern voyage the next summer. See K. G. Davies and A. M. Johnson, eds, *Letters from Hudson Bay 1703–40*, London, 1965, p. 84n., and Rich and Johnson, *Isham's Observations*, p. 326.

the Land and make Observations; but when the Time for undertaking the Voyage came on, Scroggs would not suffer me to go
with him, for what Reason I know not.[1] The Governor at Churchill was a good-natured easy Man,[2] and would not use his
Authority to oblige him to carry me against his Will. When they
returned, which was in a Months Time or thereabouts, I examined the Officers and Men, several of them having been my
Scholars in the Winter to learn Navigation. They told me they saw
nothing, at those Times they were on Shore, to hinder their going
farther; for when they were eight or ten Miles from the Point he
nam'd Whale Point, which bore E.N.E. from them, they saw an
open Sea, and the Land trench'd away to the Southward of the
West.[3] This they said to Scroggs's Face, as soon as they were got
on board our Ship at Churchill, tho' while they were under his
Command they dissembled it, and said what he pleased to have
them. From this, and all other Accounts, it appears there must be
a Passage for the Tides from the great Ocean.

This was the Copy he inclosed to me, mentioned in his Letter. In that
Paper he gave the Company, which he says was much to the same
Purpose, he was obliged to conceal great Part of his Opinion, for fear of
disobliging them; but one Point he affirms in it, which is very material,
that is, the Time of High-water in Whale Cove. He says in it: Captain
Kelsey, and likewise the Sloops that went last Year,[4] found the Tides near
the same Latitude (he was talking of the Tides at Cary's Swan's Nest)
about thirty or forty Leagues to the Westward in Whale Cove, to flow but
Ten Feet in common Tides, and a W.S.W. Moon makes a full Sea.

23. Captain Middleton to Arthur Dobbs. 22 [12?] January 1739 (OS).[5]

SIR,

As the Season is so far advanced, I thought proper to write a few

---

[1] The Company records are rather unrevealing on this. The Churchill factory
journal for 25 June 1722 simply noted 'Capt. Scroggs not thinking fitt to lett him
[Middleton] go...he saying he will Satisfie the Compy. att home for his not
proceeding wth. him....'. Ibid.

[2] Nathaniel Bishop.

[3] Again, presumably the mouth of Chesterfield Inlet.

[4] That is, in 1737.

[5] Dobbs, *Remarks*, Appendix, p. 118.

Lines to Sir Charles Wager, and delivered them into his own Hand, not having an Opportunity of discoursing him in private upon the Subject of the Discovery. I send you a Copy of my Letter inclosed. He read it while I was present, and told me that for his own Part, he was entirely for undertaking it this Spring; but he was afraid he should not be able to put it in Execution, and that the Thoughts of it must be deferr'd till next Year. As a second Letter from yourself to Sir Charles or Sir Robert Walpole may be a Means to encourage their executing it this Season, I shall leave it to your Judgment to make such farther Application about it as you think convenient; because it will be necessary for me to engage again with the Company in a very short Time, unless Sir Charles should be pleased to give some Encouragement to the other Part of my Proposal, when he has considered it.

24. Captain Middleton to Sir Charles Wager. 7 January 1739 (OS).[1]

As the Hudson's Bay Company have just given us Orders to get our Ships ready for sailing a Month sooner than usual, I beg Leave to acquaint you therewith, and with great Submission to offer a few Thoughts relating to the Expedition Mr. Dobbs proposed, that in case you should judge it not expedient to undertake it this Year in such a manner as to go through the Discovery, by wintering there; yet some Preparation may be made towards it, and at the same Time an Advantage be gain'd of the Spaniards, when they least expect it.

The Biscayers every Year send ten or twelve Ships to fish for Whales behind Resolution,[2] and these might be taken as Prizes with great Ease, together with the Fish they catch, by a Twenty-gun Ship, carrying a few Men more than ordinary to be spared for manning such Vessels as we might have the good Fortune to take in those Parts, together with a Tender about ninety Tuns. I propose a Ship of twenty or thirty Guns, as the fittest in all Respects, because they draw but little Water, and besides have a

[1] Ibid., pp. 119–20.
[2] Resolution Island, in the northern part of the Atlantic entrance of Hudson Strait.

Number of Oars, which will be extremely useful in getting thro' the Ice, and coming up with the Spaniards. We should also have Time enough to sail up the Welcome with the Ship and Tender, in order to make more certain Observations of the Course and Strength of the Tides, the Bearings of the Coast, &c. than have yet been transmitted us, which would mightily facilitate the Discovery, whenever it should hereafter be put in Execution. Another great Use of the Tender would be in case of any bad Accident in the Ice, which is sometimes unavoidable, notwithstanding the greatest Care.

In case you should be pleased to approve this Proposition, and entrust me with the Command of such a Vessel this Spring for the Purpose above-mentioned, I do assure you that I will discharge my Duty with such Care, Fidelity and Resolution, as I hope will be for the Service and Satisfaction of the Public, as well as to give you no Cause to repent assisting me with your Recommendation and Encouragement.

If this should find your Approbation, I will set down such farther Memorandums as may be proper relating to this Undertaking, and the Preparation necessary for it.

I hope, Sir, you will excuse the Freedom of this Address; and in case what I have offered be improper at this Juncture, you'll be pleased to let me know, because the Time is at hand that I must engage again with the Company, or relinquish their Service.

25. Arthur Dobbs to Sir Charles Wager. 23 January 1739 (OS).[1]

SIR,

It is with great Pleasure I hear from Captain Middleton, that he has been to wait upon you, and has laid all the latest Accounts and Journals relating to the N.W.Passage before you, which, I am persuaded you will agree with me, almost amount to a Demonstration of there being an easy Passage free from Ice, since the Welcome is the most northerly Part of the Passage.

Since this Discovery must be of great Advantage either in Peace or War, I'm persuaded you'll give your Assistance in

[1] Ibid., pp. 120–21.

having it made this Season, for by delaying it, I'm afraid lest France should get the Scent, and anticipate our Discovery. I have wrote by this Post to Sir R.Walpole upon it, and believe he will mention it to you, having referred to you in my Letter. Lord Conway has my Manuscript, which you may send to him for, if it be necessary. I depend upon your Friendship in pushing on this Attempt, which I have much at Heart. Since you agree with me it will be of great Advantage to the Public, and if any Thing can be done this next Summer, this is the proper Time to prepare for it.

26. Captain Middleton to Arthur Dobbs. 14 February 1739 (OS).[1]

The Captain's next Letter:

SIR,   London, Febr. 14, 1739.
Since my last I am favoured with yours of the 23d of January, and am highly obliged to you for writing a second Time to Sir R.Walpole and Sir Charles Wager. I have waited upon both these Gentlemen and Lord Conway several Times; and when I had not an opportunity of seeing them I was willing to put them in Mind by letters, the Copies whereof are underwritten. Yesterday I had the Honour to speak to Sir Robert Walpole for the first Time at his Levee; and he answered me with some Earnestness, repeating it twice or thrice, that the Affair was not his Business, and that I must apply myself to Sir Charles Wager. I waited of Sir Charles immediately after, to whom I have generally a free Access, and told him what Sir Robert said: He shook his Head, and said the Time for it was coming on apace, and that he would get it done if he possibly could; for my own Part, I shall continue to sollicit Sir Charles Wager about it a little while longer, and then must give it up for this Season, if nothing be done to put it into Execution very soon. I fear Sir R. Walpole has now so much Business on his Hand, that he can't spare Time to think about it; and therefore shifted it off to Sir C. Wager, who yet I believe will do nothing in it without his Consent and Advice.

[2] Ibid., pp. 121–2.

27. Captain Middleton to Arthur Dobbs. 29 March 1740.[1]

This I answered, and had the following Letter from him:

SIR,   London, March 29, 1740
I was duly favoured with your obliging Letter, together with a Copy of Sir C.Wager's, for which I return you many Thanks. I have had the Honour to discourse with Sir Charles several Times, and he has got the Copy of your Papers at Length, but he tells me 'tis impossible to proceed in the Undertaking this Season. I am now in a very great Hurry in preparing our Vessel for a Voyage to Hudson's Bay, the Company having ordered me this Year to go to Albany and Moose River. At my Return (please God) I hope to have the Honour to see you in London, being fully of Opinion that your Presence here would much facilitate the Affair, and your Interest procure the Undertaking to be set on Foot next Year.

28. Captain Middleton to Arthur Dobbs. 1 May 1740.[2]

SIR,
As we shall depart in a few Days from hence on our Voyage to Hudson's Bay, I thought it proper to assure you, that I continue my Intentions of promoting the Discovery, and making such Observations as may be useful towards it, to the utmost of my Power. At my Return (which I fear will not be till November, as we must go and come by the Orkneys, and must there wait for Orders) I hope to have the Happiness to see you in London....
P.S. Since I wrote the few Lines above, I had the Honour to see Sir Charles Wager, and he tells me he perused your Manuscript carefully, and spoke in Behalf of the Expedition to the King;[3] and his Majesty seemed to approve it very well, and said the Expence was such a Trifle, that it should not be obstructed on that Account; so that Sir Charles is of Opinion that it will be put in Execution next Year without much Difficulty, especially if

---

[1] Ibid., p. 122.
[2] Ibid., p. 123.
[3] George II (1727–60).

you should be in London to make suitable and timely Application in that Business.

29. Captain Middleton to Arthur Dobbs. 7 November 1740.[1]

Upon his Return he sent me the following Letter:

SIR,   London, Novem. 7, 1740.
I take the first Opportunity of acquainting you with my Arrival here, after a long and dangerous Voyage. Saturday Night last we had a most terrible Storm in Yarmouth Road, where I had the Misfortune to lose my Masts, and a great many Colliers and other Ships were entirely lost. As I was ordered to the Southermost Settlements, and detained a great many Weeks in the Ice in my outward-bound Passage, I have no particular Observations to communicate. I am in Hopes to have the Honour to see you in London this Winter; and then, if it should appear to be a proper Season for undertaking the Expedition, I shall be ready to concur in any Measures that may be needful....

30. Captain Middleton to Arthur Dobbs. 18 [December] 1740.[2]

SIR,
I am favoured with yours of the 29th of November, and am obliged to you for the Concern you express on Account of the Danger of the Voyage. I am likewise to ackowledge the Receipt of yours, which came in May, after my Departure.

We had a favourable Passage through the Straits of about four or five Days, and there never could have been a finer Season for attempting the Discovery, because we met there with very little Ice, and all up to the Northward in the Bay was quite open and free in the Beginning of July; but it happened otherwise to the Southward, for the Snow that had fallen and was congealed, with northerly Winds setting it to the Southward, increased it there, and retarded our Passage down the Bay....

[1] Ibid., p. 124.
[2] Ibid., pp. 124–5.

P.S. This Afternoon I waited of Sir C.Wager, and acquainted him with your Purpose of being in London next Month, to sollicit the Affair. He said you would come in a very proper Time, and made no doubt it might be accomplished.

This finishes our Correspondence until he went the Voyage, I soon after going to London, and no material Letters passing between us when I was there....

I I

PREPARATIONS FOR THE VOYAGE

INTRODUCTION

Early in 1741 Dobbs came to London to be on hand during the preparations for 'the northwest tryal',[1] although Middleton insured against a change of heart on Wager's part by keeping all mention of the venture from his employers. Together with the other regular Company captains, William Coats and George Spurrell, he busied himself preparing the Company ships for their annual voyage to the Bay. He received his long-awaited commission in the navy on 5 March; on 9 March the Admiralty Board formally approved the expedition; and the same day Middleton resigned his position with the Company.[2] The next two months passed in a flurry of activity as Middleton supervised the fitting out of his new command, the *Furnace*. Built as a bomb-vessel, with stout timbers designed to withstand the battering recoil of heavy mortars, the *Furnace* appeared well suited for Arctic work; but with only four months provisions on board her scuppers would be under water, while her deep waist might be a dangerous weakness on the long voyage. To improve both her seaworthiness and her storage capacity, Middleton asked the Navy Board to carry out extensive alterations, including the addition of another deck. With the various Admiralty departments unfamiliar with the needs of northern navigation, initiative was left largely to him, and his requests for extra boats for

---

[1] P. 75 below.
[2] HBC A 1/35, pp. 145–6. It is to the credit of the Company that when the Committee decided a few weeks later to pay a gratuity of twenty guineas to its captains, 'for the hazard of the last Voyage', Middleton as well as Coats and Spurrell received this sum. See ibid., p. 159.

work among the ice, for the latest navigational instruments, and for special provisions, were all met.[1]

At the end of April the Navy Board bought, after consulting Middleton, a 150–ton pink to act as consort vessel, and renamed her the *Discovery*. William Moor was appointed master, again Middleton's choice, for Moor was his chief mate in the Company's service. A few other Company men agreed to sail with Middleton, including Robert Wilson, who had been second mate on his voyage to the Bay in 1740. Generally, and predictably, there appears to have been little enthusiasm for the voyage among the petty officers and tradesmen allocated to the discovery vessels. Two carpenters reported on board, but left on hearing of their destination; nor did the surgeon appointed to the *Furnace* make the voyage. Instead, Edward Thompson (another Company man who was to have sailed to the Bay with Middleton that year) was appointed surgeon on the *Furnace*, 'notwithstanding his Qualification is only for a Surgeon's Mate', another surgeon's mate was made surgeon of the *Discovery*, and both were excused their examinations.[2] To prevent desertion, the forty or fifty men already on board were sent to a depot ship while the vessel was being refitted; most of them, Middleton was told, 'look ailing, having scarce any cloths'.[3] As late as 21 May Moor on the *Discovery* sat in splendid isolation, and had to borrow ten hands from another ship to take the pink downriver to join the *Furnace* at Galleon's Reach. Such problems reflected the acute manpower shortage of the wartime navy, reflected in orders making temporary appointments and relaxing the usual qualifications, and in the frequent newspaper reports on the activities of the press-gangs.[4]

The Hudson's Bay Company meanwhile was treating the expedition with the utmost seriousness, and on 9 April held a General Court 'on Special Affairs', the first for twenty-one years to be called outside the normal November annual meeting. At the meeting Sir Bibye Lake warned shareholders of the possible

---

[1] See pp. 77–81 below.
[2] See the crew lists in Adm 1/2099; also Adm 2/202, p. 276.
[3] P. 77 below.
[4] E.g. *London Evening Post*, 3 Mar 1741: 'The Press for Seamen is carry'd on with the greatest Vigour, in order to mann the Channel Fleet; and not a Man who has the Appearance of a Seaman escapes being examin'd by the several Gangs that are out.'

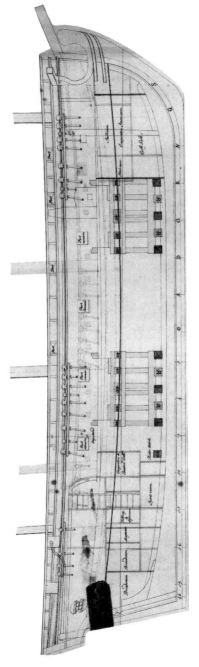

PLATE IV. Plan of the *Furnace*, 1741
(National Maritime Museum)

71

implications for the Company of Middleton's expedition, and was given a free hand 'to hinder any Encroachments on the Companys Trade, Properties, or Priviledges'.[1] Dobbs accused the Company of obstructing the expedition by enticing some of Middleton's men back into its service,[2] and at a different level the Company's anxiety that the venture might harm its trade led to a heated exchange of letters with government departments and ministers. Its only response to an Admiralty request for support in the Bay for the discovery expedition was a grudging order to its factor at Churchill that he might provide assistance should Middleton 'be brought into real Distress, and Danger of his Life, or Loss of his Ship'.[3] The Company was showing all the cautiousness of a monopolistic organization which had remained in undisturbed control of Hudson Bay since the ending of the French wars in 1713. If a Northwest Passage were discovered, the Company could do little to prevent vessels passing through Hudson Bay from engaging in trade, and its charter might prove only a frail bulwark against such activities. Dobbs had obtained from the Attorney-General an opinion that the Company 'had no Right to an Exclusive Trade, but every Merchant in England had an equal Right to trade there';[4] and was putting the matter to the test by shipping trade goods on board the discovery vessels.[5]

Middleton for his part was determined to force from the Company an order allowing him to winter at one of its factories; for if he failed to find a passage before the ice closed in the fate of Munk in 1619 and Knight a hundred years later warned of the dangers of wintering in an unprepared spot in Hudson Bay. Wager had already revealed that he was no great lover of chartered companies,[6] and in letters to the Duke of Newcastle and the Regency Council he attacked the Company's unhelpful attitude – 'very unbecoming a Company who subsist by his Majestys favour, having only an old Charter which no doubt they have made several Breaches in'.[7] Faced with the disapproval of powerful

---

[1] P. 80 below.
[2] See p. 81 below.
[3] P. 83 below.
[4] Dobbs, *Remarks*, p. 60; see also pp. 81–2 below.
[5] See p. 93 below.
[6] See p. 50 above.
[7] P. 85 below.

ministers, and a frigid note from the Admiralty in which it was informed that its conduct lay outside the usage of civilized nations, the Company capitulated. It gave Middleton a terse note in which its Bay factors were instructed 'to give him the best Assistance in your Power'.[1]

The Admiralty sent Middleton his sailing orders on 20 May.[2] They were similar to those which Dobbs had suggested in 1736 should be given to the Company's northern expedition from Churchill, and he seems to have been responsible for drafting the instructions.[3] When he reached the Bay Middleton was to sail to Ne Ultra and find the strong flood tide which the Scroggs expedition had observed coming from the west in latitude 65°N. Somewhere near there, it was hoped, lay 'a Strait or an open sea' to the west. No alternative locations were listed for exploration – an important point given the criticism levelled at Middleton after his return – and after these cursory directions for finding the passage the instructions turned to the exhilarating business of exploitation. Once through the opening, Middleton was to explore the western coast of North America, negotiate alliance with native states, and take possession of 'convenient Situations' in the King's name. If he encountered ships from Japan or any other nation, he was to bear away for home, 'that Ships of Sufficient Force may be sent out next Season to begin a Trade, or make a Settlement without any Apprehension or Disturbance from any powerfull Nation on that Side'. Breathtaking in its easy optimism, this section of Middleton's instructions anticipated events of the next reign, when naval vessels ranging the Pacific on survey work were also agents of British commercial imperialism. Middleton's instructions were one of the first tentative steps towards this policy, for they make it clear that his small expedition was but a pathfinder. If he found a navigable passage, then 'Ships of Sufficient Force' might be sent out, so that British merchants could reap the benefits of the short cut to the western shores of America, and pass on to the rich lands expected to lie beyond.

Middleton, very conscious of the short season for navigation

---

[1] P. 96 below.
[2] Pp. 86–9 below.
[3] See Christopher Middleton, *A Vindication of the Conduct of Captain Christopher Middleton*, London, 1743, pp. 6, 67; Dobbs, *Remarks*, p. 12.

in both Hudson Strait and Bay, had originally hoped to sail on 10 May (the Company ships left before the end of April), but at the beginning of June his ships were still at the Nore. There forty-three men (the complement of the *Furnace* was fixed at sixty, and that of the *Discovery* at thirty) were received from the depot ship, although several were exchanged by Middleton, 'they being very ordinary'.[1] By this time, wrote Middleton, he was only five short of his complement, but still needed petty officers. These he hoped to get as he sailed up the east coast towards the Orkneys. As the ships prepared for sailing most of the crews were paid up to 14 March, and the volunteers given two months advanced wages. The number of these was small, probably only those who had sailed with Middleton in the Company's service, and John Lanrick, 'a young gentleman' recommended to Middleton by Dobbs, and James Smith, son of Dobbs's agent Samuel Smith. Clearly, Middleton's crews were very different in character from the picked volunteers who sailed with the Arctic explorers of the next century; and if he was not encumbered with pensioners as Anson was, many of his men were in poor shape even before the ships left England.

Almost a month later than Middleton had intended, the ships set sail from the Nore on 8 June. There was no ceremony to mark the occasion, and their departure on the first naval expedition to seek the Northwest Passage was noted only in a few brief and muddled newspaper items.[2]

---

[1] Adm 51/379, f. 8.
[2] See pp. 85, 96 below.

74

PREPARATIONS FOR THE VOYAGE

DOCUMENTS

1. Arthur Dobbs to Judge Ward. 17 February 1740 (OS)[1]

I have been with Sir Chas Wager and he is to speak to Sr Robt [Walpole] and the King this week about the northwest tryal.

2. Admiralty Board Minutes. 5 March 1740 (OS)[2]

Sir Charles Wager signified the King's Pleasure that Capt. Christopher Middleton who has commanded several Merchant Ships should be appointed Captain of a Sloop. Resolved that he be appointed to the Furnace Sloop.[3]

3. Admiralty Board Minutes. 9 March 1740 (OS)[4]

Sir Charles Wager signified the King's Pleasure that one of the

---

[1] Ward Papers: D 2092/1/5/77.

[2] Adm 3/45, 5 Mar 1740 (OS). Overall control of naval affairs rested with the Lords Commissioners of the Admiralty, who formed the Board of Admiralty and met several times a week. Important orders were signed by at least three Lords Commissioners, though the Secretary usually signed for lesser matters.

[3] *Furnace* (the name, like that of *Blast, Lightning, Terror*, was a traditional one for bomb-vessels) was one of six bomb-vessels built in the summer of 1740. In September, together with two of her sister vessels, she was converted to a sloop, and was launched in October. The general dimensions of this class were: length 90 ft 6 in, keel length 73 ft 9 in, breadth 26 ft, depth in the hold 11 ft, burthen 265 tons. The vessel would normally carry a 13 in mortar forward (weighing more than four tons), and a 10 in mortar aft. For this, and other details, see Peter Goodwin, *The Bomb Vessel Granado 1742*, Annapolis, 1989. Since December *Furnace* had been engaged under Lieut. John Rankin in the press-service on the east coast.

[4] Adm 3/45, 9 Mar 1740 (OS).

Bomb Vessells should be fitted for a particular Voyage to the Northward, and that Mr. Christopher Middleton should have the command of her who is very well acquainted with these Seas; As also that a proper Vessell should be brought or hired to attend upon the Sloop, in case there is not any Vessell fitting for that Service. Resolved that Orders be sent to the Navy Board to cause the Furnace Sloop to be fitted and cleaned in such manner as they shall judge proper for that Voyage, and that she be furnished with Naval Stores for Twelve Months and victualled for that time for Fifty Men; and they are to take up a proper Vessell in the River of 100 or 150 Tuns, to attend on the said Sloop, which is also to be victualled to that time, and such part of the Provisions as the Sloop cannot take in is to be put on board the Tender.

4. Admiralty Secretary to Captain Parry (*William and Mary*). 11 March 1740 (OS)[1]

Captain Middleton, of the Furnace sloop, representing, that the said sloop is to go into dock tomorrow, and that there are between forty and fifty impressed men on board her; it is the direction of my Lords Comms. of the Admiralty that you receive the said men on board the yacht you command, & keep them in safety, til the sloop gets out of the dock.[2]

5. Admiralty Secretary to Captain Middleton. 14 March 1740 (OS)[3]

Capt Parry of the William and Mary Yacht in Longreach,

---

[1] Adm 2/473, 11 Mar 1740 (OS). For much of 1741 and 1742 Admiralty Board business was conducted by Joint Secretaries, the veteran retiring Secretary Josiah Burchett, and Thomas Corbett, who formally took over as Secretary in 1742. It was Corbett who handled the correspondence for the Middleton expedition.

[2] Lieut. Rankin's log of the *Furnace* (ADM L/F/109) shows that from January to March 1741 the sloop was pressing men off Yarmouth and Harwich. Most were taken from colliers, but there are also references to pressing 'ashore'. On occasion, force was used. So, on 3 March while in Yarmouth Roads Rankin noted, 'Fired several muskts. at a brigg to bring her too but had the misfortun to wound on [sic] man in the arm'.

[3] Adm 2/473, 14 Mar 1740 (OS).

informing my Lords Commissioners of the Admiralty that three of the men put on board the yacht from the Sloop you command, are very sick,[1] and that most of the others look ailing, having scarce any cloths; it is their Lordships direction that when you receive the said Men again, you take care to have them supplied with necessary Slop Cloths.

6. Captain Middleton to Navy Board. 17 March 1740 (OS)[2]

It is absolutely necessary to raise the said Sloop about Two foot afore and aft, and lay on her another Deck, in order to make her the more Wholesom in the Sea, as well as for the Conveniency of Stowing our men and Provisions;[3] for as she is at present, she cannot carry above four months Provisions for her designed Complement of men, and her Scuppers will then be almost in the Water, and likewise her being so Deep Waisted and long on the Main Deck may prove dangerous in that part of the World that She is going to, there often running very high and Transverse Seas, Occasioned by the Gulphs that We pass by, in going and coming from America. We are also obliged in these Voyages, to keep our men as dry as possibly we can in order to preserve their healths; The upper Deck and Timbers to be run down, may be as slight as you please, The main Occasion for Strength, being about Two foot above Water, and need not be any higher. By these Alterations, We shall be able, not only to preserve our mens health, but shall also gain one third part of our hold for Stowage, for we shall notwithstanding our having a Vessell in Company with us Endeavour to get the Bulk of our Stores on board the Sloop, for fear of any Accident or Seperation.

[1] This despite the fact that on 12 March Middleton, on his second day on board the *Furnace*, sent six men to sick quarters at Woolwich. Adm 51/379, 12 Mar 1740 (OS).

[2] ADM/B/114, 17 Mar 1740 (OS). The Board of Admiralty was assisted by several subsidiary boards with special responsibilities. Of these the most important was the Navy Board, which supervised the royal dockyards and the building, fitting, and repairing of ships.

[3] Peter Goodwin points out that accommodation on the bomb-vessels was invariably cramped. *Granado*, of approximately the same dimensions as *Furnace*, 'was built without any full-length decks, the upper deck being stepped down to maximise the cabin accommodation below the quarter-deck'. *Bomb Vessel Granado*, p. 13.

It will also be necessary to have our Windlace taken away, and have a Capstan to take up our Anchors, We having oftentimes Occasion to try the Tides in Deep Water by Anchoring.[1] I refer to your Judgement for any other alteration.[2]

7. Captain Middleton to Admiralty. 4 April 1741.[3]

Be pleased to give Orders for these following Boats to be got ready for the use of the Furnace. It being high Time they were begun to be built our Time draws near for we are obliged to sayle by the 10th May from Hence. Vizt.

> One Eight oar'd Boat   One Six oar'd   do
> One small Ice-Boat that will carry about 6 men
> One Large Launch about 25 foot long to row double bankt to go over in frame....

8. Captain Middleton to Admiralty. April 1741.[4]

> Captain Midltetons Demand for Matheml.Instruments &c.[5]
> 1 Azemuth Compass the new sort[6]

---

[1] In later bomb-vessels the windlass was replaced by a capstan. Details of Middleton's accident on 4 September 1741 (see p. 126–7 below) show that a capstan had been fitted.

[2] Middleton's journal shows that the *Furnace* 'continued in Deptford Dock refitting and altering from the 17th Day of March to the 5th of May, during which time there was a new Upper Deck lay'd, three New Masts put in, with several other Alterations.' Adm 51/379, 5 May 1741. A plan of the *Furnace* in 1741 (Illustration IV) reveals in grey lines and shading the vessel as built at Rotherhithe in 1740, and in black line the alterations requested by Middleton in 1741. These included a change from two-masted ketch rig to three-masted ship rig, the laying of an upper deck, and the replacement of the windlass by a capstan. 'For want of time', however, not all the changes Middleton had requested could be made. See report of *Furnace* council, 21 March 1742, p. 156 below.

[3] Adm 1/2099, 4 Apr 1741.

[4] Ibid. [April 1741].

[5] An unsigned note agreed to this, since 'the sloop is intended on a particuler Service'.

[6] The azimuth compass was designed to measure magnetic variation, and was also used for taking bearings from celestial objects or from known landmarks such as headlands. Middleton, together with Caleb Smith and Joseph Harrison, described an improved azimuth compass to the Royal Society in 1738. He was presumably asking for one of these. See E. G. R. Taylor, *The Mathematical Practitioners of Hanoverian England*, Cambridge, 1966, p. 186.

1 Crown Compass[1]
1 Good Loadstone[2]
1 Two foot refecting Telescope } for Jupiters
1 Fifteen foot refracting Do.   } Satellites[3]
1 Four foot Day Tellescope
1 Case of Instruments compleat for Drawing
2 Quire of drawing paper   1 Drawing Board
1 T Square
1 pair of Globes with Spiral Rhomb Lines[4]
2 Dozen of the Best Black lead penciles
Indian Ink and Camels hair pencils for Do.
1 Large parrallel Ruler
1 Marine Barometer
1 Smiths Quadrant[5]

9. General Court of the Hudson's Bay Company. 9 April 1741.[6]

The Governor acquainted the General Court that Captain

[1] This was a mariner's compass 'for the cabin', crown-shaped, hanging from the deck-head and read from below. Several examples of these are given in the lists of instrument makers of the period. See E. G. R. Taylor and M. W. Richey, *The Geometrical Seaman*, Cambridge, 1962, pp. 110–11.

[2] A lodestone for remagnetizing or 'retouching' compass needles was carried on board ships until about this time. In the mid 1740s Dr Gowin Knight introduced artificial magnets of greater consistency and longevity than lodestones. See W. E. May, *A History of Marine Navigation*, Henley-on-Thames, 1973, p. 67.

[3] In the pre-chronometer age, observation of the satellites of Jupiter was one method of determining longitude, though it was not a practical method on shipboard. Middleton used it on shore to determine the longitude of Fort Prince of Wales, Churchill, in 1742. See p. 235 below, where Middleton's description of his observations shows that the two telescopes requested here were in fact supplied.

[4] This is a slightly puzzling entry. Globes with spiral rhumb lines dated from the sixteenth century (see the description of Mercator's globe in Derek Howse and Michael Sanderson, *The Sea Chart*, Newton Abbot, 1973, p. 31) but were not part of a navigator's normal equipment in this period.

[5] Caleb Smith's 'Sea Quadrant' was a short-lived rival to Hadley's 'improved' quadrant of 1734. It did not use double reflection, but had a prism on the fixed arm. See Taylor, *Mathematical Practitioners of Hanoverian England*, p. 192, and May, *Marine Navigation*, pp. 145–6. The latter reproduces a contemporary engraving of 'Mr. Smiths New Sea-Quadrant' which includes a note that it had been 'Tried at Sea, and approved by Captain Christopher Middleton, Captain George Spurrel, Captain Joseph Harrison, and several other able and experienced Navigators'.

[6] HBC A 1/35, p. 169.

Christopher Middleton who had been Employed by the Company above twenty Years had relinquished the Companys Service, and was appointed Commander of his Majestys Bomb Vessell, called the Furnace, who with another Ship or Tender under his direction are to go on a discovery to the Northwest, and Endeavour to find out a Passage to the South Sea, China and the East Indies; The Committee being Informed thereof, and not knowing how far the same might affect their Property and be Prejudicial to the Company in their Trade, the Committee thought it necessary to lay the same before the General Court for their directions. Wherein after Deliberation by the Adventurers it was agreed Nemine Contradicente that it be left to the Committee to proceed therein, as they shall think proper, And take the best care to hinder any Encroachments on the Companys Trade, Property, or Priviledges, and to do all things necessary, for preserving the same, and whatever else they shall think Convenient to be done for the Companys advantage in this Affair.

10. Captain Middleton to Admiralty Secretary. 20 April 1741.[1]

I Beg leave to intimate to you, that it would be very proper for the Voyage we are going, instead of Twelve months Beer to be supply'd with 3 Months only of that Species, and the rest to be allowed in Brandy. The Hudson's Bay and Greenland Ships, besides their common Allowance to the Men in those cold Voyages, have an additional Quantity of Brandy, Strong Beer and Sugar supply'd to them, and given to the Men discretionally by the respective Commanders to their Ships Company; a Quart of Brandy and a proportion of Sugar once a Week to every 4 Men, but generally of a Saturday Night, and in very bad Weather, and among the Ice, which will be a great part of the Voyage, a Dram 3 or 4 times a Day to each Man. In the Hudson's Bay Service the discretional Allowance for 30 Men for 6 Months is 3 Tons of Strong Beer, and 160 Gallons of Brandy. According to that proportion the Furnace and Tender will require 8 Tons of Strong Beer and 400 Gallons of Brandy for 6 Months, which

---

[1] Adm 1/2099, 20 Apr 1741.

I beg I may be supply'd with to enable the Men to do their Duty with Cheerfulness, particularly as I shall get as many Men as possible that have already been the Voyage and know it to be a Custom; and I believe it would be of Service to the Men to have Mollasses allow'd them once a Week in lieu of Butter.

11. Arthur Dobbs to Judge Ward. 23 April 1741.[1]

As to my self I shall ly by until I know what my Expedition turns to, I have got all fixd for my Captn, he is to be fitted out with 60 men and 14 Guns with 6 Swivell Guns, in the Furnace Bomb. She is raisd and has a new deck made for the conveniency of the Men and to stow her provisions, and last Monday the Tender was bought a strong new built collier,[2] and have got his mate made Master of her[3] She is to have 30 men in her and 10 guns, in case we meet any Spanish Ships on whale fishing at the entrance of the Straits, where they generally go the Tender is calld the Discovery Pink, the Furnace came out of the dry dock on Tuesday to make Room for the Carolina yatch [sic], and is finishing in the wet dock. the design is now publick here The Hudsons Bay Company do all they can to prevent its taking effect, they took an Eskimaux Indian[4] away from my Captn who would have made a good Interpreter at ne ultra, and have given the Clerk he always had one of their Best Governmt at Albany to prevent his being an Assister to him. I have taken a Copy of their Charter from the Plantation Office to lay before Council to see if we cant open the Trade since they have none but K:Charles

[1] Ward Papers: D 2092/1/5/131.

[2] A 150–ton pink, *The Three Brothers* (to be renamed the *Discovery*). The vessel was bought after consultation with Middleton and was, the Navy Board reported, 'sound and Strong, and is a proper Vessel, when fitted, for the Service she is intended for'. ADM/B/114, 23 Apr 1741.

[3] William Moor, Middleton's cousin, who served with Middleton on Company ships, first as a boy, then as second mate, and finally in 1739 and 1740 as chief mate. For brief biographies see Rich and Johnson, *Isham's Observations*, pp. 334–6, and Glyndwr Williams in *DCB*, III, pp. 471–2.

[4] This seems to have been 'Charles', 'a young Eskemoe Boy' captured by James Bay Indians in 1736, and then bought by Company servants at Albany. From 1738 to 1741 Charles was in Middleton's care, and probably acted as interpreter on Middleton's ship when it traded with the Inuit of Hudson Strait. Charles was handed over to the Company in March 1741 after Middleton's resignation, and died in October 1741. See Davies and Johnson, *Letters from Hudson Bay*, p. 273n.

grant for an Exclusive Trade by virtue of his Prerogative Royal.[1]
Our ships will be ready to sail by the 10th of May, for I expect
next week they will be ready to take their stores and guns on
Board.

12. Governor and Committee of Hudson's Bay Company to Chief Factor and Council, Prince of Wales Fort, Churchill. 23 April 1741.[2]

...we do recommend that you will take especial Care to be always
upon your Guard; and not to suffer any Ship or Vessel to
approach our Factory, without the proper Signal; for as War still
continues with Spain, and that we are in an Uncertainty in
regard to France....

13. Admiralty to the Governor and Committee of the Hudson's Bay Company. 6 May 1741.[3]

His Majts. Sloop the Furnace commanded by Capt.Chrisr. Middleton, being fitted out at the Expence of the Government for a
Voyage to Hudsons Streights, and to endeavour to find out
some further Discoveries in those Parts, which Undertaking if
attended with Success, will not only be of great Advantage to this
Nation but to the particular Interests of the Commerce under
your Direction and Management. I am commanded by the
Lords Commrs. of the Admty to recommend the said Capt
Middleton to your favour and encouragement and to desire you
will give him Leave to confer with you on such points as may be
necessary to the Success of this Voyage, and that you will let him
carry out Orders from you to all your Factors and Agents at
your Settlements in those parts, to furnish him with what Provisions, Stores or Necessaries he shall want, and to give him all
other Assistance that he shall stand in need of, which their
Lordships will take care shall be punctually repaid to you.

---

[1] See Wager's comment on this, p. 85 below.
[2] This was a regular wartime order to all the Bayside factories.
[3] Adm 2/473, p. 376.

14. Captain Middleton to Admiralty. 12 May 1741.[1]

I this day waited of the Governor and Company of Hudsons Bay for their Answer to the Letter sent them by the Honble the Lords of the Admiralty; And I find they have only given their Factors orders to relieve us in Cases of the utmost Necessity and Extremity; without giving any particular Instructions to admit us to winter there if we shou'd have occasion;[2] I hope therefore you'l be so good to apply to Sir Charles Wager that the Board may once more desire them to give more satisfactory Directions in that Affair.

15. Captain Middleton to Admiralty. 13 May 1741.[3]

I am very much indispos'd, and have a great many Family Fatigues upon my hands, my wife being lately died, which has prevented my waiting upon you....

16. Governor and Committee of Hudson's Bay Company to James Isham and Council, Prince of Wales Fort, Churchill. 13 May 1741.[4]

Notwithstanding our Orders to you,[5] if Capt. Middleton, who is sent abroad in the Government's Service to discover a Passage to the North-West, should by inevitable Necessity be brought into real Distress, and Danger of his Life, or Loss of his Ship, and by that means forced to your Factory; in that Case you are then to give him the best Assistance and Relief you can.

---

[1] Adm 1/2099, 12 May 1741.
[2] See Document 16 below.
[3] Adm 1/2099, 13 May 1741.
[4] HBC A 1/35, p. 190.
[5] As in Document 12 above.

17. Hudson's Bay Company Secretary to Admiralty Secretary. 13 May 1741.[1]

The Gentlemen are favoured with a Letter from you, dated at the Admiralty Office the 6th Instant, by which they are informed that Captain Christr.Middleton is fitted out by the Government for a Voyage to Hudson's Streights, in which Letter their Lordships do recommend the said Captain Middleton to the Favour and Encouragement of this Company, and desire Orders from our Company to their Factors and Agents at their Settlements in those Parts, to furnish him with what Provisions, Stores, or Necessarys, he shall want, and to give him all other Assistance he shall stand in need of. They desire you will please to let their Lordships know, that our Ships have been dispatched to Hudson's Bay ever since the 27th of April last, with only the bare Provisions for the Number of Men each Ship has on Board, and for the necessary Subsistance of their Officers and Servants at Each of their Factorys, and that therefore the Company is in no wise prepared or furnished with Provisions for any greater Number of Persons than are either on Board their Ship, or now in their Factorys.

But, in case an inevitable Necessity should bring Captain Middleton, or any of the King of Great Britain's Subjects, into real Distress or Danger of their Lives, or Loss of their Ships, the Company have dispatched Letters after their Ships for the Orkneys, with Orders to their Servants and Agents, that in Case there should be such inevitable Distress as above, they should then give them the best Assistance and Relief they possibly can.

18. Sir Charles Wager to Duke of Newcastle. 17 May 1741.[2]

There having been a proposal for some years to send a small Vessel, or two, to endeavour to find a Northwest passage into the South Seas, and his Majesty having this year consented to it, two

[1] SP 42/103, 13 May 1741. The Secretary of the Hudson's Bay Company since 1737 was Thomas Burrows.
[2] SP 42/81, f. 388. The Duke of Newcastle, one of the most influential politicians of the period, was Secretary of State for the Southern Department.

Vessells have been prepared for that Expedition, viz: The Furnace Sloop (lately a Bomb Vessell) comanded by Capt. Midleton and the Discovery Pink, to carry stores and provisions, least they should be obliged to Winter in that Country. The Hudsons Bay Company having several Settlements in those Parts, where possibly the said Vessells may have occasion to stop, or Winter, a Letter has been writ from the Admiralty Board, to desire they will gave directions to their Governors that if Capt. Midleton should be in want of any necessarys or Provisions, then they should supply him. Their answer to us, is so very cool that it plainly appears, that they do not desire any further discovery in those parts than what they are in possession of: for they say, that they have no more Provisions there, than is sufficient for their own people; and I have seen a Copy of the Letter they have writ to their Governors; wherein they direct them, that if Capt. Midleton and his people should be in danger of their lives, or be in the utmost distress they may in that case releive them. I believe your Grace will think that this way of treating one of his Majestys Ships, is very unbecoming a Company who subsist by his Majestys favour, having only an old Charter which no doubt they have made several Breaches in, and which does not exclude any of his Majs. Subjects from Trading that way, in the opinion of the Attorney General.[1] If therefore your Grace should think it proper to write a Letter to the said Company, to assist Capt. Middleton, if he should stand in need of·it, when he is in those Seas, it would have more weight than that from our Board, and may possibly be of great use to Capt. Midleton and his people.

19. London Evening Post. 21–23 May 1741.

The Furnace Bomb-Ketch, that is design'd for the Discovery of the North-East [sic] Passage to India, is victualling with all Diligence: She carried 18 Months Provision, and a great Stock of Brandy, which will be of the utmost service in that cold Country.

---

[1] By now Dobbs had obtained from the Attorney-General the opinion that the Company, despite its charter, 'had no right to an exclusive Trade, but every Merchant in England had an equal Right to trade there'. Dobbs, *Remarks*, p. 60.

20. Lords Commissioners of the Admiralty to Captain Middleton. 20 May 1741.[1]

Whereas we have, in obedience to his Majesty's Commands, ordered the Furnace Sloop, whereof you are Commander, to be fitted out in a proper manner to proceed on a Voyage towards Hudson's Strait, in order to attempt the Discovery of a Passage that Way into the Western American Ocean, and have appointed the Discovery Pink, William Moor Master (who is hereby required and directed to follow your Orders) to attend you on that Service, you are hereby required and directed, so soon as the said Sloop and Pink are ready for the Sea, to fall down on the Nore, and when they have been paid what is due to their Companies, to proceed to Leith, and deliver the enclosed Packet to Captain Holburne, Commander of his Majesty's Ship the Dolphin, containing Orders to the said Captain to proceed in Company with you as far as the Islands of Orkney, for your better Security against the Privateers of the Enemy, said to be cruising thereabouts.

You are accordingly to proceed in Company with the said Ship Dolphin as far as the aforesaid Islands, and then to make the best of your Way with the Sloop and Pink under your Command towards Hudson's Strait, and after passing the same, to proceed to Cary's Swan's Nest; and then veer NoWesterly, so as to fall in with the North-west Land at Sir Thomas Roe's Welcome, or ne ultra, near the Latitude of 65 degrees North.

You are there to make the best Observations you can of the Height, Direction and Course of the Tides, bearing of the Lands, Depths and Soundings of the Sea, and Shoals, with the variation of the Needle.

When you come up with Whalebone Point[2] in 65° you are to try the best passage in doubling that Land, whether to Eastward or Westward, in case it be an Island; and on which side soever you meet the Tide at Flood, to direct your Course, so as to meet the Tide, whether NoWesterly or SoWesterly.

If after doubling that Cape, you find either a Strait or an open

[1] Adm 2/57, pp. 98–100.
[2] This was the name given by Scroggs to a cape he saw three leagues distant from his anchored sloop at the most northerly point of his voyage of 1722. See p. 58 above.

Sea, you are to keep on your Course, still meeting the Tide of Flood; and if it be so wide as to lose Sight of Land, then keep to the Larboard, or American Shore, steering SoWesterly, so as to take the Bearings of the Lands and Soundings, and observe whether there are any Inlets, Bays, or Rivers, to shelter the Ships, in case bad Weather, or contrary Winds, oblige you to take Harbour; and there make the best Plans you can of such Harbours, and Charts of the Coast.

You must make no Stay any where, whilst Wind and Weather permits, (except in making Observations for your Safety in your return) until you get to the Southward of 60 Degrees North; and then, if you continue to find an open Sea, make more careful Observations of the American Coast or Islands, and of the Head Lands, Bays, and Rivers, until you make the Latitude of 50 Degrees, or any more southerly Latitude, in case you find it convenient to Winter on the Western Side of America; but if you should find it more convenient to return into the Bay to Winter, or can make the passage home in time, after making a discovery of the Passage to the Western American Ocean, (which is the more eligible) in order to prosecute the discovery to advantage next Season, then you need proceed no farther southerly than 50 or 60 Degrees Latitude, and make all proper Observations of the Tides, Bays, Head Lands, Shoals, and Rocks on both Sides, if the Passage be narrow, or on which ever Side the Wind and Weather permits you, with the Variation, or any other curious Observations you can make.

If you find any Inhabitants upon the Coast, or any populous Nations to the Southward, you are to endeavour by all proper Means, to cultivate a Friendship and Alliance with them, presenting them with such Trifles as they value, and shewing them all possible Civility and Respect; but to take Caution, if they be numerous, not to let yourself be surprized, but to be constantly on your Guard against any Accidents.

If you find it proper to winter on the other Side of the Passage, get to a warm Climate not more northerly than 42 D. in some safe Harbour, that may be of use in a future Settlement, and rather in an Island, if there be a good Harbour, which would be safer than on the Continent for an infant Settlement.

If your Place of wintering is within a proper Distance to be supplied by the Natives on the Continent, take proper Seeds of

Fruit Trees, Plants, Grain and Pulse, and sow them in the Spring, or in case you find any civilized Nation, who wants such Kinds, you may present some to them, and make them sensible of their Use and Manner of Culture.

In Places where you meet with Inhabitants, make Purchases with their consent, and take Possession of convenient Situations in the Country, in the name of his Majesty of Great Britain. But where there are no Inhabitants, you must take Possession by setting up proper Inscriptions, as first Discoverers and Possessors.

If in your Passage you meet with any Ships trading to the Western Countries eastward of Japan, or any Japaneze Ships, and you apprehend any danger from them, either from their Force or Number, you are to proceed no farther in the Discovery, but immediately to return, that Ships of sufficient Force may be sent out next Season, to begin a Trade, or make a Settlement, without any apprehension of disturbance from any powerful Nation on that Side, lest any Accident should prevent your Return, and discourage any further Attempts to be made for the future.

If you should arrive at California without any apprehension of danger, and chuse to winter in 42 D. (where Coxton is said to have found a civilized Nation and good Harbour)[1] or more southerly, then endeavour to meet Captain Anson in the month of December, before the arrival of the Manila Ship, at Cape St. Lucas, the southern Cape of California, and leave a Copy of your Journal with him,[2] lest any Accident should happen to you upon your Return, and so the Discovery be lost, and it might

---

[1] This is a very odd reference to find in official instructions, and can be traced to Daniel Coxe's *A Description of the English Province of Carolana*, London, 1722. This contains (pp. 63–4) an account of a voyage allegedly made by 'Captain Coxton, a famous Privateer' in the 1680s along the Californian coast and northward. Looking for a harbour reported to lie in lat. 42°N, he found a convenient base on an island in the mouth of a great river. Though Coxton (if he were John Coxon, a buccaneer who raided along the South Sea coasts in 1680) was real, there is no evidence that his voyage was. As late as 1774 Lord Sandwich, First Lord of the Admiralty, received a memorandum referring to Coxton's supposed voyage, accompanied by a map. See SAN F/5/38 at the National Maritime Museum.

[2] Commodore George Anson's expedition to the South Seas had left England in September 1740. In December 1741 Anson's surviving ships were sailing north along the Mexican coast towards Acapulco, hoping to intercept the Manila galleon before she reached port.

prevent Ships being sent out to your Relief in case of Ship-wreck.

But for as much, as in an Undertaking of this Nature, several Emergencies may arise, not to be foreseen, and therefore not so particularly to be provided for by Instructions beforehand, you are in such case to proceed, as upon advice with your Officers,[1] you shall judge may be most advantageous to the Service on which you are employed.

When you return home, you are to proceed into the River of Thames, and send our Secretary an Account of your arrival and Proceedings.

21. Captain Middleton to the Admiralty. 21 May 1741.[2]

...the Furnace has very few hands, and the Discovery Pink but the Master only.

22. Admiralty Secretary to Andrew Stone, Secretary to the Regency Council. 25 May 1741.[3]

Upon his Majts. Commands to the Lords Comrs. of the Admty, they ordered one of his Sloops called the Furnace, commanded by Capt Middleton, to be fitted out for the discovery of a Passage into the Western American Ocean, through Hudson's Straits, and also appointed the Discovery Pink for a Tender to carry Provisions and other Necessarys for her Voyage; and it being uncertain whether they will be able to return this Summer, their Lordships thought proper to order my writing in their Name to the Governor and Committee of the Hudsons Bay Company to recommend Capt. Middleton to their favour, and that they would send Orders by him to their Factors and Agents at their Settlements in those Parts, to furnish him with what Provisions

---

[1] In the event, Middleton held councils of his officers on 31 July 1741, 20 March, 12 July, and 8 August 1742. On 15 August 1742 he referred, more vaguely, to the decision to return home as being 'by Consultation'.
[2] Adm 1/2099, 21 May 1741.
[3] Adm 2/473, p. 443. The Regency Council took the King's place when he was – as at this time – in Hanover.

or Necessarys he should want, for which they should be repaid, and to give him what other assistance he should be in need of.

I send you a Copy of my Letter, of their Answer, and of the Order they have given thereupon, by which it will appear how little regard they have to His Majts Ships, which they expect should protect their Trade, when there is occasion, and which has been formerly done, even to the loss of a Ship of 50 Guns in those Seas, in the War with France.[1]

This proceeding makes it seem as if they apprehended, if any further discovery should be made in those Parts, it may bring others of His Majts Subjects to trade that way to their prejudice, having (in the Opinion of the Attorney General) no exclusive right in their Charter; and their endeavouring to discourage the undertaking makes it the more probable, that a further discovery may be made, which might be a great advantage to His Maj.ts trading subjects, even though no Passage should be found that way into the South Seas, which nevertheless is thought not impracticable and once found, might be a vast benefit to the Nation.

This being the State of the Case, their Lordships desire you will lay it before their Excellencies the Lords Justices, with their request, that they will be pleased to send their Commands to the Governor and Committee of the Hudsons Bay Company, to shew a little more regard to His Maj.ts Ships than they seem willing to do, and to give more effectual Orders for supplying and assisting Capt. Middleton in what he shall want, and to send their Orders not to one Governor, or Factor only their Lordships understanding that they have more than one in those Parts.

23. Minutes of the Regency Council. 26 May 1741.[2]

In attendance: the Archbishop of Canterbury; the Lord Chancellor; the Lord Privy Seal; the Lord Steward; the Lord Chamberlain; the Duke of Richmond; the Duke of Devonshire; the

---

[1] A reference to the sinking by the French of the *Hampshire* off Hayes River, Hudson Bay, in 1697.

[2] SP 43/103, 26 May 1741.

Duke of Montagu; the Duke of Newcastle; Sir Robert Walpole; Sir Charles Wager.

A Letter was read from Mr. Corbett...Ordered, That Their Excies. Secretary do write to the Governor and Company of Hudson's Bay, to recommend to Them, in their Excies. Name, to send effectual Orders to their respective Factorys, to be assisting to His Majesty's Ships employed on the Service abovementioned, by Furnishing them with Provisions, or other Necessaries, in case there should be occasion; for which They will be punctually repaid.

24. Hudson's Bay Company Secretary to Admiralty Secretary. 27 May 1741.[1]

Herewith inclosed, pursuant to the Desire of the Lords of the Admiralty, you receive a Copy of the Orders sent by the Governor and Committee of the Hudson's-Bay Company, to their Chief and Council at Prince of Wales's Fort, Churchill River, North America; That in Case Captain Middleton (who is going abroad in the Government's Service, to discover a Passage to the North-west) should, by inevitable Necessity be brought into real Distress and Danger of his Life, or the Loss of his Majesty's Ships under his Command, and by that Means forced to the said Fort, To give him the best Assistance and Relief they can, a Duplicate of which has been delivered to Captain Middleton: The Governor and Committee humbly crave Leave to represent to their Lordships, that in case Captain Middleton should by any Means be detained or hindered from Entering the Straits early enough, to pursue the intended Expedition of a Discovery before the End of the Year, or that by any other Cause whatever (except by reason of the Distress before mentioned) he be inclined to Sail to and Winter in any of the Company's Factories; The Governor and Company apprehend the same will be the Destruction of their Trade and Factories, and will occasion the Natives to go and Trade with the French, who are very Watchful, and let no

---

[1] Printed in Middleton, *A Reply to the Remarks of Arthur Dobbs*, London, 1744, Appendix, pp. 4–6.

Opportunity slip of drawing and enticing the Natives away, and hindering them from Trading at the Company's Factories, and thereby the Company will run the utmost Hazard of loosing their Trade, which if once lost, or a Distaste or Affront be given to the Natives, it will be with great Difficulty, if ever regained; Wherefore the Governor and Committee humbly hope their Lordships will be pleased to give their Orders strictly commanding and forbidding the said Captain Middleton, That upon no Account whatever (except in Case of the before-mentioned Distress) he do attempt to come into any of the Company's Harbours, or Winter at any of their Factories; and that he be restrained from interfering in their Trade, and invading the Property, Rights, and Privileges, granted to the Company by Letters Patent by his late Majesty King Charles the Second Anno 1670, and possessed by the Company ever since, and that he be directed and enjoined not to give any Disturbance, Lett, Hindrance, or Molestation, to any of the Ships, or Sloops employed in their Service, or infringe their Liberties by Trading with any of the Natives, or Settling on any of the Lands or Territories granted to the Company by the aforesaid Letters Patent, or be permitted to Sail after he Enters the Bay to the Southward of Cape Diggs, in the Latitude of 62°45′. which the Company hope and pray their Lordships will readily Grant, in Regard there can be no Pretence of even supposing a Passage that Way, and consequently cannot in the least obstruct Captain Middleton's Expedition, if it be only to find a North-west Passage to the South Seas and Japan. The Company notwithstanding the great Losses they have sustained from time to time by the French, to the Amount of above One hundred thousand Pounds, have, with great Cost and Charges, supported the Trade, and with Care and Industry, endeavoured to preserve, secure, and encrease the same to the Benefit of this Kingdom, whereby his Majesty's Customs have been advanced, and Beaver Wool reduced to such a moderate Price, that many Thousands of his Majesty's Subjects are thereby employed in the Hatting Trade.

The Company have also expended large Sums of Money in Building Forts and Factories, and likewise Ships and Sloops, not only for carrying on the Trade, but also for making further Discoveries; two Ships whereof with all the Officers and Sailors that went from Great-Britain Anno 1719, on a Discovery of a

North-west Passage were lost, not having been heard of since;[1] the whole Charge of the Outfett of the said two Ships amounted to upwards of 2500l. and was entirely borne and paid for by the Company: And several Sloops before and since have been employed by the Company, and proceeded on such Discovery to 65 Degrees North Latitude on the Western Coast to the Bottom of Sir Thomas Roe's Welcome, and no Passage being there, they returned without Success.[2]

The Government and Committee think it would be very hard for the Company to be dispossessed of any Part of their Trade, or prejudiced in their Property, all of which is humbly submitted to their Lordships Consideration and Favour.

25. Samuel Smith to Captain Middleton. 27 May 1741.[3]

I have shipped on Board his Majesty's Ship the Furnace, whereof you are Captain, Two small Bales of Goods marked SS Stores; the one with Haberdasher's Wares, &c. and the other with five Pieces of Coarse Woollen Goods, under the Care of my Brother James Smith, who you are so kind as to take on board your Ship: As he is young, and consequently wants Experience, I beg the Favour you'll give him your Advice and Direction in the Disposal of those Goods, and in receiving Skins for Returns, which I shall always acknowledge as a particular Favour. I need not recommend my Brother to your Protection and Care; because I am convinced my Friend Mr. Dobbs's Recommendation is sufficient. When you can Advance him I don't doubt but you will do it. I wish you a happy Voyage and Success in your Discovery with all my Soul, because it must do great Honour to your Self, and be of the greatest Advantage to this Kingdom. I

[1] A reference to James Knight's expedition.
[2] A rather inflated reference to the Scroggs expedition of 1722 and the Napper expedition of 1737.
[3] Middleton, *Reply to Remarks*, Appendix, p. 3. Samuel Smith, one-time Secretary and Director of the South Sea Company, was Dobbs's agent and attorney in London. Trading goods seem also to have been taken on board the *Discovery*. Although the amount of goods taken was not great, Dobbs and Smith hoped to make 2000% profit on them. In the event, Middleton prohibited private trading while the expedition was at Churchill. See Dobbs, *Remarks*, p. 58, Middleton, *Vindication*, p. 49 and *Reply to Remarks*, p. 71.

shall be very glad to hear from you from time to time as Opportunities may offer.

If you'll please to Favour me with a Letter, direct for me in Iron-monger Lane, where I have my Counting-House.

26. Admiralty Secretary to Hudson's Bay Company Secretary. 29 May 1741.[1]

Having laid your Letter of the 27th, wrote by Order of the Governor and Committee of the Hudson's Bay Company, before the Lords Com.rs of the Admty, their Lordships command me to desire you will acquaint them that instead of the thanks they might have expected for setting on foot, by his Maj.ts Command, an Undertaking at the Expence of the Government, the Success of which must bring a general Advantage to the Nation, and in particular to their Company. They have reason to be dissatisfied with their entertaining a Suspicion of their Lordships being concerned in any design of interfering with, or dispossessing them of any Part of their Trade, or invading their Property and Rights, which is very injuriously suggested in the said Letter.

The Orders given to Capt Middleton, are not to go on a Trading Voyage, but on an Attempt after new discoveries, for the future Advantage of Trade; An Undertaking, which the Company cannot but acknowledge to be well intended, as they have themselves endeavour'd at it, tho' without Success.

Their Lordships are no less dissatisfied with the Order they have sent to their Chief and Council at the Prince of Wales's Fort, both for the severe Conditions of granting any Assistance to Capt Middleton, and that it is permitted at all but at one settlement, whereas their Lordships understand they have more in those Parts.

The Conditions prescribed in their Order are harder than is the practice of any civilized Nation towards the Subjects of another in amity with it; and it is therefore the less Excusable wth. Regard to fellow Subjects, and employed by the Government on a Work of publick Benefit.

[1] Adm 2/473, pp. 473–5.

Their Lordps. therefore hope, the Company will recall their present Order, and send out others by the Capt. to all their Chiefs, at their several Settlemts. to treat them w.th more Humanity, if they shou'd resort to them for Assistance wch. will be a more Effectual Way to prevent their Trading with the Natives, than the driving them to the necessity of it, for their own Support and Subsistance.

Capt Middleton shall be directed not to molest any Ships or Sloops empd. in the Service of the Compa. but on the Contrary, to be as Serviceable to them as Occasions offer for it, But they dont understand wt the Company wou'd mean, by confining the Progress of his Voyage, and desiring that he may not be permitted to Sail, after he enters the Bay to the So.wd of Cape Digs in the Latitude of 63. it being contrary to all good Policy, to cramp the Designs of Men empd. in new discoveries, who are better directed by their Own Observations, than they can by any Orders, given at a distance.

27. Admiralty to Captain Middleton. 29 May 1741.[1]

You are hereby required and directed during the Course of your intended Voyage not to give any disturbance or molestation to any of the Ships or Sloops employ'd in the Service of the Hudson's Bay Company, But to give them all the protection and assistance that lies in your power, whenever any opportunites offer of your being serviceable to them.

28. Hudson's Bay Company Secretary to Admiralty Secretary. 30 May 1741.[2]

I am favoured with a Letter from you, dated the 29th Instant, wherein their Lordships desire there may be some Alteration made to the Order sent by the Company to the Chief and Council at Prince of Wales's Fort, and that the same Order may be extended to their several Settlements. The Company in their

---

[1] Adm 2/57, p. 116.
[2] Middleton, *Reply to Remarks*, Appendix, p. 7.

Letter to you of the 13th Instant desired you to inform their Lordships of the impossibility they were under of making Provision for so great a Number of Persons as are intended to go with Capt. Middleton, and now beg you would assure their Lordships that they are far on their Parts from designing to give any wilful Opposition or Hinderance to the Discovery intended to be made by the said Captain: Yet they cannot but apprehend the Danger and ill Consequences that may attend the Company if Capt. Middleton should Winter at any of their Settlements. But in Obedience to their Lordships Desire, The Company have herein enclosed sent Orders for Capt. Middleton to the Chiefs of their several Factories, that if the said Captain should be obliged to resort to them for Assistance, he shall have the best the Company can give him.

29. Governor and Committee of Hudson's Bay Company to James Isham and Council at Prince of Wales Fort, Churchill. 30 May 1741.[1]

Notwithstanding our former Orders to you, if Capt. Middleton, who is sent abroad in the Government's Service to discover a Passage to the North-West should be obliged to resort to you, you are then to give him the best Assistance in your Power.

30. Daily Post. 3 June 1741.

The Furnace and Discovery, bound to Russia [sic] to find out a North-West Passage to India [sic], being compleatly victuall'd, and having taken in their Guns at the Gallions, are fallen down to the Nore, in order to proceed on their Voyage.

31. Captain Middleton to Admiralty. The Nore, 6 June 1741.[2]

I send this to acquaint their Lordships that since my Arrival here

---

[1] Ibid., Appendix, p. 6.
[2] Adm 1/2099, 6 Jun 1741.

I have been suppl'd with Men for his Majestys Sloop Furnace and the Discovery Pink under my Command with all the Dispatch possible, having within five of my Compliment for both Vessels, but can get no proper Officers for the Voyage. I have one Mate for the Discovery that will do pretty well, and I hope to supply myself to the Northward with other Officers, and complete the Number of Men allow'd me.

III

THE VOYAGE

INTRODUCTION

Furnace and *Discovery* weighed anchor from the Nore on the morning of 8 June and headed north. There was no fanfare and little public interest in their sailing. Comments in the press were confused, and reflect this lack of interest; thus in the *London Evening Post* for 21 May 1741: 'The Furnace Bomb-Ketch, that is design'd for the Discovery of the North-East Passage...' and in the *Daily Post* for 3 June 1741: 'The Furnace and Discovery, bound to Russia to find out a North-West Passage to India...'[1]

For *Discovery* at least, the beginning of the voyage was inauspicious; on the afternoon of the 8th she ran aground on Maplin Sands at the top of the tide.[2] To refloat her Middleton had to hire a passing lighter, transship the tender's guns and jettison some of her fresh water before she could be warped off. Despite the delay, by noon next day the two ships were off Cromer and by the morning of the 14th off Spurn Head. Next evening the ruins of Whitby Cathedral, on its cliff-top, were in sight and by noon on the 15th the expedition ships were lying off Sunderland. Middleton had been informed, before sailing, that a number of men would be waiting here to join the expedition and hence he sent *Furnace*'s lieutenant, John Rankin, and her master, Robert Wilson, ashore. They came aboard next morning with 'a Mate and a good Sea Man that voluntarily enter'd', but also with the frustrating news that over twenty men had been in Sunderland, hoping to join the expedition, but had dispersed when the expedition vessels had failed to arrive when they were

---

[1] Pp. 85, 96 above.
[2] Adm 51/379, 8 Jun 1741.

expected. At Sunderland, too, a number of boats came off 'with Boots and warm Cloaths for the Men'.[1] The members of both crews spent most of the money they had been paid at the Nore on these essential items of footwear and clothing; this is the first intimation that the ships' stores were less than adequate in terms of clothing for a wintering in Hudson Bay.

The two ships put to sea again on the evening of the seventeenth and by the evening of the nineteenth were off the island of Inchkeith in the Firth of Forth, bound for Leith where Middleton's instructions directed him to pick up an escort for the run north to Orkney. When a strong west-south-westerly wind sprang up, making it impossible to get into Leith:

> I call'd my Officers and Pilot together to consult what was best to be done, being a fair wind for the Orkneys. The Ebb Tide and Night coming on, the Hazard of Losing company wth. the Tender, she being almost out of Sight, and the Season of the Year far Advanc'd, it was agreed to bear away for the Orkneys, without losing any more Time to call at Leith for the Dolphin.[2]

Having taken the precaution of loading his guns in case of an encounter with privateers, Middleton pushed on northwards. By the early evening of the twenty-third the ships were off Duncansby Head and by the following morning were anchoring in Cairston Roads, off Stromness in Orkney. At noon Rankin was sent ashore with the launch to fill the ship's water casks at Logan's Well at the south end of Stromness, at which Middleton must frequently have watered his ships on his annual voyages to the Bay with the Company's vessels. Rankin returned on board in the evening having 'agreed with the shore people to keep filling as I could not trust our men ashore all night'.[3] The remainder of the water casks were filled the following day, and after a further day's delay due to a foul wind the two vessels got under way on the morning of 27 June and, heading west, dropped Hoy Head astern.

Over the next few days the expedition ships encountered a vessel inbound from Virginia, and another from New England; in each case Middleton sent a party on board them with a view to

---

[1] Ibid., 15 Jun, 16 Jun 1741.
[2] Ibid., 19 Jun 1741.
[3] ADM L/F/109, 25 Jun 1741.

pressing men, but since both were severely short-handed, let them go unscathed. Thereafter the Atlantic crossing was relatively uneventful, although quite stormy. In the early hours of 16 July Cape Farewell was sighted some eleven or twelve leagues to the north and by the twenty-fifth *Furnace* and *Discovery* were entering the eastern entrance of Hudson Strait.

Having negotiated the Strait, on 31 July Middleton called a council of his chief officers off Cary's Swan's Nest at the southeastern tip of Coats Island, at which it was decided that in view of the lateness of the season the expedition should winter at Churchill.[1] Accordingly at noon on 8 August the ships were exchanging salutes with the Hudson's Bay Company's stronghold of Fort Prince of Wales.

The stone fort (restored in the 1930s and now in the care of the Historic Sites division of Parks Canada) stands on a very exposed, low, rocky headland on the west side of the mouth of the Churchill River (see Map VII, p. 155). The headland is covered with tundra vegetation, and the closest trees are several kilometres away. By contrast the Old Factory, abandoned by the Hudson's Bay Company only the previous autumn, is in a relatively sheltered location, some five miles farther south, and also on the west side of the river. Behind it a low, rocky ridge with stunted spruce trees provides some shelter from northerly and westerly winds.

The wintering at Churchill was one of very mixed relations between the Royal Navy expedition and the Company personnel. James Isham, the governor, was of course an old colleague of Middleton's and gave him considerable assistance. Middleton and his officers were housed in the barely completed Fort Prince of Wales, and his men in the Old Factory. For the latter this cooperation from the Company was a mixed blessing. The company personnel (led by Richard Norton) had moved from the Old Factory into Fort Prince of Wales only the previous August[2] and had celebrated with a boisterous house-warming party on 27 September 1740.[3] Given the short time which had elapsed, one might have expected that the buildings at the Old Factory

---

[1] See p. 115 below.
[2] Fort Prince of Wales Journal, 1740–41, HBC B 42/a/22, 12 August 1740.
[3] Ibid., 27 Sep 1741.

would still be reasonably comfortable, but unfortunately for the Navy men, throughout the intervening winter Richard Norton had concentrated his men's efforts on dismantling the Old Factory, and transporting the lumber, nails and bricks to Fort Prince of Wales to be re-used in the buildings there. Thus, for example, on 2 February 1741 Norton recorded: 'I have 18 hands at the old factory & both the Teams. They are all employd Part ripping up the old Factory'; on 4 March: 'the Laboring men that at home a Straitening of old Nails that Come out of the old Factory'; and on 7 April: 'I sent [the masons] to the old Factory to Ripp the brest works for Sake of the Timber, we not having enough to Compleat our Parrapet at the Present Fort'.[1] It is scarcely surprising that Middleton's reaction on first seeing the Old Factory was that it was 'nothing but a Heap of Rubbish'.[2] However he gave orders to his carpenters to make the remains of the Old Factory habitable for his men as quickly as possible. One of the most useful contributions which Isham was able to make here was to lend Middleton his bricklayer to rebuild the stoves in the Old Factory. He also sent to York Factory for beaver coats to try to make good the Navy expedition's shortage of winter clothing.

The ships were warped into berths specially dug for them at Sloop Cove, where the Company traditionally wintered its sloops, about halfway between Fort Prince of Wales and the Old Factory, on the west side of the Churchill River, and the two communities settled down together for the winter. The Navy personnel numbered ninety men, whereas the Company's complement was only twenty-eight. Despite the best efforts of two Indian hunters detailed to hunt ptarmigan for Middleton and his men, this supply of fresh meat proved inadequate (or else was not reaching those who needed it most) and scurvy soon broke out. With all the officers living at Fort Prince of Wales and the men living at the Old Factory, some five miles away, lack of supervision of the men's diet and daily routine very probably was a contributory factor. The final death toll for the winter among the expedition personnel was eleven deaths from scurvy, one from drowning and one natural death; many of the others

[1] Ibid., 2 Feb, 4 Mar and 7 Apr 1741.
[2] P. 119 below.

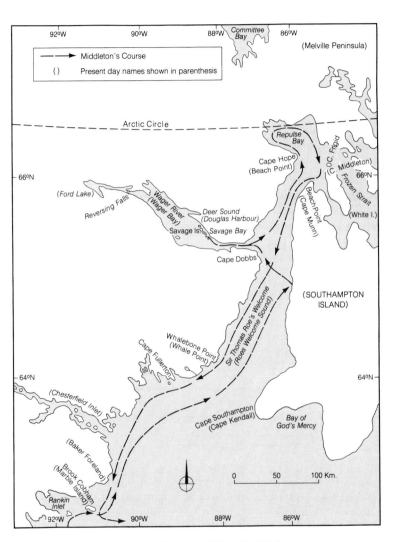

PLATE V.   The Explorations of Captain Middleton, 1742
(Drawn by Keith Bigelow and Derek Thompson)

suffered severely from frostbite. Middleton provided men with (certainly by Company standards) lavish amounts of alcohol, and was particularly generous with liquor on special occasions. On Coronation Day, the King's Birthday and Guy Fawkes Day thirty gallons of brandy were issued on each occasion for making punch. Both Middleton's journal and that of Rankin, his lieutenant, are suspiciously short on detail for several days after Christmas.

Not surprisingly Isham's recorded reactions to the presence and activities of the Navy expedition are somewhat mixed. On the one hand he stated that Middleton's armourer, who had been repairing the Indians' guns was 'very serviceable to Your Honours interest in armourrs. & smiths business, our armer. being dead & the smith not able to work as fore mentioned',[1] and on the other, he wrote in his report to the Committee in July 1742, that Middleton 'did not show himself to be a Well wisher to Your Honrs Interest'.[2] Here, he no doubt has in mind particularly the desertion of five of his men whom Middleton induced to join the expedition to offset some of his losses from scurvy, as well as the disruptions caused in the smooth running of the Company establishment by Middleton's generous use of alcohol. One can certainly sympathize with Isham's closing remarks in his report to the Committee: 'the Captn. etc. has been a Very Troublesome Guess [sic], I Humbl Desire if any Ships Comes again to winter, Your Honrs. will please to send a More fuller Order in What manner to Act'.[3] On 30 June 1742, Isham probably breathed a great sigh of relief as he watched Middleton's mastheads drop below the horizon, northward bound, and noted in his journal: '...at ¼ past 9 at Night the Furnace and Discovery, his Majesty's ships & the Churchill sloop sett sail for their voyage, whom God send safe'.[4]

Middleton's journal for the next six weeks paints a picture of a very competent piece of seamanship and exploration, effected under very difficult and frustrating conditions. On the second morning of the voyage northwards Middleton was already reporting scattered pieces of ice. By the morning of 3 July the two

[1] HBC B 42/a/23, f. 37d, 18 Jun 1742.
[2] Pp. 184–5 below.
[3] P. 185 below.
[4] HBC B 42/a/23, f. 39d. This occurred on 1 July, according to Middleton's journal, i.e. by nautical time.

ships were within sight of Marble Island, and by 3.00 a.m. on the 5th they were off Baker Foreland. Still heading north the ships encountered increasing quantites of ice and on the afternoon of 9 July *Furnace* had to alter course because of ice for the first time. Next morning, as they entered the unknown waters of the mouth of Roes Welcome Sound, they also ran into close pack ice. On the evening of the 10th both ships moored with ice anchors to a large floe and drifted helplessly with the ice; by the morning of the 11th they were getting dangerously close to the coast of Southampton Island, and were in imminent danger of being driven ashore by the ice; fortunately the ice slackened a little, and by warping, towing and even rowing the ships, their crews managed to extricate them from their hazardous predicament.

Noon of 12 July marked quite a momentous occasion; the two vessels rounded a conspicuous headland, which Middleton named Cape Dobbs, and stood in for an inlet or strait opening to the northwest beyond it. In fact it was to turn into an ice-trap, and it would take Middleton a further three weeks to extricate himself from it.

The two ships entered the inlet, which even at this stage Middleton suspected was simply the mouth of a river, to find that after a narrow entrance it widened into an extensive body of water. Middleton bestowed upon it the name of Sir Charles Wager, First Lord of the Admiralty. His description and map of it are remarkably close to the appearance of Wager Bay as it appears on the modern map: a narrow strait three to four miles in width extending for almost twenty miles, which then widens abruptly into a wide expanse fifty miles in length and up to fifteen miles wide, running away to the northwest.

The ships anchored initially inside the Savage Islands at midnight, but there they ran the gauntlet of ice floes drifting down on them with the ebb tide and, after reconnoitring, Middleton moved to a more sheltered anchorage, still inside the Savage Islands. On the evening of the 13th Rankin was sent off with an eight-oared boat to reconnoitre to the northwest, and to ascertain if it were the entrance to the Northwest Passage.

On his return in the early afternoon of 17 July Rankin reported having proceeded up the inlet until stopped by close ice; he established that the tide came from the south (i.e. from Roes

Welcome Sound), which suggested strongly that this was simply an inlet and not a strait.

Middleton next made a reconnaissance of his own; he left the ships at 6.00 a.m. the next morning and got as far as an inlet on the north shore of Wager Bay which he named Deer Sound, but is now known as Douglas Harbour; ice blocked any further progress towards the northwest. There was no improvement in the ice conditions over the next ten days. Since there was clearly no prospect of getting his ships out of Wager Bay yet, and since he still did not know its full northwesterly extent, on 28 July Middleton sent Rankin and Robert Wilson (*Furnace*'s master) to resume the exploration towards the northwest. In their absence he sent eight of his sickest men, with a few others to take care of them, to camp on a nearby island and pick the abundant scurvy grass as an antiscorbutic; this was clearly seen as a sort of rest-cure.

Early on the morning of the 31st Middleton made preparations for warping *Furnace* out of her anchorage. That evening Rankin and Wilson returned to report that they had reached the head of Wager Bay, to within sight of the reversing tidal waterfall which divides it from Ford Lake. On 2 August a reconnaissance revealed that the lower part of Wager Bay was relatively ice-free; having satisfied himself that Wager Bay did not provide a route to the Pacific Middleton now extricated himself from the ice-trap. The ships cast off their moorings around noon on 4 August and by 10.00 p.m. they had run back through the narrow entrance and were in the more open waters of Roes Welcome Sound.

They next headed northeast up the Welcome in fair weather and almost ice-free waters. Next afternoon the hopes of the expedition were raised as they rounded a prominent headland which gave promise of being the northern tip of the continent; Middleton accordingly named it Cape Hope. These hopes were soon dashed however; next morning as the sun cleared away the haze it was revealed that they were running into a deep bay, i.e. a cul-de-sac, rather than a through-passage; as an expression of his intense disappointment Middleton named it Repulse Bay.

There remained the perplexing problem of the fact that the tides had flowed south down Roes Welcome Sound. This mystery was solved on the morning of 7 August when Middleton went ashore on White Island off the northern tip of Southampton Island. Climbing to a vantage point he could see the entire length of Frozen Strait, covered with ice and impassable to his ships, separating Southampton Island from Melville Peninsula.

With this the two ships headed south again, hugging the mainland coast as closely as the treacherous reefs, shoals and currents would permit. By the twelfth they were back at Marble Island where Middleton filled his water casks and landed two of his Indian guides. Then, satisfied that he had carried out his instructions to the best of his ability, 'Myself and Men being so very ill, and I perceiving we could do no more to any Purpose, bore away for Home...'.[1]

Almost immediately Middleton found that the high incidence of scurvy among his crews had a serious impact on the functioning of the ships. The very next day he noted:'I find by our Observation that we are more to the Southward than by Account which is owing to bad Steerage, for we have not above two Men than can steer that is able to go to the Helm'.[2] Middleton had planned to stop at Cary's Swan's Nest to try the tides but the winds did not cooperate and he had to abandon this plan. By noon on the twenty-third Salisbury Island at the west entrance to Hudson Strait, was clearly visible to the east. The Straits were clear of sea ice, but were dotted with icebergs; on the morning of 25 August there were thirty in sight at once. Having avoided these hazards, however, the two ships were within sight of Cape Resolution by noon on the twenty-sixth. The following morning Middleton reported that they 'unbent our Cables, & Stow'd the Anchors',[3] in preparation for the Atlantic crossing.

The homeward voyage was uneventful but stormy, and sail-handling with crews severely depleted by scurvy did pose problems. The first landfall, on the morning of 13 September was the Butt of Lewis, and by the sixteenth the two ships were anchored in Cairston Harbour in the Orkneys. Here Middleton sent the sickest of his men ashore to sick quarters and was forced to press replacements from ships coming into harbour. On the 17th the

---

[1] Adm 51/379, pt III, 15 Aug 1742.
[2] Adm 51/379, pt II, 16 Aug 1742.
[3] Ibid., 27 Aug 1742.

Hudson's Bay Company's ship *Mary*, Captain William Coats, also anchored, homeward bound from the Bay; once Middleton had filled his water casks and the crew had had a chance to recover somewhat, the two Navy ships set sail in company with *Mary* at noon on the twenty-third.

The run south was fast and uneventful: by 4 p.m. on the twenty-sixth Mormond Hill in Buchan was in sight and a day later St Abb's Head. By noon next day Spurn Light was visible and by 10 p.m. Cromer Light. On Saturday 2 October Middleton reported : 'At ½ Past 9 Saluted the Commodore at the Nore with 9 Guns. At 5 Anchor'd at the Nore with the Best Bower in 7 fathoms Water.'[1] By 1 p.m. on 6 October the two expedition vessels were anchored in Galleons Reach. The expedition was over.

Middleton had performed a very creditable voyage of exploration, under extremely trying conditions. Apart from the fact that he had missed the entrance to Chesterfield Inlet, an oversight that can be easily understood given the existence of the curtain of low islands which mask the entrance of this inlet from a vessel cruising offshore, Middleton had accurately charted all the northwest corner of Hudson Bay. Most importantly he had established that there was no through-route from there to the Pacific.

One of the most positive testimonials as to the accuracy of Middleton's findings was written some eighty years later by Captain William Edward Parry. Having been instructed to continue the exploration of the coast northwards from Repulse Bay, in the summer of 1821 he reached that bay via Frozen Strait and having taken bearings and soundings reported:

> ...the whole account he [i.e. Middleton] has given of this bay, with the exception of its geographical position, is in general very accurate, particularly in the appearance of the lands, their relative situation, and in the nature and depth of the soundings. With respect to the Frozen Strait, through which we passed with less difficulty than usual in the navigation of those seas, ... thus, for the first time, determining by actual examination the insularity of that portion of land which by anticipation has long been called Southampton Island, ... there can be little doubt that the account Middleton has given of its appearance, as

[1] Ibid., 2 Oct 1742.

seen from Cape Frigid, is in the main a faithful one. In that view it would seem to be 'almost full of long, small islands', nor is there any improbability of its having been, at the time of his visit, covered with ice, which might appear to be 'fast to both shores', presenting to a person so situated a hopeless prospect of penetrating through it to the northward... our subsequent experience has not left the smallest doubt of Repulse Bay and the northern part of the Welcome being filled by a rapid tide flowing into it from the eastward through Frozen Strait.[1]

---

[1] W. E. Parry, *Journal of a Second Voyage for the Discovery of a North-West Passage from the Atlantic to the Pacific; performed in the years 1821–22–23 in His Majesty's Ships Fury and Hecla*, London, 1824, p. 54.

THE VOYAGE

DOCUMENTS

1. The Journal of Captain Christopher Middleton 1741–42[1]

[OUTWARD BOUND]

Friday 24th [July 1741]. *SbE, SEbE, SbE. Course W29°S. Lat. 61°21'; long. 64°07'W Var. 40W. Cape Resolution, the East end bore N28E, 8 Miles per Account. Cape Farewell E12S, 192 leagues.* Fresh Gales with a Continual Fog and much Rain. We are very near Hudson's Straits, or rather enter'd, by the Whirling Tides. At Noon we Sounded; Had ground 200 fathom Water; some small Stones and Coral Came up. Kept working to Windward in the Opening of the Straits; its about 13 Leagues wide from side to Side of its Entrance. The Tides are very Strong & dangerous, running about 7 Miles an hour WSW & ENE across the mouth of the Straits, and sets you from side to side in one Tide. Cape Resolution is in Longitude 64 degrees West from London, and the Latitude of the South Part thereof 61°25′N. So by our

---

[1] Adm 51/379, pts I and II. The full title is 'A Journal of the Proceedings on board his Majesty's Ship Furnace Under my Command in a Voyage for the Discovery of a Passage thro' Hudsons Bay to the South Sea'. The entries in italics represent the navigational and other information given in tabular form on the left-hand page. The right-hand page contains the daily entries (here in Roman) under the heading of 'Remarkable Observations and Accidents'. The sections of the journal covering the outward voyage to Cape Resolution at the eastern entrance to Hudson Strait, and the homeward voyage from Marble Island, have been omitted. Interspersed with the journal entries as printed are various relevant reports, instructions, minutes and letters from the voyage, shown here in square brackets. The Admiralty records also contain Middleton's 'Log Journal' for the section of the voyage from 1 July 1742 (departure from Churchill) to 18 August 1742 (shortly after leaving Marble Island on the homeward voyage) (Adm 51/379, pt III). This was published by Middleton in his *Vindication*, and is not reproduced here, apart from a few items of information not included in the journal, which are introduced here as notes.

Longitude made we are 7 miles to the Westward of the Cape, and about 4 miles to the Southward of it. I am sure by the Tides which we try'd by the Current Log[1] that we are so near it, but as it is a very bold Shore I shall not work near it, untill it clears up a little, for at this time it is so foggy wee cannot See a quarter of a Mile off.

Saturday 25th. *SbE to SE. Course W17N. Dist. in miles 79. Lat. 61°45'; long. 66°46W. Var. 40°W. Cape Resolution, the East End bore E17S, 26 leagues.* Hard Gales right on Shore, with a Continual wet Fog. At ½ Past 4 p.m. we made Cape Resolution, which bore NbE by the Compass, one Mile distant. We were Standing off to the Eastwd. when we made it, the Wind being at SE and foggy Weather. We Put our Helm a-weather, & bore in for the Straits. We were already enter'd 3 or 4 Leagues as I mention'd at Noon. Steer'd NWbN the Course up the Straits one mile off Shore; the East end of the Cape bore at the Same time NEbE about 4 Leagues per Account for we could not see so far for the Fog. The Ebb Tide Runs at the Rate of 6 Miles an Hour against us. Shortened Sail for the Tender; fir'd 3 Guns being very Foggy. No Ice in our Way, only some Isles lying close in shore.[2] At 3 a.m. out all Reefs and Set the Topgallant Sails. At Noon little wind and foggy.

Sunday 26th. *SE. Course W21N. Dist. in miles 94. Lat. obsd. 62°21'; long. 69°54'W. Var. 40°W. Cape Resolution E19S 59 leagues. Upper Savage Islands NEbE 5 Leagues.* Moderate Gales and Clear Weather for the Most Part. Saw many Isles of Ice all round us when the Fog Clear'd up but no Ledges of ditto.[3] Past in sight of

---

[1] In his journal entry three days earlier Middleton had explained: 'The Method I have to find the Tides & Currents will always discover when you draw near the Land without Sounding, or Where there is no ground to be got, wch. is by a new Current Log, and is of great use in these Parts of the world, or any other of the like kind, as also getting the time of High Water, and the Course of the Tide, any where unknown without Puting out a Boat, or going ashore, almost in any Weather'.

[2] In his journal William Moor, master of *Discovery*, comments on the unusual lack of ice: 'The Entering of the Straits is clearer now, than we've had for this many Years past, commonly being Choak'd with Heavy Ice from Side to Side' (Adm 51/290 pt IV, 25 Jul 1741).

[3] Here Middleton is distinguishing between icebergs ('Isles of Ice') and sea ice ('Ledges').

the North Shore about 4 Leagues of; fir'd 4 Guns, a Signal for the Savages to come off,[1] as is usual here.

Monday 27th. *SE, NNE to SEbS. W21N. Dist. in miles 90. Lat. 62°53'; long. 72°56'W. Var. 40°W. Cape Resolution bore E19S, 89 leagues. Cape Charles bore NW¾W 8 leagues dist. by Compass.* Moderate and fair for the most Part. At 4 p.m. try'd the Tide and found it Set NbW 4 fathom. At 8 Cape Hope[2] bore SWbS 7 Leagues; the said Cape is on the South. We Pass'd several Isles of Ice; fir'd 2 Guns for the Savages to come off, but none to be seen any where yet. At 10 a.m. Hall'd up our small Bower Cable and clear'd between Decks. At 11 ditto got our Boat out, & Sent Her towards the Shore with the Lieut. in her to try the Tides. Light Airs of Wind & clear.

Tuesday 28th. *So., SSE & SE. Course W8°N. Dist. in miles 108. Lat. obsd. 63°07'; long. 76°51'W. Var. 40°W. Cape Resolution bore E16S, dist. 126 leagues.* Little Wind, fair and Clear Weather the first Part; the middle and latter fresh Gales and Hazy, foggy Weather. At 3 p.m. not being got the length of Cape Charles,[3] and finding the Boat Could not keep up with the Ship with Sails and Oars, & Night coming on, made the Signal for her. At 4 the Boat Came on board. Sounded Close under the East of the Cape, Had 90 fathom Water, Sand & Small Stones 2 Miles from the Shore. At 8 ditto the East End of the Cape bore S the West End W½N, the Nearest Part WbS 9 Miles. Fresh Gales. At ½ Past 9 ditto Wm. Clark, our Sail Maker, going up to Reef the Foretopsail afore the Wind, fell from the Shrouds over board. We brought to immediately, lower'd our Ice boat from our Quarter, but lost him. At 4 a.m. in 1st Reef of the M'topsail. Saw several Isles of Ice.

Wednesday 29th. *SEbS, So., to ENE. Course W20S. Dist. in miles 102. Lat. obsd. 62°27'; long. 80°31'W. Var. 41°.* Variable Winds and fair Weather, but Hazy. At 2 p.m. saw the high land of

---

[1] The reference here is to the Inuit of southern Baffin Island, who regularly came out from shore in kayaks and umiaks to trade with the Company's ships on their way through the Straits.

[2] Cape Hope's Advance, on the south shore of Hudson Strait.

[3] I.e. Rankin had not managed to reach shore to try the tides.

Walsingham.[1] At 4 the Westernmost Isle of Digges bore SW¼W 10 Miles. At the Same time Cape Walsingham bore S½E. At 6 ditto it bore SSE and the West Island of Digges SSW 5 leagues; also the North End of Mansels Isle at 8 p.m. bore NWbW 5 leagues. At 9 ditto lay to for the Tender; at 10 she came up with us, made Sail. At 4 in the Morning the North End of Mansels Isle bore S½W4 leagues. I find by this Account Cape Diggs is in the Longitude of 77°45′ West from London and bears from Cape Resolution W12°N, dist. 140 Leagues, which is the Length of Hudson's Straits. Also the North End of Mansels Isle is dist. from Diggs 12 leagues, and is in the Latd. of 62°40′ North and Longitude from the Meridian of London 79°05′ West.

Thursday 30th. *East, NNE, NEbE. Course W15S. Dist. in miles 75. Lat. 62°05′; 83°05W. Var. 38°W. Mansels Isle the North End bore E19N, dist. 41 leagues. Cape Churchill W32°S 110 Leagues.* Moderate and Hazy. At 6 p.m. a thick fog; fir'd 2 Guns & Short'd Sail for the Tender. At 8 ditto sounded 104 fathom. At 12 at Night 86 fathom, small brown Stones. At 2 a.m. sounded 70 fathom; lay to for the Tender till Day-light; a thick Fog. Try'd the Tide; set SW 4 faths. At 6 ditto made Sail; bore away. At 8 sounded 50 fathom; small Stones. At 10 ditto clear'd up; saw the land; the Westermost Part NWbW, the Nearest NbW 9 or 10 Miles. Hazy. Sounded from 45 to 48 and then to 40 fathom; Shells and Small Stones with Dents in the Tallow. These last Soundings at Noon.

Friday 31st. *East, ENE. Course W35S. Dist. in miles 113. Lat. obsd. 61°02′; long. 86°11′W. Var. 35°W. Mansels Isle the North End E26N 76 leagues.* Moderate & foggy Weather for the most part. At 2 pm. sounded 43 fathom Water with Some Stones and Mud off Carey's Swans Nest.[2] At 6 ditto sounded 86 fathom Water; steering a-long Shore 3 Miles dist.; the Land lies WbN. At 10 ditto sounded 98 fathm., ouzey soft Mudd. Little Wind. At 12 at Night shortned Sail for the Tender. Sounded 112 fathm. Water; rocky Ground. At 4 a.m. 111 fathom, ouzey Ground; at Noon 112 fathom, rocky Ground. Hazy Weather.

[1] Cape Wolstenholme.
[2] The southeastern tip of Coats Island. This rather strange name, bestowed by Sir Thomas Button in 1612, still survives. For a discussion of possible origins see Christy, *Voyages of Foxe and James*, I, 165n.

This Day a Council was Held on Board[1] in Latitude, Longitude etc. as per Margent.

The Question was Put & taken into Consideration, whether it would be Proper to proceed upon a Discovery of a Passage from Hudson's Bay to the South Sea directly, or to repair with His Majesty's ships Furnace & Discovery to Churchill River in Hudson's Bay, as the Season of the Year is too far advanced to Proceed any farther, and there being a Necessity of Secureing the Vessels and Providing Necessaries for Wintering, as soon as Possible, and it was unanimously Resolv'd, Considering the Rigors of the Winter in these Parts of the World, the want of everything necessary for building Lodgings for the Men, a convenient Place for secureing the Vessels from the dangers of the Ice, the Necessity of digging Store Rooms for the Provisions, no Brandy, Spirits or Strong beer being Proof against the Severity of the Winter above Ground, the Uncertainty of Secureing the Vessels after the Frost comes on, which usually Happens in the Beginning of September, and the Obstructions we may Probably meet with in our Passage by Fogs, Calms, Ice, & contrary Winds.

That it would be the best and surest Method for the Service in general, to Proceed directly for Churchill River in Hudson's Bay, there to secure His Majesty's Vessels Furnace & Discovery, with their Provisions, Stores and Ammunition, and to Provide convenient Winter Quarters, Firing and Necessary Cloathing for their respective Companies, and to wait the breaking up of the Ice next Year, and then to attempt the Discovery of a Passage from Hud's. Bay to the South Sea.

Saturday, August 1st. *Ne, NbW to NW. Course W39S. Dist. in miles 61. Lat. 60°22'; long. 87°49'W. Var. 30°W. Mansels Isle the North End bore E31°N dist. 100 Leagues.* Moderate Gales and a Continual Wet Fog, firing every Half Hour. At 8 p.m. Sounded 112 fathom Mud; Shortned Sail for the Tender. At 12 at Night 120 fathom Mud; at 4 a.m. 115 fathm. ditto. At 10 ditto saw a Ledge of Ice a-Head; Shorten'd Sail. At Noon Sounded 100 fathm, blue Clay; enter'd the Ledge of Ice at the Same Time. We have

---

[1] Those present (apart from Middleton) were William Moor, John Rankin and Robert Wilson (Middleton, *Vindication*, p. 104).

fir'd these 24 Hours 26 Signal Guns for the Tender,[1] being a very thick Fog & tacking among the Ice etc.

Sunday 2nd. *SW to ENE. Course W40S. Dist. in miles 61. Lat. obsd. 59°23'; long. 89°23'W. Var. 28°W. Mansels Isle the North End bore E24N, 110 leagues.* A Continual Fog and variable Winds. At 4 p.m. got out of the Ledge of Ice into a Clear Sea. A very thick Fog, or we might have avoided this Ice. At 4 p.m. Sounded 96 fathom. At 8 ditto 79 fathm; at 10 ditto 80 fathm. At 12 in the Night 80 fathm; at Noon 83 fathm; all soft Sticking Mud. Fir'd 8 Guns these 24 Hours for the Tender.

Monday 3rd. *ENE, N, NbW. Course W40S. Dist in miles 54. Lat. 59°06'; long. 90°41'. Var. 26° W. Mansel's Isle the North End bore E33°N dist. 132 Leagues.* Moderate Gales and Foggy Weather for the Most Part. At 10 p.m. sounded 73 fathom; at 12 at Night Sounded 55 fathom. Working to windd. under a Ledge of Ice to the SW of us. At 10 a.m. sounded 53 fathom; much Ice and Fog. These Soundings are on a Bank 25 or 30 leagues from Churchill. Fir'd 7 Guns these 24 Hours for tacking etc. in a Fog.

Tuesday 4th. *WNW to NNW. Course W3°N. Dist. in miles 28. Lat. 59°08' ; long. 91°38'W. Var. 26°W. Mansel's Isle E31°N 144 Leagues.* Since last Noon hazy, foggy Weather for the most part;[2] meeting with much Ice; turning to Windward & to the Norward of it, appearing Clearest that Way. At Noon in 63 fathm. Water, blue Clay, with Small Stones. Fir'd 10 Guns for tacking and Keeping Company these 24 Hours.

Wensday 5th. *NW, W to WSW. Course N25°W. Dist. in miles 24. Lat. obsd. 59°24'; long. 92°10'W. Var. obsd. 24°W. Mansel's Isle E*

---

[1] The latter responded in kind; Moor noted 'these 24 [hours] we have fired 24 Guns', Adm 51/390, pt IV, 1 Aug 1741.

[2] In his journal John Rankin, *Furnace*'s lieutenant, reports what might well have been a serious accident. Christopher Row fell from the main topmasthead, bounced off the main top lantern and from there into the main chains, but did himself no harm (ADM L/F/109, 4 Aug 1741).

26N 141 Leagues. Little Wind and fair Weather. Continued working to Windward. Saw many Ledges of Ice to the Southwd. & Northwd. of us.[1] At Noon little Wind, almost Calm. Sounded 60 fathom, sticking Ground.

Thursday 6th. *W, WNW, SW to West. Course S37°W. Dist. in miles 22. Lat. obsd. 59°17'; long. 92°26'. Var. 24°W. Mansel's Isle E28N, 146 Leagues.* Light Airs variable, almost Calm, with Hazy Weather. Working to Windwd. under Ice, of which we Saw much to the Southward. Had 53 fathom Water at Noon.

Friday 7th. *WSW, West, SW, West. Course W10N. Dist. in miles 43. Lat. obsd. 59°25'; long. 94°48'W. Var. 22° W. Mansel's Isle East 23N, 166 Leagues.* Moderate Gales and Hazy for the Most Part. At Noon bore down & took the Tender in Tow. At 4 p.m. tack'd. Sounded 38 fathom; working to Windwd. under much Ice to the Southward of us. At Noon Saw the Land about 30 Miles to the Eastward of Churchill.[2] Sounded 28 fathom Water, Hazy; 4 or 5 Leagues off Shore.

[WINTERING AT CHURCHILL]

Saturday 8th. *North, East to NbW. Course W32S. Dist. in miles 46. Lat. 59°02'; long. 94°48'. Mansel's Isle the North End bore from Churchill Harbour E24N dist. 180 Leagues.* Little Wind & Calms with Hazy, foggy Weather and Rain. Sounded from 38 to 49 fathom along shore. At ½ past 9 p.m. anchor'd to Stop the Tide of Ebb. Foggy. The Soundings are Small Stones and Shells with white Clay. At 4 a.m. it Clear'd up; weigh'd and Stood in for

[1] Rankin records the baffling information: 'The Master is verie bad and three Men down in the Small Poxe, having died of the same (ADM L/F/109, 5 Aug 1741)'. It is hard to know how to interpret this entry; it is quite conceivable that the master (Robert Wilson) was ill. But if there were three deaths by disease on board it seems very strange that Middleton would not also have recorded them. It is even less likely that the disease was small pox, given the extremely contagious nature of that disease, and the fact that there is no other reference to it.

[2] Moor identifies this landfall as Knight's Hill, which lies just west of Cape Churchill (Adm 51/290, pt IX, 7 Aug 1741).

Churchill Harbr. The Fort Bore West about 4 Leagues.[1] At 9 ditto the Lieutt. was sent ashore to acquaint the Governer & Council Here who we were, and to deliver the Hudson's Bay Company's orders to them.[2] It being Calm we row'd & tow'd. At Noon the Boat Return'd; we were then off the Harbours Mouth abt. a Mile distant rowing and all our Boats a-head towing in with the Flood. It floweth Here in the Harbour WNW nearest from 10 to 14 foot neap & Spring Tides. At Noon Pass'd by the Fort,[3] saluted them with 9 Guns, who return'd the Same Number.

Sunday 9th. *Calm, ENE, NE. Moor'd in Churchill Harbour in 8 fathm. at High Water; the New Fort bore N½W; the Point of Cape Merry*[4] *& Eskimay Point in one bore NbE; Ward's Mount*[5] *SSW. We are a Quartr. of a Mile dist. from the Shore on Cape Merry Side.* Little Wind & Calms, for the Most Part. At 2 p.m. anchor'd just withn. the Harbour to stop the Tide of Ebb, it running very Strong and no Wind. At 8 ditto weigh'd, it being Calm, Warp'd into Her birth; by 12 at Night got her Moor'd with the two Bowers. They

---

[1] At this point they had already been observed from shore. Robert Pilgrim, temporarily in command at Fort Prince of Wales, recorded their approach as follows: 'Aug. 8 1741. Saturday at Break of Day Saw two Ships in the Offing a small Breeze of wind at North. I immediately shotted all our Guns & made all ready for a vigorous Defence. Sent for all our Men home' (HBC B 42/a/23 f. 4d). This wary reaction should be seen in the light of the original orders which Pilgrim had received from the Governor and Committee, dated 23 April (see p. 82 above), and of the fact that Middleton's were the first non-Company ships seen in the Bay for almost thirty years (Williams, *British Search*, p. 59).

[2] Here Middleton is referring to the rather grudging instructions issued by the Governor and Committee on 13 May 1741, to the effect that Middleton should be given assistance if he were 'forced to your Factory' (see p. 83 above). Pilgrim's account of Rankin's landing is as follows: '...about 10 of the Clock saw a Boat abrest the Rivers Mouth. I fir'd a Gun at her, when she spred a white Flagg & about 11 she came ashore with an Officer. I talk't to him over the Parapet when he show'd me Your Honours Letter. I then lett him in & found your Honours new orders to admitt Capt. Middleton etc. to come here' (HBC B 42/a/23, f. 4d). Rankin (ADM L/F/109, 8 Aug 1741) confirms that his boat was fired upon.

[3] The massive stone fortifications of Fort Prince of Wales, which still dominate the entrance to Churchill Harbour with their forty-two guns, were barely completed after ten years of construction.

[4] The rocky cape on the east side of the river mouth, i.e. across the river mouth from Fort Prince of Wales and due north of the present townsite of Churchill.

[5] The low rocky hill immediately behind Sloop Cove.

told me from the Shore they had Pull'd down the Old Fort,[1] for which I was very Sorry. At 4 a.m. I sent the Lieutt. and a Pilot out to bring in the Tender. A fresh Gale at NE. At 8 ditto the Tender got in and moor'd by us; Loos'd all our Sails to dry.[2] I went to see what Condition the Old Fort was in, and found it nothing but a Heap of Rubbish; Order'd our Carpenters to get ready, and use all the Dispatch Possible to make Lodgings for the Men before the Winter Sets in.

Monday 10th. *ENE, East, a hard Gale. Moor'd in Churchill Harbour.* Moderate & fair, with variable Winds. At 4 this Morning up all Hands. Order'd the Boatswain and 18 Hands to The Old Factory to clean away the Rubbish, that the Carpenters and Bricklayers might repair it. Sent the Carpenters & Sawyers to cut Boards for ditto; the Rest employ'd in getting Drift Wood against Winter. Towards Noon blowing Hard; struck Yards and topmasts. Hazy with Rain.

Tuesday 11th. *ESE.* The first and Middle Parts fresh Gales with Rain; the latter more moderate. Continued employing all Hands as above.

Wednesday 12th. *ESE, NNW, West.* Moderate Weather & variable Winds. Some of our Men employ'd in rigging & getting the Same ashore, Having but 2 Hours in a Tide that we can land any Stores, being a long way flat and dry off the Shores.[3]

---

[1] The original post established by James Knight in the summer of 1717 (James F. Kenney, *ed., The Founding of Churchill. Being the journal of Captain James Knight, Governor-in-Chief in Hudson Bay, from the 14th of July to the 13th of September, 1717,* Toronto, 1932) was located on the west bank of the river mouth five miles SSW of Fort Prince of Wales, and out of sight from it. It lay on the south-facing slope of a rocky headland with stunted spruce trees and fronted by a vast expanse of boulder-strewn tidal mud flats. The previous factor, Richard Norton, had moved his operations from the Old Factory to Fort Prince of Wales only the previous August 12 and demolition of the buildings had represented the major work-project of the winter. The timber, bricks and even nails were transported to Fort Prince of Wales to be reused (HBC B 42/a/22).

[2] His mind now set at rest, Pilgrim sent away the men he had summoned into the fort to repel a possible attack, 'being 20 hay makers and rafters' (HBC B 42/a/23 f.5).

[3] Pilgrim sent the Company's yawl *Quicohatch* to help with the unloading.

Thursday 13th. *West*. Ditto Weather. Our Men employ'd as before.[1]

Friday 14th. *WNW*. Moderate and fair. Our Carpenters employ'd as before; the rest of our Men getting the Powder out of the Furnace into the Magazine at the New Fort, & the Rigging, Mast, yards etc. ashore under a Tent where the Ships are to Winter.

Saturday 15th. *South, East, Calm*. Moderate and Hazy, variable Winds and Calms. Continued at work as before, getting our Provisions and Stores to the Old and New Factories where we must winter.[2]

Sunday 16th. *Calm*. Moderate and Fair, with Calms. This Day the Company's Sloop returned from York Fort, with their Factor for this Place,[3] who gives us an Account of their Ship Having Sail'd from thence three or four Days before for England.

Monday 17th. *Calm, NW. Moor'd in Churchill Harbour*. Ditto Weather. Continued getting the Provisions ashore. Employ'd 20 Men to dig and clear away Stones, in order to make a Dock in the Cove where the Ships are to winter,[4] and secure them from the

---

[1] Pilgrim contributed further by lending the Navy expedition his horse team for hauling provisions up from the shore to the fort (ibid.).

[2] The officers were to spend the winter in relative comfort at Fort Prince of Wales, while the men would be housed in the 'refurbished' Old Factory.

[3] Middleton made the diplomatic gesture of going out to meet the Company's sloop, *Churchill*, bringing the new factor (ibid.). This was James Isham who till now had been in charge at York Factory and whose term of office at Churchill would last until 1745 (Rich and Johnson, *Isham's Observations*, p. 319). Had he had any misgivings about the welcome extended by Pilgrim to Middleton's expedition thus far, there was not much he could do about it, being thus faced with a *fait accompli*.

[4] Sloop Cove, located on the east side of a rocky headland on the west side of the river mouth and two miles almost due south from Fort Prince of Wales. The ships' masts would have been clearly visible from the fort as they lay in the cove. Due to glacio-isostatic rebound, which is causing the whole of the Hudson Bay area to rise steadily, the cove is now a grassy meadow with a small freshwater pond, its surface about three feet above the level of high spring tides. The most recent estimate of the present rate of uplift (A. Mark Tushingham, 'Observations of Postglacial Uplift at Churchill, Manitoba', *Canadian Journal of Earth Sciences*, Vol. 29 (1992), pp. 2418–25) is 2.6 to 2.9 feet per century. Since this type of movement decelerates with time, this means that the land has risen at

Tides and Ice. It flows in the Cove 7 or 8 foot at Common Spring Tides, and we draw near 11 foot when all is out. We find it very Difficult digging the Ground being all froze when we get 6 Inches below the Surface[1] and meet with many Rocks and large Stones, which we are Oblidg'd to blow up.

Tuesday 18th. *WNW*. Ditto Weather & Wind. Most of our Men employ'd with Spades & Pickaxes, but Have not been able to dig above 4 Inches below the Surface in two Days. Some of our Men are digging a Pit at the New Fort 6 feet deep to bury some of our Strong Beer in order to Preserve it till the next Spring. The Governer and Council Here this Day came on board, when we consulted the Properest methods we could for Lodging the two Ships Companies, and Preserving their Healths in Winter, most of their Men Having Had the Scurvy last Winter.[2] I drew up a case to shew the Necessity of it, and desired their Assistance to get the Indians to kill what fresh Provisions they could for us, but the Indians of this Province being all gone into the Country, the Governer Sent to York Fort for Some; notwithstanding which I find I Shall Lose this Season for Killing of Geese.[3]

---

least 6.5 feet since the time of Middleton's visit, an amount which is consistent with his description of the cove and with the amount by which his men deepened it. Set into the rocks on either side of the meadow and pond are the mooring rings to which the Company's sloop captains used to moor their sloops, and to which *Furnace* and *Discovery* possibly also moored. On the rock face overlooking the 'cove' are carved the names of Middleton's vessels and the date '1741' (see Frontispiece).

[1] Churchill lies near the southern limit of continuous permafrost, which in this area reaches depths of approximately 195 feet. This represents one of the earliest references to problems encountered in excavation or construction in Northern Canada due to permafrost.

[2] The previous winter the first report of illness was from a timber-cutting camp some distance from Fort Prince of Wales, in early March 1741 (HBC B 42/a/22, 7 Mar 1741). By 1 April a total of six men was sick and ultimately one man died (on 9 April). However it should be noted that the complaint is not identified in the post journal as scurvy but rather as 'Violent Pains in their Limbs etc, wch. is occasioned by Colds' (ibid., 1 May 1741).

[3] Isham recorded in his journal that he visited the Old Factory with Middleton at noon to decide on the repairs needed before the men could winter there. He also noted that he had allocated Middleton a quarter of the dwelling house in Fort Prince of Wales to accommodate the officers and some of the men. Confirming Middleton's comments, in a further attempt to assist the expedition Isham 'this morning sent an old Indian to York Fort to acquaint them of Captn. Middleton's arrival and to send some Indians to hunt for Factory use, we having no Indians here, & to send some Beavr. coats for clothing for the Ship's compay. if they can spare any not having Indians here' (HBC B 42/a/23, f. 6).

Wensday 19th. *South, West. Moor'd in Churchill Harbour.* Moderate and fair, with variable Winds. Most of our Men empld. in digging and blowing up of Rocks in the aforesaid Cove, and getting Stores and Provisions ashore.[1]

Thursday 20th. *West & WNW.* Ditto Weather. Continued every Tide clearing and blowing up Rocks as we dig down, to get the Ships in the next Spring Tides, if Possible, before the Winter comes on. The Spring Tides fall out the last of this Month.[2]

Friday 21st. *ENE.* Dark Cloudy Weather for the Most Part. At 3 a.m. I went ashore along with my People, as I have done every Tide, who dug till 8, when the Flood Put us off, also at 3 in the Afternoon blowing up several large Stones as we dug down. We make but a Poor Hand of it, for after we come down 2 feet, we meet with a Hard frozen white Clay like Fuller's Earth.

Saturday 22nd. *ENE to WNW.* Moderate and fair. Continued digging every Tide with 20 Men being as many as we could get Pickaxes, Spades, etc. for, the rest of our men repairing the Old Fort, loading the Small Sloops I hired, and unlading and carting up the Provisions, etc. from the Shore to Warehouses a Quarter of a Mile distant from the Landing Place.

Sunday 23rd. *SW, calms. Moor'd in Churchill Harbour.* Moderate and fair, with variable Winds, employ'd as before, & getting about 12 Tons of Ballast out of the Furnace, leaving in her about 9 Tons of ditto with 25 Tons of Iron Ballast which I Propose to shift her with, when She comes aground. She now draws 11 feet Water abaft and 10 feet afore, with nothing in but Cables, 3 Anchors and her lower Mast with the aforesaid Ballast, which must be kept in until She takes the Ground for the Reason above Mention'd.

---

[1] Isham's journal records some further examples of mutual co-operation in the entry for this date: '...the Capts. carptr. a fitting up Cabbins for him & officers [at Fort Prince of Wales]... Sent the Bricklayer to the old Factory to repair the Stoves...' (ibid.).

[2] Another record of mutual co-operation appears in Isham's journal: The Company's team was hauling 'our dry goods from the houses on the hill to make room for the Captns. stores etc.' (ibid.). Meanwhile the Navy men were still burying their beer in a hole in the yard at Fort Prince of Wales.

Monday 24th. *NW. Squally Weather*. Part of the Men employ'd in digging at the Cove, Part lading and unlading Provisions into & from the 2 Sloops, and Part Stowing away the Strong Beer in a Pit dug for it at the New Factory, and covering it with Earth and Horse dung from the Frost, being 6 feet under ground, and a Covering of 8 or 9 feet above, no Liquors being Proof against the Winter, except in Cellars, under the House in the Area within the Fort where there are constantly two or three large fires kept, but those Cellars are quite fill'd, chiefly with Vessels belonging to the Factory and some few belonging to the Ships.[1]

Tuesday 25th. *SE*. Moderate Weather & Calms for the first Part, the latter Squally with Rain. Our Men employ'd as above.[2]

Wensday 26th. *SE, ESE, East*. Strong Gales and frequent Squalls with variable Winds. Bent the Sheat Cable, got the Sheat Anchor over the Side. Continued digging and blowing up the large Stones we meet with in digging down. The Weather being very bad in the Afternoon we could not get ashore, A very Storm of Wind and Rain. In the Night one of our Boats sunk astern but lost Nothing but one burden board, the Oars being taken out before Night, and the Ice Boat up in the Tackles.

Thursday 27th. *ESE. Moor'd in Churchill Harbour*. Continued a Storm of Wind & Rain wth. Hard Squalls. Got up 2 Boats in the Tackles alongside. They would not keep from Sinking when astern.

Friday 28th. *East*. The first Part Hard Gales and frequent Squalls with Heavy Rains; the Middle the Storm abated, but continued fresh Gales and Hazy Weather with Rain. At 4 a.m. sent 20 Men ashore for digging, the Spring Tides being near at Hand, Having a New moon to-Morrow Night, and must endeavour to get the Ships it [in] if the Wind and Tide will Permit

[1] Isham records that the Navy carpenter, presumably having finished work on the officers' quarters in the Fort, was now helping the Company's carpenter to put a new keel on the Company's sloop, *Churchill* (ibid.).

[2] The Company's team of horses was now being used to haul the Navy's beer supply from the shore up to the Fort (ibid.). It appears that this may not entirely have met with the approval of the Committee in London. A marginal note reads: 'Why did not the Capt. make the sailors draw or carry this & other things'.

us; the Shores very dangerous, being all lin'd with large Stones, and it doth not flow above 13 feet at the River's Mouth on Common Spring Tides unless help'd with Northerly Winds.

Saturday 29th. *ENE*. Moderate Weather, the Wind variable. Unmoor'd the Discovery ready to get her into the Cove before us, there not being room for two Ships to lie abreast; by 7 a.m. got her into the Cove as far as she would fleet this Tide.[1]

Sunday 30th. *NNW. In Churchill River near our Wintering Cove.* Ditto Weather. By Noon got the Furnace unmoor'd. At 2 p.m. Hall'd her into Shoal Water near the Cove ready to get her in the next Tide; Hove out all our Ballast & got everything out of Her.[2]

Monday 31st. *NW. At the Mouth of our Wintering Cove Churchill River.* Moderate and fair. At 3 a.m. being Moor'd with our Small Bower and Stream Cable, unmoor'd, hove short, and by 6 weigh'd being the Half Flood. At 7 hove her into the Cove's mouth as far as the Tide would fleet her. We broke 4 Ice Poles, by the Ship's running foul of them, several being Set up as Marks for transporting Her into the Cove. At Low water the Ship being Dry, and taking the Ground made a great heel or list, and thereby slipt off Half her false Keels[3] from close aft to Her Midships. The two false Keels were very Rank, being 12 Inches deep, and on no Hold but the Keel Staples or Clamps, and here and there a Treenail about an Inch or two Hold. So we must be oblig'd to get it quite off.[4]

---

[1] On board *Discovery* Moor noted: 'At 3 AM unmoor'd and just get enterd the Cove before the Tide faild us' (Adm 51/290, pt IX, 29 Aug. 1741).

[2] Rankin's log records that *Furnace* now drew 9′ 10″ forward and aft (ADM L/ F/109, 30 Aug 1741).

[3] False keel: an additional keel fitted outside the main keel usually for protection in the event of grounding.

[4] The co-operation between the Company and the Navy was still continuing: on this date Isham noted: 'The ship's Carptr. about the Sloop, the Captns. cooper a making us some pails'. (HBC B 42/a/23, f. 7d).

PLATE VI. Fort Prince of Wales, Churchill, 1777
From Samuel Hearne, *A Journey to the Northern Ocean....*, 1795
(Special Collections, University of Saskatchewan Library)

SEPTEMBER 1741

Tuesday 1st. *NW.* Cloudy with Snow and Northerly Winds. All Hands employ'd in digging the Dock deeper for the two Ships; the Discovery just enter'd, the Furnace her Length without. Very bad Tides tho' at their Height.

Wensday 2nd. *NE.* Frequent Showers of Snow. Our People employ'd in digging the Dock deeper for the Ships, the Ground very near as Hard as portland Stone, & Scarce to be enter'd with Pickaxes. The Carpenters & Bricklayers belonging to the New Fort repairing & fitting up the Old Factory and Some Apartments at the New Fort for my Self and some of my Officers.[1]

Thursday 3rd. *NNW. At the Mouth of our Wintering Cove.* Very Cold Weather, with frequent Showers of Snow. Our Men employ'd night & Day Tides digging and blowing up the large Stones we meet wth. in digging. Yesterday Morning sent some Provisions & Sick Men to the Old Factory, with the Surgeon of the Discovery to take Care of them, with Orders to get what fresh Provisions and Necessaries they could for them. Our Ship Has not fleeted since we Hall'd ashore, so that we must continue digging the Ground Lower, on Account of getting the Ships off in the Spring of the Year, being the Tides is much lower in the Spring than the Fall. Large Flocks of Geese and Ducks have been seen flying here for this fortnight Past, tho' none to be seen these three Days, but we shall lose the Opportunity of getting any, having no Indians to Kill them.

Friday 4th. *NWbN.* Cold Weather with Sleet and Snow; the Winds variable. Continued our Men at Work as above; every Tide as we dig down we meet wth. Rocks and Stones which we are oblig'd to blow up. We got our Anchors above high Water Mark. Yesterday Morning as I was going forwards and the Men running round with the Capston, I was jamm'd between the End of one of the Bars and the Companion wch. took my breast and

---

[1] In return Navy sawyers were sawing 2½" planks to make platforms for the guns on the Fort's ramparts (ibid., f. 8).

Back Bone, so that I fell down senseless for some time, and when recover'd a little was in great Pain & Difficulty of breathing, but don't find any Damage Inwardly. I hope I shall in a short time recover again thro' the Assistance of Providence.

Saturday 5. *NbW.* Fresh Gales and frequent Squalls with much Snow & freezing cold Weather. Continued a Dock a-head of both Ships that we fleet in against the next Spring Tides. It is better digging now than in the Spring of the Year, tho' bad enough. Sent some Stores to the New Fort.

Sunday 6th. *No., NNW.* Ditto Wear. with frequent Showers of Hail & Snow. Continued both Tides digging & blowing up Rocks as long as the Water would Premit us. Our whole false Keel off a-fore & abaft, yet she doth not fleet these Neap Tides. Sent the Launch with Provisions from the Tender to the Old Factory, where most of our Men and Officers are to Winter.[1]

Monday 7th. *NNW. At our Wintering Cove in Churchill River.* Cold, Piercing Weather with frequent Showers of Hail and Snow. Continued as above every Tide. The Ground very Hard and Many Stones to blow up. Sent 16 men to cut Firewood & pile it up, ready for drawing Home in the Winter upon a Sled when the Ground is froze, it being now very marshy and boggy.[2]

Tuesday 8th. *NNW, SSW.* First Part Moderate and fair, the Middle and latter fresh Gales; our Men employ'd as above, but the Tides ebbing out very little, could not come to drill the Rocks.[3] Sent our Launch to the Old Fort with Provisions.

Wensday 9th. *SSE.* Hard Gales; the Ground all Cover'd with

---

[1] At noon on the 6th the Company's bricklayer returned to Fort Prince of Wales from the Old Factory 'having almost rebuilt the Stoves at that place' (ibid.).

[2] Middleton's cooper was now 'making coolers for brewing' (ibid.).

[3] This despite the fact that, as Rankin records, 'wee damed the lower Part of the Dock and hove the Water out with buckets and Scoops. The Tide forced the Dam before we could drill three or four Holes to blow it up'. (ADM L/F/109, 8 Sep 1741). On shore the co-operation between Navy and Company still continued: Isham records: 'the Smith & Captns. Armrr. a making Bolts for the Sloop' (HBC B 42/a/23, f. 9).

Snow. Continued digging till 8 p.m. and from 5 till 8 this Morning. There are two large Stones in our Way, but the Tides not ebbing out to come at them, we could not blow them up. The Ships Have not fleeted for several Days Past.

Thursday 10th. *WNW.* A very Hard Gale with Snow and freezing. Continued at work as before. Our Men almost benumb'd with digging in the Water.[1]

Friday 11th. *Ditto.* Much Snow fell last Night, and Sleet still continues with a Storm and freezing. We are in Hopes, if we can get up one Rock that lies in our Way which we have been Six Days about, to get the Furnace into Safety for the Winter. The Weather is very Cold and Pinching to the Officers and Men, being Oblig'd to work in the Wet and freezing.

Saturday 12th. *NNW.* Fresh Gales and frequent Showers of Snow. Continued digging and blowing up Rocks. Sent the Launch with Bread and other Provisions to the Old Fort the Morning Tide and Return'd in the Afternoon.

Sunday 13th. *Variable. At our Wintering Cove, Churchill River.* Moderate Weather; the Wind Variable. Order'd all our Men from the Shore, to come and receive Slops,[2] Bedding and Dead Mens' Cloaths which were issued out to those that wanted by 2 o'Clock p.m. We finished our Dock for the Furnace. At 7 in the Evening, being High Water, got her into it as high as we durst go that she might Fleet in the Spring of the Year, and Moor'd Her between 6 Cable ends, viz. one of the Discovery's Cables for the Quarters, our Stream Cable on each Bow, and another ahead and right a-stern, all well serv'd[3] and rounded to Prevent Damages from the Ice. We broke in Heaving the Ship into the Cove & Dock, 2 Hawsers of 4 & 5 Inch, and the 7 Outrigging Pendants of the Careening Geer.

---

[1] On this date the Company's bricklayer returned from the Old Factory for good, 'having made 3 Stoves and plastered one of the Houses leaving their labourer to do the rest, I wanting him home to mend our own Stoves, etc.' (ibid.).

[2] Slops: ready-made clothing issued to seamen against their pay.

[3] To serve a cable is to wind spunyarn tightly around it to help make it impervious to water.

Monday 14th. Moderate and fair Warm Weather, tho' much Snow on the Ground.[1] Got the Cables and Rigging on board both Ships, together with some of our Iron Ballast to Prevent them from Fleeting at the Spring Tides, there being a Swell with the Wind from ENE to NNW, we being but two Miles from the Harbour's Mouth and no Place in the whole River so secure from the Dangers of the Ice as this Cove. Here they Winter the three Sloops belonging to the Hudson's Bay Company, that draw about 6 feet each, but we were oblig'd to dig down 4 feet to get the two Ships into the Cove. We got the Discovery in first. Expended 50 Pounds of Powder at different times in blowing up the Rocks in our Winter Cove.

Tuesday 15th. *Ditto.* Moderate Weather with Thunder, Rain & Lightning. Our Men employ'd from 4 this Morning till 8 at Night getting the Remainder of our Iron Ballast and Rigging on board & Sending Provisions to the Old Factory. The best of our Men Cutting wood ready to Haul home for firing in the Winter.

Wensday 16th. *SW. At our Wintering Cove in Churchill River.* Moderate and fair. Continued getting our Boatswain's and Carpenter's Stores on board to keep the Ship from fleeting on Common Tides.

Thursday 17th. *NNW.* Ditto Weather. Sent Several of our Men's Chests and Bedding to the Old Fort in the Launch. Got our Cables serv'd and Hove Tort. Expended 4 old Hammacoes for the Service. this Afternoon I went on Shore with my Bedding and lay at the New Fort[2] after having secured the Ships as well as Possible. There are about 10 Hands at the New Factory, the Rest at the Old, Most of the men being order'd to their Winter Quarters.

Friday 18th. *NW, NNW.* A Strong Gale and very Cold with some Snow.

---

[1] Isham reports that three of the Company's boats and the Navy boats, with a total of forty men, set off upriver to bring home rafts of timber for firewood (HBC B 42/a/23, f. 9d).
[2] I.e. Middleton now took up residence at Fort Prince of Wales.

Saturday 19th. *NWbN.* More Moderate Weather; a cold Air and cloudy. In the Night the Tender's Cutter went adrift from the Old Factory about the last Quarter Flood Having in Her the Masts, Sails, Spreets[1] and Oars belonging to her, together with the Grapnel and Grapnel Rope belonging to the Furnace's Pinnace. I sent Men on both Sides of the River to look for her, but they could see nothing of her.[2]

Sunday 20th.[3] *No., Calm.* Close, Cloudy Weather, almost Calm. Sent 20 Men from Each Fort in Search of the Boat from the River's mouth as high up as any Tide runs on both Sides, and to look for her diligently from low water to High Water Mark, but no appearance of Her. Our Carpenter Having got Cold, lost the Sight of His Eyes for some time.

Monday 21st. *Variable.* Hazy Weather, variable Winds and Cold Air.[4]

Tuesday 22nd. *NNW. At our Wintering Cove in Churchill River.* Fresh Gales and freezing, with Cold Air.

Wensday 23rd. *NE, NEbE.* Hazy Weather & variable Winds. I sent 8 Men along Shore without the River to see if the Boat was drove out of the Harbour to Sea, but the [sic] find Nothing of her.

---

[1] Spreet or sprit: a long spar extending diagonally across a spritsail, i.e. a four-sided fore-and-aft sail.

[2] On this date Isham reports that: '... at noon our Carptr. came from the Sloop, he and the rest of the Carptrs. having finnish'd putting in the new Keel & shifted severall of her Plank...' (ibid.).

[3] This was the date on which the Indian whom Isham had sent to York Factory returned with bad news. He had 'stayed 7 days at the north side of Port Nelson & cou'd not get over' (ibid.). In the same journal entry Isham explains that the situation is even worse than it might appear, since Richard Norton, his predecessor, had apparently given the Indians normally trading at Churchill an unusually large amount of ammunition, and hence they were not likely to come in again for some considerable time, i.e. there would be fewer Indians than usual available to hunt for either the Company post or for the Navy expedition. In this predicament Isham tried again: 'therefore have sent 2 young men again to York Fort to acquaint them of our disappointment & to desire Mr. White to send us as many Beaver Coats as he can spare and to supply us with 10 Familys of Indians against the Spring to hunt for us, not being able to see or here from any Indians this fall' (ibid.).

[4] The Company's shipwright and the Navy carpenters now began work on the Company's launch *Quicohatch* (ibid.).

Thursday 24th. *NE to East.* Ditto Weather and Small Snow.[1]

Friday 25th. *ENE.* The first Part little Wind, the Middle & latter fresh Gales, and cold Weather.

Saturday 26th. *East.* Snow and Cold Weather with freezing, the Wind Variable.

Sunday 27th. *East to NNW.* A very Hard Gale, the Wind Variable, and very cold Weather, the Thermometer as low as in the Hard Frost that Happen'd in England two Years ago.

Monday 28th. *NW.* A strong Gale, the Wind variable, and very Cold Weather. This Day I Went to the Old Factory to see what order they were in at that Place and what Wood they had Haul'd home for their Winter firing. In my Return from thence I stop'd at the Ships, and found they lay very well.[2]

Tuesday 29th. *NW to NNW.* Moderate Winds and Cold freezing Weather, the Wind variable. We Kill'd about 100 white Partridges[3] before the Cold Weather Set in, but since that time they are all gone into the Woods farther in-land.

Wensday 30th. *NNW to SW.* Little Wind and variable, froze very Hard, the River almost full of Ice, but driving out Every Ebb. I sent People to see if the Ships were afloat at the Height of the Spring Tides but the [sic] were not.[4]

---

[1] Isham notes that he is keeping two families of Indians at the Fort 'to knitt snow shoes, we not having above 15 pair in the Factory, much more [sic] our neighbours' (ibid., f. 11).

[2] On this date Isham records co-operation from the Navy in laying in firewood for the following winter, i.e. 1742–43: 'Early this morning sent 11 Men up the River for to fall our next Winters Firewood & pile it in Heaps, 4 of wch. is the Captns men, likewise sent 9 Men over the River to Bears point to fall Stockades & pile them in Heaps, 4 of wch. is the Captns Men' (ibid., f. 11d). He also sent his bricklayer back to the Old Factory to make further repairs to the stoves.

[3] Middleton is referring to either Willow Ptarmigan (*Lagopus lagopus*) or Rock Ptarmigan (*Lagopus mutus*). Only the former nests in the Churchill area, but both flock south to the shelter of the forest edge in winter.

[4] William Moor was in charge of this inspection party (Adm 51/290, pt IX).

OCTOBER 1741

Thursday 1st. *N to W.* For the Most Part fair freezing Weather & almost Calm. At 10 p.m. a fresh Gale with the Ice in the River fast along the Shore two Miles off.[1]

Friday 2nd. *Calm, ESE. In our Wintering Cove Churchill River.* Since last Noon moderate and cloudy for the Most Part with variable Wind, all round the Compass.[2]

Saturday 3rd. *Variable.* Fresh Gales and Cold freezing Weather.

Sunday 4th. *WNW.* A Strong Gale with Some Snow and Hard Frost. Sent the Lieutenant and several of our People this Morning to get our Guns in Readiness against Sunday the 11th, to solemnize that Day, being His Majesty's Coron. Day.

Monday 5th. *NNW, SSE.* Ditto Weather; much Ice drove out of the River.

Tuesday 6th. *SSE, North.* A very Hard Gale with Snow and freezing; the Wind variable. Much Ice driving out of the River.[3]

Wensday 7th. *N, NE.* More Moderate, freezing very Hard. The River almost full of Ice.

Thursday 8th. *NW.* Ditto Weather. Not much Snow upon the Ground as Yet, but very cold.

Friday 9th. *Ditto.* Cold, Freezing Weather, with Snow.

Saturday 10th. *Ditto.* Clear Air, with variable Winds and great Frost.

---

[1] It is clear from Moor's journal, however, that there was still a channel of open water down the middle of the estuary (ibid., 1 Oct 1741).

[2] The Company's bricklayer completed his work at the Old Factory and returned to Fort Prince of Wales.

[3] The carpenters, presumably including the Navy men, were again working on the *Quicohatch* (HBC B 42/a/23, f. 12).

Sunday 11th. *Ditto. In our Wintering Cove, Churchill River.* Ditto cold Weather. This being the Anniversary of His Majesty's Coronation Day we solemnized it in a Particular Manner. We March'd all our Men from the New Fort, under Arms, to the Cove where the Ships lay, being above two Miles distant, and at Noon discharg'd 28 Guns belonging to both Ships that were lay'd in order on the shore for that purpose where the two Ships Winter. The Officers drank to His Majesty's Health & Success to the British Arms, as the Guns were firing. It was observ'd at the Same time that the Wine, with which the Officers drank the aforesaid Healths, and which was good Port wine, froze in the Glass as soon as Pour'd out of the Bottle. They March'd back in the same order with Drums beating and Colours flying. When they Arriv'd at the New Fort they were drawn up in the Middle of the Area, where they Went thro' their Exercise, fir'd several Vollies, and drank to the Health of His Majesty, the Prince and Princess of Wales and all the Royal Family. The Articles of War and Orders of the Navy were read to them. In the Evening His Majesty's Officers and those of the Hudson's Bay Company were Plentifully regal'd and the Men belonging to both Ships and the Factory Men had thirty Gallons of Brandy made into Punch to drink the aforesaid Healths, to which the Natives were invited, and Evening concluded with all possible Demonstrations of Joy to the great Pleasure and Satisfaction of the Natives.[1]

Monday 12th. *NW, So., SW.* Variable Winds with Snow. Most of the Ice that lin'd the Shores of the River and Bays for 3 or 4 Leagues round, drove out to Sea. Continued freezing very hard.

Tuesday 13th. *SW, NNW. Churchill Fort.* Moderate, Warm Weather. Much Snow fell last Night; the Wind variable. All the Ice that lin'd the Shores without and for two Miles up the River, drove out of Sight to Sea, the rest fast froze. People Have Crossed the River upon the Ice 8 Miles up 4 Days ago. I observe

---

[1] While the details of this rather grand celebration are recorded at length by both Middleton and Rankin, Isham makes no mention of it. Instead he records some rather sobering news: '...this forenoon the Indians that went for York Factory 21st last month came back, who inform us all was well at that place, and that Mr. White could spare no Coats, but assures me that he will procure me all the Indians he possible can for to come in the Spring to hunt for us' (ibid., f. 12d).

How so much Ice is made every Year in the Bay, Straits and Shores in these Parts, and why there is more made some Years than others. It's caus'd in the fall of the Year, before the Rivers, Bays and Inlets are froze fast, for the Ice that is Made on the several Lee shores increase at a great Rate, near one Mile in 24 Hours, which at the Flux and Reflux of the Tides break off and when the Wind blows from the Shore is all Carryed out to sea where it fastens together & more increases with it. And as we find in the Straits and Bay Greater Quantities of Ice some Years than others, it is owing to the Length of Time these several Rivers, Inlets, Bays etc. are freezing fast, for the Sea is not, nor can freeze without something to fasten upon, and if the Rivers Should keep open untill the latter End of October, in [sic] would go near to fill Hudsons Bay one Quarter full of Ice. Now all the Ice that's drove into the open Bay, let the Wind blow from any Part of the Compass, will have one side of it a Weather side, which makes a great Increase by the Wash of the Sea against it; and as the Winter continues for nine months there must be great Quantities made in that Time.[1]

Wensday 14th. The first Part Moderate Weather and Hazy, the Middle and Latter fresh Gales with Snow, the Wind variable and very cold with freezing. At 4 in the Afternoon the Surgeon went out and Kill'd two white Hares; they weigh'd about 12 or 14 Pound each, and were very fine eating.[2]

Thursday 15th. *Churchill Fort.* Fresh Gales with Frost and Snow. Most of the Men came down from the Old Factory to the New, in order to be supply'd with Cloath to make themselves Stockings, Caps, Mittins and Socks, and a Coarse Blanket to wear over

---

[1] This is an interesting but fallacious hypothesis as to the formation of sea ice, the critical erroneous link in the argument being: 'for the Sea is not, nor can freeze without something to fasten upon'. At sufficiently low temperatures vast areas of open sea can freeze very quickly, with the progressive formation of grease ice, frazil ice and young ice. See also Margaret Montgomery, 'Does the Bay freeze?', *The Beaver* (Outfit 282, June 1951), pp. 12–15.

[2] Most probably the white winter phase of the snowshoe hare (*Lepus americanus*) but possibly the arctic hare (*Lepus arcticus*). The ranges of the two species overlap in the Churchill area (A. W. F. Banfield, *The Mammals of Canada*, Toronto, 1974). But even if arctic hares these must have been giants since the average weight of adults of that species is only 10 lb.

their other Cloaths.[1] No Person could endure the Cold in the Country without this Contrivance. The Shoes they wear here are of the Leather of Deer-Skins or Canvas, made big enough to contn. their Feet, when cover'd with Yarn Stockings and three pair of Socks of Coarse Duffield over them. On their Legs they wear a large Pr. of Cloath Stockings, which covers their other stockings & Breeches; upon their Hands they wear a Pair of Cloath Mittins lin'd with Beaver or Duffield, which reach up to their Elbows, and when they go abroad a Pair of Snow Shoes 5 foot long & 18 Inches broad to keep them from Sinking in the Snow, and on their Head a Cap of Beaver, which lets down round their Shoulders, yet all this will not Prevent their freezing some Days. These things they were oblidg'd to take up of the Factory Here, as we were not Provided.[2]

Friday 16th. Fresh Gales and Cloudy with Snow and Frost; the Wind variable. One Day the River's Mouth is quite full on the Flood with Ice, & the Ebb Carries it out again; if the wind blows for a Day or two on the Shore, it freezes for 3 or 4 Miles all round. When the Wind comes off the Land & the Tides break it loose, it is all Carried out to Sea. The River is not fast with Ice at the Entrance yet, tho' full every Tide, & for several leagues without, when the Winds blow on the Shore

Saturday 17th. The first Part Moderate Weather, the latter fresh Gales & Much Snow. The Ice drives all off the Shore for many leagues.

Sunday 18th. Ditto Weather with much drifting Snow. Towards Evening the Wind Shifting it blew, snowed and froze hard all Night. Very cold Weather now with all Winds. Much Ice out at Sea.

Monday 19th. *NNW. Churchill Fort.* Moderate Weather for the

---

[1] In all clothing and goods to the value of £146–3–6 (Bay prices) were supplied to the expedition by Isham (Committee Minutes, 2 Dec 1742, HBC A 1/35, p. 344).

[2] Given the experience and knowledge which Middleton and several of his officers must have accumulated while employed by the Company as to winter conditions in the Bay, this lack of adequate winter clothing is one of the major mysteries concerning the expedition.

Most Part and Clear Air, freezing very hard. I sent this Morning to see how the Ships lay; they brought me word they were very Safe in their Docks, and all our Ropes moderately tort. We have Had for these 3 or 4 Days past very great Tides (occasion'd by the last Northerly Gale) several feet higher than have been this Year.

Tuesday 20th. *Ditto.* Ditto Weather with Hard Frost. The River's Mouth Continues open a little Way. All full of Ice out in the Bay farther than we can see.

Wensday 21st. *No, NNW.* Ditto Weather with very Hard Frost. The Water, Ink and every thing freezing by the Fireside. Much Snow this afternoon, & extream Cold.

Thursday 22nd. *Ditto.* Moderate Gales, freezing hard. Several Places in the River open, but no Water to be seen out at sea, Every Night the People belonging to the Factory take several white Foxes[1] with traps, being very Plenty here.

Friday 23rd. *No, NW.* Light Airs and Moderate Weather. This Day the Lieut. & Master of the Tender went to see how the Ships lay in their Winter Cove and found they lay very well, all jamm'd up with Ice for a mile without them, so now I fear no sea hurting them, but dread getting them off in the Spring of the Year, for the Tides, they tell us are very different then.

Saturday 24th. *Almost Calm.* Fair Weather & almost Calm, but freezing Hard continually. Several of the Men that are employ'd in the Woods, cutting the Winter firing, came here for Brandy in lieu of Beer. Sent several Men for Bread on board the Discovery.

Sunday 25th. *NW.* Little wind, a Cold freezing. No going any Distance from the Fort or off the Rocks without Snow Shoes to wear; for the Snow in Many Places is 10 or 12 feet deep.[2]

---

[1] Arctic fox (*Alopex lagopus*).

[2] Even as early as this in the winter the Navy men were beginning to feel the lack of proper clothing. Isham reports: 'Severall of the Ships' Compays. at times come for Necessarys to keep them warm, having no wearing Apperall for this Country' (HBC B 42/a/23, f. 14).

Monday 26th. *SE*. Little Wind and Hazy with Snow and freezing Weather.

Tuesday 27th. *EbN to SE*. Fresh Gales and Much Snow; the River open at its Mouth, but much Ice all without, farther than we can see.

Wensday 28th. *No, NNE*. Fresh Gales and a Continual Snow.

Thursday 29th. *NNW*. *Churchill Fort*. A very Hard Gale; snow'd all Night. Our Men which we have here & the Factory's People employ'd in wheeling out the Snow from the Area within the Fort, being 3 feet deep in many places.

Friday 30th. *Ditto*. Fresh Gales and clear Weather, freezing very Hard. This being the Anniversary of His Majesty's Birth Day, we solemnized it in the Same manner we did the Coronation, firing 17 Guns, the Tender 11; drank to His Majesty's Health, and the Royal Family and distributed 30 Gallons of Brandy made into Punch together with strong Beer, among our People, the Factory's Men and Natives, as before on the Coronation Day.

Saturday 31st. *Calm*. The Weather very cold and Calm with a thick Fog. Several Men belonging to the Factory, came Home from Hunting and Wooding, with their Necks and Faces froze.

NOVEMBER 1741

Sunday 1st. *Ditto*. Calm Weather & foggy, the Air something Milder.

Monday 2nd. *N*. Very Cold freezing Weather with fresh Gales and much Snow drifting with the Wind towards the Evening. The Ice drives out and in at the River's Mouth with every Tide, but no water to be seen without, nor a Mile up the River, all full of Ice.

Tuesday 3rd. *NW*. Moderate and fair, but freezing hard. Two of our Men froze their faces in going to the Woods.

Wensday 4th. *N*. Fresh Gales and fair weather, with Snow towards the Evening.

Thursday 5th. *N*. Hard Gales with much Snow and freezing. This being the Anniversary of Gun Powder Treason,[1] and our Guns being cover'd with Snow, we play'd off some fire works at the New Fort, and gave our Men and Officers 30 Galls. of Brandy and Sugar to make Punch as before.

Friday 6th. *NW*. *Churchill Fort*. Moderate Weather, freezing Hard.[2]

Saturday 7th. *NbW*. Fresh Gales with Snow and freezing cold Weather. The River is not quite fast at the Mouth yet, the Ice driving in and out with the Tides, but all the Flatts round the Shores and several Miles out at Sea cover'd with Ice.

Sunday 8th. *NbW to SW*. Moderate Weather. Most of the Ice drove out to Sea from the Shores, as the Wind shifts off the Land, & only What is fast to the flats left.

Monday 9th. *NNW*. A Hard Gale with Some Snow, freezing very Hard. I sat a Bottle of English Sprits without the House this Night, and it was Hard froze in the Morng.; the Sprits were full Proof. The Factory People took several White Foxes in Traps, and shot some White Partridges, as they do every week but they are very scarce to what they are some Winters here.

Tuesday 10th. *Ditto*. Continued a Hard Gale with much snow drifting & severe Frost. Freezes everything in our Bed Places, except Brandy. Wine, Strong Beer etc. is all Congealed to Ice in one Night's time when the Fire is out.[3]

Wensday 11th. *NbW*. Fresh Gales & Stormy Cold Weather. It is

---

[1] Guy Fawkes Day.

[2] In yet another display of his genuine desire to assist the Navy expedition, on this date Isham 'sent 2 Indian lads to the northeast to kill partridges for the Captain' (ibid., f. 15).

[3] The two Indian hunters had been quite successful: Isham reports that they brought in fifty ptarmigan and one hare for Middleton (ibid., f. 15d).

Hardly Possible to go 40 Yds. without the Doors and escape freezing the Face and every Part of the Body that is not cover'd with double cloathing.

Thursday 12th. *Ditto.* Fresh Gales and cold Weather. The River is now quite froze fast from Side to Side as low as its Entrance.

Friday 13th. *Ditto.* Fresh Gales with Snow and cold Freezing Weather.

Saturday 14th. *NE.* Moderate and fair, with little Wind.

Sunday 15th. *SE.* Mild Weather. Set up Beacons at a small Dist. one from the other quite Cross the River near the Mouth, as a Guide for Passengers in foggy Weather. The Ice is 4 or 5 feet thick.[1]

Monday 16th. *SE. Churchill Fort.* Fair, moderate Weather, very cold and freezing.

Tuesday 17th. *Ditto.* Mild Weather, and light Airs. The Ice drives without from the Land, where it is not fast. It's not fast above a mile from the Shore Seawards.

Wensday 18th. *WSW, W to NE.* The first Part fair Weather with Calms & variable Winds, the latter fresh Gales and Snow with hard freezing.

Thursday 19th. *Calms.* Fresh and Snow. This Day the Indians brought in an Hundred white Partridges, which I bought from them, as I had done several times before, for the Use of the Sick, we having had several of our Men dangerously Ill since they came ashore; some of them Continues so.

Friday 20th. *West, NE.* Fresh Gales & Snow, with variable winds, and hard Frost.

---

[1] The Indians brought in a further ninety ptarmigan for Captain Middleton (ibid., f. 16).

Saturday 21st. *NE to NW*. Little wind and Calms, with Snow & freezing.

Sunday 22nd. *ENE to ESE*. Modert. Gales all Day; in the Night fresh Gales and drifting Snow, freezing very Hard.

Monday 23rd. *NE, calms to NbW*. Fresh Gales the wind variable, the Snow drifting and freezing very hard. The Snow very deep in many Places; no going a Quarter of a Mile without Snow Shoes.[1]

Tuesday 24th. *NNW & SE*. Fresh Gales in the Day; more moderate in the Night with Snow.

Wensday 25th. *SE, SW*. Moderate Weather, some snow, and freezing hard.

Thursday 26th. *WSW*. Very cold Hazy Weather, some snow in the Night.

Friday 27th. *East*. Moderate and fair; some snow and a Hard Frost.

Saturday 28th. *Ditto*. Moderate and Hazy Weather with some snow.

Friday 29th. *Ditto*. Fair clear Weather & very Sharp cold Air; the Sea all froze as far as we can see; the Ice about 4 foot thick in the Middle of the River, but upon the Shoals, and all along the Shores in great Heaps.

Saturday 30th. *NNW*. Strong gales and drifting snow, the wind at NNW extream cold freezing everything by the fire in the Night. We can very well perceive in the Beams of the Sun the Air to be fill'd with icy Particles extreamly Sharp & Angular.[2]

---

[1] Isham's journal again records a mixed work crew of Company men and Navy men clearing snow out of the yard at Fort Prince of Wales; the young Indian hunters brought the captain a further twenty ptarmigan (ibid., f. 16d).

[2] Middleton was supplied with another 144 ptarmigan by his Indian hunters (ibid., f. 17).

DECEMBER 1741

Tuesday 1st. *NW. Churchill Fort.* Strong Gales, drifting Snow & cold freezing Weather.

Wensday 2nd. *NNW.* Very Hard Gales last Night; extream cold & clear Weather.

Thursday 3rd. *NW.* Fresh Gales and cold Weather.

Friday 4th. *Ditto.* More moderate and fair, but very cold.

Saturday 5th. *Ditto.* Little wind variable, fair & clear with hard freezing.

Sunday 6th. *Ditto.* Ditto Weather.[1]

Monday 7th. *NNW.* The first Part Moderate, the latter fresh Gales and Squally. Very cold

Tuesday 8th. *Ditto.* Ditto Wind and extream cold, but fair & Clear. Cut a large Hole in the Ice 15 feet over, in the Stream of the River, to freshen our Salt Meat. The Ice in that Place is 5 or 6 feet thick.

Wensday 9th. *NNW.* Ditto Weather and Wind.

Thursday 10th. *Ditto.* Fresh Gales and extream Cold Weather. I went out Yesterday to Observe the Sun's Altitude in order to find the Refraction. The Spirit in Elton's Quadrant[2] froze in less than 10 Minutes so No liquid is Proof against the Extremity of the Weather.

Friday 11th. *Soly.* Fair Weather but very cold. We have recd. from the Indians since the Winter set in at several times about

---

[1] A further eighty ptarmigan arrived for Middleton (ibid., f. 17d).
[2] John Elton developed an improved quadrant in 1732 whose two spirit levels helped provide an artificial horizon when the actual horizon was obscured. See May, *Marine Navigation*, pp. 128–9.

1500 White Partridges,[1] which Have been of great Service to our Sick People, having had no other fresh Provisions, except some few Jack fish[2] which I got from the Natives and Country People for my own Table. Both the Fish & Partridges will keep 7 or 8 Months froze as Hard as Ice.

Saturday 12th. *So. to WNW*. Very Cold Weather. Many of the Factory's Men, who lie in the Woods & are employ'd in cutting their Next Winter's firing, freeze their Hands and Faces.

Sunday 13th. *No. to ESE*. Extream cold Weather with fresh Gales. This Morning I bought 100 Partridges which the Indians brought in.

Monday 14th. *ESE*. Moderate and fair the 1st and Middle parts; the latter fresh Gales; so Extream Cold that one of the Home Indians, and [sic] Old Man about 70 froze in His Tent to death under the Walls of the Fort.[3]

Tuesday 15th. *E*. Fresh Gales with Some Snow. Very cold.

Wensday 16th. *NNW*. Ditto Weather and Variable Winds.

Thursday 17th. *WNW*. Ditto Weather & Hazy. Many of the Factory's People & some of ours froze their Hands and Faces in going Half a Mile.

Friday 18th. *E, ESE*. Moderate Gales, the Winds Variable.

Saturday 19th. *SE*. Have had a Moderate Warm Day, Considering the Time & Place. Sent the Sled to the Ship for some Bread and a Cask of Vinegar that was forgot on board, all froze to Solid Ice. Sent up 100 Partridges to the Sick Men at the Old Factory, and a Cask of Brandy for their Christmas Cheer, with orders for

[1] Rankin adds the information that the ptarmigan were served out at a rate of two per man per day in lieu of salt provisions (ADM L/F/109, 11 Dec 1741).

[2] Pike, presumably from nearby lakes.

[3] Isham corroborates this but adds the significant information that the old Indian was 'a little in liquor' at the time of his death (HBC B 42/a/23, f. 18). The Company's men dug a grave for him, which must have been a major undertaking.

them to broach four Casks of Strong Beer, and sent them Sugar to their Brandy.

Sunday 20th. *NNW.* Variable Wind and hard freezing Weather.[1]

Monday 21st. *NW.* Moderate Gales but very Sharp Air.

Tuesday 22nd. *Ditto.* Ditto Weather. Most of the Factory Men and Indians that were hunting and fishing for the Ships' Companies, & the Factory, are returned to keep their Christmas according to Custom, for 12 or 14 Days. We shall give our People Strong Beer & Brandy every Day all the time.

Wensday 23rd. *WNW.* Fresh Gales and hazy drifting Weather with Some Snow.

Thursday 24th. *Ditto.* Most of our People at the Old Factory are very well excepting two or three that are afflicted with the Scurvy,[2] & were ailing before they came on shore in this Place. I have given them, ever since our English Beer has been expended, Spruce Beer and Brandy, the only Means us'd here to prevent the Scurvy.[3]

[1] Middleton's liberal provision of alcohol to both his own men and the Company's men provoked a serious disciplinary problem for Isham, as the latter recorded in his journal for this date: 'this Forenoon Jn. Armaunt, Wm. Allen & Robt. Irvin came here for some Things they wanted, got drunk, & one offering to go away, run the Risque of his Life by lying down to sleep by the River, brought him in. Irvin we put in Irons for scanderlizing my Chief Officer & making a Disturbance, about 6 at night he broke the Lock of his Irons.
Dec. 21st. Mon.... Brought Irvin this morng. to the Bar; gave him 12 Lashes and sent him away that he might behave better for the Future, but the other 2, Allen & Armaunt got over the Works at break of Day & run away to the Woods, by which for showing such bad Examples, the next time I see them I hope I shall bring them to their Good Behaviour' (ibid., f. 18d). Isham also notes that on the 21st the two Indian lads brought in 120 ptarmigan for Middleton.
[2] This early appearance of scurvy makes one wonder how many of the men were in fact eating the ptarmigan and fish supplied to them. It is not unlikely that with the conservatism of the eighteenth-century seaman with regard to diet, some were refusing to touch the fresh supplies. The fact that all the officers were housed in Fort Prince of Wales, some five miles away, and out of sight of the Old Factory, would make this even more probable.
[3] Justice caught up with the two fugitives from Fort Prince of Wales on this date: '...at the same time brought the 2 Men that ran away, Jno. Armaunt & Wm. Allen, to the Barr, gave them 20 Lashes apiece for a Warning to them, & the rest all being present, not to do the like again' (ibid., f. 19).

Friday 25th. *ESE*. Very Cold Weather with frequent Squalls, Snow & drifting.[1]

Saturday 26th. *SW*. Fresh Gales and hard freezing Weather.

Sunday 27th. *SW*. Fresh Gales variable with Snow.

Monday 28th. *Soerly*. Continued cold freezing Weather and variable Winds.

Tuesday 29th. *NW*. Moderate Warm Weather but the Snow drifting very much. Paskler Bennet, one of our Men, Died this Day, after being a long time ill.[2]

Wensday 30th. *NNW*. Moderate Warm Weather. Six Indians came here from the North & brought with them some Buffalo's Flesh,[3] & goods to Trade with the Factor. These are what they call Home Indians, but have been from the Factory these 5 Months. They were 20 Days coming from their Families. I examin'd them concerning the Country they Hunt in, & find by the Description they give of it, that it is barren and without Woods. I desir'd them to bring me a more Particular Account when they came in May Next.

Thursday 31st. *NNW, Soly, NNW*. Moderate Weather all the Day, but in the Night a Hard Gale & Snow. The six Indians went away this Morning in order to Return to their Families having got their Guns mended, & their Goods exchang'd with the Factor.[4]

---

[1] It seems a little strange that Middleton makes no reference to Christmas celebrations.

[2] Bennet had been living at the Old Factory (ibid., f. 19d). Moor noted that he had been 'long ill of the Scurvy' (Adm 51/290, pt IX, 29 Dec 1741).

[3] This was very probably muskox meat. This species had been referred to as 'buffalo' ever since the first known encounter of a Company employee with the species, namely that of Henry Kelsey in 1689 (A. G. Doughty and C. Martin, eds, *The Kelsey Papers*, Ottawa, 1929, p. 27). Later in the eighteenth century Samuel Hearne (Samuel Hearne, *A journey from Prince of Wales's Fort in Hudson's Bay, to the northern ocean undertaken by order of the Hudson's Bay Company, for the discovery of copper mines, a North West Passage... in the years 1769, 1770, 1771 & 1772*, London, 1795, p. 135) reported that he found muskox tracks within only nine miles of Fort Prince of Wales, although this must have been the extreme southern limit of their range.

[4] The lack of any reference to New Year's celebrations is again somewhat surprising.

JANUARY 1742

Friday 1st. *N, NNW. Churchill Fort.* The first Part Moderate; the latter hard Gales & drifting Weather with Snow. I sent three Men to the Ship to see how all was on board; in coming back they lost their Way by the Weather's changing, and drifting so much they could not see many Yards before them. They were a little froze but no great Damage.

Saturday 2nd. *North.* A hard Gale all Night and drifting Snow; very cold, freezing everything in my Cabin, tho' a fire kept in from 5 in the Morning till 9 at Night, and when the Fire is out, a red hot Shot 24 lb Weight hung up at the Window to thaw it; on the outside there are Shutters to every Window 6 Inches thick, four large fires made in the Stoves every Day, a Cart Load of wood for each, yet all this will not keep things from freezing within door.

Sunday 3rd. *NNW.* Cold, freezing, drifting Weather.

Monday 4th. *NW.* Fair & clear Weather, but extream cold. I went out this Forenoon with a Design to take a Walk, but had not gone 200 Yards before my Face was froze all over in a Blister, so was oblig'd to return.

Tuesday 5th. *NNW.* A Very Hard Gale and extream Cold Weather; everything freezing Close by the Fire. No stirring out of the Factory without freezing.

Wensday 6th. *N & NW.* Hard Gales in the Night & very cold; less wind in the Day. Several of our Men Sick at the Old Factory of the Scurvy and Fever.

Thursday 7th. *NNW.* Fresh Gales & drifting Snow, very cold, & no stirring abroad witht. freezing.

Friday 8th. *North.* Ditto Weather with thick Snow. Extream Cold.

Saturday 9th. *NW.* Ditto Weathr. Recd. 50 Partridges this Morning.

Sunday 10th. *NW. Churchill Fort.* Fresh Gales and very thick Snowy Weather, freezing hard.

Monday 11th. *WNW.* More Moderate & Clear, but extream Cold. Mr. Thompson, my surgn. has been at the Old Factory these three Days past to visit the Sick Men there and is not yet return'd.[1] Twenty Men came down from there with the Sledge by which I sent up thither 5 Casks of Brandy & Half a Barrel of Gunpowder, with Shot answerable, for every Man to kill what Partridges they can over and above their Allowance. I sent up at the Same Time 50 Partridges for the Sick Men.

Tuesday 12th. *NW.* Moderate & fair. This Day our Surgeon return'd from the Old Factory with Six Sick Men which were brought from thence on a Sledge, for whom I have appointed a convenient Place for an Hospital, with fresh Provisions & Proper Attendance. Two Men were left behind so dangerously ill that the Surgeon would not venture to bring them Down with the others. I have sent the fresh Provisions & the Surgeon of the Pink takes Care of them.

Wensday 13th. *NNW.* Fair, Moderate Weathr. but extream cold.

Thursday 14th. *Soly.* Fair & moderate, but very cold. I have been abroad every Day these three Weeks, and this Day as far as the Ships, but could scarce keep my Face from freezing. I could not stir out for some time before being very ill and the Weather Extream Cold.

Friday 15th. *WNW.* Close hazy Weather and extream cold.

Saturday 16th. *NNW.* Ditto Weather.

Sunday 17th. *NNW. Churchill Fort.* Close Weather and Foggy, with drifting Snow. Eight of our Men very ill in the Scurvy, and a Slow Fever. Our Surgeon makes Decoctions of Spruce and baths their Limbs therein, applies the best Medicines for their

---

[1] In other words Thompson had been sent to assist the *Discovery*'s surgeon in countering the outbreak of scurvy at the Old Factory.

Disorders, & they have fresh Meat and Broth for their Common Dyet.

Monday 18th. *Variable & Calm.* Fair & clear but very cold. At 9 this Morning I went to the Old Factory, having been out every Day This week past 3 or 4 Miles. The Distance between both Factories is 5 Miles; return'd in the evening having given orders for empng. all Hands in getting Fire-wood for their own burning & freshening the Salt Provisions to keep them Clear of the Scurvy.[1]

Tuesday 19th. *Ditto.* Much Snow all Day and Night. At 4 this Morning I was taken ill with a violent Pain in my breast, and is what they call the Country Distemper here,[2] several People in this Country being subject to it. I continued 24 Hours in much Pain & Agony, sweating all the time, & great Difficulty of breathing. It's worse for the time it lasts than the Stone or Gravel. It reduced me so low that I fainted twice, and brought my Fever and Ague on again, which I had been clear of this Week past.

Wensday 20th. *NNW.* Continued Snowing & Blowing. Very cold Weather.

Thursday 21st. *NW.* Fair & Clear. All Hands employ'd in clearing the Snow out of the Area withn. the Fort. Several of our Men came down from the Old Factory for Socks, Mittins and other things to keep them Warm; they likewise gave in a Memorandum of what Slops Cloaths they wanted from the Ship, when I could Send anybody on board. The Weather is extream cold, tho' very clear. I use all Means to get what fresh Provisions I can from the Indians & others. I gave Orders some time before Christmass that any Man who would go out and Shoot Partridges should have their whole allowance, Powdr. & Shot & all they could kill to themselves, tho' I am at great Trouble &

---

[1] As Rankin explained (ADM L/F/109, 18 Jan 1742) Middleton meant that they should cut a hole in the river ice and soak their salt meat in the fresh water for a while, keeping the hole clear of ice every day.

[2] Moor's journal for this date notes that Middleton 'was taken ill of the Pleuratis [presumably pleurisy]'; he repeated this on 5 February (Adm 51/290, pt IX, 19 Jan, 5 Feb 1742).

Charges in getting them Indian Shoes, without which they Cannot go into the Woods.

Friday 22nd. *NW.* Fair & Clear, but extream cold freezing Weather.

Saturday 23rd. *Ditto.* Fair & Clear with Hard Frost. Rec'd. 100 Partridges from the Indian Hunters.

Sunday 24th. *Ditto.* Ditto Weather, the Snow drifting. Extream Cold.

Monday 25th. *Ditto.* Fresh Gales and Hazy with Some Snow.

Tuesday 26th. *NNW.* The Morning Fair & Clear, the Middle and all Night Snow and hard Gales. Most of our People at the Old Factory employ'd in cutting a Hole thro' the Ice in the Middle of the River to freshen their Salt Meat, the rest getting Home Wood; 8 or 10 of them froze their Hands, Faces, Toes, Arms etc. in a Miserable Manner, 5 or 6 More very bad & down with the Scurvy. This Day I was taken ill with the Country Distemper in as violent a Manner as before; it continued upon me 24 Hours, and oblig'd to sit up all the Time. No Medicine can be found to give any ease. It leaves a soreness in the Breast for three Days after.

Wensday 27th. *NW.* Moderate & fair, but cold freezing Weather.

Thursday 28th. *Ditto.* Fresh Gales & cold freezing weather. Rec'd. 150 Partridges from the Indians.

Friday 29th. *Ditto.* Fresh Gales and freezing Hard, the Snow drifting. Several of the Factory's Men came Home from the Woods for a Fortnight's Provisions. Most of them lie in the Woods all the Winter cutting Fire-wood, fishing and Shooting Partridges. Rec'd. 14 Fish from one of the Factory Men that lay out all Winter catching Fish, which is done by cutting Holes thro' the Ice, and Passing Nets from Hole to Hole under the Ice; some they Catch with Hooks. The Greater Part they take in Winter is Jack fish.

Saturday 30th. *Sly.* Moderate & fair Weather; the Wind Variable to the So'ard but it Seldom Continues 24 hours that Way or another, except between the NE & NW, wch. generally blows for 9 months; the Frost continues as long, with much Snow.

Sunday 31st. *NNW. Churchill Fort.* Fresh Gales and the Snow drifting for the most Part. Most of the Men that came to the Factory for Provisions are return'd to the Woods to Haul their Wood to the River side ready to raft Home by Water in the Summer for next Winter's Firing.

FEBRUARY 1742

Monday 1st. *NW.* Fresh Gales & Cold freezing Weather. Sent Mr. Thompson, our Surgeon, to the Old Factory to cut off some of the Mens Toes that are Mortify'd with being Froze.

Tuesday 2nd. *NW.* Very Cold, but clear and Moderate Gales.

Wensday 3rd. *NW.* Fresh Gales and Fair Weather, Very Cold.

Thursday 4th. *NW.* Fair clear Weather but very cold. This Evening our Surgeon came down from the Old Factory, after cutting off the Men's Toes & the flesh of Several that were froze and mortify'd. There are 4 men at the Old Factory very bad wth the Scurvy, 12 at the New Factory very ill with the Scurvy, the Country Distemper and froze, 25 at both Places belonging to both Ships not able to go abroad, and several not able to Help themselves. I get fresh Provisions for those in the Scurvy, & the Surgeon uses all Possible Means to save them. In the Spring of the Year we shall supply 'em with green Herbs, the best remedy known here for the Scurvy.

Friday 5th. *Ditto.* Moderate and fair, but very cold. This Morning I was a third time afflicted with the Country Distemper; it is a violent Pain while it Continues, & generally last 24 Hours. Several of our People are often afflicted with it.

Saturday 6th. *Ditto.* Moderate Gales and Clear Weather, freezing very hard in the Night.

Sunday 7th. *NNW*. Ditto Weather.

Munday 8th. *Ditto*. Extream Cold freezing Weather.

Tuesday 9th. *Ditto*. Wind variable wth. Snow this Day. Rec'd. 129 Partridges from the Natives, they having been out trying for Deer,[1] but could get none.

Wensday 10th. *From N to South & EbS. Churchill Fort.* A very Storm all Night and continues this Day with much Snow. Could not see 10 Yards for snow & drift.

Thursday 11th. *N & NNW*. Continued blowing hard all Night wth. a Whistling Wind; this Morning more moderate. Sent 4 Men to the Old Factory to assist in Hauling Home the Firewood, there being not above 15 able to go abroad, the rest laid up with the before mention'd Disorders. I likewise sent our Surgeon up to visit them, & assist Mr. Shaw, Surgeon of the Discovery with his Advice.

Friday 12th. *NW & NNW*. Fresh Gales and Fair Weather. This Day our Surgeon return'd from the Old Factory; brought down with him three Men, two of which Has the Scurvy, the other miserably froze.

Saturday 13th. *NNW*. Moderate and fair, but freezing very Hard, being colder now than any time this Winter. This Day Christopher Row, one of our Men died of the Scurvy, being very ill these two Months.[2] We have 15 or 16 more very bad with that Distemper, Fevers & Froze.

Sunday 14th.[3] *NW*. Fair Clear Weather, little or no Wind; when Calm Moderately Warm, but when the Wind blows a little, very cold. I Observ'd the Sun's Rising & Setting for several Days past,

---

[1] I.e. caribou (*Rangifer tarandus groenlandicus*).

[2] This was the same man who fell from the main topmasthead into the chains on 4 August 1741, in the middle of the Bay, but had the amazing luck to escape without injury.

[3] Rankin went to Sloop Cove to check the ships after the recent gales and found them in good order, although the snow had drifted up to the quarter rails (ADM L/F/109, 14 Feb 1742).

& find he continues 18 or 20 Minutes longer above the Horizon than he should, which makes the Refraction above double to what is generally allow'd near the Horizon, but I shall be more particular when I can get out and use an Instrument to take the Altitude to every Degree above the Horizon, with the Time compared with the true appar'nt Altitude.

Monday 15th. *NW.* Fair & clear Weather but very cold. Two Men were sent down here from the Old Factory for cure, one having his Arm very Dangerously Froze, the other his Toe in the same Condition. Rec'd. 100 Partridges from the Indians for the use of the Sick.

Tuesday 16th. *NNW.* Fresh Gales & very cold, but fair & Clear Weather.

Wensday 17th. *Ditto.* Ditto Gales & cold Weather. About 25 of our Men at the Old Fort employ'd getting home Firewood which are all that are able to go out,[1] besides 10 Here Officers and Boys.

Thursday 18th. *NW.* Light Airs and fair Weather. Our People employ'd in fetching Ice & Fire-wood home, for those that lie in but one Week, without Exercise, are sure of being down with the Scurvy. Most of the Factory Men are out all the Winter cutting Fire-wood for the Next Year, fowling, hunting and fishing, and not one of them troubled with any Distemper, so that it is really for want of more Exercise that Disorders attend our Men.

Friday 19th. *Ditto.* Light Gales & fair Weather.[2]

Saturday 20th. *Ditto.* Moderate, as before, but very cold.

Sunday 21st. *WNW.* Fresh Gales and Cold freezing Weather. This Day Ewd. Matthews died, after being a long time ill of the Scurvy. Those which die of that Distemper are generally taken

---

[1] Out of a total of 88 men at the Old Factory, according to Rankin (ibid.).
[2] Isham notes that three of the Navy men were employed at clearing the snow from the yard at Fort Prince of Wales (HBC B 42/a/23, f. 23d).

with a Purging 4 or 5 Days before it carries them off and is a certain forerunner of Death. I use all means to get fresh Provisions for them.

Monday 22nd. *Almost calm.* Moderate & fair Weather. Somewhat Warm while Calm.

Tuesday 23rd. *Calm.* Ditto Weather; almost calm.

Wensday 24th. *Sly & Variable.* Mild Weather. This Day being somewhat well, I went out, & survey'd Part of the River.

Thursday 25th. *Etly.* Ditto Weather. Continued Surveying, with Some of my Officers and Men.

Friday 26th. *SE. Churchill Fort.* Ditto Weather. Continued our Surveying as high up as the Old Factory. In the Afternoon the Sprits in the Theodolite froze, tho' it was a Mild Warm Day. As many of our Men as could go abroad were employ'd in getting home Firewood. At 8 this Morning, as the Sun was ascending from the Horizon (and in his Descent towards it) he was crown'd with Arches of Circles of various Colours like a Rain-Bow. In the Corona appear'd two Parhelia, one on each side of the Sun and in a Line with it, with Whitish Tails Pointing from the Sun. Nearer the Zenith, where the Corona was a little faint & imperfect, there Shone out another Arch, which was inverted, having a third Parhelion in the Middle of it, which appear'd somewhat Obscure. This Phenomenon lasted untill Sun-Set, the Sky being very Clear. The Inverted Arch & upper Parhelion disappeare'd first, the other two set with the Sun. The Diameter of the Corona round about the Sun was near 40 Degrees, as I Observ'd with an Instrument.[1]

Saturday 27th. *SE.* Little Wind and fair pleasant Weather. Rec'd two Sick Men from the Old Factory. The Same Phenomenon, as

[1] This is an excellent description of a particularly spectacular display of parhelia (or 'sun-dogs') and haloes, phenomena which occur quite commonly in clear calm conditions in cold climates in winter, and are caused by refraction of the sun's light by ice crystals in the air. See Middleton's further discussion, p. 229 below.

before, appear'd all this Day, but more faint. Many of these are seen here in the Winter.

Sunday 28th. *Calm & Variable.* Moderate & fair.[1]

MARCH 1742

Monday 1st. *SE.* Little wind and fair Weather.[2]

Tuesday 2nd. *NNW.* Fresh Gales & Cold Weather.

Wensday 3rd. *Ditto.* Ditto Weather.

Thursday 4th. *SSE.* Moderate, but very Cold Weather. Some Snow in the Night.

Friday 5th. *NE.* Fresh Gales & Very Hard freezing.

Saturday 6th. *N, NNW.* Extream Cold Weather, with Hard Gales.

Sunday 7th. *Ditto.* Continues blowing very Hard, and is as Cold as any time this Winter. Several Men have Froze their Faces.[3]

Monday 8th. *NNW. Churchill River.* Very hard Gales, with Cold freezing Weather.

Tuesday 9th. *NW.* Ditto Winds and Weather. Our People employ'd in Halling down Fire-wood And brush to bream the Ship with,[4] which will serve likewise to keep the Sun from her. Several Indians are come down here almost starv'd for want of Food.

---

[1] According to Rankin another two sick men, William Potter and John Blair, were hauled down from the Old Factory on a sledge (ADM L/F/109, 28 Feb 1742).

[2] Rankin records that on this date both crews were placed on a reduced bread ration (ibid., 1 Mar).

[3] The Indians brought in two caribou, one of which Isham gave to the Captain (HBC B 42/a/23, f. 25).

[4] Breaming: the operation of cleaning a ship's hull by burning off the weeds, barnacles etc., either in a dock or by careening the ship. It was an operation that could prove dangerous.

Wensday 10th. *NNW & NW*. Fresh Gales & fair Clear Weather, but extream Cold. Partridges are So Scarce, we can scarce get enough for our Sick Men.

Thursday 11th. *NW*. Moderate & fair but very Cold.

Friday 12th. *Ditto*. Ditto weather. Several Wolves came down near the Factory.

Saturday 13th. *NW & NNW*. Light Gales and fair Clear Weather but very Cold. This Day Abraham Page departed this Life after a long Illness with a fever and Scurvy; a very stout able bodied Man, and a good Seaman. We have at this time 15 or 16 very ill, several of them cannot Live Long, so extream Cold there is no stirring abroad. This Day we rec'd 50 Partridges and 22 Fish, the latter are taken with Nets & Hooks under the Ice, 25 Miles up the River, by a Servant of Mine, who is in the Hudson's Bay Company's Service, and has been employ'd all the Winter to fish for us.

Sunday 14th. *NNW*. Fresh Gales & very thick Weather, with Snow & Drift. Extream cold.

Monday 15th. *No*. Fresh Gales & drifting Snow.[1]

Tuesday 16th. *Variable & Calm*. Moderate Weather.

Wensday 17th. *NW*. Ditto Weather and Clear.

Thursday 18th. *NNW*. Fresh Gales with Some Snow and Drift.[2]

---

[1] Rankin reports that he and Middleton went to Sloop Cove in the afternoon and found the carpenters making a 'logg tent' to live in, presumably while they were breaming the ship. Log tents were commonly used by the Company's men; they consisted of tent-shaped huts made of poles leaning against a ridge pole and caulked with moss and mud. Detailed descriptions may be found in Rich and Johnson, *Isham's Observations*, pp. 90–91 and in 'Clerk of the *California*', Account, I, pp. 135–7.

[2] The mutual assistance was still continuing. Isham's journal entries for 18–22 March record that Captain Middleton's armourer was repairing the Company's hunting guns (HBC B 42/a/23, f. 26d, 27). This was particularly appreciated by Isham in that his armourer, John Hancock had died the previous October (see p. 185 below).

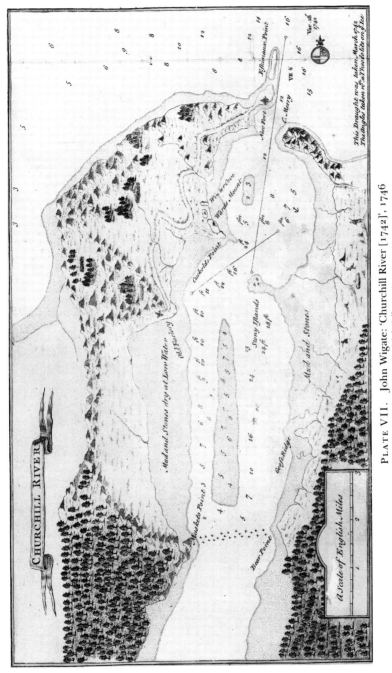

PLATE VII. John Wigate: 'Churchill River [1742]', 1746
(British Library)

155

Friday 19th. *WNW.* Fresh Gales and fair Weather.

Saturday 20th. *NW. Churchill River.* Fresh Gales with some Snow in the Night, and Very Cold Freezing Weather.

Sunday 21st. *Ditto.* Fresh Gales, fair & Clear but very Cold.

[*On this date Middleton called a council meeting, attended by himself, John Rankin, William Moor, master of* Discovery, *and* Furnace's *master, Robert Wilson, to discuss alterations which should be made to* Furnace *before the navigation season began. The outcome of their deliberations was as follows:*

'It is taken into Consideration, Whether it would be necessary for the Service his Majesty's Sloop *Furnace* is ordered upon to make the following alterations, which were mentioned by a Letter from Capt. Middleton to Sir Jacob Ackworth, and for want of time could not be affected,[1] *viz.* the Quarter-Deck to be made flush with the present main Deck, by having a slight one laid over the former, and a Companion Way thereupon made to go down into the Steerage; the former Passage thereto being not only inconvenient, but very dangerous for Persons coming from below to go forwards, when the Capston is in use, as Capt. *Middleton* by sad Experience found, being jamm'd between the End of a Capston Bar and the Companion.

And it was Resolved, That considering the high and traverse Seas in this Part of the World, and the Probability of shipping large Quantities of Water, it is absolutely necessary to have the Quarter-Deck made flush with the Main-Deck, the Sloop to be steer'd with a Wheel, dead Lights hung with Hinges to be fixed to the great Cabbin Windows, which will make more room for the Capston than is at present, and which we shall be obliged to use very frequently upon our entering or coming out of Harbours, warping among Ice, and upon Account of trying the Tides; and it is our Opinions those Alterations ought to be made before his Majesty's Sloop *Furnace* proceeds to Sea. Given under our Hands this 21st Day of *March* 1741/2'.][2]

Monday 22nd. *SE.* Fair and Moderate Weather; in the Morning Calm, at Noon veer'd to SE. John Blair, an able Seaman died last Night of the Scurvy, after a long illness, 14 or 15 more continue

---

[1] See p. 77 above.
[2] Middleton, *Vindication*, pp. 106–7.

very ill of the Same Distemper. We continue serving them with fresh provisions and Strong Beer; those that are well are serv'd with half Brandy and half Spruce Beer, and a Bottle of Brandy and Sugar to every 4 Men once a Week over and above their Allowance. Our Carpenters are at work repairing the Ships against the time of our Proceeding on our Discovery, which will be as soon as the River breaks up.

Tuesday 23rd. *ESE*. Fresh Gales, with some snow in the Night, and Moderately Warm.

Wensday 24th. *Variable*. Little Wind and Mild Weather.

Thursday 25th. *NW*. Ditto with Snow.

Friday 26th. *SE*. Moderate Weather & Snow.

Saturday 27th. *Variable*. Little Wind from the SE to NW and round to ENE with Some Snow in the Afternoon. Last Night Henry Spencer died of the Scurvy, being long ill. Most of them are carried off with a Looseness. The Weather begins to be Somewhat Milder. Our Carpenters Can work 2 or 3 Days in a week at the Ship in Tents that have built for that Purpose.

Sunday 28th. *WNW*. Strong Gales and Much Snow. This Day Died James Thrumshaw, being long ill with the Scurvy.[1] Two of the Factory's Men lost their Way, and lay out all night in the Snow, the Weather being so thick they could not find their way home.

Monday 29th. *NNW. Churchill Fort*. Continues a very Storm of Wind and Snow. No Stirring out of doors; the Fort full of Snow within, & on the outside as high up as the Top of the Parapets. No Seeing 50 Yards Dist. these 30 Hours for Drift & Snow.

Tuesday 30th. *Ditto*. The Weather abating Somewhat, yet very Cold; order'd the Lieutenant to Clear the Ship of Ice and Snow,

---

[1] Isham notes that Henry Spencer had died at Fort Prince of Wales and James Thrumshaw at the Old Factory (HBC B 42/a/23, f. 28).

by Making Several Fires to melt the Ice within-board & air her, the Ice being 3 or 4 Inches thick all under our Deck, and at the Heads of the Nails and Bolts within her. The Factory's Men that Lay out in the Woods all the Winter are come Home, and ours must lie on board to make Room for them.

Wensday 31st. *Ditto.* Fair, but very Cold Weather & fresh Gales. Our men all employ'd cleaning and clearing away the Ice within-board, some hauling Brush and small Wood to bream and Grave the Ship.[1]

APRIL 1742

Thursday 1st. *NW.* Very Cold Sharp Weather. Our Men continued to make Fires in the Ship to thaw the Ice in our Cabins, and between Decks before our People lie on bd.

Friday 2nd. *Calms.* Light Airs & Calms, with fine pleasant warm Weather, and a Clear Sky; it is so commonly when there is no wind. The Sun this Day Makes some Places thaw, where it falls on it.

Saturday 3rd. *Soly & NW.* Moderate Warm Weather all Night, and warm Air, the Wind being Soly. till 10 in the forenoon, then the wind coming about to NW it grew Hazy, the Snow drifting, and by Noon blew a strong Gale.

Sunday 4th. *Ditto.* Thick Hazy Weather, with drift & Snow, but not so cold as usual. Our Men Mov'd some of their Chests and bedding on board. They keep 6 or 8 Fires in the Cook Room and between Decks in Stoves, to Air the Ship against the Officers and Men lie on board.

Monday 5th. *NNW & NW. Churchill Fort.* Cold freezing Weather, but clear Air. The Lieutt. and most of the Officers & Men lay on board last Night,[2] and kept good Coal Fires, & the Gratins Close

---

[1] Graving: synonymous with breaming (see above, p. 153).
[2] The exceptions, as recorded by Rankin, were Mr Shaw, *Discovery's* surgeon, and the sick men under his care at the Old Factory (ADM L/F/109, 5 Apr 1742).

Cover'd, but found the Ship very Cold. I Observ'd the Emersion of the first Satellite of Jupiter this Evening, but the Moon shining too bright, and the Northern Lights appearing, as they do here every Clear Night, hindred my seeing the Emersion.

Tuesday 6th. *NNW*. Fresh Gales and cold freezing Weather. Our Men employ'd cutting away the Ice, to get the Ship farther a-stern, as soon as we can have Water to fleet her from where She is, before the River breaks up, for as long as the Northerly Trade wind blows I do not expect the Tides to fall, nor the River to break up, but rather to be much augmented by the in-land Floods which always come down before the Ice is quite loose here.[1]

Wensday 7th. *Nly.* Cold freezing Weather with fresh Gales and drifting Snow. Our People have dug down, close to the Ship's Stern, to the Ground, and found 9 or 10 foot water flow'd in at High Water. The Ice is 10 foot thick, and the Snow above is 13 foot. The Ship is bedded round with Ice and Snow up to her top & Quarter Rails. She appears more like a lump of Ice than a Ship. All our Men (except some that are Sick, and not able to stir abroad) are on bd.

Thursday 8. *NW*. Fresh Gales and Cold Weather. Our People employ'd as before. Read the Articles of War and an Order of mine to prohibit the Men from trading with the Indians.

Friday 9th. *WNW, W, SW & SSW. Churchill Fort.* Moderate Weather. This Day I went to the Ships; the People employ'd in cutting the Ice from the Ship; the Carpenters in brimming and caulking the Ships, and laying the Beams over the Old Quarter Deck.[2] Ralph Pearce, the Carpenter's Mate of the Tender died this day of a Scurvy and Fever after 3 months illness. We shall find a great Loss of him in the Spring for fitting the Ships for the Sea.

[1] On 6 April the Navy's blacksmith was mending a leaking copper for Isham. Next day Isham 'sent sevll. Indians to the Factory to kill Partridges for the Captn' (HBC B 42/a/23, f. 29).

[2] As Rankin notes (ADM L/F/109, 9 Apr 1742), the quarter deck had been 19″ lower than the main deck and tended to be awash if there was much of a sea. The modifications now being made (and approved at the Council on 21 March) would make both decks of equal height.

Saturday 10th. *SSE*. Moderate Warm Weather, to what we generally have here, with some hail and large Flakes of Snow, a certain Sign of the Winter's being far spent, for the Snow that has fell for these 6 Months past was as fine as Dust. Our Men employ'd as before.

Sunday 11th. *NE & No*. Moderate Gales, and dark, hazy, cloudy Weather. I bought from the Inds. above 300 Partridges, and Sent the Major Part to the Ships for the Use of the Men.

Monday 12th. *No. & NNW*. Fresh Gales and drifting Snow. All Hands continue as above, the Cooper trimming the Cask, and the Smith making Iron Work for the Ships, as hath done all the Winter, and mending Shovels and Pickaxes for digging the Ships out of the Ice.

Tuesday 13th. *Ditto*. Ditto Weather. Our People employ'd as before, and Carpenters laying the Water-Way Planks[1] of the Quarter Deck; Ice froze in the Dock this Night 2 Inches thick.

Wensday 14th. *NW*. Ditto Gales and cold Weather, with some Sleet and Snow. Our People continue to work as above except 10 or 12 that are froze & ill of the Scurvy, 3 or 4 of whom will Hardly recover. The Spring of the Year seems very backward, and no Greens to be had, or can be expected this Month or 5 Weeks without a Change of Wind & that for a continuance. Our Carpenters began to caulk the old Quarter Deck.

Thursday 15th. *NW & WNW*. *Churchill Fort*. Fresh Gales and drifting Snow; So cold that our Men could not Stand an Hour digging in the Dock without going to the fire. It froze 2½ Inches in the Dock. There was a Sail Hung at the Bow of the Ship to keep off the drifting Snow, yet the Men were almost Numb'd with Cold. One of them fell into the Dock among the loose Ice, and was almost dead before they could get him out & carried to the Fire.

---

[1] The outermost planks of the deck, often with a groove cut to carry the water to the scuppers.

Friday 16th. *NW*. Weather as above. Our People at Work as before. The Ink, tho' standing by the Fire, froze Solid.

Saturday 17th. *NW, WNW, NNW & NE*. Moderate Gales, variable & Hazy Weather with Hard Frost. Our Men employ'd as before, and the Carpenters Caulking the Quarter Deck. Last Night the Dock Froze 2 Inches thick. Several of our Men taken ill, thro' the Severity of the Weather.

Sunday 18th. *NE & No*. The first Little Winds with much Snow and freezing Hard, the Middle & latter Clear & Moderate warm Air, the Sun Shining. Several of our Men are Numb'd with the Cold. The Carpenters employ'd in laying the New Quarter Deck Beams.[1]

Monday 19th. *NW, SW & South*. Light Airs and Calm. Moderately Warm in the Daytime when the Sun Shines and there's little Wind, but very cold in the Night, freezing Hard. This Day John Armount, a good Sailor, one of the Factory's Men, enter'd.[2] Brought our Sick Men from the Old Factory on a Sledge,[3] and the Surgeon of the Discovery came with them.

Tuesday 20th. *SW & WSW*. Continues Clear Warm Weather in the Day Time, with fresh Gales. The Ice without the Harbour, that is not fast to the Main Body, is all driven off the Land by the Wind, but I expect its Return the Next Northerly Wind. When the Wind is on the Shore there is no End to be seen to it & I believe it may reach 9 or 10 leagues from the Shore. Haul'd on bd. some Plank from the New Fort for the Qr. Deck & 2 of our Sick Men that were not able to Walk, being very ill with the Scurvy.

[1] The Indians delivered a further 240 ptarmigan (HBC B 42/a/23, f. 30d).

[2] John Armaunt was the first of the Company men to desert the Company in order to enlist in the Navy and join Middleton's expedition; it was he who had received 20 lashes on 24 December for getting drunk and then running away. Isham's reporting of his desertion is as follows: 'Early this Morning unbeknown to any body John Armaunt went from hence, & at Noon I Understood he has enter'd himself in His Majesty's Service on board the Furnace, Captn. Middleton Commandr. And am informed they have try'd to allure several of our Men into the same Service, but can get no more at present, in their right Senses to comply' (ibid.). Isham's closing phrase is a telling one.

[3] A total of nine men according to Rankin (ADM L/F/109, 19 Apr 1742).

Wensday 21st. *SW & WSW. Churchill Fort.* Moderate & Pleasant Warm Weather in the Day time. Continue cutting the Ice from the Ship against the Change of the Moon, which Happen the 24 Inst. Haul'd from the New Fort some Plank & the wheel for our Ship. At 4 in the Afternoon we Had a small Shower of Rain, and had none 7 Months before.

Thursday 22nd. *W, NW, SE & South.* Little Wind and Cloudy Warm Weather, with Some Showers of Rain. Our Men and Carpenters employ'd as before. The Tide flow'd 9 feet this Morning. Sent the Sledge to the Old Factory for some Beef.

Friday 23rd. *SE, ESE, NE & NW.* Fresh Gales and Cloudy Weather, with Frost & Snow. The men all employ'd, the Carpenters laying the Quarter Deck, Part of the Men Clearing the Hold of the Rigging and Cordage, and getting our Cables and Part of our Iron Ballast ashore, and Part cutting the Ship out of the Ice.

Saturday 24th. *North, NE & East.* Ditto Weather. All Hands employ'd in getting the Discovery's Cables ashore & Part of the Iron Ballast, reeving ditto Cables thro' the Viol Block[1] that is lash'd to the Anchor Stock let down in the Ice, back'd with another, and an Eight fold Tackle to the End of the Cable brought to the Capston to heave the Ship astern in the Dock that is cut for her in the Ice. We've cut all the Ice round her, and in under the Keel afore and abaft, as far as a Man could Reach with a Pole Axx, but being froze fast to the Ground could not move her in the least, tho' the Tide flow'd 10 foot 3 Inches astern & 9 foot ahead.

Sunday 25th. *East, ESE & SE. Churchill Fort.* Fresh Gales and Cloudy Weather with Frost & Snow the first and Middle Parts; the latter fresh Gales and Clear Weather. Our People continue cutting the Ice under her Bulge,[2] being oblig'd to lie along upon a Board lay'd upon the Ice and Water, and to reach under the

---

[1] Viol block: a large single-sheaved block usually lashed to the mainmast. Through it was rove the viol, a large, endless loop of rope, made fast to the anchor cable and used in weighing the anchor where the anchor cable was too thick to go round the barrel of the capstan.

[2] I.e. bilge.

Bulge as far as they are able. She's fast froze to the Ground; the Men almost numb'd with the Cold in clearing the Ice from her, and several not able to Work. One Man this Day had one of his Toes so much mortify'd with the Cold that the Surgeon was oblig'd to cut away almost all the flesh from it. The Tide flow'd last Night 9 foot 6 Inches. This Morning 9 foot 4 Inches.

Monday 26th. *ESE to East*. Moderate Gales & clear Weather. Employ'd as before. The Tides flow'd 9 foot 4 Inches at Night & 9 foot 11 Inches in the Morning. Our Purchasing Tackle Blocks and Falls[1] were so much froze that they would neither heave or reeve thro' the Blocks till they were thaw'd by a Fire made on Purpose. Haul'd two Days allowance of fresh Partridges from the New Fort for the use of the Companies of the two Ships.

Tuesday 27th. *ESE to SE*. Ditto Weather the first Part, the Middle and latter fresh Gales and cloudy. Read the Articles of War and an order of mine to prohibit the Officers and Men having any Commerce or Traffick with the Indians. The People employ'd as before.

Wensday 28th. *SE, So. & SW*. Moderate Gales and Clear Weather, with Some Showers of Rain. Our Men employ'd late and early in cutting the Ice from the Ships, the Carpenters Caulking her Sides. Sent 2 Sledges to the Old Factory for the Remainder of the Provisions and the People's Chests. Saw a Goose fly over the Ship at Noon.[2] One of our Men kill'd a Goose about 4 Miles distant from the Ship being the first that was kill'd this Season in this Part of the Country.

Thursday 29th. *N, NE & ENE*. Ditto Weather the first Part, the Middle and latter fresh Gales, variable & cloudy Weather. Employ'd as before. At 5 a.m. sent the Sledge to the Old Factory for some Stores.

Friday 30th. *E, ESE*. Fresh Gales and Cloudy Weather with

[1] Fall: the end of a rope which is passed through a block and on which the pull is exerted in order to achieve power.
[2] This must have been a very welcome sight, since it gave promise of a reliable supply of fresh meat.

Rain. Employ'd as before. The Ice froze 2 Inches thick on the Ship's Bottom afore and abaft.

MAY 1742

Saturday 1st. *E, ENE. Churchill Fort.* Fresh Gales and Foggy Weather, with much Sleet, Rain, and hard frost. The Men at work from 6 a.m. to 12, but could stand it no longer for the Cold.

Sunday 2nd. *N, NW.* Ditto Weather, with Thunder, Rain, Lightning and Some Showers of Hail. Employ'd our People as before.[1]

Monday 3rd. *NW to W.* Fresh Gales, foggy Weather, and very cold. The Major Part of our People employ'd in cutting the Ice from the Ship, the rest in Getting Brandy, Cheese and Partridges from the New Factory for our Men.

Tuesday 4th. *WbN to ENE.* First Part Moderate Gales and Clear Weather with Frost; the latter cloudy with little Wind. All hands employ'd cutting away the Ice, making several Purchases,[2] and getting the Iron Ballast and everything of Great weight out of the Ship, in order to lighten her and get her farther astern the next High Tides.

Wensday 5th. *ENE to NNE.* Moderate Gales and cloudy Weather the 1st and Middle Parts, the latter little Winds and thick fogs with Rain. Our People employ'd in digging the Dock Deeper, and cutting [ice] from the Ship's Bottom, it being 6 Inches thick.

Thursday 6th. *E, ESE & SE.* The first Part little Wind and foggy

---

[1] Rankin reports that on this date two more of the Company men, John Morgan and David Thomas, enlisted in the Navy and joined the expedition (ADM L/F/109, 2 May 1742).

[2] In his journal Rankin is a little more explicit: they embedded an anchor in the ice on each side of the ship, and led purchases to them. They also began preparing empty casks which would be secured to the ships to give them extra buoyancy (ibid., 4 May 1742).

Weather, the Middle and latter fresh Gales with some frost and Snow. The men employ'd in cutting the Ice from the Ship's Bottom on the Larboard Side as far under as they can reach with Pole-axxes; found She's hard froze to the Ground. The Men are obliged to lie upon the Ice at full Length to reach in under her Bulge. Dug under her Keel, and reev'd a Six Inch Hawser double for a Runner thro' three Blocks and the Standing Part to the Sheer Head[1] on both Bows to lead on Board the Discovery with a Six-fold Tackle to their Windless.

Friday 7th. *ESE, SE & EbS. Churchill.* Fresh Gales and foggy Weather with frost and much Snow; our Men employ'd as before. Rais'd a pair of Sheers on each Bow for a Purchase and Swifting[2] the Ship for Cask to lift her. Tide 7 foot 10 Inches.

Saturday 8th. *ESE.* Moderate Winds and much Snow for the most Part. At 11 p.m. got 60 Cask into the Dock, and lash'd them to the Swifter. At 6 a.m. began to heave upon all our Purchasing Tackles; stranded the Discovery's Cable in three Places,[3] and bent the Shank of our Bower Anchor that was let down into the Ice, broke the Wood of the Viol Block and bent the Iron Pin so that the Sheeve went upon the Axle of the Block, and was of no more service to us.

Sunday 9th. *West to NWbW.* The first part little Wind with some Snow; the Middle and latter fresh Gales and cloudy weather with frost. At 6 p.m. hove a great Strain with all our Purchasses, but could not move her. The Tide flow'd Morning and Evening 8 foot 10 Inches. At 8 a.m. sent all our Men to the New Factory for empty Casks to put under the Ship's Bottom.

Monday 10th. *WNW to NWbN.* Moderate Gales & fair Weather, with frost. At 7 p.m. hove all our Purchases but to no Purpose. The Tide flow'd 9 foot. At 7 a.m. hove a great Strain with 75 Cask under her Bulge.[4]

---

[1] Sheers or sheer legs: a tripod of spars used for lifting heavy weights.
[2] Swifting: rigging a rope cradle under the hull, to which the empty casks would be secured to give extra buoyancy.
[3] At least one strand of the cable broke.
[4] This included quite a range of sizes: puncheons, hogsheads and half hogsheads, according to Rankin (ibid., 10 May 1742).

Tuesday 11th. *NW to NNW.* Moderate Gales and cloudy Weather, with Some Showers of Hail and Snow. Lash'd 27½ Tons of Cask to the Ship. Our Men still Digging the Ice on the larboard Side. At 8 p.m. hove a great Strain with all our Purchasses but could not in the Least move her, her Keel and 4 or 5 Strakes[1] being froze to the Ground. The Tide flow'd 9 foot 3 Inches.

Wensday 12th. *NW to WNW. Churchill.* Fresh Gales and cloudy, with hard frost and some Snow. At 8 p.m. hove a great Strain with all our Purchasses, and broke one of the Runners that was to the Sheers. At 4 a.m. shifted it end for end. Sent to the Old Factory for empty Cask.

Thursday 13th. *So., SE & ESE.* The first and Middle Parts fresh Gales and cloudy with Frost and Some Hail, the latter moderate Gales and fair Weather. At 2 p.m. our Men return'd from the Old Factory with empty Cask, and unlash'd all the Casks from the Swifter. At 4 a.m. the Carpenters began to caulk the Discovery's Sides. Our People employ'd in digging the Ice on the Larboard side of the Ship to make the Dock Wider. At 8 ditto sent the Viol Block to New Factory to be mended; ditto serv'd out fresh Geese to both Ships Companies in lieu of Salt Provisions, which will be continued every Day as long as any are to be Purchas'd from the Indian Hunters. The allowance is three geese for every four Men, Banjon[2] as well as Meat Days. There are two Sorts of Geese, the one Call'd Grey Geese,[3] the other Whaways;[4] the former weigh with the Feathers, Necks, Gibblets and Guts taken away, from 6 to 10 Pound each. The lesser sort, Call'd Whaways, the Aforementioned Apurtinances being taken away, are from 4 to 6 Pound Weight.

Friday 14th. *SSW, So., SE & East.* The first and Middle Parts Moderate Gales and Clear Weather, the latter fresh Gales and Cloudy with frost and some Showers of Hail. At 3 p.m. began to dig the Ground down with Pickaxxes to get in under her Keel on

---

[1] Strakes: the lines of planking running the length of the hull.
[2] Banyan days, when seamen were usually given fish or cheese instead of meat.
[3] Canada goose (*Branta canadensis*).
[4] Snow goose (*Chen caerulescens*).

the Larboard Side. We find the Ground very Hard froze, and difficult to get at her Keel, the Tide Seldom going out from the Ship.

Saturday 15th. *So., SE & East. Churchill.* For the Most Part fresh Gales and cloudy Weather with Small Rain. Our Men employ'd as before & overhauling the Blocks and Tarring the Rigging.

Sunday 16th. *ESE, SE & South.* Moderate Gales and cloudy Weather. Employ'd in digging the Ground and Ice away from the Larboard Side. At 9 a.m. sent some hands to the New Factory for fresh Geese for the Ship's Company. Ditto tarr'd the Mastheads.

Monday 17th. *ESE to South.* Ditto Weather. Employ'd as before. At 8 a.m. Got some fresh Geese and Bread from the New Factory.

Tuesday 18th. *SW, West & WNW.* Fresh Gales and Cloudy Weather. At 2 p.m. sent to the New Factory for some Brandy, the Men employ'd as above. At 10 a.m. sent for the Viol Block, and employ'd the Rest in cutting the Discovery's Cable out of the Ice to get the other End of the Cable that was stranded for a Runner for our Purchase to see if we can get her farther astern.

Wensday 19th. *SW & NW.* Ditto Weather. Our Men employ'd as before and Slinging the Casks to lash under the Ship to lift her. At Noon read the Articles of War; and an order of mine as before mention'd.[1]

Thursday 20th. *NbW to ENE* . The first Part fresh Gales and cloudy Weather; the Middle and latter moderate and hazy with some Rain. Employ'd as above. At 5 a.m. sent to the New Factory for fresh Geese.

Friday 21st. *E to ESE. Churchill.* Fresh Gales and Cloudy Weather with Frost, Hail and Much Rain for the Most Part. At 2 p.m. tarr'd the Tops and Yards, and reev'd the other end of the

---

[1] I.e. his prohibition against any trading with the Indians.

Discovery's Cable, as a Runner for our Purchassing Tackle. Our People employ'd in digging under the Starboard Bulge and lashing the Cask on the Larboard Side.[1]

Saturday 22nd. *ESE, SE & South.* Ditto Weather. Employ'd digging the Ice under the Discovery's Stern & lashing the Cask under the Starboard Side of the Furnace. At 6 a.m. Hove a great Strain on all our Purchasses, swifted the Ship under the Mizen Chains, and rais'd a Pair of Sheers with a Purchassing Tackle to shake her loose aft, having a Pair on each Bow before, but could not move her.[2]

Sunday 23rd. *So., NW, No. & NE.* Little Winds and cloudy hazy Weather for the most Part. At 6 a.m. hove all our Purchasses, with 35 Ton of Empty Cask under her, yet could not move her, having 6 Strakes froze fast to the Ground, then were oblig'd to unlash the Cask, and dig the Ground & Ice from the Starboard Side, where She was free from Rocks.

Monday 24th. *NE.* Ditto Weather. Employ'd as before. At 5 a.m. Sent to the New Factory for Geese for the Ships Companies. Tarr'd the Fore Shrouds.

Tuesday 25th. *WSW, W & NW.* Ditto Weather with Small Rain. At 4 p.m. Sent to the New Factory for some Bread. At 8 a.m. hove our Stern Purchass, being a High Tide but to no Purpose, for reasons above mention'd.

Wensday 26th. *NW to No.* Fresh Gales and cloudy the Major Part of these 24 Hours. Wind from NW to No. having High Tides. Got in our Iron Ballast on our lower Deck, & the Cables on the Upper Deck to Prevent the Ship from Straining, her Bottom being fast froze to the Ground on the Starbd. Side. Shor'd her up on both Sides with Balgs & other Shores. Continued Digging

---

[1] Rankin reports that fresh geese were being served to both ships' companies, i.e. a total of 98 men, every day this week (ibid., 21 May 1742).

[2] Rankin records in his journal that since the ship was heeled to starboard her starboard bilge was frozen to the ground, and that even with pole axes they could not reach the seven or eight strakes closest to the keel to cut the hull loose (ibid., 22 May 1742).

quite under her. The River open a little above in the Channel,[1] but is fast from Side to Side below, & at the River's Mouth.[2]

Thursday 27th. *East to North. Churchill.* The first and Middle Parts little Wind variable, the latter fresh Gales and Cloudy. Our Men employ'd as before, the Carpenters Caulking the out Side.

Friday 28th. *Variable.* Little Wind variable and Calms. Employ'd as before. At 8 a.m. got all our Cables on Shore again, the Tides taken off. Fleeted[3] our Rigging, tarr'd and tallow'd our lower Masts and Rigging.

Saturday 29th. *NNW to W.* The two first Parts little Wind and Calms, the latter fresh Gales and clear. Our Men employ'd as before. At 4 a.m. Sent a Sledge a Quarter of a Mile over the Ice with the Ship's Iron Tiller to be made Strait by the Smith at the New Fort. Rec'd. from ditto 5 Barrels of Tar and one of Pitch for the use of the Ships.

Sunday 30th. *WSW.* Moderate & fair Weather. At 1 p.m. fir'd 21 Guns from a Platform, it being the Anniversary of King Charles the Second's Restoration. Drank to His Majesty's Health, and to the Health of the Prince and Princess of Wales, and all the Royal Family, & gave a Cask of Strong Beer to the Ships Companies to do the like.

Monday 31st. *Variable.* Little wind, variable & clear Weather. At 2 p.m. Robt. Rattery departed this life.[4] Our Men employ'd as before.

[1] According to Rankin the open water of the main channel came to within half a mile of Sloop Cove (ibid., 26 May 1742).

[2] James Isham records that another of the Navy men had 'departed this life' (HBC B 42/a/23, f. 34d). According to Moor his name was John Furnix, and he died on the 24th of scurvy (Adm 51/290, pt IX). It seems strange that neither Middleton nor Rankin mentions this death.

[3] Fleeting: in this connection refers to moving the upper set of deadeyes up the shrouds, which would have become stretched over the winter, so that there would be room to haul them tauter.

[4] Rankin provides the additional information that he had died of scurvy (ADM L/F/109, 31 May 1742). He also records that most of the Indians had returned to the Fort from the camps where they had been shooting geese. They had killed 5000 geese for the expedition. Between 11 and 27 May 554 geese had been consumed by the Navy men. Presumably the remainder had been salted down.

JUNE 1742

Tuesday 1st. *Ditto. Churchill.* The first two Parts little Wind, variable & Clear, the latter foggy. At 3 a.m. the Ice that Cover'd the River gave way in the Channel and drove out at the River's Mouth, but continues all fast on the Flats for near a Mile from the Shore all round. At 8 Wm. McCulla came on board from the Goose Tent where he had been forwarding the Indian Hunters to Kill Geese for us. He voluntarily enter'd with me above two months ago. By Noon got all our Iron Ballast on Shore in Readiness to get the Ship off the Next Spring Tides. We have almost dug all the Ice from under her now, having had tedious Job of it. The Ground is as hard as a Rock almost that we are forc'd to get through.

Wensday 2nd. *East, So., SSW & NE.* Moderate Gales and fair Weather. The People employ'd in cutting the Discovery out of the Ice, and Some digging under our Starboard Bulge in under the Keel when the Tide is out. At 10 a.m. rattled our Fore Shrouds.[1] Ditto a great deal of Ice drives in & out with the Tides in the River.[2]

Thursday 3rd. *ENE, SE, S, WSW, WNW.* The first Part little Winds & Cloudy. At 2 p.m. thunder and Lightning and a very Great Shower of Hail, with Large Hail Stones, wch. lasted about a Quarter of an Hour.[3] The Weather was very hot after the Shower. The Middle Part little wind and fair; the latter fresh Gales and Clear Weather. The Men employ'd as before. The Ice continues driving in and out with the Tides, but all fast on the Flats.

Friday 4th. *West, ENE, East.* The first Part Moderate Gales &

---

[1] To rattle: to secure the ratlines to the shrouds.

[2] On 2 June Isham 'sent Mr. Ferdinand Jacobs on board His Majesty's ships to take particular care there is no clandestine dealing between His Majesty's subjects & the Natives' (HBC B 42/a/23, f. 35d). This could only have been arranged with Captain Middleton's approval which says much for his continued desire to maintain amicable relations.

[3] According to Rankin one hailstone measured 1.5″ in diameter or 4.5″ in circumference (ADM L/F/109, 3 Jun 1742).

Cloudy Weather. At 3 p.m. Squally with Thunder, Lightning & Rain; the Middle and latter Parts Moderate Gales and cloudy. Rattled our lower Shrouds. Ditto employ'd in cutting the Discovery out of the Ice. This Day I Shot a White Whale and got a Barrel of Oil out of it.[1] At 10 a.m. got 33 Ton of Cask under the Ship to lift her.

Saturday 5th. *ENE, East. Churchill.* The first Part Moderate Gales & Cloudy. At 6 p.m. hove all our Purchases. Ditto the Ice gave Way Where our Anchor Was let down, & the lashing broke of the Kedge that back'd the Discovery's Anchor. Our Anchor fell to the Ground, but did not Hold. Ditto cut a Hole in the Ice, and let an Anchor in on the Starboard Quarter, and Made a Purchass with our Viol for a Runner in at the Bow Port, & a Tackle to it. Ditto a great deal of Ice came in with the Flood Tide. Ditto most of the Ice broke loose on the Flats. The Middle & latter Parts fresh Gales and cloudy with Some Showers of Rain. At 6 a.m. a great deal of Ice drove off the Flats. At 11 ditto let an Anchor down in the Ice on the Larbd. Quarter for a Purchass to get the Ship astern. Ditto some employ'd in digging about the Discovery. Ditto carried our Stream Anchor & Cable out to the Full length of the Cable right astern.

Sunday 6th. *SE, SEbE.* The 1st & middle Pts. fresh Gales & cloudy. The latter Part some Squalls and Hard Showers of Hail, Sleet and Rain. At 5 a.m. very much Ice came in wth. the Flood. Ditto employ'd in digging the Discovery out & forcing the Ice out of the Dock.

Monday 7th. *W, SW, S, SSE.* Little Wind, & fair Weather. At 1 p.m. knock'd all our Shores away, except 3 or 4 of the upper Shores. At 6 ditto hove all our Purchasses, but could not move her. Ditto broke the Shank of our Kedge Anchor. At 2 a.m. mov'd all the Cleats lower down on the Starbd. Side, on Acct. of lashing more Cask under the Ship having Heel'd her to Port. At 6 ditto hove all our Purchases, & by the Strain broke the Arm of our Stream Anchor that was let down in the Ice.

[1] Schools of beluga (*Delphinaptera leucas*) still run into the mouth of the Churchill River every summer; indeed whale-watching has become an important tourist attraction.

Tuesday 8th. *NW, No. & NE.* The 1st & Middle Parts fresh Gales & Squally with Showers of Rain; the latter pt moderate Gales and fair Weather. At 8 a.m. hove all our Purchases, & mov'd the Ship about 11 foot astern in her Dock. Ditto broke our Viol we had to our Anchor for a Runner to heave the Ship off. The Flats are almost Clear of Ice, tho' a great deal drives in and out every Tide.

Wensday 9th. *East, WSW, SW.* The 1st & Middle Pts. fresh Gales & fair Weather. At 1 p.m. carried our best Bower Anchor to a large Stone astern, and lash'd our Viol Block to it, & used the Discovery's Cable for a Runner wth. 2 treble Blocks for a Purchasing Tackle to heave the Ship astern. Ditto broke the Double block all to pieces that was to the Stream Cable, & the Runner Block that was for the Purchases to the Anchor on the Starbd. Qr. The Latter Part Moderate Gales & hazy. At 8 a.m. hove all our Purchass but could not move her, having but a poor Tide. Drilled a large Stone, and blow'd it up at 2 Difft. times. Large Cakes of Ice 10 or 12 foot thick drives in and out every Tide.

Thursday 10th. *WSW, SW, SSW. Churchill.* Moderate Gales and hazy Weather. At 9 p.m. hove all our Purchasses & got the Ship her length astern in her Dock, & Carried out Anchors & Ropes, and moor'd her between four, & took all the Cask from under her. A great deal of Ice comes in with the Tide. At 2 a.m. bream'd and Pay'd ye Starboard, and employ'd the Carpenters in caulking & Greaving her. The whole Suit of Careening Gear has been render'd unserviceable by getting them in & out of her Winter Dock, & 2 Viols, 2 of the Furnace's Anchors, & 2 of the Discovery's Anchors, several Hawsers, Towlines etc. in getting her off.[1]

Friday 11th. *SW, NW, NE, East.* The 1st and Middle parts little Winds & fair Weather, the latter Part fresh Gales & very thick Fogs. At 2 p.m. came in to trade with the Hudson's Bay Company Factor at Prince of Wales's Fort several of the Northern

---

[1] A Company representative was still stationed on board the ships. Isham reports: '... call'd Mr. Jacobs home upon business, having ordered Mr. Smith to see no Indians goes anigh the Ships...' (HBC B 42/a/23, f. 36d).

Indians.[1] At 5 ditto very Hard Showers of Rain, with much Thunder & Lightning & variable Winds all round the Compass. A great many large Cakes of Ice came in wth. the Flood Tide. Ditto hove the Ship about 20 or 30 foot farther out. Ditto the Carpenters breaming Part of the Larboard Side, & caulk'd & pay'd it. At 9 a.m. sent 2 Small Sloops belonging to the Hudson's Bay Company[2] to ballast our Ship when out in the River, & to bring our Provisions on board. I this Day wth. Present & large Promises prevail'd on 2 Northern Indians to be Linguists.[3]

Saturday 12th. *East, ESE, SE*. The 1st & middle Parts fresh Gales & dark Fogs, the latter part moderate Gales & foggy. Made an end of Breaming, caulking & Paying the Ship; got our best & Small Bower Anchors & Cables to the Ship's Bows for mooring her when off in the Stream.[4] Several Northern Indians went to the New Factory to trade. I prevail'd on one of them to accompany the other two I had before got, who I believe will be very Serviceable on the Voyage, knowing the Country a great way to the Northwd. & one of whom speaks Engh. tolerably well.[5]

Sunday 13th. *SE, SEbE. Churchill*. The 1st & Middle Parts fresh Gales & foggy. At 2 p.m. carry'd out the Discovery's Bower Anchor, Cable, Stream Cable, and 2 Viols bent to them to heave the Ships over the Flats into the Stream. At 9 ditto began to heave out. Slip'd all our Hawsers & hove out into the Stream.

[1] These were Chipewyans and totalled 27 by Rankin's count (ADM L/F/109, 11 Jun 1742).

[2] *Bear* and *Quicohatch* (HBC B 42/a/23, f. 36d).

[3] According to Rankin the three Indians recruited were a man called Pissquatanu (referred to simply as an Indian) and two others, Claydiddy and Clayhulla, described as Northern Indians (ADM L/F/109, 11 Jun 1742). For further details see Middleton's letter of 28 June, p. 183 below.

[4] Rankin reports that beacons were set up on the large rocks on the mud flats so that they could be avoided while the ships were being warped out into the channel (ibid., 12 June 1742).

[5] Another Company employee appears to have tried to join the expedition on this date. Isham's version of the sequence of events is as follows: '... this morning the Master of the Sloop & Jno. England Shipwright having some Words by his not getting up to work, he went on board His Majesty's Ship Furnace & entered in His Majesty's Service, but at Noon he returned again on board of the Sloop but did no work all Day. Would have agreed wth. another in his room wth. Captn. Middleton but none would stay. This England I shall send home not being fitt for the Service being an indolent Person & knows Nothing' (HBC B 42/a/23, f. 36d–37).

Ditto came off with the Kedge Anchor & 2 Warps, which we carried out to heave the Ship over wth. Let go the Small Bower Anchor, and moor'd a Cable each Way. Ditto got in Some Iron Ballast. At 4 a.m. took up the Kedge Anchor, and sent the Launch ashore for the best Bower Anchor and some Iron Ballast. Ditto sent the Master & 12 Men to load the Hudson's Bay Company's Sloop with Shingle Ballast. Ditto the River Clear of Ice. Ditto the Carpenters employ'd in caulking the Qr. Deck. The Latter Part Calm & Hazy. At Noon the Launch came on board wth. the best Bower Anchor & Iron Ballast. The Northern Indians return'd to their own Country.

Monday 14. *ESE, SE, South.* Little Winds & Hazy. The Launch employ'd in bringing off the Iron Ballast and Rigging. At 2 p.m. sent the Yaul For the Tops.[1] At 4 ditto got our Fore, Main & Mizen Tops over the Mastheads. At 7 ditto sent for the Caps & got them up in the Tops. Ditto bent the Best Bower Cable. At 9 ditto one of the Sloops came on board with 15 Tons of Shingle Ballast. Ditto came on board our Topmasts. At 11 a.m. got our Caps over the Mast Heads & Topmast thro' them. Ditto got the Mizen topmast up & Rigged.[2]

Tuesday 15th. *South, SSW.* Moderate Gales & hazy. At 2 p.m. rigg'd our Fore and Main Topmasts. Ditto sent the Launch for Shingle Ballast, and at 9 return'd with 6 Tons. At 6 a.m. got the Cross-Jack Yard across & Mizen Topsail Yard & bent the Sail. At 11 the Launch came on board with the Remainder of the Iron Ballast, & the lower & Topsail Yards, and Top G't Masts. Ditto came on board two Sloops wth. Shingle Ballast, one 12 Tons, the other 9 Tons. Our people employ'd in Rigging the Ship.

Wensday 16th. *SSW, NE, NbW.* The first Part Squally with Thunder, Lightning & Rain. At 3 p.m. sent the Master and 8 Men, together with the Mate of the Factory's Sloop to the Goose Tent, which is about 7 Leagues from this River, and the Place where most of The Geese are Kill'd by the Indians for the

---

[1] Tops: topmasts.
[2] Even with all the activity on board Middleton managed to lend Isham the services of his carpenter to caulk the sloops *Bear* and *Quicohatch*, which, however, he was using to ballast his ships (ibid., f. 37).

Factory's Use in the Spring & Fall of the Year, and their Salted & Put in Cask. Employ'd in Rigging the Ship. The Latter Part fresh Gales with Some Rain.

Thursday 17th. *NE, ESE, SE.* The first Part fresh Gales and Cloudy, the Middle and latter Parts little Winds and Cloudy. At 4 p.m. rattled the Fore & Main Topmast Shrouds, and Sent the Launch for Ballast, who return'd with 8 Tons. At 9 a.m. Parrell'd¹ our Yards. Ditto Scrap'd the Topmasts & Topgallt Masts & tallow'd them. Ditto came down the River about 30 Canoes of the Upland Indians to trade with the Factor here.²

Friday 18th. The first Part fresh Gales and Cloudy. At 4 p.m. the Launch brought on board 6 Tons of Shingle Ballast, and employ'd her afterwards in getting 8 Chaldrons of Coals out of the Tender to repay the Factory part of our Winter firing. The Middle and latter Parts fresh Gales with Rain.³

Saturday 19th. Moderate Gales & cloudy Weather. Came on board Some of our Sails and bent the Fore and Main topsails. The Sloop return'd with Salted Geese from the Goose Tent. At 6 a.m. bent the Topgallant Sails, & loos'd the topsails to dry. Employ'd in Rigging the Ship.

Sunday 20th. Moderate Gales and Hazy. At 4 p.m. came on board the Sloop with 16 Casks of Salt Geese. Ditto sent 2 Sloops for Water & the Launch for Sails & Rigging. At 4 a.m. a Sloop

---

¹ Parrel: a rope threaded through a number of wooden balls, by which the yard is held against the mast, permitting the yard to be braced round to the wind.

² According to Isham it was on this date that the three Indians whom Middleton had hired moved aboard *Furnace*, 'to be assistant in getting provisions etc. in his Voyage to the northward, he proposing to return them in the Fall within 3 or 4 Days travel of their Country, wch. will be time enough for them to get Goods for the winter' (ibid., f. 37d). Isham was still keeping a close watch for any trading betwen the Navy men and the Indians. Presumably because of the great influx of Indians from upriver he stationed Ferdinand Jacobs on board *Furnace* again.

³ Even now the mutual co-operation was still continuing. On the 18th Isham noted: '... the Captn's armer. a-mending the Indians guns, he being very serviceable to Your Honrs. interest in armours. & smith's Business, our Armer. being dead & the Smith not able to work as fore mentioned' (ibid.).

came on board with 10 Casks of Water. John Matthews[1] in Heaving the Lead on board the Sloop fell over Board & was drown'd. At 10 ditto came on board 6 Casks of Beef & 6 of Pork. Employ'd some of our Men in digging Beer out of the Ground, which was found hard Froze to a Lump of Ice in Shape like the Cask.[2]

Monday 21st. Moderate Gales & hazy. Our People employ'd in getting Provisions out of the Tender, and bringing them on board, in order to lighten her.[3]

Tuesday 22nd. Moderate Gales & fair Weather. At 6 p.m. the Discovery hove a-stern into our Dock.[4] Ditto 2 Sloops employ'd in bringing our Provisns. from the New Factory, & the Men in stowing them away.[5]

Wensday 23rd. The 1st Part fresh Gales with much thunder, Lightning and hard Showers of Rain; the Middle & latter fresh Gales. At 4 a.m. the Launch Came on board with 12 Casks of Water, & a Sloop with 8 Casks of Beer & other Provisions.

Thursday 24th. Moderate Gales and Cloudy. Our Men employ'd in Stowing the Hold, bringing on board Provisions,[6] setting up the Rigging, and getting all Clear for Sailing.

Friday 25th. Moderate Gales and fair Weather the 1st & middle Parts, the latter fresh Gales & Cloudy. The 2 Sloops employ'd in bringing Provisions & Stores on board.[7] This Day had a

---

[1] Identified as the master's servant by Rankin (ADM L/F/109, 20 Jun 1742).

[2] On both the 20th and 21st the Company's team of horses was busy hauling ships' provisions from Fort Prince of Wales down to the shore to be loaded on board the sloops to be ferried over to Sloop Cove (HBC B 42/a/23, f. 38).

[3] Rankin reports that a total of 35 casks of bread, 22 of flour and 15 of beef and pork was transshipped with this end in view (ADM L/F/109, 21 Jun 1742).

[4] After two tiers of casks had first been swifted under her starboard side to reduce her draft, as reported by William Moor (Adm 51/290, pt IX, 22 Jun 1742).

[5] By Rankin's count these included 3 casks of strong beer and 11 of small beer (ADM L/F/109, 22 Jun 1742).

[6] According to Rankin these included 1 cask of peas, 6 of bread and 4 of groats from Fort Prince of Wales (ibid., 24 Jun 1742). At the same time 7 casks of flour, 8 of strong beer and 5 of small beer were transshipped from *Furnace* to *Discovery*.

[7] The provisions included 13 casks of bread, 11 of peas, 5 of groats and 1 of raisins, by Rankin's count (ibid., 25 Jun 1742). The stores included cables, spare anchor stocks and some 4-inch plank.

Survy [sic] on the Brandy, the Cask being very Defective, and thro' the Extream Frost in the Winter Prov'd leaky.[1]

Saturday 26th. The first Part fresh Gales with Some Rain; the Middle & latter little Wind & cloudy. At 8 p.m. the Sloop came on board with the Brandy.[2] At 11 a.m. the Launch brought Some of the Guns and Carriages on board.[3]

Sunday 27th. The 1st & Middle Parts Moderate Gales and Cloudy Weather. At 9 p.m. the Sloop brought the Remainder of the Provisions from the New Factory.[4] At 11 ditto the Launch and Sloop came on board with the Guns and Carriages. At Sunrising fir'd a Gun & loos'd the Fore topsail.

Monday 28th. *E. Churchill River.* Moderate Gales and fair Weather. Got every thing on board[5] & the Ship ready for Sailing and only wait for a Wind to carry us out of the River. I have hereto annex'd a Plan of this River for the better Explanation of anything thereto relating mentioned in this Journal.[6] Wind NE.[7]

---

[1] In his journal Moor added: 'came down the River about 50 Trading Canoes all loaded with Furrs' (Adm 51/290, pt IX, 25 Jun 1742).

[2] Rankin notes that this totalled 49 casks (ADM L/F/109, 26 Jun 1742).

[3] According to Isham's journal this was the day on which 'Captn. Middleton went on board the Furnace wth. all his household goods etc. for his voyage to the South Seas' (HBC B 42/a/23, f. 39). He also noted that another two of the Company men, John Morgan and John Mackbeath, had left the Company to join the expedition; this made a total of four such desertions. Isham comments: 'I have talkt to the Captn. concerning this entertaining your Servts. & all the Satisfaction I can gett is he cannot refuse any Man that enters, at the same time refused Jno. England on the last of the month'. Given the circumstances one can fully understand Isham's closing request: '... and desire if any more of His Majesty's Ships winters here I may have more fuller Orders in what manner to act' (ibid.).

[4] By Rankin's count these included 10 casks of bread, 3 of peas, 1 of groats, 2 of flour, 2 of cheese, 3 of strong beer and 1 puncheon of salt (ADM L/F/109, 27 Jun 1742).

[5] Including the sheet anchor and the swivel guns, as noted by Rankin (ibid., 28 Jun 1742).

[6] This map does not appear to have survived unless it was the one issued under the name of John Wigate, Middleton's clerk, 1746. See p. 155 above.

[7] Isham's cooperation continued right to the end: the Company's team was being used to haul the last of Middleton's supplies and equipment from Fort Prince of Wales down to the shore. In the light of this, it must have been particularly galling to Isham that yet another of his men, David Thomas, threw in his lot with the expedition that morning (HBC B 42/a/23, f. 39).

Tuesday 29th. *East.* Fresh Gales. The Men employ'd in getting every thing well Stow'd.[1]

Wensday 30th. *Variable.* Moderate and Variable Winds. At 3 a.m. fir'd a Gun a Signal for unmooring. At 7 unmoor'd. At 9 warp'd over towards the East Side of the River, and at 12 came to an Anchor in 7 fathom Water.

JULY 1742

Thursday 1st. *SSE to SEbS. Course N15E. Dist. in miles 89. Lat. obsd. 60°00′. Long from London 96°17′.*[2] *Var. N18°W. Churchill River bore S15°W, dist. 30 Leagues.* The 1st Part light airs of Wind variable; the Middle & latter fresh Gales and Hazy. At 4 p.m. made the Signal to weigh, & hove Short. At ½ Past 8 Weigh'd; at 9 got out of the Harbour of Churchill[3] and Sent the Boat ashore with the Pacquet, directed to the Honble. the Principle [sic] Officers & Commissioners of His Mjy's Navy, London, & lay to for the Boat & Tender.[4] At 11 our Boat return'd. Sounded & found 17 fathom Water. At 1 a.m. bore away, The Tender in Company. At 2 ditto the New Fort bore SWbW, dist. 4 Leagues. At 4 ditto Sounded and found 20, 15 & 24 fathoms. At 5 Sounded & Had 25 & 26 fathoms. Ditto set the Foresail. At 8 Sounded & had no Ground at 40 fathom. Set the Topgallant Sails. Saw several Pieces of Ice.

[1] Rankin records that the very last items came on board from Fort Prince of Wales, namely 41 barrels of gunpowder (ADM L/F/109, 29 Jun 1742).

[2] All Middleton's longitudes from this point onwards show an error of 2°. At the beginning of his journal he explains: 'Note, that in the Tables I made use of for Computing the Time of the Emersion of Jupiter's first Satellite at London March 20, 1742, there was an Error of the Press; The Mean time for March 20 being sett down 15 h 36′ 20″ instead of 15 h 26′ 20″ which is the Reason that the Longd. of Churchill is put 97° instead of 95° in my Journal. And on this Accot. two Degrees are to be taken from all the Longitudes in my Journal, from our Departure from Churchill, as far as Cape Diggs homeward. This Correction is allready made in the Logg Book'. Hence Middleton's log for 1 July 1742 gives the longitude as 94°17′W.

[3] No doubt with a sigh of relief Isham noted: '...at 9 p.m. at night the Furnace & Discovery, his Majesty's ships ... sett Sail for their Voyage, whom God send safe...' (HBC B 42/a/23, f. 39d).

[4] In his log entry for 10 o'clock Middleton adds the information: 'Put a Cable and one of the Tender's Anchors on Board of her, which we had borrowed for Mooring, two of our own being broken' (Adm 51/379, pt III, 1 Jul 1742).

[Among the letters taken ashore, to be forwarded to England via the Company's ships was the following letter from Middleton to Sir Charles Wager, dated 28 June 1742, from Churchill River, summarizing the major events of the wintering:

The last that I wrote to you from the Isles of Orkney was dated June the 25th 1741. On the 27th I sail'd from thence, the Tender in Company. The first and second Day after we were out had Calms and contrary Winds, spoke with two Ships, the one from New England, the other from Virginia, both bound to London: after that had favourable Winds and Weather. On the 16th of July made Cape Farewell, the East Entrance of Davis's Straits, being very high ragged Land, cover'd with Snow. It's in the Latitude of 59°45′ N and Longitude from the Meridian of London about 46° W which Meridian I shall account my Longitude for the rest of the Voyage.

On the 21st saw several large Isles of Ice in Latitude 60°30′ and Longd. 61°00′W. On the 25th made the South part of Cape Resolution, the North Entrance of Hudson's Straits, being in the Latitude of 61°25′N and Long. 64°00′W. and at the same time sail'd into the Straits with a fair Wind but thick Fog. The Variation of the Compass in this Strait is N40° Westerly. Very strong and dangerous Tides run in here, with Overfalls, Riplings and Whirlings, yet very deep Water, 200 fathom not far from the Shore. The Tides flow in Change Days ESE and WNW in the Harbours on Shore, and five Fathom: the Flood comes from the Eastward, and thither it returns.

The 29th got the Length of Cape Diggs in the South Side and West End of the Straits, in Lat. 62°50′N. and Long. 78W. about 140 Leagues from Cape Resolution which is the Length of these Straits. Found our Passage very clear of Ice, only large Isles that are forever seen on the Coasts here. The Land on both Sides is very high: the North Side appears to be nothing but Islands and broken Land, cover'd all the Year with Snow, and pester'd with Ice impassable excepting three Months in the Year. The same Evening we past by the North End of Mansel's Island, which is distant from Cape Diggs 14 Leagues, and is in Length 20 Leagues, tho' in most places not above 3 Leagues broad; very low and dangerous coming near it in the Night and foggy Weather, being deep Water close to, and cannot be seen above 3 or 4 Miles from the Deck in clear Weather.

We made Careys Swan's-Nest on the 31st in Long. 88W and Latit. 62° forty Leagues from the No. End of Mansels Isle, having thick foggy Weather, blowing hard, the Wind Easterly and on the Shore, could not try the Tides or make bold with the Land. Off this place I

PLATE VIII. Christopher Middleton: manuscript chart of his explorations, 1742
(Ministry of Defence Library, Whitehall)

180

NORTH

MAIN.

Q. Anne's Foreland

Salisbury Island

Variation 60 degrees

XI

Variation 60 degrees

C. *Charles*

C. *Walsing Sevan*

C. *Digs*

PART of HUDSON'S STRAIT

PART of the LABRADORE:

OR, THE

COUNTRY

OF THE

USKIMAYS.

Graff Island

TO THE
Right Honourable
THE
LORDS COMMISSION
*for Executing the Office of
Lord High Admiral of Great
Brittain, Ireland, &c.
This Chart is Moſt Humbly
Dedicated by
Capt. C. Middleton,
Commander of His Majeſtie
Ship Furnace, 1743.*

181

held a Council, where it was unanimously agreed to repair to Churchill River for Reasons given in my Journal to which I refer your Lordship.

August the 2d it continued foggy, and meeting with much Ice retarded us very much in our Course. On the 7th made the Land thirty miles to the Eastward of Churchill River, having had much Ice, contrary Winds, Calms and Fogs for 4 Days past. On the 9th got both Ships into Churchill River, and employ'd our Men in preparing Winter Quarters for the Ships, themselves and provisions, by repairing an Old Fort that was in Ruins, cutting Fire-Wood to burn in the long Winter, digging a Dock for the two Ships, and places underground to secure our Ships from the extream Frost.

On the 31st hall'd the two Ships o'shore on Account of the Spring Tides, and to be out of the way of Ice. September the 17th got both Ships securely moor'd, free from the Dangers of Ice, and sent the Men to their Winter Quarters. We had for the most part from the first of this Month, Hail, Snow and cold pinching Weather, the Land all cover'd with Snow, and the Shores lin'd with Ice. The Dock that we were oblig'd to dig for our Ships was done with great Labour and Toil to our Men Night and Day, had much ado to compleat it before the Winter came on, the Ground being hard frost all the Year, except three or four foot down, and many large Stones and Rocks we were oblig'd to blow up. By the 29th the River was almost full of Ice, and the Northerly Trade Winds set in, making it extream cold. The Wind blows between the NNE and NW until the Latter End of May. Most of our Men employ'd in cutting Wood for Burning in Stoves, which they hall home upon Sledges, over the frozen Snow, when there is any thing of moderate Weather, and they can stir abroad; for many Days there is no looking out of Doors for the Drifting Snow and extream Frost.

We continued 4 Fires in our Dwelling-house every Day in large Brick Stoves that will hold a good Cart-load of wood each time, and at Night when burnt down, stop the Top of the Chimney to keep he Heat in our Apartments. After Christmas several of our Men got the Scurvy, with Pains all over their Limbs. By March they almost all had it and several dy'd. The Frost is so extream for four or five Months in the Winter that we can hardly look abroad without freezing our Faces, Hands or Feet, and then lying in for Cure brings on the Scurvy, and whoever takes to his Bed hardly ever gets abroad again, but falls into a Looseness which generally carries him off in 8 or 10 days. Tho' in 20 Years that I have us'd this Voyage I never heard of or knew any afflicted with this or any other Distemper before the last and this Year.

April the 7th I ordered my Officers and Men to the Ships. I mean such as were able to do any thing; for we were very weak and sickly at that Time, and employ'd them in clearing the Ice from the Inside of the Ship which was several Inches thick and airing the same with 4 or 5 large Coal Fires made in the Iron Stoves we had for that purpose. The Carpenters were employ'd in fitting the Ship for Sea again, and about the Middle of April set all Hands to work in digging a Dock in the Ice to heave the Ship farther a-stern before the River broke up, for the Tides generally take off when the Ice is gone. They work'd with great Labour Night and Day as the Tides would permit in digging the Dock, and cutting the Ice from the Ship, but it was the 10th of June before I could get her into the River, where I lay'd her o'ground for the Carpenters to bream and caulk. I have us'd the utmost Dispatch in getting both the Ships ready for Sea, and propose, if Winds and Weather permit, to sail this Day and diligently obey my Instructions in proceeding on the Voyage for the Discovery of a Passage from this Place to the South Sea...

[P.S.] A little before the Ships were ready for Sailing some Northern Indians came here to trade, and I prevailed on three of them with presents and promises to accompany me in my Voyage. Two of these Indians speak several Dialects of the Indian Tongue, and have, as far as I can understand been at Ne Ultra, the Third is one who was brought up about the Factory here, but has been among the Northern Indians, speaks their Language and English tolerably well, and I hope will be of great service to the Main Design. I have herewith inclos'd the Observations I made here this winter.[1]

On the same date Middleton had written a briefer account of the winter-ing, addressed to the Secretaries of the Admiralty Board:

I Beg the Favour you will acquaint their Lordships that I sail'd with his Majesty's Ship Furnace, the Discovery Tender in Company, from the Isles of Orkney the 27th day of June 1741, and put into Churchill River the 9th of August following, where I secur'd the Ships, and wintered the Companies in the best manner I could provide for them. Most of the Men were afflicted with the Scurvy in Winter, and 10 of them died of that Distemper. I have since got five of the Men belonging to the Factory here, who voluntarily enter'd with me, and have with presents and large promises prevail'd on three Indians, one of whom speaks English tolerably well, and who are acquaint'd with the Land to the Northward of this place to accompany me in my

---

[1] Presumably Middleton's observations on the 'Effects of Cold'; see pp. 225–37 below. The letter itself is in Adm 1/2099.

Voyage. I shall sail this Day, and carefully put in execution my Instructions, and for my Proceedings hitherto I humbly refer their Lordships to my Journal. I have got what Provisions and Stores the Factory here could spare, which added to what I before had makes 34 Weeks of all Species at whole Allowance, as by the inclos'd Weekly Account.[1]

Middleton's letter to Sir Charles Wager travelled to London in the same ship as Isham's annual report to the London Committee of the Company, dated July 1742. An extract from that report, relevant to Middleton's expedition reads as follows:

We Recd. your Honrs. Letter Dated May the 30th by Captn. Christopher Middleton in the Furnace with the Tender in Compa. Mr Wm. Moor Master on the 8th of Augst. 1741 wherein Your Honrs Orders that in case Captn. Middleton shou'd Resort here for us to give him the Best assistance in Our Power, I have Comply'd wth. the said Order, and have assisted them to the best of my Knowledge, without any Determent to Your Honrs. Interest. Part of our Dwelling wth. the Old Fort he had, to winter his men in; the Team and Sloop for to assist in Loading and Unloading there Ships fall and Spring etc, Provisions, Stores wearing Aparel for the men wch they Stood greatly in Need of, I have took care here Inclos'd to Send the books of Debts with the Mens Names and prizes fixed as currant in the Country, with a Receipt from Captn Middleton and all other Books and Papers of any Dealings I have had wth him concerning your Honrs affairs, with a packet for the Honrble Commissioners of the Navy Board. Eleven of men Died this year belonging to the said Ships of the Scurvy, And several very bad, one Drowned and One a Natural Death, by wch and other Reasons Captn Middleton and his Officers have been continually Induceing Our Men with Liquor, fine words and Preferments, to enter on board his Majestys Ships and has Succeeded, so farr as to gett 5 men to Enter in his Majestys Service, who left the Fort unknown to me, Vizt. Jn. Armount, Sailor, April the 19, Wm MacKenlock Labr. June the 1st, John Morgan Labr. and Jn Mackbeath Sailor, June the 26th, and David Thomas Labr June the 28th, and at Captain Middletons Departure he informed me he wou'd make Such a Seizure of my men wch would be Very unpleasing to me, and all because I wou'd not Comply with his taking an Indian on board to Whip him etc. I must needs say he did not show himself to be a Well

---

[1] Ibid. This letter is endorsed 'recd. and read 10/18 Sepr. 1742'. The letter and Middleton's of the same date to Wager, were carried back to England by Captain George Spurrell in the *Sea Horse*. See HBC A 1/35, p. 313.

wisher to Your Honrs Interest, in the winter the Officers and Men under his Commd did Cutt burn and Distroy the Cover of the Lime Kiln at the Old Factory, as Likewise he did Suffer them under his Command to Cutt and distroy the Lime House at the Same place, all which may be computed at nigh Ten Pounds Damage, was it to be repaired in England. Captain Middleton Saild from here for his Discovery to the South Seas on the 30th of June with the Tender in Compa, as likewise your Honrs. Sloop who made but a poor Trade, wch May be imputed to the Sloops not Going last year, the Captn etc. has been a Very Troublesome Guess, I Humbly Desire if any Ships Come again to winter, Your Honrs will please to send a More fuller Order in What manner to Act.

Our Armourer Jn. Hancock Dying October the 13th, 1741, wou'd have been a great hinderance in Promoting the Trade at this place, had not Captn Middletons Armourer Mended all the Trading Indians Guns, who was very handy in that Point in Perticular.[1]]

[ON DISCOVERY]

Friday 2nd. *SbE to SEbS. Course N2oE. Dist. in miles 128. Lat. obsd. 62°04'. Long. 94°42'. Var. N21°W. Ditto S21°W, dist. 65 Leagues.* Fresh Gales & hazy Weather for the Most Part. At 2 p.m. Shortn'd Sail for the Tender. At 6 sounded 63 fathom. At 12 sound 43 fath., rocky Ground. Ditto took in the 1st Reef of the Foretopsail. At 2 a.m. sounded, & had from 46 to 42 fathom. At 8 sounded 43 fathom soft Sticking Ground. At 10 had 43 fathom soft Ground; at 12 45 fathom. Haul'd up the Foresail. At 5 this Morning Saw 3 Islands in Lat. 61°40',[2] the Wmost bearing NWbN & the Emost NbW, abt. 3 Leagues dist, but the Weather being very Hazy and the Wind on the Shore we could not come any Nearer, or see the Main Land. At the Same time Sounded, and found 27 fathom Water.

Saturday 3rd. *SSE, NEbN to East. Course N36°E. Dist. in miles 46. Lat. obsd. 62°47'. Long. 93°43'. Var. N25W. Churchill River bore S24West, dist. 83 Leagues.* The first pt moderate Gales & Hazy

[1] HBC A 11/13, ff. 75–6.
[2] The three islands lying off Bibby Island.

Weather; the Middle little Winds & wet Fogs; the latter fresh Gales and Hazy. At 4 p.m. sounded & had 45 fathm. At 5 bore down 2 miles NNE for the Tender; fir'd a Gun for ditto. Sounded 52 fathom. At 7 bore down 2 Glasses for the Tender. Fir'd 6 Guns it being foggy. Sounded 56 fath. At 10 ditto 44 fath; at 12 ditto 43 fath., soft Clay. These last 3 hours fir'd 6 Guns more for the Tender. At 1 a.m. Tack'd & Sounded 38 fathom. Fir'd 3 Guns as a signal for the Tender, and one every half Hour afterwards till 6 in the Morning, being 9 Guns More. At 2 a.m. sounded 30 fathom; at 3 ditto 43 fathom; at 4 ditto 49 fathm. At ½ Past 5 Tack'd. At 6 Saw an Island, the two Extremities bearing NbE & EbN, lying in the Latitude of 63°00′ and Longitde. from the Meridian of London 93°40′W, which I take to be the Same Capt. Fox called Brook Cobham.[1] It's about 8 Leagues Long and 3 broad, pretty bold and good Soundings near it, and Stretches away NW & SE by Compass, having much Snow upon it. At 10 ditto tack'd and Sounded; had 15 fathom 5 or 6 Miles from the Shore. At Noon the Said Island, the Eastmost Part bore East, the Westmost Part NbE, and the Nearest pt NNE dist. 5 Miles.

Sunday 4th. *NEbE, WNW to NNE. Course E20N. Dist. in miles 54. Lat obsd. 62°58′. Long. 91°55′. Var. N27W. Ditto bore S33W, dist. 95 Leagues.* For the Most Part, have had light Gales and variable Weather. At ½ Past 12 Sounded & had from 25 to 29, 31 & 34 fathoms. At 2 the East End of Brook Cobham bore NEbE dist. 4 or 5 Leagues; at 4 p.m. the South End of ditto bore NE½E, dist 5 Leagues. Sold Dead Men's Cloaths.[2] At 5 ditto sounded & had 35 fathom. At 6 ditto the East End of Brook Cobham bore NE 7 or 8 Miles Dist., & the Northmst. Part NbW dist. 8 or 9 Leagues. Sound & had 3 fathom soft Ground. At 8 ditto sounded 33 to 35 & 40 fathom, soft Sticking Ground; at 10 sounded & had 40 fath. ditto Ground. At 11 let the 1st Reef out of the Topsails. Sounded from 45 to 46 fathom. At Noon the Island bore WSW

---

[1] This is Marble Island, lying off Rankin Inlet. One wonders at the reference to there being snow on it so late in the season. The island consists entirely of a white quartzite with a great deal of rock outcropping, and this could easily have been mistaken by Middleton for snow.

[2] I.e. the clothing of men who had died during the wintering. This was standard Navy practice, the proceeds being forwarded to the next of kin.

7 or 8 Leagues. Set the Foresail & Staysails. At 2 a.m. sounded, and Had from 54 to 55 fm. Water. At 4 ditto Sounded from 52 to 60 fathom. At ½ Past 5 ditto set the Mainsail & sounded 60 fathom. At 7 ditto Haul'd up the Mainsail for the Tender, & sounded from 75 to 74 fathom; bore down to the Tender five Glasses.

Monday 5th. N & NEbE. Course W33N. Dist. in miles 30. Lat. obsd. 63°14'. Long. 92°50'. Var. obsd. N30W. Churchill River bore S25W, dist 94 Leagues. The first Part Light Airs and fair Weather; the Middle fresh Gales & Squally; the Latter little Wind and Hazy. At 4 p.m. sounded 80 fathoms. At 8 took in the 1st Reef of the Topsails; at ½ past 8 tack'd, fired a Gun, & handed the Fore topsail. At 10 Set the Fore-topsail, and sounded 75 fathom. A great Sea from the Eastward. At Noon Sounded 75 fathom. At 2 a.m. Sounded from 75 to 70 fathm. At 3 this Morning saw a Head-land on the North Side of the Welcome,[1] bearing NWbN 7 or 8 Leagues dist. I try'd the tide Several times, and found it to run 2 Miles an Hr. from the NEbE by Compass the Day before the Change or the Full Moon, and I take it to be the Flood from the Eastwd.,[2] but have not Stop'd any where to go on Shore. Sounded and found 23 fathom three Leagues from the Land. I should have Sent my boat ashore here but it is coming on foggy. This Head-land is in the Latitude 63°20'N and Longitude from London 93°00' or 4 degrees east from Churchill.[3] At 4 Let the Reefs out of the Topsails, and Set the Small Sails. At 5 Sounded 70 fathom; at 8 ditto 72 fathom; at 10 ditto from 60 to 43. At Noon the Westmost Part of the Head-land in Sight bore NWbW 6 or 7 Leagues dist., the Eastmost NbE 5 Leagues dist. Sounded from 42 to 35 fathom.[4]

---

[1] Roes Welcome Sound, between Southampton Island and the Keewatin mainland. By the north side Middleton means the west or northwest side.

[2] Middleton is hoping to prove or disprove Dobbs's deductions as to the existence of a Northwest Passage on the basis of the height of the tides and the direction of the tidal current. See his instructions, p. 86 above.

[3] Taking into consideration the 2° error in Middleton's longitudes these coordinates match those of Baker Foreland quite accurately.

[4] On this date Moor in *Discovery* reported that he could not spare time to take soundings, 'what with Making and Shortng. Sail for the Furnace, and then being so badly Man'd' (Adm 51/290, pt IX, 5 Jul 1742).

Tuesday 6th. *NEbN, NbW to NNE. Course E5°N. Dist. in miles 31. Lat. obsd. 63°16'. Long. 91°44'. Var. N30°W. Ditto Bore S 31°W, dist. 99 Leagues.* Light Gales of Wind & fair Weather for the Most Part. Continued Sounding the first 4 hours & had 42, 40, 42, 38, 38, 35, 38, 35 fath. Water. At ½ past 2 p.m. tack'd. At ½ pt. 3 ditto the Emst. Part of the Headland in Sight, bearing NbE, the Westernmost WbS, the Nearest dist. 5 or 6 Leagues, working along shore, the flood from the NEbN & the ebb from the SWbS. At ½ Past 5 Tack'd & Sounded from 23 to 33 fathom. At 8 ditto Sounded 32 fathom; the Island Brook Cobham in Sight, bearing WbS 9 Leagues. Set topgallant Sails. At 10 the Easternmost Part of the Headland in Sight bore NW dist. 4 or 5 Leagues. At 11 Handed the Small Sails, and Sounded 60 fathom. At 2 a.m. Sounded 73 fathom; at 4 ditto 78 fathoms. At 5 tack'd & Sounded from 78 to 70 fathoms. Lower'd the Small Boat, try'd the Tide & found it Set NNE 2 fathm. At ½ Past 7 tack'd. Sounded 70 fathom. At 8 ditto the Eastmst. Part of the Headland above mentioned bore WNW½N dist. 8 or 9 Leagues. Set the Topgallant Sails. Unbent the Jibb, and alter'd its Foot to make it Stand, being too deep by the Leech, & scrap'd the Yaul. I found the Tide close in with the Head Land before Mentioned to run 2 Miles an hour from the NEbE which I take to be the Flood. By the Slacks from several Trials I found it to flow near W or WbN having a Full Moon this Day.

Wensday 7th. *WNW, NNE, ENE. Course E28°N. Dist. in miles 38. Lat. 63°39'. Long. 90°38'. Var. N31W. Churchill River Bore S32W, 110 Leagues.* Light Gales, with Hazy & foggy Weather. At 2 p.m. shortned Sail for the Tender. At 4 sounded 65 fathom. At 6 ditto 60 fathm. At 8 ditto from 70 to 75 fathm. At 10 ditto from 70 to 68 fathm. Tack'd and fir'd a Gun being foggy. At 12 Sounded 70 fathoms. At ½ Past 1 a.m. fir'd a Gun, Tack'd, and Sounded 60 fathom. At 4 ditto sounded & found 78, 76 & 73 fathom. At 6 ditto 72 & 70 fathom, Soft Sticking Ground. At 8 ditto 71 to 73 fathom soft Ground. At 10 ditto 85 to 90 fathm. At Noon Sounded and found 90 fathom. I have try'd the Tides several times since I was in-shore at Brook Cobham, & find little or none, but that may be owing to the Distance from the Land, as we find it happens in other Places. I have seen no Whales or

Large Fish of any Sort , except one White Whale as big as a Grampus,[1] and about 4 or 5 Seals.

Thursday 8th. *NNW, NEbE, Calm, WSW. Course N32E. Dist. in miles 30. Lat. obsd. 63°55'. Long. 90°00'. Var. N34W. Ditto bore S35W, dist. 120 Leagues.* For the Most Part little Wind, Hazy Weather, Calms & much Ice, all to the Northwd. of us, close inshore for several Leagues. At 2 p.m. sounded & had 92 fathom, soft Ground. At 4 ditto sounded 90 fathom. At 6 ditto 83 & 82 fathm. At 8 ditto 82 fathm., soft Ground. At 10 ditto 83 fathm., ditto Ground. At 12 ditto 83 to 88 fathm. Tack'd. At 2 a.m. Sounded and had from 80 to 74 fathoms. At 3 ditto Saw the N Side of the Welcome, and much Ice in Shore;[2] the Nearest Part of the Land bore NW about 7 or 8 Leagues. At 4 ditto Sounded; had 75 fathom. At 8 ditto try'd the Tide; found it Set ENE 2 fathom. Exercis'd the Small Arms. The Westmst. Land on the North Side of the Welcome bore at Noon NW, the Eastmst. NE, the nearest Dist. 7 or 8 Leagues. Sounded 57 fath.

Friday 9th. *WNW, SWbW. Course N 36°E. Dist. in miles 62. Lat. obsd. 64°51'. Long. 88°34'. Var. N34W. Churchill River Bore S36°West, dist. 136 Leagues.* Little Wind, with foggy, Hazy Weather. Sailing along a Ledge of Ice. At 11 p.m. sounded 72 fathom. At 2 ditto alter'd our Course for the Ice, fir'd a Gun, & Shortned Sail for the Tender. At 4 ditto sounded 38 fathoms, the North Shore in Sight. At 5 the Tender Came up with us; made Sail; Sounded 43 to 54 fathom. At 6 the Westmst. Land in Sight from WNW to NEbE the nearest dist. 7 Leagues. Past Several Pieces of Ice; fir'd a Gun to alter the Course at 8 ditto and Set the Top Gallant Sails. At 10 Sounded 80 fathom. At 2 a.m. saw much Ice a-Head, then in Sight of the North Shore. At 4 ditto Past much Shatter'd Ice; Sounded 68 fathm. Saw the East Side of the Welcome from the SbE to the NEbE, the nearest

---

[1] Grampus: the killer whale (*Orca orca*).

[2] Moor's journal, unusually, is fuller than Middleton's here: 'At 4 PM Fell in with a Ledge of Ice Streaching from the WNW to the ENE which obliges us to stand to the Et.ward in hopes of geting the Sooner clear on't for we know that all the Ice Driven towards the Southwards, for oftentimes in the Company's ships when we meet with Ice in the Bay in coming to Churchill, we were forc'd to go to the North'ard of all before that we can get in with the West Shore, that we Run sometimes 2 or more Degrees of Latitd. to the Northward' (ibid., 8 Jul 1742).

distance 4 Leagues, low, even Land.[1] The West Side bore at the Same time from WNW to N, the nearest Dist. 7 or 8 Leagues, so that the Welcome is 11 or 12 Leagues broad here. Sounded 44, 45, 47, 57, 55, 57, 40 & 44 fathom. At 10 a.m. enter'd a Ledge of Ice, Sailing amongst it. At 12 a thick Fog; lay'd to for the Tender, fir'd a Gun, & Sounded 74 fathom. At Noon the Tender Came up with us. Continued lying to till the Weather clear'd up. We find very good Soundings along both Shores at 3 or 4 Leagues dist. but little or no Tide here on the Shore. We are fast jamm'd up with Ice, and [no] Oppertunity to get on Shore to try the Height of the Tides, the Welcome being full of Ice from Side to Side.

Saturday 10th. SWbW to SWbS. Course NE. Dist. in miles 15. Lat. obsd. 65°00'. Long. 88°10'. Var. obsd. N36W. Churchill River. Foggy, Hazy Weather, sometimes fresh Gales; jamm'd up amongst much heavy Ice. At ½ past 12 p.m. the Fog clear up a little; made Sail towards the North Shore amongst thin Ice. Sounded from 60 to 54 fathom, much Ice all round. At 2 ditto sounded 65 fathom. Try'd the Tide & found it Set NEbE one Mile an Hour. At 4 ditto made the Signal to Grapple; fir'd two Guns. At 5 ditto grappled both the Ship & the Tender to a large piece of Ice, to keep off from the Shore, the Wind blowing on the South Side. At 8 set the Land on both Sides of the Welcome, the East or South Shore from the SSE round to the NEbE; the West or North Shore from the West to the No., the nearest Dist. 6 or 7 Leagues, the South Side dist. 5 Leagues at Least. Fill'd all our empty Casks with fresh Water from off the Piece of Ice we Grappled to.[2] At 12 Sounded 58 fathoms. At 2 a.m. fair but hazy, with a fresh Gale at SWbS driving all the Ice we came thro' upon us, which is now jamm'd fast to both Sides of the Welcome. Sounded 56 fathom. At 4 a.m. Sounded 46 to 45 fathoms. At 5 ditto 49 fathom. At 6 ditto 51 fathm.; fresh Gales and Hazy. At 8 ditto got down Topgallant Yards. Sounded 50 fathom. At 10 ditto 53 fathom. At Noon Sounded 55 fathom. We are using Means to keep us from being forc'd upon Shore and to Prevent our Separation, by making fast to the Largest Piece of Ice we can

---

[1] This is the first sighting of the coast of Southampton Island.
[2] I.e. from fresh melt pools on top of the floe ice.

come at. I find by frequent Trials with the Current Log, there is neither flood nor Ebb on this South Side. Our way made by driving in the Ice with the Wind, allowing the Variation, is NE 15 Miles. It is so Hazy that we can not see the West Shore, and we are not above 3 Leagues from the Eastern Shore, wch. is in sight from the SbW to NEbE, and we drive ENE by Compass, but I hope the Ice will fill between us and it to prevent our being a-shore, for we are not able to help our Selves untill the Wind Shifts, or it is Calm.[1]

Sunday 11th. *SSW, SW. Course NE. Dist. in miles 15. Lat. obsd. 65°11'. Long. 87°45'. Var. obsd. N36W.* Have had for the Most Part fresh Gales with Wet fogs & Rain, much Ice all round from Side to Side the Wellcome, and for 10 Leagues to Windward of us. At 1 p.m. the Current set NEbE 4 fathom; at the Same time Sounded 47 fathom. At 2 ditto 54 fathom. At 3 ditto 47 to 45 fm. At 4 ditto 49 fm. At 5 ditto 48 to 45 fm. At 8 ditto 48 to 44 fm. At 10 ditto 44 to 45 fm. At 12 ditto 40 to 44 fm. Continued driving on the South Shore. At 2 a.m. Sounded 43 to 42 fathm., rocky, Stoney Ground. At 4 ditto 43 fm. At 6 ditto from 43 to 40 fm., rocky & Stoney. At 7 ditto 38 faths.; at the Same time found the Tide set NNE 4 fathm. At 10 ditto the Tide Set East 6 fath.; Sounded & had 28 fm. The Weather Clearing up a little we found ourselves within 2 miles of the South Shore. It pleased God that it came Calm, then the Ice opened as usual, and we began to Warp off from the Shore, by Carrying out Warps and Grapplings from Piece to Piece of Ice. The Tender did the Same. We shall make but little Way unless the Wind Shifts to favour us, the Tide Constantly setting to the Eastward. Our Drift, by Acct., since noon last, when the Variation is allowed, is 15 Miles NE, and makes us in the Longitude & Latitude as per Margent. I Shall Endeavour to get out towards Whalebone Point to try for a Straits or Passage, according to my Instructions as soon as the Ice & Wind will favour us.

Monday 12. *NE to ESE. Course N11W. Lat. 65°30'. Long. 87°55'. Var. N36W.* Calms, Light Airs, & little Winds, with foggy & Hazy

---

[1] Middleton was only too well aware of the dangers his ships were exposed to, namely of being driven helplessly ashore or onto a reef while beset in the ice.

Weather. Continued Warping & Setting with our Ice Poles amongst the Ice being quite Calm. At 4 p.m. Sounded 31 fathoms. At 5 ditto had a Small Breeze, set the Staysails and got up the topgallant Yards and set the Sails; rowing, warping, Setting the Ice open, & towing with our Boats ahead. At 8 ditto the Ice opened more. Continued as above. At 9 ditto Grappled 5 Miles off the Shore, to wait for the Tender. This East Shore lyeth by Compass NNE & SSW, low, even Land. At 11 ditto the Tender came up with us; Cast off our Grapplings & made Sail. At 2 a.m. Grappled to a large Piece, a thick Fog coming on, and sent our Boat to Help the Tender. By 3 ditto got her fast to the Same Piece of Ice. At 4 ditto Sounded 35 to 38 fathm. At 6 ditto 39 fathm; try'd the Tide; found it Set NE 2 fathom. At ½ Past 7 it clear'd up a little. Cast off our Grapplings; made one Warp, and Set Sail. At 8 ditto the Ice opened towards the North Shore. Sounded 43 fathom. Half Way between the two Shores we had 49, 48 & 46 faths., grey Sand, Shells & Some Stones. At Noon the Eastmost Land on the North Shore bore NE, the nearest dist. 4 Leagues. At the Same time a fair Point, Cape or Head-land appear'd to the Northwd. of Whale-bone Point and bore from us SWbW, dist. 8 or 9 Leagues in Latd. 65°10′N and Longitude from the Meridian of London, by our Acct. 88°06′ West, which I Shall Name **Cape Dobbs**, after my worthy friend, the Honble. Arthur Dobbs Esqr. of Castle Dobbs in Ireland.[1] I am now Standing in for an Inlet or Straits that makes a fair opening NW from us, but not very wide,[2] to secure the Ships from the Ice in the Welcome, there being no Safety lying here, or Proceeding any farther untill the Ice is gone.

[*Middleton reached this decision after calling a council, attended by himself, Lieutenant Rankin, William Moor, master of the* Discovery, *and Robert Wilson, master of the* Furnace. *The outcome of their deliber-ations reads as follows:*

The manifest Hazard of his Majesty's Ships *Furnace* and *Discovery*, from the vast Quantities of Ice that surrounded them, the Sea being covered for ten Leagues to Windward, and the Ships driving every Tide nearer the Land, and at that time within two Miles of the Shore;

---

[1] Still named Cape Dobbs.
[2] The entrance to Wager Bay.

that there was a Necessity of turning back or seeking some Harbour, as soon as might be, to secure the Ships, was taken seriously into Consideration, and it was unanimously Resolv'd, that it would be the most eligible and safest Method for the Preservation of his Majesty's said Ships, and the Lives of the Men, to make the best of our way to an Inlet or Strait, that appear'd beyond *Whalebone-Point*, there to seek out some convenient Place to secure the Ships, till such time as the *Welcome* should be clear'd of Ice, and then use our utmost Endeavours for proceeding on our Discovery. In witness whereof we have hereunto set our Hands the Date and Year above-written'.[1]]

Tuesday 13th. *ENE & Calm. Var. N36°W.* Light Winds & Calms, with Hazy Weather. At 1 p.m. sounded & had 43 fathm., Sand, Shells and Small Stones. At 2 ditto Cape Dobbs bore SWbS 7 or 8 Leagues; the Easternmost Land on the North Side of the Opening ENE (which makes this Bay) 8 or 9 Leagues. At 4 ditto the Entrance of the River bore NWbW dist. 4 Leagues; Stood in for the River amongst Sailing Ice, and order'd the Tender to lie to, or Stand off, untill we could make the River, and then if we went in, She was to follow.[2] At 6 ditto made the Signal for the Tender to come in after us. At 10 ditto almost Calm, much Ice about us, rowing & towing with our Boats ahead, to get into Some Place of Safety. At 12 ditto Anchor'd on the North Shore in 34 fathoms, within Some Islands to Stop the Tide. Much Ice drove down with the Tide of Ebb, and several Pieces came foul of us, tho' we Steer'd all the Tide, Had a Whole Cable out, and all hands Setting with Poles to fend off, and clear the Pieces of Ice when they took us. Several of the Uskimay Savages came along Side in their Boats. At 6 a.m. being low water, hove in the Cable to the Short Service. At 8 ditto veer'd out to the Long Service. At 10 ditto I sent the Lieut. & the 8 oar'd Boat to Sound within some Islands about 2 or 3 Miles from us, in order to find some secure Place where we might ride free from the Dangers of the Ice. At the Same time I sent the Master with the Ice Boat to help the Tender in to anchor by us out of the Ice & Strong tides.

---

[1] Middleton, *Vindication*, pp. 107–8.

[2] Moor's version is slightly different: 'sailing thro much Ice for an Opening in the Land like a River or an Inlet... at ½ past 3 the Furnace under our Stern. when Capt. Middleton told me, that he wou'd Run up as far as he cou'd with Safety, to see whether it was a Bay or no what it was, and that I might not Follow unless that he shou'd Run first out of Sight' (Adm 51/290, pt IX, 13 Jul 1742).

At 11 ditto we got the Sheat Cable bent. Many large Pieces of Ice came foul of us, & one of them brought the Anchor home, but She brought up again. Entering this River which I shall name the River **Wager**, after the Right Honble. Sr. Charles Wager, one of His Majesty's Most Honble. Privy Council, First Lord Commissioner of the Admiralty etc., we had very good Soundings as high as we went, from 16 to 20, 30 & 44 fathm. This River at its Entrance & about 4 or 5 Miles higher up, is 6 or 8 Miles broad;[1] but after you get 4 Leagues up, it is then 4 or 5 Leagues Broad. It was just flood when we enter'd it, and we found the Tide in the Narrows to run 5 or 6 Miles an Hour, on the Neap, but much easier where we anchor'd. There are Several islands in the Middle, and Some Rocks that we escap'd, it being high Water, when we went over them. The Land on both Sides is as high as any I have Seen in England.[2] The Soundings from the River's Mouth to this Place where we Anchor'd are as follows: 16, 21, 24, 28, 25, 25, 24, 24, 24, 21, 26, 28, 27, 28, 34, 36, 44, 40, 40, 42, 40, 38, 39, 38, 39, 38, 35, 18, 14, 15, 25, 32, 40, 44, 42, 38, 33, 34, 36, 34 and 34 fathoms, then Anchor'd. These Soundings were taken in the Middle of the River, as fast as the Deep-Sea Lead could be thrown. The Tender has drove with the Tide All Night, and now she is driving down with the Ebb, it being Calm, and Surrounded with Ice in the Middle of the River, and in no little Danger.

Wensday 14th. *SSE. Moor'd in Savage Sound.* These 24 Hours have had little Wind, and much Ice driving down the River on the Ebb. The River, Higher up, as far as we can see, is full of Ice from Side to Side.[3] Many of the Savages came on board of us; I gave them Several Toys, but they had. nothing to exchange

---

[1] This is a slight exaggeration; at its narrowest point the entrance to Wager Bay is about 4.5 miles in width, but as Middleton indicates it widens out considerably farther west.

[2] This is again rather an exaggeration; the highest land visible on either side of the narrows of Wager Bay is barely 500' high; farther to the west the land on the south side rises to 1500' but even this is a lot lower than the highest land Middleton could have seen in England.

[3] Moor reports that at 2 p.m. Middleton sent the ship's master and two hands in the ice boat 'to Acquaint me that they had got the Furnace safe Moor'd out of the Tides way under several Islands, over towards the Et. shore' (ibid., 14 Jul 1742).

except their old Cloaths, & about 20 Gallons of Train Oyl, which latter we excepted of for the Use of the Boatswain & Carpenter. At 4 p.m. weigh'd our best Bower Anchor to get into a better Road, within Some Islands, and found one of the Arms of the Anchor broke off. We Sail'd about 4 Miles Higher up, and Anchor'd in a Sound between Some islands[1] & the North Main in 16 fathom Water and moor'd with our broken Anchr. near those Islands. At 8 ditto the Discovery Tender came to Anchor by us. Much Ice continues driving Past us, several Pieces of Which Came foul of us, without doing any Damage, there being more Eddy than Tide here. This Place I have Nam'd Savage Sound. At 12 ditto drew the Splice of the Best Bower, & Shift'd it from the Starboard to the Larboard Side. At 7 a.m. I Sent the Lieut. wth the 8 oar'd Boat, & 9 men Well Arm'd, with Provisions for 48 Hours to discover this River, & to observe the Course, Direction & height of the Tides, with Orders to return within the above-mention'd time. The three Indians I have Sent along with him, to know whether they were acquainted with this Country.

Thursday 15th. *SEbS to ESE.* Fresh Gales & Cloudy, the Wind at ESE. This Wind hath drove the Ice out of the Welcome into this River, & fill'd it quite Full. Our People employ'd in serving the Cables to Preserve them from being Cut by the Ice that drives in & out by the Tides. At 11 a.m. I went on Shore upon some of the Islands, found them quite bare, no Bush or Tree of any Kind, some Short Grass & Moss in the Valies, & a small Quantity of Scurvy Grass[2] & Sorrel amongst the Stones above High Water Mark, wch. we brought on board for the Sick Men. Set our fishing nets but Caught no fish. Many of the Men are very ill with their old Distemper, the Scurvy. Those that were on their Recovery when we left Churchill are relaps'd, so that near Half of them are unserviceable.

Friday 16th. *ESE to SEbE. Lat. obsd. 65°30′.* The first Part fresh Gales & Hazy; the Middle Hard Gales with Rain; the latter fair & Clear. Our People employ'd in Coiling down the Cables in the

---

[1] The Savage Islands so called after the encounter with the Inuit.
[2] *Cochlearia officinalis*, a shore plant well known for its antiscorbutic properties.

Hold, & getting up the Spare one to coil between Decks. At 3 p.m. I return'd on board. At 6 ditto Bent the Best Bower Cable to the Spare Anchor. Much Ice driving up and down the River. At 10 ditto lower'd our Yards a-Port-last,[1] and got the Boat up in the Tackles. At 4 a.m. got up the lower Yards, the Weather being more Moderate, and clean'd the Decks. At 6 ditto loos'd our Sails to dry.[2] I find the Tide at the Mouth of the River, flows on Change Days 5 Hours, & rises from 10 to 15 foot Water. The Flood without Comes from the East by compass, the Course of the Land, but in the Mid-channel ENE by ditto. I have found here a good Cove, with 10 or 12 fathm. Water in it,[3] where I intend to secure the Ships from the Ice before the Spring Tides come on; for where we now lie we are oblig'd to keep all Hands up all the Ebb, fending off the Ice with Poles to save our Selves.

Saturday 17th. *ESE to SEbE*. Moderate Gales & Clear Weather. The River Continuing full of Ice. At 1 p.m. the Lieut. & the three Indians return'd having been up the River as far as the ice would Permit them, all above being fast from Side to Side. He found good Soundings in the Chanel from 70 to 80 fathom. He likewise try'd the Tides when he was up the River, and found the flood Came from the Southward. I am preparing to go up that way myself to see if any other outlet may be found to the Sea or Welcome. Where the Lieut. has been he found it to flow 13 foot it being then Neap Tides. The 3 Indians know nothing of this Part of the Country. At 6 a.m. made the signal to unmoor, & fir'd a Gun. At the Same time I went away with the Boat & 8 Hands,[4] taking the two Northern Indians along with me, and order'd the Ship into the Cove. At 8 ditto unmoor'd & got out Warps to Warp her in. Broke the Tender's Kedge Anchor in warping among the Ice. Set the Foretopsail.

Sunday 18th. *ESE. In the Cove in Savage Sound*. Fine, moderate, clear Weather. Our People employ'd in Scraping the Ship For

---

[1] Level with the bulwarks.

[2] In his log entry for noon Middleton adds the information: 'Our People employed in drawing and knotting Yarn' (Adm 51/379, pt III, 16 Jul 1742).

[3] In his log entry Middleton notes that cove is about 2 miles from his present anchorage (ibid., 16 Jul 1742).

[4] Middleton was accompanied by William Moor, and four of the hands were from *Discovery* (Adm 51/290, pt IX, 17 Jul 1742).

tarring. At 2 p.m. the Ship got into the Cove & moor'd in 9½ fathm. Water between four. At 8 the Master & 8 Men got the Discovery in, and moor'd by us. Serv'd all the Hawsers two or three fathoms under Water to keep the Ice from rubbing them. By 8 this Evening I got up the River Wager 15 Miles, & found the Tide flow'd 12 foot, & a West Moon Makes full Sea, that the Tide came in at the Mouth of the River where the Ships came in at and run SSE. This Evening the Indians Kill'd a Small Deer,[1] where we lay all Night. Heard several of the Savages making an uncommon Crying in the Night, as they always do when they See Strangers, but none Came Near us.

Monday 19. *SSE.* Moderate, hazy Weather with Some Rain. Pay'd the Ship's Outsides wth. Tar. Stay'd the Fore & Main top Mast, and Set up the Rigging. At 2 this Morning Got all things in the Boat & went five Miles Higher up the River and got into a Small River or Sound about 6 or 7 Miles broad[2] but how far it may run in-land we know not. The Main River is 6 or 7 Leagues wide at this Place but so full of Ice, that we can't go Much Higher up. The land on both Sides is very high. I went up on one of the Highest Mountains about 24 Miles from Savage Sound from whence I could See the River Wager as far down as where the Ships lay, and about 8 or 10 Leagues farther up than the Place I Stood upon. I Observ'd that the River run NbW by Compass, but grew narrower in its Course upwards, & full of Ice.[3]

Tuesday 20. *ESE. Deer Sound.* Moderate & Hazy Weather. Much Ice where our Ships lay before they were haul'd into the Cove. Our People employ'd in filling Water, and overhauling the Rigging, Scarping the Masts, etc. At ½ past 8 p.m. I return'd on board, and brought with me 6 Deer that the Indians shot while I was making my Observations, which I distributed among the Sick People in both Ships over & above their Allowance for (which is very strange) in all their Sickness even a Day or two before they dy'd, they could eat their Whole Allowance & a great deal more if they had it. The Place where the Indians Kill'd the

[1] I.e. Barren-grounds caribou (*Rangifer tarandus groenlandicus*).
[2] Douglas Harbour (Middleton's Deer Sound) on the north side of Wager Bay.
[3] In his log entry Middleton adds: 'We got 5 other Deer we had killed into the Boat, and prepared to return to our ships.' (Adm 51/379, pt III, 19 Jul 1742)

Deer I nam'd Deer Sound, from the Plenty of Deer we Saw there. The Land is very Mountainous & barren with Rocks of the Marble Kind; in the Vallies a great many Lakes, some Grass, & Numbers of Large Deer as big as a small Horse 12 or 13 hands high. Upon small Islands, not half a Mile round, there is Generally Seen a Small Herd.[1] At 7 a.m. I went down the River wth. the same Boat to Search for a Harbour for the Ships near the River's Mouth, if we Should be taken Short in going out, & to see if the Welcome clear'd any thing of Ice.

Wensday 21. *ESE*. Clear Weather, light Airs & Hazy. Our People employ'd about the Ship Rigging & Masts & fitting and Mending the Quarter Netting. At 4 this Morning I got on Board wth the Boat, with much Hazard of Staving her with the Ice in the Strong Tides below. No getting out to Sea untill the River & Welcome is more Clear of Ice; for when I was within 4 Miles of the River's Mouth I got upon a High Hill from Which I could see the Welcome, & perceiv'd it full of Ice from Side to Side.[2]

Thursday 22nd. *NNE to NNW*. Moderate & fair with Small Rain. At 1 p.m. hove tort the Moorings, and clear'd away the Ice. Tarr'd the lower Masts & Pumps. At 6 a.m. loos'd all the Sails to dry. Got up the topgallant Yards. At 10 up all Chests & Hammocks and Scrap'd, & Clean'd between Decks. The Ice continues very thick in the River as far as we can See above and below, and more drives in every Tide, if the Wind comes from the Welcome. At 2 p.m. sent the Lieut. with the 6 oar'd Boat up the River.

Friday 23rd. *NNW to NNE*. Little Wind and Hazy, with frequent Showers of Rain. There is more Ice in the River now than hath been seen before. No sending a Boat any distance Downwds. Put more Service on our Cables to save them from the Ice.

---

[1] Rankin reports that there were also large numbers of ducks and other waterfowl and that they saw 9 whales (ADM L/F/109, 20 Jul 1742).

[2] Middleton's log supplies the additional information that at 6 p.m. the men were clearing ice away from the cables, and that when Middleton's boat returned at 4 p.m. it had difficulty in getting into the cove due to ice (Adm 51/379, pt III, 21 Jul 1742).

Saturday 24th. *NbW*. Fresh Gales with Rain. Our People em-ploy'd about the Rigging & filling of Water. At 6 a.m. the Lieut-enant return'd with the Boat, having been gone 48 Hours to Sound amongst the Island near Deer Sound. Found the river full of Ice.[1] He brought on board with him 3 Deer the Indians Kill'd, which I distributed among the Sick People & Officers of both Ships as before.

Sunday 25th. *Ditto*. Little Wind wth. Hazy Weather. At 2 p.m. we found the Stock of our Best Bower Anchor to be broke wth. the Ice grounding upon it in 4 fathm. Water, being the Same Anchor that one of the Arms broke off before, so that it is now quite useless. Put it on board the Tender. At 8 ditto got one of the Discovery's Anchors,[2] & new Stock'd it for our Use.[3] At 10 a.m. I sent the Lieut. and Master down the River to its mouth, to observe whether the Ice was clearer below & in the Welcome, intending to get out if Possible before the Spring Tides put in, and to Search for a Cove or Harbour near its Entrance.

Monday 26th. *North*. Moderate Gales and Hazy Weather.[4] The River Continues very full of Ice from Side to Side, as far as we can see. The Longitude of Savage Bay,[5] where we now lie, by account from the Meridian of London, is 89°28′West. The Variation of the Compass I have Observ'd Several Times, and found it 35 degrees Westerly. The Latitude of the Entrance of this River Wager is 65°32′N. The Latd. of Deer Sound is

[1] Rankin's journal is a little more detailed: 'At 6 am I returned with the Boat and seven Deer with the Northern Indians, having been 25 Leags and better up the River, finding deep Water all the way; no Ground 67 fam. I found severall Islands in the Middle with 30 fam. Water close long side of them. I saw a Fall or a Fresh on the west Side of them. I went to the Top of the highest Mountain I could see and saw a very high Mountain and Land on both sides of the River away to the westward. The River is as full of Ice as ever.' (ADM L/F/109, 24 Jul 1742).

[2] In his log Middleton provides the additional information that this anchor had been bent at Churchill (Adm 51/379, pt III, 25 Jul 1742).

[3] Middleton's log entry for 4 a.m. records: 'Our men employed making Plats for our Cables' (ibid., 25 Jul 1742).

[4] In his log entry for 6 a.m. Middleton reports: 'The Anchor abovementioned being compleatly stock'd, got it over the Side, and tarred it. The Weight of it 7 C. 03 qrs. oo lb.' (ibid., 26 Jul 1742).

[5] In the log entry for this date Middleton refers to it as 'Savage Sound' so named 'from the Natives coming to us there' (ibid., 26 Jul 1742).

65°50'N. The Course to the Said Sound from Savage Bay is NW by Compass; the Dist. about 24 Miles.

Sunday 27th. *Ditto.* Small Breezes of Wind, and Hazy. Hauled up our Sheat Cable, got up our spare Sails & Air'd them. At ½ Past 9 p.m. the Lieut. & Master return'd on board, & gave an acct. that the River was much choak'd up with Ice, quite out to Sea, that they were in great Danger of Losing the Boat and themselves with the Strong Tides, being jamm'd up fast in Ice, and Carried 6 or 7 Leagues out of the River in the Strength of the Tides where the great Pieces of Ice overset one upon another. When they got into the Welcome, the Tide was easy, and the Ice thinner. They row'd round to the North Shore, and got in upon the Flood, with some Damage to the Boat, but not much.

[*Rankin's report, written on his return, reads as follows:*

I was ordered to take the Master with me in the eight oar'd Boat, to sound in the Channel to the northward of the Islands in the River, and to see for a Harbour for our Ships, near the Mouth of the River, for a safe Retreat, if need be, but I could find none on the north Side; but I saw several Openings or Coves on the south Side, but I could not get near them; for the River was very full of Ice from Side to Side. I made the best of my way up to the Ships from near the River's Mouth; I got up to the Island off the Mouth of *Savage* Sound or River, the Tide came down upon me, and all the Ice, with such Force and Swiftness, that our Boat must have been smashed into a thousand Pieces, if we had not got her instantly into a Cove, or large Field of Ice:[1] we were inclosed with so much Ice, many large Pieces, some of them drew nine or ten Fathoms Water; we were forced upon the south Shore with great Swiftness, and many Pieces were forced upon the Rocks, and others against them with great Force; we were forced off again near the Middle of the River, and carried out of the River's Mouth with the Tide of Ebb above five Leagues, before we could see the least Opening among the Ice, to get the Boat out. About four or five in the Morning, the 26th, the Ice opened a little, I got the Boat out of the Cove, and forced her through the Ice, it having little or no

---

[1] As it stands this part of the report does not make much sense, but it is clear from Rankin's own journal that he managed to get the boat into an embayment or cove in the edge of a large floe; hence the boat, while drifting with that floe, was relatively safe.

Motion, the Flood Tide being made, we got among loose Ice, and sailed towards the north Shore. About twelve at Noon, the 26th, we lay the Tide off Ebb, and got on board of the Ship at half an Hour past nine at Night. *July 27th, 1742. John Rankin*][1]

By this Account, there is no getting out wth. the Ship untill the River is Pretty Clear, and if we were out, there is so much Ice to the Northwd. and the Welcome Constantly full, that we could not Proceed any farther Yet, so I hope there is no Time lost by our being in Safety here.

Wensday 28th. *South & SSW*. Moderate & Hazy. At 1 p.m. the Lieut. & Master went up the River to try if they could find any way out of it into the Welcome, besides that we came in at, on Account they have seen many black Whale[2] and other Fish the last time they were up, and none seen where we lie, or any where below. I likewise order'd them to try Deer Sound & every Opening, to find whether the Flood came in any other way than that we came in at. This we may do as there is no going out untill the ice is clear in the River & Welcome.

[*Middleton's complete orders to Rankin concerning this trip read as follows:*

Whereas I ordered you and the Master to sound in the Channel on the north Side of the Islands in this River, and to look out for a Harbour for the Ships near the Mouth thereof, but finding by your Report, that there is none to be found on the north Side, and the River being very full of Ice, there was no approaching the south Side; it also having been hinted to me, that there was some hopes of a Passage or Inlet into the Sea, from the Risings of the Tides at or near *Deer Sound*, black Whales having been seen thereabouts, and it being impossible to move the Ships with Safety, while such Bodies of Ice are now in the River, and continue to drive with the Tides; you and the Master are hereby required and directed to take the six-oar'd boat, and proceed up the River *Wager* as far as *Deer Sound* before-mentioned, and to be as particular as may be of the Flux of the Tides, their Direction and Height at that Place and near it, and particularly to note whether the Flood in the River *Deer Sound* comes from this River or some other, and to make strict Enquiry, whether the black

---

[1] Middleton, *Vindication*, pp. 108–9.
[2] I.e. Bowhead whales (*Balaena mysticetus*).

Whales can have any other Passage from this Sea into this River, than that where his Majesty's Ships *Furnace* and *Discovery* came in at, and to report to me, under your Hands, at your Return, which is to be as speedy as the Nature of the Service you are ordered upon will permit, what Observations you make thereof, and for so doing this shall be your sufficient Warrant. Dated on board his Majesty's Ship *Furnace*, the 27th Day of July 1742][1]

At 6 this Morning sent our Boat with 8 of our Sick Men, and several that were Lame wth. the Scurvy to an Island about 5 Miles off, having Plenty of Scurvy-Grass & Sorrel on it, & left them there wth. Tenting & Necessaries. The Tide flow'd 12 foot 6 Inches.

Thursday. 29th. *Variable.* Moderate & Hazy. our People employ'd in making Plats[2] for the Cables. The Tide flow'd 13 foot this Day, and it was high Water at one o'Clock. I had not found above 15 foot Water on the Highest Tides. This Day I went upon one of the Highest Hills, as I have done every Day since the Ship has been in the Cove, to observe if the Ice clear'd in the River, but I find it all full below, but something thinner above.

Friday 30th. *WbN to North.* Light Airs & variable Winds. Our People employ'd in making Plats etc. At 8 a.m. got on board our Head Anchor, ready to get out of the Cove. The Ice, I perceiv'd from the Hills as usual, was all fast below and for 8 or ten Miles above without the Islands, tho' it is Pretty clear just without the Cove.

Saturday 31st. *North to WbN.* Moderate & fair Weather, with some Rain. Our People employ'd in filling Water. Got our Stern Anchor on board, and got it ahead ready to heave the Ship out of the Cove. At 8 a.m. a fresh Gale blowing into the Cove. Hove all our Moorings tort again. Abundance of Ice has drove out of the Welcome by this Wind, and almost fill'd the Bay without us.

---

[1] Ibid., pp. 109–10.
[2] Plats: braided rope to be wound around the cable to prevent wear on it where it passes through the hawse-hole or elsewhere.

AUGUST 1742

Sunday 1st. *South & SW.* The first Part fresh Gales and much Rain; the Middle & Latter moderate & fair with variable Winds. At 1 p.m. carry'd out an Anchor astern to Secure the Ship. At 5 the Boat came on board wth. the Lieut. & Master, who gave me An Acct. that they had been 10 or 12 Leagues above Deer Sound, saw a great many black Whale of the Whale-bone Kind, try'd every Opening they saw, & constantly found the Tide of Flood came from the Eastward, or in at the Mouth of the River Wager.[1]

[The full report submitted by Rankin and Wilson reads as follows:

'We, whose Names are hereunto subscrib'd took the *Furnace*'s six-oar'd Boat, and went from *Savage Sound*, where his Majesty's Ships *Furnace* and *Discovery* then lay; and on the 28th, at one in the Morning, arriv'd at *Deer Sound*, where we tried the Tide, and found the Flood to come into that Place from the River *Wager*, and rose at that time ten Feet. At six o'Clock the same Morning we left *Deer Sound*, (where we put the two northern *Indians* ashore to kill some Deer for our sick Men) and sailed for a high bluff Land on the N.W. Side of the River *Wager*. Our Course from the Islands on the north Side of *Deer Sound* to the high bluff Land, was N.W.b.N. by Compass; we sounded frequently, and had no Ground with a Line of sixty-Eight Fathoms all the way over. When we were a-breast of the high bluff Land, we steer'd W.N.W. keeping the mid-Channel, and still found no Ground at 98 Fathom, except nigh some Islands that lay in the fair Way about one third over the River, and 30 Fathoms within a League of one of them.[2] This Course we kept till we got about 15 Leagues from *Deer Sound*, but finding the Tide or Fresh against us, and the Wind coming fair, we were afraid to stay any longer, for fear of hindering the Ships from going to Sea; however, we came to a Grapnell with the Boat, and went upon a high mountainous Land,

---

[1] In his log Middleton reported: 'The Lieutenant and Masr. brought on board by my Order two Bottles of Water taken up alongside. One at Deer Sound, the other 10 or 12 Leags above it, being the highest they went up. This latter tasted but barely brackish. The Tide flowed there no more than 6 Feet' (Adm 51/379, pt III, 1 Aug 1742).

[2] Moor added: 'the Course they steerd after they left that Bluff was WNW, and they Believ'd it Flow'd not above 6 or 8 Foot there' (Adm 51/290, pt IX, 1 Aug 1742).

where we had a very fair View of the River. From thence we saw a great Run or Fall of Water[1] between the suppos'd main Land and the aforesaid Islands, very narrow, seemingly not a Mile broad, and about a League from where the Boat lay; but to the northwards we discovered a large Collection of Water, in which were several Islands, and high mountainous Land on both Sides of it, the west Side having many bluff Points, and broken Land. In our Return towards the Ships, and not far from *Deer Sound*, we saw several large black Whales of the Whalebone kind, some of which came very near the Boat. So that upon the whole, we think there may be some other Passage into the Sea from the River *Wager*, besides that which his Majesty's Ships *Furnace* and *Discovery* came in at, and imagine there is a great Probability of an Opening or Inlet into the Sea, somewhere on the east Side thereof, tho' we cannot fix the Place, Given unto our Hands this first Day of *August*, 1742. John Rankin, Robert Wilson.][2]

At 4 a.m. unmoor'd, and Warp'd out of the Cove towards Savage Bay. At the Same time our Sick & Lame Men came on board from Scurvy Island.

Monday 2nd. *SSE, SEbS. Moor'd in Savage Bay, Wager River. Scurvy Island, So., Eastern point of Savage Bay SEbS.* The first Part fresh Gales, and variable Winds; the Middle more moderate & cloudy; the Latter fresh Gales with Rain. Much Ice driving up & down with the Tides. Continued warping out of the Cove. At 4 p.m. moor'd in Savage Bay, two Miles without the Cove in 20 fathm. Water, clear Sandy Ground.[3] At Noon sent our 6 oar'd Boat & 7 hands to help the Tender out of the Cove. At 3 a.m. I went down the River to see Whether the Welcome was any thing clear of Ice, intending to carry the Ships out the first Shift of Wind.[4]

Tuesday 3rd. *SEbS to East.* The 1st part fresh Gales & hazy with Rain; the Middle moderate & fair; the latter little Wind & hazy.

[1] The fall described here is very probably the reversing tidal fall between Ford Lake and the head of Wager Bay.

[2] Middleton, *Vindication*, pp. 110–11.

[3] In his log entry Middleton notes that from this anchorage 'Scurvy-grass Island bore S. the Eastmost Point in the Sound bore SEbS; the N. Point of the Cove NbE.' (Adm 51/379, pt III, 2 Aug 1742)

[4] Middleton's log adds the additional information: 'Find the Ice much thinned above in the River without the Islands' (ibid., 2 Aug 1742).

At 4 p.m. I return'd on board with the boat, found the Ice pretty Clear in the Offing & River; if we cannot get out in one Tide there's no Anchoring by the Way, while the Ice is driving with Such Strong Tides as we had here, & it is now near the Spring Tides, but please God, I will try as Soon as the Wind will permit me.[1]

Wensday 4th. *NW, SSW, ESE, NE. Course E20°N. Dist. in miles 40. Lat. obsd. 65°38'. Long. 87°7'W. Var. N38W.* Little Wind variable. At ½ Past 12 Unmoor'd. At 1 p.m. got under Sail, running down the River against the Tide of Flood. At 5 ditto almost Calm; got the Pinnace ahead & tow'd & row'd with the Ship's Oars. By 6 ditto abreast of the lowermst. Islands, and Perceiv'd the Tide was then fallen a foot. Continued rowing and Towing being Calm.[2] By 10 got out of the River, the Tide setting us out at the Rate of 5 Miles an Hour. The River's Mouth at 12 bore NWbW dist. 4 Leagues. Fell in with a Ledge of Ice; got in our 8 oar'd Boat. At 2 a.m. sounded 30 to 36 fathom; found the Flood came from the East. At the Same time the River's Mouth bore NWbW 5 or 6 Leagues; Cape Dobbs WNW 9 Leagues. The Easternmst Land on the North Side in Sight, NE 6 Leagues; the nearest NNW 4 or 5 leagues. At 4 Sounded 37 to 34 fathoms. Almost Calm.[3] At 8 Sounded 30, 22, 20 fathm. Tackd. Light airs, variable. At 9 Lay'd too for the Tender. Up SSE, off SW. At 10 Sounded 37 to 45 fathoms. At 12 Sounded 47 to 46 fathom. The Southermt. Land on the South Shore in Sight, bore South, the nearest Distance 4 Leagues SEbE; the Eastermst. Part bore EbN. On the North Shore, the Eastmost Part bore NbE, the nearest dist. NW½N 8 Leagues; the Westmost part of ditto in Sight bore West at Noon. Allowing the River Wager's Mouth to be in the Latitude & Longitude of 65°24'N & Longitude from the Meridian of London 88°87'W makes in Latitude & Longitude as Per Margin. I several times try'd the Tides, and found the Flood to

---

[1] Middleton's log entries add several additional minor points: at 12 midnight 'Cleared Harse ready for unmooring'; at 8 a.m. 'Loosed all our Sails to dry. Little Wind and variable'; and at noon: 'At 12 made a Signal to unmoor' (ibid., 3 Aug 1742).

[2] In his log entry for 8 p.m. Middleton offers the additional information: 'The Tender in Company' (ibid., 4 Aug 1742).

[3] At 6 a.m. Middleton recorded in his log: 'Saw two or three black Whales blow this Watch' (ibid., 4 Aug 1742).

Come from the E or EbN near the Middle of this Strait, and an East Moon makes full Sea or High Water here as well as in the River's Mouth, working to the East to meet the Tide of Flood in this Strait, which is about 13 Leagues from Side to Side. Saw Several Ledges of Ice, but not much in our Way.

Thursday 5th. *EbS to NW. Course N29°E. Lat. obsd. 66°14′. Longitude 86°28′. Var. N40W. The Mouth of the River Wager bore W44°S, Dist. 73 Miles.* Moderate & fair. Standing over to the South Shore;[1] Sounded from 41 to 40 & 35 fathom. At 4 Tack'd. Sounded 35, 36, 34 fathom. The Eastermt. Point on the South Side bore NEbE, the Westermt. SSW½W, 2 Leagues the Nearest; the Northmst. part on the North Side in Sight bore NEbE dist. 8 or 9 Leagues. At 6 pm. Sounded 35, 36, 35, 36 faths., Hard, rocky Ground. At 8 ditto the Easternmost pt of the South Shore bore EbS; the Southermt. Part SWbS the nearest Distance 3 Leagues; the Land on the North Side NE, the Westermt part WbN, the Mouth of the River Wager NW. At ½ past 8 Tack'd. At 9 Set the Mainsl. & Sounded 34 fathoms. At 12 Sounded across the Strait, and found from 46 to 48 fathom the greatest Depth. At ½ Past 12 haul'd up the Msail & Tack'd. Standing along the North Shore. At 2 a.m. sounded 38, 40 & 38 fathom; small brown stones, hard Ground, with Dark Colour'd Shells. At 4 a.m. Sounded 37, 34, & 41 fathm., ditto Ground. The Northermt. Part of the Land in Sight on the North Side bore NNE dist. 4 or 5 Leagues. At ½ past 6 Haul'd up the Foresail; Sounded from 33 to 25 fathom. At 8 Sounded 27, 44, & 43 fathm.[2] At 10 Saw much Ice to the Northward of us, near the Land, and about 3 Leagues from us. Sounded 37, 36, 38 & 40 fathoms. At 12 Sailing amongst Shatter'd Ice. Sounded 37 to 39 fathom, Hard rocky Ground. The Eastermost Point on the South Side bears NEbE, the Northermost Point on the North Side in Sight N½E. South is a low Beach, running EbN & WbS for 7 Leagues, low & even, and of the Shingle or Gravely Kind.[3]

---

[1] This is a little confusing, in that Middleton is referring to the coast of Southampton Island, which here runs north-south.

[2] Middleton's log entry for 8 a.m. also includes the comment 'The Tide runs all in eddies' (ibid., 5 Aug 1742).

[3] Middleton's log entry expands a little on this: '...a fine low even Beach like Dungeness. All the South Side, which I have yet seen, is of the same sort of Shingle or Gravel' (ibid., 5 Aug 1742).

At the East end of this Beach a very High, Mountainous, ragged Land, like Some Part of Hudsons Straits appears in Sight.[1] The Narrows or Straits, where we now are, is not above 8 or 9 Leagues broad; the Tide runs very Strong, with Eddies & Whirlings, that the Ship will Hardly Steer, and I find that the Flood Comes from the EbN by Compass. There is very good Soundings in this Strait, especially on the South Side, where you have 25 fathom ½ a Mile from the shore.

Friday 6th. NbE to NNW. Course North. Dist. in miles 36. Lat. obsd. 66°44'. Long. 87°21'. Var. N50W. Cape Hope bore SW, Distance 6 or 7 Leagues. Moderate & Hazy. Lay too [sic] from 12 to 1 for the Tender; try'd the Tide & found the Flood to come from the EbS; Sounded 45 fathom. The End or point of the beach[2] at 2 p.m. bore 4 or 5 Miles dist. At ½ Past 2 Sent the Lieut. with The 6 oar'd Boat on Shore to try what time of Tide it was, and found it had Ebb'd two foot, and that the Flood Came from the Eastward. At 3 made a Signal for the boat to come on board; Much Ice. At 4 made Sail; the Northermst. Land on the North Side in sight bore N½W, the Eastmst. on this Side ENE. At 6 Tack'd, a Ledge of Ice being a-Head, & stood a-Cross the Channel. Sounded 48, 44 & 48 fathom, Stoney Ground. The High Land in Sight, joining the low Beach, bore SbW dist. 6 Leagues. The Point of Land I nam'd Cape Hope NbE½E 5 Leagues. At 8 Sounded 32 & 35 fathom. At 9 Tack'd. Sounded 30 to 34 fathom, hard, rocky Ground. Much Ice in our Way. At 11 Sounded and had no Ground at 50 fathom. At 12 Cape Hope bore NWbW, working among Ice. At 2 sounded 35 to 38 fathom; much Ice in our Way, and Oblig'd often to tack for it. At 4 a.m. sounded 38 to 40 fathom, working & Sailing among Ice. At 5 Sounded 96 fathom well over to the Eastern Shore; Very High Land in this Bay. At 6 sounded 96 fathom, Shells. Sailing among Shatter'd Ice. Sounded 66 fathm. At ½ past 7 Tack'd. The Northermt. Point on the East NbW; ditto on the West Side NWbN 5 or 6 Leagues dist. Sailing among Ice. At 10 Sounded 66 fathm. Try'd the Tide & found little or none. At ½ Past 10

[1] This was the relatively high land of White Island (reaching heights of 1250') seen beyond the low, northern tip of Southampton Island.
[2] This, the northernmost tip of Southampton Island was named Beach Point on Middleton's map, but at some point it has been renamed Cape Munn.

Tack'd. Sounded 66, 68 & 70 fathom. At noon Cape Hope bore SW½S dist. 6 or 7 Leagues. At 4 in the Afternoon we saw a fair Cape or Head-land on the West or North Shore bearing from us as above, the Land trenching away from the EbN to the NbW making 8 Points of the Compass. This gave us Great Joy and Hopes of its being the Extream Part of America, and thereupon nam'd it Cape Hope.[1] We work'd up round it thro' much Stragling Ice all night. In the Morning when the Sun Clear'd away the Haze, to our Great Disappmt. we Saw the Land all round quite from the Low Beach to the Westward of the North, meeting the Western Shore, & made a deep Bay.[2] Then our Hopes of a Passage that way was all over, but, to make Sure, we kept on our Course to the Codd of it, untill two the Next Afternoon, when every one on board saw Plainly it was nothing but a Bay, and that we could not go above 6 or 8 Miles farther. We try'd the Tide Several times in the Fore & afternoon, and Still found it Slack water. So we concluded we had pass'd by Some Opening where the Tide came in at from the Eastward.

Saturday 7th. *WSW to SE. Lat. obsd. 66°21'. Long. 86°41'. Var. obsd. N45W. Ditto cape bore N½E, Dist. 5 or 6 Leagues.* Little Wind & fair Weather. At 2 p.m. tack'd in the Codd of the Bay, which bore NbW dist. 3 Leagues, and is about 6 or 7 Leagues from Side to Side, very High Land;[3] Cape Hope bore SW¾S. At 4 Sounded 74 fathom. Cape Hope then bore SW by Compass, dist. 6 or 7 Leagues. Sailing among Stragling Ice. At 12 Cape Hope bore WbN 4 or 5 Leagues dist. Sounded 105 fathom. At 4

---

[1] Unfortunately this very significant name appears to have been downgraded on the modern map. The culprit appears to have been Captain William Edward Parry; it is clear from both the text and the map in the account of his visit to Repulse Bay in 1821 that he misunderstood Middleton's descriptions and clearly did not have his map available. As a result he transferred the name Beach Point from the northern tip of Southampton Island across Roes Welcome Sound to Middleton's 'Cape Hope' and the name 'Cape Hope' to another headland a few miles to the west (Parry, *Journal of a Second Voyage for the Discovery of a North-West Passage*, p. 54).

[2] Repulse Bay. In his journal entry for the following day Moor confirms this report and also notes Middleton's naming of the bay: 'At 2 PM came up with the Furnace, lying too and trying the Tide, But cou'd find neither Ebb nor Flood to Run, for we cou'd see the Land all Round to the Northward for the furthermost part of it bore NNW from us and not above 4 Leagues Distance, which Capt. Middleton has named Repulse Bay' (Adm 51/290, pt IX, 7 Aug 1742).

[3] The land both west and south of Repulse Bay rises to about 750'.

Sounded 55 fathom. Continued Sailing among Ice. At ½ Past 5 Tack'd for the Tender. Sounded from 55 to 40 fathom. Much Ice to the Eastwd. of us. At 8 a.m. Tack'd, Cape Hope bearing NW½W dist. 6 Leagues; the Low Beach SW 4 or 5 Leagues; Sounded 55 fathom. At 10 I went ashore with the Boat taking my Gunner, Carpenter & Clerk[1] along with me, to try if I could find from whence the Flood Came in at to this Strait or Bay. At ½ Past 11 the Ship lay to for the Return of the Boat, and took a Reef in each Topsail. At Noon Cape Hope bore N½E 5 or 6 Leagues. The Beach WSW 4 Leagues. The Entrance of the Frozen Straits amongst the Islands on the East Side bore East 2 Leagues.

Sunday 8th. SE to ESE. Course S30°W. Dist 47 miles. Lat. obsd. 65°41'. Long. 87°42'. Var. obsd. N38°W. The South shore SWbW, Dist. 3 or 4 Leagues. Fresh Gales & Hazy Weather. At ½ Past 2 p.m. made Sail and Stood in Shore. Sounded from 33 to 27 fathom. At 4 Tack'd, Cape Hope Bearing N½E dist. 6 Leagues; the Beech SW½W, the Middle of the Frozen Straits ESE 3 Leagues. At 6 Tack'd & Stood in for the Boat. Sounded 60 fathom. At ½ Past 6 lay to for the Boat. At 8 Cape Hope Bore N½E or N; the low Beech Point WSW 4 or 5 Leagues. At ½ Past 9 I return'd on Board with the Boat. Continued Lying too; Much Ice all round us. At 2 a.m. bore away; fir'd a Gun for the Tender to do the Same. At 3 Sounded 35 fathom, dist. from the Beach one Mile. Cape Hope bore NEbN dist. 6 Leagues, the Point of the low Beech SEbE 9 Miles. Sailing along the South Shore, and about 3 Leagues dist. at 8 this Morning, which lieth as far as we can now see to the Westward WSW. At ½ Past 9 Lay'd to for the Tender. Much Ice on the West Shore, near one third over. At 12 the nearest Distance from the North Shore 8 or 9 Leagues; the South Shore SWbW dist. 3 or 4 Leagues. Sounded 33 fathom. I return'd on Board, as above mention'd, after having travelled in-land with the Gunner, Carpenter, my Clerk & one Indian, from one Mountain to another, about 15 Miles, untill we came to a very high one that overlook'd the Frozen Straits, and the East Bay on the Other Side, and could

---

[1] George Axx, John Hodgson, John Wigate.

See the Passage where the Flood came in at.[1] The narrowest Part of this Strait is 4 or 5 Leagues, and 5, 6, or 7 Leagues in the broadest, almost full of long, small Islands, and in Length about 16 or 18 Leagues. It stretches SE round to the South, and to the Westward we could see the Said Strait from the Beggining to the Ending all full of Ice not Yet broke up, all fast to both Shores, and the Islands therein. We saw very high Land about 15 or 20 Leagues to the Southd. of where we Stood[2] which I take to run toward the Head-land Bylot name'd Cape Comfort, being the farthest he went, and the Bay between this and the Cape Fox call'd Lord Weston's Portland & is Part of Hudson's North Bay, about NW from the West End of Nottingham Island, by comparing our Longitude with that of Fox or Bylot. This last mention'd Strait, being full of Ice, not yet broke up, and very Probably may Remain so this Year, if it breaks up at all, must be a Fortnight or three Weeks Hence, and then the Winter in these Parts set in. It was resolv'd in Council to try the other Side of the Welcome from Cape Dobbs to Brook Cobham, if we might happily find an Opening there, and then return to England.

[*The full record of the deliberations of this council reads as follows:*

At a Council held the 8th Day of *August*, 1742, on Board His Majesty's Ship *Furnace*. PRESENT, Capt. *Christopher Middleton*, President, *Wm. Moor*, Master and Commander of the *Discovery*, *John Rankin*, Lieutenant, *Robert Wilson*, Master, *The following Transactions were read, and unanimously agreed to*, viz.

August the 3rd, 1742. Unmoor'd and sailed out of *Wager* River, that River and the Straits being pretty clear of Ice, in pursuit of our Discovery. The 4th having contrary Winds and Calms, made but little Northing. On the 5th by Noon, got into the Latitude of 66°14', but met with much Ice and strong Tides. The same Day in the Evening, we discovered on the north Side of our new Straits, a Cape or Head Land bearing N, the Land on the south Side lyeth E.b.N. and W.b.S. and on the other Side N.b.W. which gave us all great Joy and Hopes of its being the extream north Part of *America*. We could see little or no Land to the northward of it, and deep Waters, very high Land, and strong Tides, when we were 4 or 5 Leagues short of it. This Capt.

---

[1] Middleton had hiked across White Island and back.
[2] This is the high northeast coast of Southampton Island, which does indeed extend southeast to Cape Comfort.

Middleton named *Cape Hope*. We turn'd or work'd round it the same night, and got 5 or 6 Leagues to the N.by W. before we could see any otherwise than fair and wide Straits, but the 6th Day about Noon, after having got into the Latitude of 66°40′, found we were embay'd, and by 2 in the Afternoon, could not go above 3 Leagues farther, having tried the Tides all the Forenoon till 2 o'Clock in the Afternoon but found neither Ebb nor Flood, yet deep Water. From this it was concluded, that we had overshot the Straits on the north Shore, where we found strong Tides that came from the E.b.S. but apparently no Passage; and as there was no proceeding above 3 or 4 Leagues farther, it was agreed upon by all to return back and search narrowly for the Straits, by finding from whence the Floods came. On the 7th, at 10 in the Forenoon, after we were confirmed the Flood came in on the north Side from E.b.S. Capt. *Middleton* went on Shore in the Boat, and found it flowed 15 Feet three Days after the Full, and a W.b.S. Moon made high Water. Capt. *Middleton*, together with the Gunner and Carpenter (who were two of the Boat's Crew, many of our People being very ill) went 12 or 15 Miles on the south Side of these Straits, and on the highest Hills they could find, saw the Passage that this Flood came in at, the Mountain they stood upon being pretty near 9 Leagues from the Entrance of this Strait out of the Bay the Ships were in, and from whence they could see about 12 or 15 Leagues farther; but for the 18 or 20 Leagues, it was fast with Ice not yet broke up, and running away S.E. and S.S.E. by Compass, with very high Land on both Sides, about 4 Leagues broad in the narrowest, and about 6 in the widest Part, with above 20 small Islands in the Middle and Sides, and it being then the 7th of *August*, and no Appearance of its clearing this Year, and near the 67th Degree of Latitude, no anchoring the Ship, being very near deep Water close to the Shore, and much Ice driving with the Ebb and Flood; but little Room if thick Weather should happen, which we could not but expect very soon, having had much clear Weather; for which Reasons it is agreed upon to make the best of our way out of this cold, dangerous and narrow Strait, and to make farther Observations between the Latitude of 64° and 63°, on the north Side of the *Welcome*, having seen large Openings, broken Land and Islands, with strong Tides, but had not Opportunity of trying from whence the Flood came in our Passage hither. Given under our Hands this 8th Day of *August*, 1742. *Christopher Middleton, John Rankin, William Moor, Robert Wilson, George Axe, John Hodgson.*][1]

Monday 9th. *EbN to NEbE. Course S25W. Dist. in miles 94. Lat.*

----

[1] Middleton, *Vindication*, pp. 112–14.

obsd. 64°10'. Long. 88°56'. Var. obsd. N33W. Cape Dobbs bore
N23°E, Dist. 21 Leagues. Fresh Gales and Clear Weather; sometimes Hazy. At ½ Past 12 made Sail, & bore away. At 2 p.m. the
Mouth of the River Wager bore NW¾N, 8 or 9 Leagues. At 4 set
all the Small Sails. Cape Dobbs bore NW¾W, dist. 6 Leagues. At
10 Sounded 50 fathom; at 12 Sounded 60 to 65 fathom. At 1
a.m. 56 to 50 fathm. At 4 ditto 43 to 25 fathm. Alter'd the
Course to deepen the Water. Haul'd up the Foresail. Sounded
34 fathom, 5 Leagues off the North Shore. At 6 reef'd the
Topsails, & lay to for moderate Weather. At 8 Sounded 66 to 70
fathom, Rocks & Stones. At 10 Sounded 68 fathom, ditto
Ground. At 12 Sounded 70 to 65 fathom. The Land on the
South Side in Sight bore EbS to South. It is about 16 or 18
Leagues broad here.

Tuesday 10th. *East to ENE. Course WbS. Dist in miles 53. Lat. obsd.
63°56'. Long. 90°53'. Var. obsd. N32W. Ditto bore N44East, Dist. 35
Leagues.* The first Part fresh Gales and Hazy; the Middle more
Moderate; the latter fresh Gales and hazy. At 1 p.m. Sounded 35
to 36 fathom. At 2 Wore Ship and lay'd to with her Head to the
Northward. At 4 Sounded 45, 44, 43 fathom. The Extream Points
of the South Shore in Sight bore from S to SEbE dist. 6 or 7
Leagues. At 7 Made Sail, and Stood in for the North Shore. At 8
Saw that & the So. Shore at the Same time. Sounded 60 fathom
in the Midway. At 10 Sounded 47, 46 and 45 fathom, then lay'd
to with her Head to the Northward. At 12 Sounded 45 to 43
fathom. At 2 a.m. sounded 47 to 45 fathom. At 4 Sounded 45 to
35 fathom. Wore Ship; the North Shore from NE to NNW, the
nearest Distance 4 or 5 Leagues. At 5 Made Sail; Sounded 45
fathm. At 8 Sounded 40, 39, 36, & 37 fathom, the North Shore
bearing from NbE to EbN. Kept as near the Shore as we Could
to see if there was any Openings or Passages in the Land. At 10
Sounded 29, 24, & 26 fathom, Rocky Stony Ground and Some
Sand. At 12 Sounded 35, 35, 34, 35 fathm. Let out the first Reef
of the Topsails.

Wensday 11th. *Ditto. Course W42S. Dist. in miles 54. Lat. obsd.
63°14'. Long. 92°25'. Var. obsd. N28W. Cape Dobbs bore N44E, Dist.
55 Leagues.* The first Part little Wind & fair Weather; the Middle
fresh Gales & Hazy; the Latter moderate and fair. At 2 p.m.

sounded from 30 to 34 & 36 fathm. At 4 Sounded 39 to 34 fathom. Set the Foresail. Continued Sailing in Sight of the Main Land of the North Shore quite from Cape Hope. Haul'd off to deepen our Water; Sounded at 6 & found 34 to 28 fathom Water. At 8 Sounded 29 to 35 & 40 fathom. Haul'd up the Foresail & double Reef'd both Topsails, then lay'd to till Day light. Sounded every hour & had from 44 to 65 fathom. At 4 a.m. made Sail. At 6 Stood in with a headland 9 or 10 Leagues to the East of Brook Cobham.[1] It bore NWbN 5 or 6 Leagues. Sounded 60 to 49 fathm. At 7 set the Foresail; sounded from 60 to 50 fathom. At 10 Sounded from 49 to 9 fathom, standing in for the Headland.[2] At 12 Haul'd off from the Head-Land to deepen our Water. At Noon saw the Island of Brook Cobham, which bore WbS 8 or 9 Leagues. Sounded 20 fathm, 4 Leagues off Shore. I find, by coasting along the Shore of the Welcome from the Frozen Strait to this Place, that it is the Main Land, tho' there are Several Small Islands & deep Bays. This Head-Land and the other in 64°[3] makes a Deep Bay. In our Passage out, we did not see the Bottom of it, as we have done Since,[4] and by keeping Closer in-shore we have seen many Large black Whales of the Right Whalebone Kind.

Thursday 12th. *NEbE to NE. Course W35S. Dist. in miles 40. Lat. obsd. 62°49'. Long. 93°43'. Var. N28W. The Middle of the Island of Brook Cobham bore NEbE, Dist. 4 or 5 Leagues.* Moderate and clear Weather. From Noon till 2 p.m. sounded 39, 30, 31, 25, 23, 17 fathm. Between 2 & four Sounded, 23, 20, 34, 38, 40 & 45 fathom. At 4 the South End of Brook Cobham Island bore WNW dist. 4 Leagues. At 6 Sounded 38, 24 & 25 fathom. At 8 brac'd to, and try'd the Tide, and found it came from the Eastward. Tack'd. At 10 Sounded 34, 37, 39 fathm. Lay to till Day light. At 12 Sounded 38, 37, & 35 fathom. At 2 Sounded 35, 36, 37, 39 fathom. At 4 Made Sail & Work'd to Windward. At 6

---

[1] Baker Foreland.

[2] Middleton's log entry for 10 a.m. includes the additional information: 'Two Leagues off saw several black Whales playing in shoal Water' (Adm 51/379, pt III, 11 Aug 1742).

[3] Cape Fullerton.

[4] Middleton is only partly correct here; he may well have seen the head of Daly Bay (the large embayment between Cape Fullerton and Baker Foreland) but he had not spotted the entrance of the long, narrow inlet of Chersterfield Inlet.

Tack'd & Stood in for the Island. At 8 Sounded 50, 46, 43 and 43 fathom. At noon the Island of Brook Cobham bore NEbE dist. 4 or 5 Leagues. At 3 a.m. I sent the Lieut. ashore[1] to try the Tides at Brook Cobham, and to See if we could Water the Ships there. The two Northern Indians went ashore with him. This Island is about 3 Leagues from the Main Land, about 7 Leagues Long, lying NWbW & SEbS by Compass, and is 3 Leagues over in the broadest Part. It is in the Latitude of 63°00' & Longitude from the Meridian of London 93°40'W; all white Hard Stone like Marble.

Friday 13th. *ENE. At Anchor. The Middle of the Island of Brook Cobham bore NEbE, Dist. 4 Leagues*. Moderate & Hazy. Continued working up towards the Island. Sounded 3 leagues off Shore; had 23, 15, 19, 16 & 15 fathom Water. At 2 Tack'd, the Body of the Island bearing ENE dist. 7 Miles, in 15 fathom Water. At 6 p.m. came to with our Small Anchor in 24 fathm. Water to Stop the Tide, and Wait for the Boat. The Tender by us. The Middle of the Island bore NEbE, dist. 4 Leagues. Fir'd a Gun every Half Hour from 8 to 12 Signals for the Boat. At 1 a.m. the Boat return'd. At 5 ditto I sent the Master & the 6 oar'd Boat for Water. At 12 made the Signal for the Boat to Come off. When the Lieut. return'd he gave me an Account that he had not been above 2 or 3 Hours Time on Shore, that it was neither High nor Low Water while he Staid there. At his first Landing he saw three Deer one of Which the Indians Shot, together wth. a White Bear.[2] They likewise Saw several Swans & Ducks.[3]

[1] Rankin took the six-oared boat (Adm 51/379, pt III, 12 Aug 1742).
[2] In his log Middleton mentions that the bear was brought on board, 'but it was very poor' (ibid., 13 Aug 1742).
[3] William Moor reports that at 9 a.m. on the 13th he too sent his yawl ashore for water. It returned at 6 pm with the intriguing news 'that there is a great Deal of the Wreck of Capt. Barlows Ship and Sloop, which were Supposed to be Lost near this Latit.' (Adm 51/290, pt IX, 13 Aug 1742). George Berley (or Barlow) was captain of James Knight's ship *Albany*, abandoned along with her consort *Discovery* at Marble Island in 1719, and hence if Moor's men were reporting seeing the actual wrecks, rather than just wreckage, this is the first known report of the sighting of the wrecks of Knight's vessels. Although Scroggs had found ample evidence of the shipwrecks in 1722 the discovery of the wrecks themselves in five fathoms of water is usually ascribed to Samuel Hearne during a sloop voyage to Marble Island in 1767. The wrecks are located in the almost land-locked body of water between Marble Island and Quartzite Island, i.e. at the east end of the former. Hence, since Rankin and party were ashore watering at the

Satturday 14. *NW to NNW*. Moderate Weather & variable Winds. At 4 p.m. the Boat Came on board wth. a Tun of Water. At 5 I sent her away for more. Fir'd a Gun Every Half Hour from 8 to 12. At 2 a.m. the Boat got on board with the Water. At 4 I sent the Boat away for More Water, together with the two Northern Indians who being desirous to [be] left near their own Country, I let them have a small Boat the Tender was Supply'd with at Churchill, which I caus'd them to be taught the Use of, and loaded it with Powder, Shot, Provision, Hatchets, Tobacco, & Toys of every Kind I had on board.

Sunday 15th. *NW to NNE. Course S21E. Dist. in miles 102. Lat. 61°25'. Long. 92°25'. Var. obsd. N26W. Brook Cobham bore N21W, dist. 34 Leagues*. The first Part little Wind & Calms, the Middle fresh Gales & Hazy; the latter fresh Gales with much Rain. At 4 p.m. weigh'd & Made a Signal for the Boat to come off. At 8 bore away, having got the Water & Boat in, the Body of the Island Brook Cobham bearing NEbN dist. 15 or 16 Miles. Sounded 55 fathom. At 12 Sounded 60 fathom. At 2 a.m. Sounded & found no Ground at 60 fathom. At 4 Sounded 70 to 76 fathom; again at 6 & 8 & found Still 70 fathm. At 10 Sounded 65 fathom; took the first Reef in each Topsail & took in the Mizen Topsail. At 12 Sounded 75 fathom. Our Boat return'd as above, and brought me an Account that by the Marks left on the Shore by the Tides, it flows there Some times 22 foot, & that a West or WbN Moon makes high. They left the two Northern Indians in the Island Brook Cobham,[1] who, as their Linguist

---

harbour at the west end of the island (quite unmistakable from his sketch map, Middleton, *Vindication*, p. 153) it is clear that the two parties explored a good deal of the island. What is surprising is that the watering party from *Discovery* did not see the abundant remains on shore which were discovered 25 years later by the crews of the HBC sloops *Success* and *Churchill* (including Samuel Hearne). These included the remains of a brick house, a large heap of coal, an anvil, cannon, shot and large quantities of wood chips (Williams, *British Search*, pp. 26–7; Kenney, *Founding of Churchill*). For a fuller discussion, and for the results of recent searches for relics of the Knight expedition see Geiger and Beattie, *Dead Silence*, especially ch. 7.

[1] Having first provided them with a boat. Moor records: 'Sent the two Northn. Indians and gave them our Yaul and everything else, that any of the two Ships Companys, cou'd think wou'd be of any Service to them' (Adm 51/290, pt IX, 15 Aug 1742).

told me, intended to go to the Main Land the first Oppertunity. The Indian Linguist being far from His Own Country, and desirous of Seeing England,[1] desir'd he might work as a Common Man on board, and wanting Some of my Compliment I enter'd him on the Ship's Book. I find I can do no more to the Purpose I am order'd upon, and my Men are Most of them very Much distemper'd, so that by Consultation we find the best Method to bear away for England.

[*The two ships reached the Orkneys on 15 September, and from here Middleton sent several reports and letters south. On the 19th he wrote the following letter to the Secretaries to the Admiralty Board from his anchorage at Cairston:*]

I beg leave to acquaint you for their Lordships Information, that on the 15th of September I arriv'd with his Majesty's Ship Furnace under my Command and the Discovery Tender, at the Isles of Orkney, where I have been oblig'd to put several of my Men Sick on shore being much distemper'd with the Scurvy, as indeed most of the Men of both Ships are. I only wait here to recruit them again after the Fatigues of the Voyage, and to impress Men to bring the Ships up, intending to proceed to the River Thames in a few Days, according to my Instructions.[2]

By 2 October when he reached the Thames, Middleton had compiled an abstract of the major events of the summer's voyage:

I sailed from Churchill the first Day of July, being the first Spurt of Wind I could get for sailing out of the Harbour, and continued sailing with a fair Wind, till the third, when we saw an Island, the two Extremities bearing N.b.E. and E.b.N lying in the Latitude of 63°00 north, and Longitude from Churchill 3°40 east, which I take to be the same which Fox named Brook Cobham. On the fifth Day, I saw a Head-Land on the north Side of the Welcome, bearing N.W.b.E. seven or eight Leagues distance, in the Latitude of 63°20, and Longitude from Churchill 4°00 east. Here I tried the Tides several times, and found close in with the Land the Tide to run two Miles an Hour from the N.b.E. which I take to be the Flood, and by the Slacks, from

---

[1] In his log entry Middleton adds the further information, 'and I having his Friends and the Governor's Consent to it' (Adm 51/379, pt III, 15 Aug 1742). 'His Friends' presumably refers to the other two Indians, and 'the Governor' one assumes, is Isham. For more on the Indians and their fate see pp. 308–11 below.

[2] Adm 1/2099, 19 Sep 1742.

several Trials, I found that a West or W.b.N. Moon made high Water, having a full Moon that Day. On the 8th Day, saw the north Side of the Welcome, with much Ice in Shore. I tried the Tide, and found it to set E.N.E. two Fathoms. On the ninth, continuing my Course, and sailing through much Ice, I was obliged at length to grapple to a large Piece. The Tender did the same to keep off from the Shore, the Wind blowing us right upon it. I tried the Tide frequently, and could discover neither Ebb nor Flood by my current Log. Here we were fast jamm'd up in the Ice, being totally surrounded for many Miles, and the Wind setting it right upon us, it was all Ice for ten leagues to Windward, and were in great Danger of being forc'd a-shore; but it happily falling calm, after we had lain in this Condition two or three days, the Pieces of Ice separated, or made small Openings, we being then within two Miles of the Shore, and with no little Difficulty haul'd the Ships from one Piece to another, till we got amongst what we call Sailing Ice: that is, where there are such Intervals of Water, as a Ship, by several Traverses, may get forwards towards the intended Course. In this manner we continued till we saw a fair Cape or Head Land to the northward of Whalebone-Point, in the Latitude of 65°10'N and Longitude from Churchill 8°54' East. This I named, after my worthy Friend, Cape Dobbs. I had very good Soundings between the two Shores of the Welcome, having 46, 48 and 49 Fathoms Water. At the same time that I saw Cape Dobbs, I saw a fair Opening bearing N.W. which, according to my Instructions, I stood in for among the sailing Ice. It was just Flood when we entered it; the Tide running very strong, which, by Observations afterwards, I found to run five or six Miles an Hour. I run over some Rocks on the north Side of it very luckily, being just high Water, and anchored in about 34 Fathoms; but as soon as the Tide of Ebb was made, it ran so strong, and such Quantities and Bodies of Ice came down upon us, that we were obliged to steer the Ship all the time, and keep all Hands upon their Guard with Ice-poles to shove off the Ice; notwithstanding which it brought our Anchor home, and taking hold again, one of the Arms of the Anchor was broke off.

The next day, I sent my Lieutenant in the Boat to seek out some securer Place for the Ships, it being impossible to keep a-float where we were. Some Uskimay Savages came off to us, but had nothing to trade, I us'd them civilly, made them some Presents, and dismissed them. As soon as I got the Ships secur'd, I employ'd all my Officers and Boats, having myself no little Share in the Labour, in trying the Tides, and discovering the Course and Nature of this Opening, and after repeated Trials for three weeks successively, I found the Flood constantly to come from the eastward, and that it was a large River we were got into, but so full of Ice, there was no stirring the Ships, with any probability of Safety, while the Ice was driving up and down with the strong Tides. Here I lay not a little impatient to get out; went several times in my Boat towards the Mouth of the River, and from a Hill that over-look'd Part of the Welcome, saw that Place full of Ice; so that I found there was no time lost by our being in Security; however, I sent my Lieutenant and Master in the eight-oar'd Boat to look out for a Harbour near the Entrance of the River, but they found none, and it was a small Miracle they got on board again; for they were so jamm'd up with Ice, which driving, the strong Tides would inevitably have stove the Boat to-pieces, and all must have perished, had it not been for an Opening in a large Piece of Ice into which they got the Boat, and with it drove out of the River's Mouth; but when the Tides lack'd [sic], the Ice open'd as usual, and they row'd over to the north Shore, so got in with the Flood. I several times sent the Indians on shore, to see if they knew any thing of the Land; but they were quite ignorant of it. In this vexatious Condition I continued for 3 Weeks, resolving to get out the first Opportunity the River was any thing clear of Ice, and make what Discoveries I could by meeting the Flood-Tide. This River, which, by frequent Trials of the Lands, Soundings, Tides, etc. I was able to take a Draught of, I nam'd the River Wager, after the Right Honourable Sir Charles Wager, etc.

On the third of August, the River for the first time was a little clear of Ice, and accordingly in pursuit of our Discovery, and on the fifth by Noon got into the Latitude of 66°14′. We had then got into a new Strait, much pester'd with Ice, and on the north Side of which we saw a Cape or Head Land bearing north; we had deep Water, and very strong Tides within four or five Leagues of it. I named this Head Land Cape Hope, as it gave us all great Joy and Hopes of its being the extreme north part of America, seeing little or no Land to the northward of it. We turned or worked round it the same Night, and got five or six Leagues to the N.b.W. before we could perceive any otherwise than a fair and wide Opening; but about Noon the sixth Day, after having got into the Latitude of 66°40′, found we were imbay'd, and by two in the Afternoon could not go above three Leagues farther, and having tried the Tides, all the Forenoon, every two Hours until two o'clock in the Afternoon, found neither Ebb nor Flood, yet deep Waters. From this it was concluded, that we had over-shot the Straits on the north-east Shore, from whence the Flood came; and as there was no proceeding above 3 or 4 Leagues further, it was agreed upon by all to return back and search narrowly for a Strait or Opening near where we found the strong Tides. On the seventh, after we were confirmed the Flood came in at the north-east from the E.b.S. I went on Shore in the Boat, and found it flowed 15 Feet, three Days after the Full, and a W.b.S. Moon made high water. I travelled twelve or fifteen Miles from Hill to Hill inland, till I came to a very high Mountain, from whence I plainly saw a Strait or Opening the Flood came in at, and the Mountain I stood upon being pretty near the Middle of this Strait, I could see both Ends of it; the whole being about 18 or 20 Leagues broad, and very high Land on both Sides of it, having many small Islands in the Middle and on the Sides of it; but it was all froze fast from Side to Side, and no Appearance of its clearing this Year, and near the 67th Degree of Latitude, and no anchoring the Ships, being very deep Water close to the Shore, and much large Ice driving with the Ebb and Flood, and but little Room if thick Weather should happen, which we continually expect in these Parts; it was agreed upon in Council to make the best of our way out of this dangerous narrow Strait, and to make Observations between the 64th and 62d Degree of Latitude. The Frozen Strait I take to run towards that which Bylot named Cape Comfort; and the Bay where Fox had named a Place Lord Weston's Portland. It is in the Latitude of 66°40, and 12°49 east from Churchill.

Pursuant to this Resolution we bore away, and tried the Tides on the other Side of the Welcome, sounding and observing close in there, but met with little Encouragement. On the 11th of August, I once more saw the Island of Brook Cobham, and continued trying the Tide, and still finding the Flood came from the eastward, and by coasting along the Welcome, was certain of its being the main Land, tho' there are several small Islands and deep Bays, and saw several Black Whales of the right Whalebone kind. I work'd off and on by Brook Cobham, sent the northern Indians a-shore upon the Island, who, at their Return, gave me to understand it was not far from their Country, and desir'd I would let them go home, being tired of the Sea. I kept them with Assurances, that I would act according to my Promise; and finding no Probability of a Passage in two or three Days after, I gave them a small Boat, well fitted with Sails and Oars, the Use of which they had been taught, and loaded it with Fire-Arms, Powder, Shot, Hatchets, and everything desirable to them. They took their leave of me, and I sent another Boat for Water, which accompanid them a-shore, the southern Indian being with them. The southern Indian, who was Linguist for the northern ones, returned with the Boat, being used to the English Customs at the Factory, and desirous of seeing England, being a willing, handy Man, I brought him with me.[1] And the same Evening,

---

[1] The 'Southern' or Cree Indian did not survive long. On 5 May 1743 the Hudson's Bay Company wrote to Isham at Churchill that 'Scooth the other Indian arrived here but died soon after in Capt. Middletons Service' (HBC A 6/7, f. 23d).

which was the 15th of August, I bore away for England, thinking to have tried the Tide at Carey's Swan's Nest, but could not fetch it. On the 20th saw Mansel's Isle. On the 21st Cape Diggs was in sight. On the 26th made Cape Resolution, and arrived at Cairston in Pomona, one of the Islands of Orkney; most of my Men being so very much afflicted with the Scurvy, and otherwise sick and distempered, that I shall be obliged to leave Part of them behind me, and only wait to impress Hands to carry the Ships safe to London. For the Particulars, I must refer you to my journal and Draught I shall send to the Admiralty, this Sheet of Paper being not sufficient for the particular Accidents.[1]

According to Middleton copies were sent 'to the Admiralty, the Navy, and to Mr. D...- in Ireland'. More probably this means copies to the Admiralty, to Sir Charles Wager personally, and to Dobbs. The copy in the Admiralty files has an additional two sentences at the end: 'I sail'd from the Orkneys the 24th of the same Month [September], and having variable Winds and Weather, am now working up the River Thames to moor at Galleons Reach, there to wait farther Orders. For the particulars of the Voyage I humbly refer their Lordships to my Journal and Draught'.[2] Over the next two months in at least three letters to Thomas Corbett, one of the Secretaries to the Admiralty, Middleton had occasion to make reference to the calibre of the men with whom he had made the voyage to Hudson Bay:

Middleton to Thomas Corbett, 16 October 1742, Woolwich.

I beg leave to acquaint you for the Information of my Lds Commrs of the Admiralty that this Day I receiv'd their Lordships Order of the 15th Instant in Relation to the five Men,[3] who are thereby directed to be discharg'd into the Cornwall; and, in Answer thereto I desire their Lordships may be acquainted, that I should have been glad to have got rid of them long ago, and I am only sorry Capt. Stapylton is to be troubled with such Villains; for notwithstanding I have used them all the Voyage with great Lenity, and Indulgence, and have order'd them near a third more Provisions than his Majts. Allowance, they have broke open and plundered almost every Cask in the Ship, by which I am no small Sufferer, and now have deserted the Ship under my Command without any Leave or Notice, and intic'd all the common Hands to do the same, who, I believe did not want much

---

[1] Middleton, *Vindication*, pp. 114–19.

[2] Adm 1/2099 [2 Oct 1742].

[3] Four names are given in the margin: Jn Exelby, Wm French, Wm Miller, Wm Gay.

Invitation; for, certainly no Ship was ever pester'd with such a Set of Rogues, most of them having deserv'd hanging before they entered with me, and not three Seamen among the whole Number of private Men, so that had it not been for the Officers, who, every one of them, work'd like common Men, I should have found no little difficulty to get the Ships to England...[1]

Middleton to Thomas Corbett, 28 October 1742, Woolwich

...We were oblig'd to put 8 of our Hands to sick Quarters at the Orkneys, and being 10 short of our Compliment besides; nay even of those we had aboard, officers excepted, not above 3 or 4 that were able either to go aloft or stand at the Helm, being so afflicted with the Scurvy...[2]

Middleton to Thomas Corbett, 24 November 1742, Woolwich

... of those Men whom I carry'd out with me, not one third of them were Seamen; that 14 of the very best died in the Country where I winter'd; that it was a small Miracle to preserve the Vessels afterwards upon my Voyage, and bring them safe home, having at that Time not above two Men that could go to the Helm; above one half being afflicted with the Scurvy in a miserable Manner.[3]

At almost exactly the same time as Middleton was writing his summaries, the general public was provided with an account of the expedition, in the form of two letters written (one at Churchill and the other at the Orkneys on the return voyage) by John Lanrick, one of the 'young gentlemen' who had participated in it, which appeared in The Gentleman's Magazine:

From on Board his Majesty's Ship the Furnace, in Churchill River, North America, June 21, 1742.

The 27th of June we left the Orkneys. The 16th of July we made Cape Farewell, about 446 Leagues to the Westward of the Orkneys, and about four or five Leagues distant from us. The Land, which was rocky and high, was cover'd with Snow. The 25th of July we made the Island of Resolution, which makes one Side of the Straits Mouth; and here we were pretty much in Danger, on Account of the thick Fogs, being close upon the Land before we could perceive it, and having a Fresh Wind right in upon the Shore. In the Straits we met with a great many Islands of Ice, some of them 50 Fathoms perpendicular

---

[1] Ibid. [16 Oct 1742].
[2] Ibid. [28 Oct 1742].
[3] Ibid. [24 Nov 1742].

above Water, and three Times as much under; these Islands make Yearly from the Northward away to the Southward, where they melt and decay. The 3d of August we fell in with a grest deal of broken Ice, but, soon got clear of it. On the 5th we saw a large Cake or Field of Ice, which from the Top mast Head we could not see over; but by standing to the Windward for 84 Hours we got clear of it, and the 7th of Aug. made the Land about Churchill River, which lies in 59°10 N. Latitude and Longitude from London above 83 Deg. W. The 8th we got into the River's Mouth and moor'd Ship. Here is an English Settlement, or Factory, belonging to the Hudson's-bay Company, with a strong Fort, where we resolved to winter, seeing the Season was then too far spent for proceding on our intended Discovery.

The Winter sets in here about the Beginning of Sept. and continues till June, during which the Ground is all covered with Snow and Ice. But it is impossible to give a just Idea of the Severity óf the Weather, to those who have never personally seen or felt its Effects; it generally frezes to such a Degree, that no Man whatsoever is able to face the Weather with any Part of his Body naked or exposed, but in the shortest Space of Time he is exposed, in such a Manner, that the Part turns whitish and solid like Ice, and when thaw'd, blisters like scalding or burning. Several of our Men have lost their Toes and Fingers by being froze, nay, the Spirit of Wine or Brandy freeze and turn solid; our Cloathing is a Beaver or Skin tuggy,[1] above our other Cloaths, Shoes of Deer-Skin, with three or four Socks of thick Blanketting or warm Cloth above our Stockings; Mittens of Beaver lined with Duffield or thick Cloth; and a Beaver Cap with a Chin Cloth which covers the greatest Part of the Face; and when we walk out, we use a Pair of Snow Shoes, made of Thongs of Deer-Skin, about six Foot in Length, and a Foot and a half in Breadth, to support us from sinking in the Snow; the Ice we found to be seven Foot thick in the Middle of the Stream in the River. There is no Disease or Distemper prevails here, unless it be the Scurvy, of which we have lost ten of the best of our Seamen; there are great Plenty of Partridges in the Winter Time, which are entirely white, and a Vast Flight of Wild Geese in the Fall of [sic] the Spring. We have had no less than 6000 Geese killed this Spring, by about 20 Indians, 3000 we have got salted for Use, besides 5 or 600 we used fresh. The Soil is but a barren Kind, tho' Plenty of Wood, such as Pine, which is the only Tree that grows here. The Native Indians are a very active People, but unmindful of Futurity, only careful of the present; they are of a swarthy Colour, and middle Stature.

They trade in all Kinds of Furs with the English, for Brandy,

---

[1] A calf-length beaver coat.

Tobacco, Guns, Powder, Shot, and little nice Fineries, of which they
are very proud; but Opportunity won't allow me to give a particular
Description of them. They dwell in Tents and remove from Place to
Place as best suits their Turn. The 1st of June the River broke up, and
in a few Days after we get the Ships out into the Stream after two
Months unspeakable Toil, in cutting them clear of the Ice; and now
we have got all Things ready for Sea, full of Hopes of Success, and
desirous to get rid of this dismal Country. In Case we meet with
Success we shall be out another Winter, and lie at California, on the
other Side of the Continent.

I am, etc. J. L.

Orkneys, Sept. 19.

The 1st Day of July we set out from Churchill Fort, on our intended Discovery. The 8th we enter'd Sir Tho. Roe's Welcome, which
is about 14 Leagues across; the 9th we fell in with a vast Body of
broken Ice, in which we were inveigled three Days, being obliged to
ply our Warps and Grapnels; the 12th, having got amongst thinner
Ice, we set Sail, and stood over for the North Shore. In the Latitude
65. 10. we named a high Land CAPE DOBBS, in Honour of 'Squire
Dobbs. Observing an Opening to the Northward of the Cape, we
stood in for it, designing to come to an Anchor to try the Tides; but
finding that it was the Mouth of a great River, we run eight Leagues
up it, and at last were obliged to come to an Anchor amongst broken
Ice, where we rode in the greatest Danger. Here several Usquemays
came off in their Canoes, who saluted us with their Shrieks and
hideous Yells, and brought us some Whalebone and Train Oil, which
they gave us for little Bits of Iron, of which they are wonderfully
fond. They are People of a very swarthy Complexion, well made,
vigorous and active, but by Accounts of them, of savage Dispositions,
tho' I think quite otherwise; they wander from Place to Place, and live
by hunting and fishing, in which they are very expert in their own
Way. During our Stay in the River Wager, we killed a good many
Deer; we were obliged to stay here for 16 Days and could not possibly
put to Sea on Account of the prodigious Quantity of Ice. The 4th of
Aug. we left the River, and stood away for the Northward, being
blessed with fine Weather; we had a full Prospect of the Land on each
Side; in the Latitude 66°30 we saw the Land stretch away to the
Westward, which gave us great Hopes, but afterwards found it to be
nothing but a Bay Land all round; then standing away for another
Opening on the East Side, we laid the Ship to, and went ashore to

take a Survey, from the Top of a high Mountain, when we could see the Sea all froze in one solid Body for about 20 Leagues to the S.E. and finding at the same Time that the Flood Tide came from thence, we were fully confirmed that it had a Communication with the East Sea, and that there was no such Thing as a Passage into the Western Ocean, as was expected. The 8th of August we bore away to the Southward, and made some further Search about the Latitude of 64°. Thus having travers'd all along the Bay, the 15th we took our Farewell of the Bay; the 20th we made the Head of the Strait; the 26th got clear of them, and lost Sight of Land. In the Passage from the Straits we had very strong Gales, tho' pretty fair. The 15th of September we came in at Hoy Sound, and anchor'd in Stormness [*sic*] Harbour.

Never were Ships worse manned; several of our Men are dead in the Country, the one Half of the Remainder so taken with the Scurvy, that they have been uncapable of doing Duty.

I am, etc., J. L.[1]]

---

[1] *The Gentleman's Magazine*, XII (November 1742), pp. 586–7.

2. Captain Middleton's Paper to the Royal Society, October 1742

CAPTAIN MIDDLETON'S ACCOUNT OF THE EXTRAORDINARY DEGREES AND SURPRIZING EFFECTS OF COLD IN HUDSON'S-BAY, NORTH AMERICA,[1]

read before the Royal Society, Oct. 28. 1742

I Observed, that the *hares, Rabbits,*[2] *Foxes* and *Partridges,*[3] in *September,* and the Beginning of *October,* changed their native Colour to a snowy White; and that for six Months, in the severest Part of the Winter, I never saw any but what were all white, except some *Foxes* of a different Sort, which were grizled, and some half red, half white.[4]

That Lakes and standing Waters, which are not above 10 or 12 Feet deep, are frozen to the ground in Winter, and the Fishes therein all perish.

Yet in Rivers near the Sea, and Lakes of a greater Depth than

---

[1] Printed in *Philosophical Transactions,* XLII (1742–3), 157–71. To place Middleton's discussion of the climate of Churchill in perspective it may be useful to review the present-day climatic data. The January mean temperature at Churchill is −27.6°C and the extreme minimum is −45°C. In summer the July mean temperature is 12°C and the extreme maximum is 32.7°C. Mean annual temperature is −7.3°C. Mean annual precipitation is 390.3 mm. Since Middleton's expedition occurred at the height of the colder phase known as the Little Ice Age, or Neoglacial, temperatures then were probably a few degrees lower than at present.

[2] It is difficult to be sure as to the distinction Middleton is making between hares and rabbits. However it seems likely that he is differentiating between the smaller snowshoe hare (*Lepus americanus*), whose average weight is about 3.3 lb and the much larger Arctic hare (*Lepus arcticus*), whose average weight is about 10.3 lb. The ranges of the two species overlap in the Churchill area (Banfield, *Mammals of Canada,* pp. 80–88).

[3] By partridges Middleton is referring to the willow ptarmigan (*Lagopus lagopus*) and/or the rock ptarmigan (*Lagopus mutus*). Only the former nests in the Churchill area but the winter ranges overlap here; the rock ptarmigan, generally a tundra species, moves south of the treeline in winter to some extent (W. E. Godfrey, *The Birds of Canada,* Ottawa, 1966, pp. 110–12).

[4] Here the white foxes to which Middleton refers are unquestionably arctic foxes (*Lagopus lagopus*), the 'different sort' might be either individual arctic foxes which were slow in changing colour, or more probably silver foxes or cross foxes, i.e. colour phases of the red fox, *Vulpes vulpes,* which also occurs in the Churchill area (Banfield, *Mammals of Canada,* pp. 295–301).

10 or 12 Feet, Fishes are caught all the Winter, by cutting Holes through the Ice down to the Water, and therein putting Lines and Hooks. But if they are to be taken with Nets, they cut several Holes in a strait Line the Length of the Net, and pass the Net, with a Stick fastened to the Head-line, from Hole to Hole, till it reaches the utmost Extent; and what Fishes come to these Holes for Air, are thereby entangled in the Net; and these Fish, as soon as brought into the open Air, are instantaneously frozen as stiff as Stock-fish.[1] The Seamen likewise freshen their salt Provisions, by cutting a large Hole through the Ice in the Stream or Tide of the River, which they do at the Beginning of the Winter, and keep it open all that Season. In this Hole they put their salt Meat, and the Minute it is immersed under Water, it becomes pliable and soft, though before its Immersion it was hard frozen.

Beef, *Pork*, *Mutton*, and *Venison*, that are killed at the Beginning of the Winter, are preserved by the Frost, for six or seven Months, intirely free from Putrefaction, and prove tolerable good Eating. Likewise *Geese*, *Partridges*, and other Fowl, that are killed at the same time, and kept with their Feathers on, and Guts in, require no other Preservative but the Frost to make them good wholesome Eating, as long as the Winter continues. All kinds of Fish are preserved in the like Manner.

In large Lakes and Rivers, the Ice is sometimes broken by imprisoned Vapours; and the Rocks, Trees, Joists and Rafters of our Buildings, are burst with a Noise not less terrible than the firing off a great many Guns together. The Rocks which are split by the Frost, are heaved up in great Heaps, leaving large Cavities behind; which I take to be caused by imprisoned watery Vapours, that require more Room, when frozen, than they occupy in their fluid State. Neither do I think its is unaccountable, that the Frost should be able to tear up Rocks and Trees, and split the Beams of our Houses, when I consider the great Force and Elasticity thereof. If Beer or Water is left in Mugs,

---

[1] This technique of ice-fishing is described in greater detail by Samuel Hearne on the basis of his travels with the Chipewyan in 1770–72 (Hearne, *Journey to the Northern Ocean*, pp. 11–12). It is still widely used across the North American Subarctic; see for example illustrations and discussion in E. S. Rogers and J. G. E. Smith, 'Environment and Culture in the Shield and Mackenzie Borderlands' in: J. Helm, ed., *Handbook of North American Indians*, Vol. 6, *Subarctic*, Washington, 1981, p. 136.

Cans, Bottles, nay in Copper-pots, though they were put by our Bed-sides, in a severe Night, they are surely split to pieces before Morning, not being able to withstand the expansive force of the inclosed Ice.

The Air is filled with innumerable Particles of Ice, very sharp and angular, and plainly perceptible to the naked Eye. I have several times this Winter tried to make Observations of some celestial Bodies, particularly the Emersions of the Satellites of *Jupiter*, with reflecting and refracting Telescopes; but the Metals and Glasses, by that Time I could fix them to the Object, were covered by a quarter of an Inch thick with Ice, and thereby the Object rendered indistinct, so that it is not without great Difficulties that any Observations can be taken.

Bottles of *strong Beer, Brandy, strong Brine, Spirits of Wine*, set out in the open Air for three or four Hours, freeze to solid Ice. I have tried to get the Sun's Refraction here to every Degree above the Horizon, with *Elton*'s Quadrant, but to no purpose, for the Spirits froze almost as soon as brought into open Air.

The Frost is never out of the Ground, how deep we cannot be certain. We have dug down 10 or 12 Feet, and found the Earth hard frozen in the two Summer Months; and what moisture we find five or Six feet down, is white like Ice.[1]

The Waters or Rivers near the Sea, where the Current of the Tide flows strong, do not freeze above 9 or 10 Feet deep.

All the Water we use for Cooking, Brewing, etc. is melted Snow and Ice; no Spring is yet found free from freezing, though dug never so deep down. All Waters inland are frozen fast by the Beginning of *October*, and continue so till the Middle of *May*.

The Walls of the House we live in[2] are of Stone, two Feet thick, the Windows very small, with thick wooden Shutters, which are close shut 18 Hours every Day in the Winter. There are Cellars under the house, wherein we put our *Wines, Brandy, strong Beer, Butter, Cheese* etc. Four large Fires are made in great

[1] Churchill lies at the southern limit of continuous permafrost, i.e. the area within which 100% of the land surface is underlain by permafrost. With the exception of a surface layer known as the active layer and varying in depth between a few inches and perhaps six feet, the ground is frozen to a depth (in the Churchill area) of approximately 195 feet.
[2] This was the two-storey stone house inside the court-yard at Fort Prince of Wales, of which only the first storey has been restored.

Stoves, built on purpose, every Day: As soon as the Wood is burnt down to a Coal, the Tops of the Chimneys are close stopped with an iron Cover: This keeps the Heat within the House (though at the same time the Smoke makes our Heads ake, and is very offensive and unwholsome); notwithstanding which, in four or five Hours after the Fire is out, the Inside of the Walls of our House and Bed-places will be two or three Inches thick with Ice, which is every Morning cut away with a Hatchet. Three or four times a Day we make Iron Shot of 24 Pounds Weight red-hot, and hang them up in the Windows of our Apartments. I have a good Fire in my Room the major Part of the 24 Hours; yet all this will not preserve my *Beer, Wine, ink,* etc. from freezing.

For our Winter Dress we make use of three Pair of Socks of coarse Blanketing or Duffield for the Feet, with a Pair of *Deer-skin*[1] Shoes over them; two Pair of thick *English* Stockings, and a Pair of Cloth Stockings upon them; Breeches lined with Flannel; two or three *English* Jackets, and a Fur or Leather Gown over them; a large Beaver Cap, double, to come over the Face and Shoulders, and a Cloth of Blanketing under the Chin; with Yarn Gloves, and a large Pair of Beaver Mittings hanging down from the Shoulders before, to put our Hands in, which reach up as high as our Elbows; yet notwithstanding this warm Cloathing, almost every Day, some of the Men that stir abroad, if any Wind blows from the northward,[2] are dreadfully frozen; some have their Arms, Hands, and Face blister'd and frozen in a terrible manner, the Skin coming off soon after they enter a warm House, and some have lost their Toes. Now their lying-in for the Cure of these frozen parts, brings on the Scurvy in a lamentable manner. Many have died of it, and few are free from that Distemper. I have procured them all the Helps I could, from the Diet this Country affords in Winter, such as fresh Fish, Part-ridges, etc. and the Doctors have used their utmost Skill in vain; for I find nothing will prevent that Distemper from being mor-tal, but Exercise and stirring abroad.

Coronae and *Parhelia,* commonly called *Halo's,* and *Mock-Suns,*

---

[1] I.e. caribou-skin.
[2] Fort Prince of Wales is located on a particularly exposed headland, and experiences extreme wind-chill conditions in winter.

appear frequently about the Sun and Moon here. They are seen once or twice a Week about the Sun, and once or twice a Month about the Moon, for four or five Months in the Winter, several *Coronae* of different Diameters appearing at the same time.

I have seen five or six parallel *Coronae* concentric with the Sun several times in the Winter, being for the most part very bright, and always attended with *Parhelia* or *Mock-Suns*. The *Parhelia* are always accompanied with *Coronae*, if the Weather is clear; and continue for several Days together, from the Sun's Rising to his Setting. These Rings are of various Colours, and about 40 or 50 Degrees in Diameter.

The frequent Appearance of these *Phaenomena* in this frozen Clime seems to confirm *Descartes's* Hypothesis, who supposes them to proceed from Ice suspended in the Air.[1]

The *Aurora Borealis* is much oftner seen here than in *England;*[2] seldom a Night passes in the Winter free from their Appearance. They shine with a suprising Brightness, extinguishing all the Stars and Planets, and covering the whole Hemisphere: Their tremulous Motion from all Parts, their Beauty and Lustre, are much the same as in the northern Parts of *Scotland, Denmark*, etc.

The dreadful long Winters here may almost be compared to the Polar Parts, where the Absence of the Sun continues for six Months; the Air being perpetually chilled and frozen by the northerly Winds in Winter, and the cold Fogs and Mists obstructing the Sun's Beams in the short Summer we have here; for notwithstanding the Snow and Ice is then dissolved in the Low-lands and Plains, yet the Mountains are perpetually covered with Snow, and incredibly large Bodies of Ice continue in the adjacent Seas. If the Wind blows from the southern Parts, the Air is tolerably warm, but insufferably cold when it comes from the northward, and it seldom blows otherwise than between the north-east and the north-west, except in the two Summer Months, when we have, for the major part, light Gales between the east and the north, and Calms.

---

[1] The occurrence of parhelia is indeed usually associated with ice crystals in the air.

[2] Churchill lies within the circumpolar belt of maximum auroral activity (or auroral oval) and, on average experiences auora on 243 days per year. The incidence of aurora decreases both north and south from this belt of maximum occurrence. See: C. Störmer, *The Polar Aurora*, Oxford, 1955, fig. 17, p. 15.

The northerly Winds being so extremely Cold, is owing to the Neighbourhood of high Mountains,[1] whose Tops are perpetually covered with Snow, which exceedingly chills the Air passing over them. The Fogs and Mists that are brought here from the Polar Parts, in Winter, appear visible to the naked eye in Icicles innumerable, as small as fine Hairs or Threads, and pointed as sharp as Needles. These Icicles lodge in our Cloaths, and if our Faces be uncovered, they presently raise Blisters as white as Linnen Cloth, and as hard as Horn. Yet if we immediately turn our Backs to the Weather, and can bear our Hand out of our Mitten, and with it rub the blistered Part for a small time, we sometimes bring the Skin to its former State: If not, we make the best of our way to a Fire, and get warm Water, wherewith we bathe it, and therby dissipate the Humours raised by the frozen Air; otherwise the Skin would be off in a short time, with much hot, serous, watry Matter coming from under along with the Skin; and this happens to some almost every time they go abroad for five or six Months in the Winter, so extreme cold is the Air when the Wind blows any thing strong.[2]

Now I have observed, that when it has been extreme hard Frost by the Thermometer, and little or no Wind that Day, the Cold has not near so sensibly affected us, as when the Thermometer has shewed much less freezing, having a brisk Gale of northerly Wind at the same time. This Difference may perhaps be occasioned by those sharp-pointed Icicles before-mentioned striking more forcibly in a windy Day, than in calm Weather, thereby penetrating the naked Skin, or Parts but thinly covered, and causing an acute Sensation of Pain or Cold: And the same Reason, I think, will hold good in other Places; for should the Wind blow northerly any thing hard for many Days together in *England*, the Icicles that would be brought from the Polar Parts by the Continuance of such a Wind, though imperceptible to the naked Eye, would more sensibly affect the naked Skin, or Parts but slightly covered, than when the Therometer has shewn a

---

[1] Middleton is in error here; there are no high mountains to the north or northwest of Churchill. The low winter temperatures are due to a combination of continentality and high latitude.

[2] This is an accurate description of the occurrence and appearance of frostbite, but it is purely due to the flesh freezing and is not caused directly by the ice particles in the air.

greater Degree of freezing, and there has been little or no Wind at the same time.[1]

It is not a little surprising to many, that such extreme Cold should be felt in these Parts of America, more than in Places of the same Latitude on the Coast of *Norway*; but the Difference I take to be occasioned by the Wind blowing constantly here, for seven Months in the twelve, between the north-east and north-west, and passing over a large Tract of Land, and exceeding high Mountains, etc. as before mentioned: Whereas at *Drunton*[2] in *Norway*, as I observed some Years ago in wintering there, the Wind all the Winter comes from the north and north north-west, and crosses a great Part of the Ocean clear of those large Bodies of Ice we find here perpetually.[3] At this Place we have constantly every Year nine Months Frost and Snow, and unsufferable Cold from *October* till the Beginning of *May*. In the long Winter, as the Air becomes less ponderous towards the *Polar Parts*, and nearer to an *Aequilibrium*, as it happens about one Day in a Week, we then have Calms and light Airs all round the Compass, continuing sometimes 24 Hours, and then back to its Old Place again, in the same manner as it happens every Night in the *West-Indies*, near some of the Islands.

The Snow that falls here is as fine as Dust, but never any Hail, except at the Beginning and End of Winter. Almost every Full and Change of the Moon, very hard Gales from the north.

The constant Trade Winds[4] in these northern Parts I think undoubtedly to proceed from the same Principle, which our

---

[1] Middleton's observations as to the effects of wind-chill are quite sound, i.e. the accelerated loss of heat from the skin caused by mechanical advection of heat from the skin as well as by conduction and radiation. It has little to do with ice crystals, as he attempts to argue.

[2] Trondheim.

[3] Middleton is correct in ascribing the milder winters of the Norwegian coast in the same latitude as Churchill to the moderating influence of the ocean, but it should be noted that that particular coast experiences an unusually mild winter (i.e. has a large positive temperature anomaly) even for a coastal area due to the benign influence of the North Atlantic Drift, originating (as the Gulf Stream) in the Gulf of Mexico.

[4] This is a peculiar use of the term 'Trade Winds'. It is now customarily applied to what Middleton refers to as the 'Trade Winds near the Equator', namely the Northeast and Southeast Trade Winds, driven by the pressure gradient between the Subtropical Highs and the low-pressure belt of the Intertropical Convergence.

learned Dr. *Halley* conceives to be the Cause of the Trade Winds near the Equator, and their Variations.

'Wind,' says he, 'is most properly defined to be the Stream or Current of the Air; and where such Current is perpetual and fixed in its Course, it is necessary, that it proceed from a permanent and unin-termitting Cause, capable of producing a like constant Effect, and agreeable to the known Properties of Air and Water, and the Laws of Motion of fluid Bodies. Such an one is, I conceive, the Action of the Sun's Beams upon the Air and Water as he passes every Day over the Oceans, considered together with the Nature of the Soil and Situation of the adjoining Continents. I say, therefore, first, that according to the Laws of *Statics*, the Air which is less rarefied or expanded by Heat, and consequently more ponderous, must have a Motion towards those Parts thereof which are more rarefied, and less ponderous, to bring it to an *Equilibrium*, etc.'[1]

Now, that the cold dense Air, by reason of its greater Gravity, continually presses from the Polar Parts towards the Equator, where the Air is more rarefied, to preserve an *Aequilibrium* or Balance of the Atmosphere, I think, is very evident from the Wind in those frozen Regions blowing from the north and north-west, from the Beginning of *October* until *May*;[2] for we find, that when the Sun, at the Beginning of *June*, has warmed those Countries to the northward, then the south-east, east and variable Winds continue till *October* again; and I do not doubt but the Trade Winds and hard Gales may be found in the southern Polar Parts to blow towards the Equator, when the Sun is in the northern Signs, from the same Principle.

The Limit of these Winds from the polar Parts, towards the Equator, is seldom known to reach beyond the 30th Degree of Latitude; and the nearer they approach to that Limit, the shorter is the Continuance of those Winds. In *New-England* it blows from the north near four Months in the Winter; at *Canada*, about five Months; at the *Danes's* Settlement in *Streights Davis*, in

---

[1] See Edmond Halley, 'An Historical Account of the Trade Winds....', *Philosophical Transactions*, XVI (1686), pp. 153–68.

[2] This attempt at explaining the wind systems of a very wide latitudinal belt, although hinting at the significance of pressure gradients as part of the wind-provoking mechanism, is a gross oversimplification, neglecting entirely such complications as air masses, frontal systems and travelling low and high pressure systems. But given the state of meteorology at the time Middleton's ideas are quite reasonable.

the 63rd Degree of Latitude, near seven Months; on the Coast of *Norway*, in 64, not above 5 Months and a half, by reason of blowing over a great Part of the Ocean, as was before-mentioned; for those northerly Winds continue a longer or shorter Space of time, according to the Air's being more or less rarefied, which may very probably be altered several Degrees, by the Nature of the Soil, and the Situation of the adjoining Continents.

The vast Bodies of Ice we meet with in our Passage from *England* to *Hudson's Bay*,[1] are very surprising, not only as to their Number, but Magnitude. It is in truth unaccountable how they are formed of so great a Bulk, some of them being immersed 100 Fathom or more under the Surface of the Ocean; and a fifth or sixth Part above, and three or four Miles in Circumference. Some hundreds of these we sometimes see in our Voyage here, all in sight at once, if the Weather is clear. Some of them are frequently seen on the Coasts and Banks of *Newfoundland* and *New-England*, though much diminished.

When I have been becalmed in *Hudson's Streights* for three or four Tides together, I have taken my Boat, and laid close to the Side of one of them, sounded, and found 100 Fathom Water all round it. The Tide floweth here above four Fathom; and I have observed, by Marks upon a Body of Ice, the Tide to rise and fall that Difference, which was a Certainty of its being aground. Likewise in a Harbour in the Island of *Resolution*,[2] where I continued four Days, three of these Isles of Ice (as we call them) came aground. I sounded along by the Side of one of them, quite round it, and found 32 Fathom Water, and the Height above the Surface but ten Yards; another was 28 Fathom under, and the perpendicular Height but nine Yards above the Water.

I can in no other manner account for the Aggregation of such large Bodies of Ice but this: All along the Coasts of *Streights Davis*, both Sides of *Baffin's Bay*, *Hudson's Streights*, *Anticosti*, or *Labradore*, the Land is very high and bold, and 100 Fathoms, or more, close to the Shore. These Shores have many Inlets or Fuirs, the Cavities of which are filled up with Ice and Snow, by the almost perpetual Winters there, and frozen to the Ground,

---

[1] Here Middleton is referring to icebergs rather than sea ice.
[2] Resolution Island forms the north side of the eastern entrance to Hudson Strait.

increasing for four, five, or seven Years, till a kind of Deluge or Land-flood, which commonly happenms in that Space of time throughout those Parts, breaks them loose, and launches them into the Streights or Ocean, where they are driven about by the variable Winds and Currents in the Months of *June, July*, and *August*, rather increasing than diminishing in Bulk, being surrounded (except in four or five Points of the Compass) with smaller Ice for many hundred Leagues, and Land covered all the Year with Snow, the Weather being extremely cold, for the most part, in those Summer Months.[1] The smaller Ice that almost fills the Streights and Bays, and covers many Leagues out into the Ocean along the Coast, is from four to ten Fathom thick,[2] and chills the Air to that Degree, that there is a constant Increase to the large Isles by the Sea's washing against them, and the perpetual wet Fogs, like small Rain, freezing as they settle upon the Ice; and their being so deeply immersed under Water, and such a small Part above, prevents the Wind's having much power to move them: For though it blows from the north-west Quarter near nine Months in twelve, and consequently those Isles are driven towards a warmer Climate, yet the progressive Motion is so slow, that it must take up many Years before they can get five or six hundred Leagues to the southward:[3] I am of Opinion some hundreds of Years are requir'd; for they cannot, I think, dissolve before they come between the 50th and 40th Degree of Latitude, where the Heat of the Sun consuming the upper Parts, they lighten and waste in Time: Yet there is a

[1] Icebergs in fact represent masses of ice which have broken away from the floating tongues of glaciers which reach the sea. But even in areas such as the Alps, where glaciers are a fairly commonplace feature of the environment, the concept that glacier ice flows was not generally understood until the latter part of the eighteenth century, hence Middleton may be excused his mistake.

[2] Middleton is now discussing sea ice, although his estimates of thickness are rather exaggerated.

[3] Middleton is greatly underestimating the rate of drift of icebergs. Although they were on a floe rather than on an iceberg, the party marooned on a floe from *Polaris*, the expedition ship of Charles Hall's expedition, drifted a distance of well over 2000 miles (from Smith Sound to almost the Strait of Belle Isle) between 15 October 1872 and 30 April 1873, i.e. over a period of just over six months (E. V. Blake, ed., *Arctic Experiences: containing Capt. George E. Tyson's Wonderful Drift on the Ice-Floe, a History of the Polaris Expedition, the Cruise of the Tigris and Rescue of the Polaris Survivors. To which is added a general Arctic Chronology*, New York, 1874). Icebergs, being deeper-drafted would tend to drift more slowly, but certainly not as slowly as Middleton would suggest.

perpetual Supply from the northern Parts, which will so continue as long as it pleases the Author of all Beings to keep things in their present State.

Observations of the Longitude, Latitude, *and the* Declination *of the* Magnetic Needle, *at* Prince of Wales's Fort, Churchill River

Having observed the apparent Time of an Emersion of *Jupiter's* first *Satellite* at *Fort Churchill*, on *Saturday* the 20th of *March* last 1741–2, at 11 hours, 55 min., 50 sec., I find the same Emersion happened at *London*, by Mr. *Pound's* Tables,[1] compared with some Emersions actually observed in *England* near the same Time at 18 hours, 15 min., 10 sec, Whence the horary Difference of Meridians, between *Fort Churchill* and *London*, comes out 6 hours, 19 min., 20 sec., Which converted into Degrees of the Equator, gives for the Distance of the same Meridians 94° 50′.

Wherefore, since the Time at *London* was later in Denomination than that at *Churchill*, it follows that, according to this Observation, *Churchill* is 94 Degrees 50 Minutes in Longitude west of *London*.

I took several other Observations, which agreed one with another to less than a Minute, but this I look upon as the most distinct and best.

The Observation was made with a good 15 Foot refracting Telescope, and a two Foot Reflector of *Gregory's*[2] Kind, having a good Watch of Mr. *Graham's*[3] that I could depend upon; for I have frequent Opportunities of discovering how much its Variation amounted to, and constantly found its daily Deviation or Error to be 15 Seconds too slow; by which means it was as useful to me for all Purposes, as if it had gone most constantly true without any Change. This Watch I kept in my Fob in the Day, and in Bed in the Night, to preserve it from the Severity of the

---

[1] James Pound (1669–1724) drew up new tables predicting the instant of eclipse of the satellites of Jupiter after it was discovered that Cassini's tables were incorrect.

[2] James Gregory (1638–75), who invented the Gregorian (reflecting) telescope.

[3] George Graham (1673–1751), one of the best-known instrument-makers of the period.

Weather; for I observed, that all other Watches were spoiled by the extreme Cold.

I have found, from repeated observations, a Method of obtaining the true Time of the Day at Sea, by taking eight or ten different Altitudes of the Sun or Stars, when near the Prime Vertical, by Mr. *Smiths*'s or Mr. *Hadley*'s Quadrant,[1] which I have practised these three or four Years past, and never found from the Calculations, that they differed one from another more than 10 or 15 Seconds of Time. This Certainty of the true Time at Sea is of greater Use in the Practice of Navigation, than may appear at first Sight; for you thereby not only get the Variation of the Compass without the help of Altitudes, but likewise the Variation of the Needle from the true Meridian, every time the Sun or Star is seen to transit the same. Also having the true Time of Day or Night, you may be sure of the Meridian Altitude of the Sun or Star, if you get a Sight 15 or 20 Minutes before or after it passes the Meridian; and the Latitude may be obtained to less than five Minutes: With several other Uses in astronomical Observations; as the Refraction of the Atmosphere, and to allow for it, by getting the Sun's apparent Rising and Setting, which any body is capable of doing, and from thence you will have the Refraction.

If we hadd such a Telescope contrived as Mr. *Smith*[2] recommends to be used on Shipboard at Sea, now we can have an exact Knowledge of the true Time of the Day or Night from the above Instruments and a good Watch, we should probably be able to observe the Eclipses of the first *Satellite* of *Jupiter*, or any other *Phaenomenon* of the like Kind, and thereby find the Distance of Meridians, or Longitude at Sea.[3]

The Variation of the Magnetic Needle, or Sea-Compass, observed by me at *Churchill* in 1725, (as in No. 393 of the *Philosophical Transactions* for the Months of *March* and *April* 1726) was at that time north 21 Degrees westerly, and this Winter I have carefully observed it at the same Place, and find it no more than 17 Degrees, so that it has differed about one Degree in four Years; for in 1738, I observed it here, and found

[1] See above, p. 79 n. 5.
[2] Caleb Smith.
[3] On the limitations of determining longitude by this method see p. 73 n. 3 above.

its Declination 18 Degrees westerly.[1] I have carefully observed, and made proper Allowance for the Sun's Declination and Refraction, and find the Latitude here to be 58 Degrees 56 Minutes north: But in most Parts of the World, where the Latitudes are fixed by Seamen, they are for the most part falsly laid down, for want of having regard to the Variation of the Sun's Declination, which, computed at a distant Meridian, when the Sun is near the Equator, may make a great Error in the Sun's rising and setting *Azimuths*, etc.

These things I thought proper to take notice of as they may be of Service to Navigators, and the Curious in natural Inquiries.

The foregoing Relation having been given by Capt. *Middleton* to the late worthy President of the Royal Society, Sir *Hans Sloane*, Bart.[2] he was pleased to communicate the same to the Society, and at the same time, as the surviving Trustee of the late Sir *Godfrey Copley*, to nominate Capt. *Middleton* to receive this Year the Prize Medal, given annually by the Royal Society, in consequence of Sir *Godfrey*'s Benefaction; and the same was accordingly presented to the Captain on St. *Andrew*'s Day last, 1742.

---

[1] Middleton's 'Declination' is the present-day scientific term for what was more generally known in the eighteenth century as 'variation'. It is perhaps worth remarking here that variation or declination alters both with time and in space.

[2] 'Late' in the sense that Sloane had retired as President of the Royal Society in 1741.

IV

CONTROVERSY

INTRODUCTION

When the dispirited Middleton expedition reached the Thames in October 1742 Dobbs was in Ireland. His first reaction to Middleton's report of the voyage was one of shared disappointment. 'All the fine Hopes' prompted by the observations of Foxe and Scroggs had vanished, he wrote.[1] A lingering curiosity about the tidal flows in the Welcome and the whales sighted near Brook Cobham prompted further queries to Middleton, but they were half-hearted at best. More alluring was a prospect which Dobbs had evidently been mulling over during the expedition's absence – the opening of the trade to Hudson Bay, expansion into the interior, and the dissolving of the obstructive Hudson's Bay Company. In letters to Middleton in October and December 1742 Dobbs sought to enlist the captain's interest and support.[2] In reply, Middleton, who despite the award by the Royal Society of its prestigious Copley Gold Medal for his paper on the effects of cold, was out of employment, out of pocket, and in poor health, patiently explained the difficulties in the way of Dobbs's grand scheme.[3] Before Dobbs received this discouraging response, he had studied Middleton's journal, which he had received in December, and wrote to him with exciting news. 'You have made a much greater Progress in the Discovery of the Passage, than you imagined when there...I realy think that you have prov'd the Passage, tho' you were not at once able to perfect it...I think I may congratulate you upon your having

[1] P. 251 below.
[2] See pp. 254, 257–9 below.
[3] See p. 262 below.

found the so-much-wish'd-for Passage'.[1] The Wager was not a river but a strait, and the only reason why Middleton had not found a flood tide from the west there was because he had not sailed far enough up it. He had found only its northerly entrance, obstructed by ice, but to the south there was a larger, ice-free entrance.

It was at this point in his exchanges with an increasingly irritated Middleton that Dobbs claimed to have received a letter from London, signed by 'Messrs Brook and Cobham', which accused the captain of deliberately concealing the existence of a passage. On the receipt of a second letter, which ended with the cryptic salute – 'Fox was an honest man' – Dobbs hurried to London.[2] There, he said, the mysterious 'Brook and Cobham' disclosed themselves as Edward Thompson, surgeon of the *Furnace*, and John Wigate the clerk, who convinced him that Middleton had falsified his journal and chart. By coincidence, it seemed, three months after the return of the expedition, Dobbs in Ireland and two members of Middleton's crew in London were independently seized with doubts about its explorations. It could have come as no surprise to Middleton to learn in April that there was a 'close Design' against him by Dobbs, Thompson, Wigate, and Lieutenant John Rankin.[3]

At the beginning of May the Board of Admiralty summoned Thompson, Wigate and Rankin, together with Robert Wilson, master of the *Furnace*, and demanded their reponses in writing to Dobbs's 'queries' about the events of the voyage.[4] Three weeks later it sent both queries and answers to Middleton, and requested 'a very particular and clear Answer' to Dobbs's charges.[5] This answer took the form of a 150–page manuscript, delivered to the Admiralty in July, and then published by Middleton as part of his *Vindication*.[6] It marked the beginning of a two-year pamphlet war between him and Dobbs. Any explanation of Dobbs's conduct at this time must refer back to his letter of 22 January when he told Middleton that if it was agreed that

[1] Pp. 263–5 below.
[2] For the anonymous letters, see pp. 259–61 below.
[3] Middleton, *Vindication*, p. 12.
[4] See p. 270 below.
[5] P. 271 below.
[6] See pp. 273–310 below.

a passage might yet be found, 'the Presumption will be a great Inducement to open the Trade to the Bay'.[1] Here was the key to the matter. The Northwest Passage was part of a wider scheme to abolish the monopoly of the Hudson's Bay Company and expand trade in and beyond the Bay. Middleton's refusal to accept that a passage existed meant that his conduct of the expedition had to be questioned, for in looking to official and mercantile circles for support for his new plans Dobbs would be faced with considerable scepticism after the failure of the recent expedition to find a passage in the place he had confidently predicted. To shift the blame to Middleton would help to clear his own reputation, and open the way for a second expedition to the Bay, this time under a commander less scrupulous of the Company's interests than Middleton.

Although the attack on Middleton was a cynical exercise which sacrificed a man's reputation to commercial gain, it is possible that Dobbs genuinely thought that a passage might yet be found. This would not be on the basis of the unbelievable pseudonymous letters (although Dobbs claimed to have received them in early 1743 he made no mention of them in his correspondence with the Admiralty that spring), but through his close study of Middleton's journal. This showed him that the expedition had not sailed close enough to the west coast of the Bay between the Wager and Marble Island to have made a through examination, and he was firmly persuaded that it had missed the entrance to the passage along that stretch of coast. Twenty years and another expedition later Dobbs, at the age of seventy-four, was still hoping for the 'discovery of the passage to the Western American Ocean, which I have labour'd to obtain these thirty Years, and then I should die in peace'.[2] Intuition, however, would hardly gain Dobbs the support he was looking for in 1743, and he needed to discredit both Middleton and the Hudson's Bay Company. The accusation that Middleton had been bribed by his former employers not only explained why he had not found the passage. If believed, it would lead to a further weakening of the Company's position, already undermined by its initial reluctance to help Middleton in 1741, and by the widespread distrust of monopolistic companies.

[1] P. 266 below.
[2] Dobbs to Earl of Egremont, 17 Jul 1763. C.O.5/310, f.27d.

Dobbs produced four main witnesses to testify against Middleton: Thompson, Rankin, Wigate, and more surprisingly, William Moor.[1] They accused the captain of concealing the existence of a passage by leaving the Wager when the discovery was almost made, of inventing a Frozen Strait to explain the high tides and whales in the Welcome, and of bringing the explorations to a premature close. The four men repeated these charges in published statements, in affidavits, and in evidence given before committees of enquiry; yet unless we accept the authenticity of the anonymous letters there is no evidence that they held these opinions before the arrival of Dobbs in London in the spring of 1743. Rankin's journal, which mysteriously disappeared when Middleton wanted to borrow it during the controversy,[2] confirms the captain's account of the voyage, while a letter from the lieutenant in February 1743 praised Middleton in the most effusive terms.[3] Middleton's own journal has a note on the fly-leaf, signed by Rankin as well as Wilson and James Smith, testifying that it was 'a true Coppy from the Original Logbook'.[4] Moor's log, sparse though it is, contains no hint of disagreement with the handling of the expedition, and in letters of April and May 1743 he was scornful of the insistence of Thompson, Wigate and Rankin that there was a passage.[5] When Moor next appeared in print, it was this very assertion which he solemnly repeated.[6]

The affirmations of these four witnesses, together with several petty officers and tradesmen who also gave evidence against Middleton, were incorrect on almost all counts. The most likely explanation of their willingness to swear false statements is that they were bribed; and it is difficult to see who could have been responsible but Dobbs. Money was not necessarily involved. Middleton maintained that the hostile witnesses were promised posts of one kind and another, and it is significant that Moor commanded Dobbs's privately financed expedition to Hudson Bay in

---

[1] Middleton later wrote sadly of Moor's part in the campaign against him as that of 'the Man whom I have brought up, as my Child, from the Age of 12 or 14'. Middleton, *Rejoinder*, p. 122.

[2] Christopher Middleton, *A Reply to Mr. Dobbs's Answer to a Pamphlet Entitled Forgery Detected*, London, 1745, p. 3.

[3] See pp. 268–9 below.

[4] P. 269 below.

[5] See pp. 270–71 below.

[6] Arthur Dobbs, *A Reply to Capt. Middleton's Answer*, London, 1745, pp. 121–8.

1746. It is a sign of the unscrupulous way in which the campaign against Middleton was conducted that Moor, in his published letter to Dobbs, insisted 'I have no future Views of a Command',[1] although Dobbs had already told Judge Ward that Moor was to be given command of the proposed private expedition to Hudson Bay, as he was 'very sober and carefull and will also be an Adventurer [investor] himself'.[2] It is also significant that Thompson, perhaps the most virulent of the witnesses against Middleton, sailed on the expedition as surgeon and member of the council.

To combat the attack on his reputation Middleton produced fifteen witnesses from the discovery crews, together with a rather unexpected letter of support from James Isham.[3] It is doubtful if the way in which Middleton obtained some of the affidavits he later printed would bear close examination. Some show a suspicious similarity of wording, while others demonstrate remarkable feats of memory by witnesses on points of detail. None of this alters the fact that a considerable group from the discovery crews was willing to stand by Middleton at a time when he must have seemed to them to be under attack by persons of power and authority. Dobbs accused Middleton of using his influence to procure advancement for his witnesses; but far from achieving this Middleton could do little for himself, and was not offered another command until May 1745. His three further years of service were not untroubled, for in 1747 he was investigated on charges of fraud and assault, and found guilty of striking his boatswain. It was no surprise that when peace came in 1748 he was placed on the half-pay list, where he remained until his death in 1770. The promise of his early years and his skill as a navigator and explorer make the story of his wasted career after 1742 a sad one.[4]

[1] Ibid., p. 128.

[2] Dobbs to Ward, 31 Mar 1744. Ward Papers: D 2092/1/6/100. For affidavits relating to promises of posts allegedly made by Dobbs to Rankin and Wigate see Middleton, *Vindication*, pp. 140, 148.

[3] See pp. 310–11 below.

[4] *The Monthly Review* for 1784 claimed that Middleton had died 'in the utmost penury and distress', having sold his Copley Gold Medal, and with all his children dead. The evidence of Middleton's will throws doubt on this. Drawn up in December 1769, only a few weeks before his death, it refers to a second wife and four children, and made provision for the distribution among them of his books, instruments, Copley Medal, and an unspecified amount in South Sea annuities. See PRO, Probate 11/963.

The arguments between Dobbs and Middleton over the conduct of the expedition were to fill the twelve hundred pages of eight books or pamphlets published by the disputants between 1743 and 1745. In the end, the charges and counter-charges had become confused and repetitive, an 'abundance of rubbage and impertinance' in the words of the Company ship-captain William Coats.[1] Characteristic of pamphlet warfare, the exchanges developed their own momentum, generating much heat but little light. As the subject-matter of the publications became thinner so their titles lengthened. In 1744 Dobbs published his *Remarks upon Capt. Middleton's Defence: wherein His Conduct during the late Voyage For discovering a Passage from Hudson's Bay to the South-Sea is impartially Examin'd; His Neglect and Omissions in that Affair fully Prov'd; The Falsities and Evasions in his Defence Expos'd; The Errors of his Charts laid open, And His Accounts of Currents, Streights, and Rivers, Confuted; Whereby it will appear, with the highest Probability, That there is such a Passage as he went in search of.* Not to be outdone, Middleton responded with a fearsome counter-blast of his own: *A Rejoinder to Mr. Dobbs's Reply to Captain Middleton; In which is expos'd, Both his Jesuitical Prevarications, Evasions, Falsities, and false Reasoning; his avoiding taking Notice of Facts, formerly detected and charged upon him as Inventions of him or his Witnesses; the Character of the latter, and the present Views of the former, which gave rise to the present Dispute. In a Word, An unparalelled Disingenuity, and (and to make use of a Verodobbsical Flowering of Rhetoric) a Glaring Impudence, are set in a fair Light.* A few nuggets of information can be prised out of the later pamphlets, but the main areas of controversy are already clear to see in the original charges brought by Dobbs in 1743 and by Middleton's replies, as printed in his *Vindication* (Document 15 below).

The most important points were summed up in the rival charts produced by Middleton and Wigate.[2] A comparison of them shows four main differences. Middleton marks an unbroken coastline north from Eskimo Point, the Wager as a river, and to the north the tide flowing through Frozen Strait down the west coast of the Bay. Wigate's chart shows several openings along the coastline north of Eskimo Point, a strait to the west

---

[1] Coats, *Geography of Hudson's Bay*, p. 2.
[2] See Maps IX and X.

through the Wager, but none to the north where Middleton placed Frozen Strait, and the tide flowing east and northeast from the Wager and the other inlets. On all but one of these points Middleton was substantially correct. The discovery expedition of 1747 found the Wager to be a closed inlet. Parry in 1821 discovered the Frozen Strait just as Middleton had described it,[1] and later navigators found the tide and whales passing through it into the Welcome. But Middleton's one error was to keep alive hopes of a passage through Hudson Bay. Despite his assertions to the contrary, he had not sailed near enough the coast south of the Wager on his return leg to have made a close examination, and so had missed the entrance of Chesterfield Inlet. His lapse, if such it was (Middleton's instructions ordered him to look for a passage *north* of 65°N.) was understandable, and he expressed his feelings on a landlubber's criticism with some asperity: 'Could the very knowing Mr. Dobbs imagine that the Ship was to coast a shore, where Land is as high as that over Torbay or above Plymouth, in the manner Boats do, at half a Mile Distance, especially with a Wind, most part of the time, two or more Points on the Shore, and a Tender which was a bad Sailer?'[2] With his crews discouraged and sickly, Middleton had made only a perfunctory examination of the broken coast south of the Wager. After the disappointments of the Wager and Repulse Bay, the main desire of all concerned was to finish the work of discovery and return to England. There is a ring of conviction about Robert Wilson's remarks on the crews' reactions: when the 'poor scorbutick Creatures heard it was agreed to return from the Frozen Strait, they were overjoy'd, and ready to leap out of their Skins, as the Saying is.'[3]

At the same time as he was engaged in pamphlet warfare with Middleton, Dobbs was pushing ahead with his plans for a privately-financed discovery expedition to Hudson Bay. As part of the effort to create a favourable climate of opinion for this, and for the wider design to open the trade of Hudson Bay and its hinterland, Dobbs published in 1744 *An Account of the Countries adjoining to Hudson's Bay*. In this work Dobbs dovetailed

---

[1] See pp. 108–9 above.
[2] Middleton, *Reply to Remarks*, p. 38.
[3] Quoted in Middleton, *Vindication*, p. 163.

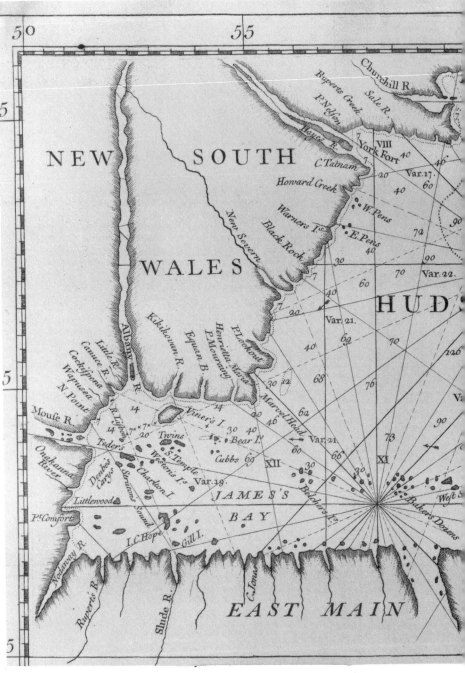

PLATE IX. Christopher Middleton: 'Chart of Hudson's Bay and Straits....', 1743
(Ministry of Defence Library, Whitehall)

246

In this Bay
John Monk he said
winterid in the Year 1619.
but I rather think it was in
Churchill River, from the
Marks of a Wreck of a Danish
Ship & some Brass & Copper Guns
I took up in the Year 1742, with X'tian
the 4th. upon 'em. dated 1610.

C. Ushamay

Whale Cove

49

40

60   60

Outward bound Passage

VI. 29
Brook   Cobham
Var. 27   40
30

PRINCE

89   90   90   80   60

70

Home

Inward bound Passage

120   122   70   80   60

N'S BAY   St. ROE's Welcome   70   60
120   109   96   90   50   60   60
50

C. Southampton
Carey's Swans Nest
C. Nesdrake   A low Singley Beach like Dungeness
Var. 37   C. Pembrook   Sea Horse P.
120   C. Comfort
70   70   90   120   30   50   30
30   120
30   70   120

Var. 33   Mansel's I.   Var. 43
80   30   90
60   30
N. Sleepers   Diggs Is.
76
X
Nottingham I.
C. Walsingham   30

Ille of C. Charles
24
Salisbury I.
Var. 43

C. of H.
ITS

Chesterton
Whale P.
C. Dobbs
VI. The New Strait
Var. 35
50

Wager   River
Discover'd in 1742
70
70
70
Deer   Sound
Savage   So. C. Hope
50
Repulse Bay discover'd
40   80
40   Var. 50   80   90
VI.   100
The Frozen Strait

L

Mill's I.

Queen Mary's Cape
Ld. Weston's
Portland

ST

NORTH

Queen Ann's Foreland

247

several themes: the probability of a Northwest Passage; the opening of the trade of the Bay and the settling of colonies in the interior; and in general the substitution of a forceful and expansionist policy for the sluggish attitude of the Hudson's Bay Company. 'By the unaccountable Behaviour of the Hudson's Bay Company', Dobbs wrote, 'the Government and Parliament have a just and legal Right to lay open that Trade to all the Merchants in Britain'.[1] His emphasis on the crucial importance of the struggle between Britain and France for the great central plain of North America showed that he was more than ever conscious of the danger he had first noted in his memorandum to Walpole fifteen years earlier – that the enterprising French would confine English traders and settlers to the coastal fringes of the Atlantic coasts and Hudson Bay. His knowledge of current French publications with their reports of a River of the West heightened his fears that the French would smell out his own plans for reaching the Pacific, or perhaps anticipate him by discovering a more southerly route to the great ocean.

In England there were those familiar with the Bay region who could point out, as Middleton had done in his letter to Dobbs of January 1743, the problems of expansion inland from the Bayside posts. Captain Coats grumbled that 'what Mr. Dobbs has thought fitt to call a discription of Hudson's Bay, is so erronius, so superficial, and so trifling, in almost every circumstance. So contrary to the experience and concurrent testimony of every person who have resided in that country....'[2] But while the observations of Coats, Isham and other Company servants lay unpublished, and unread outside Company or family circles, and while commentators were denied knowledge about the Company's activities,[3] then the field was left open to potential rivals and hostile critics. As Dobbs began to enlist help among his mercantile and political associates for a second discovery expedition to the Bay, it was clear that much more than exploration was involved.

---

[1] Dobbs, *Account of Hudson's Bay*, p. 158.

[2] Coats, *Geography of Hudson's Bay*, p. 2.

[3] When John Oldmixon was revising his *British Empire in America* he complained that despite his 'pressing instance' he could obtain no information from the Company about its history since 1714. John Oldmixon, *The British Empire in America*, 2nd edn., London, 1741, I, pp. 566–7.

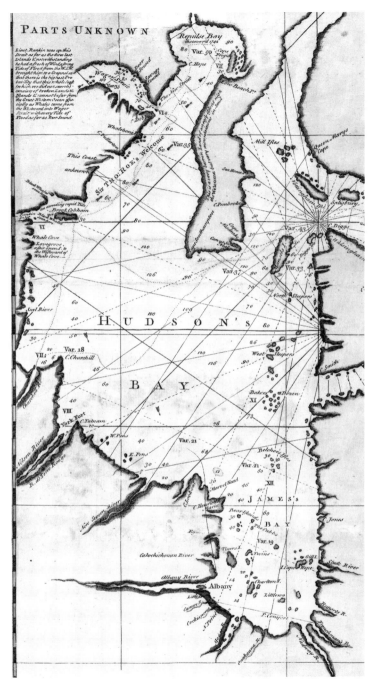

PLATE X. John Wigate: 'Chart of the Seas, Straits &c. thro' which his Majesty's Sloop "Furnace" pass'd for discovering a Passage from Hudson's Bay to the South Sea', 1746
(British Library)

CONTROVERSY

DOCUMENTS

1. Arthur Dobbs to Captain Middleton. 20 October 1742.[1]

Dear SIR,

I had the Favour of yours from Churchill[2] by Capt. Spurrel, and also your last from the Orkneys,[3] and the Duplicate from London, and congratulate you upon your safe Arrival with the Ships after so dangerous a Voyage; but 'tis with Concern I find we have been disappointed of our Hopes of an easy Passage from the Welcome or Whalebone Point, as we had Reason to have expected, had the Account been true, which Fox laid down in his Journal, and which had in some Measure confirmed by Scroggs, from his Manuscript Journal; but as your Observation of the Height and Direction of the Tides there, and Quantity of Ice, is directly contrary to their Account; all the fine Hopes formed from their Accounts are quite vanished, nothing being agreeable to their Journals, but the black Whales you observed near Brook Cobham, and that the Time of the Tides flowing at the Welcome from the N.E. agrees pretty much with Fox's Account;[4] since you found a W. or W. by N. Moon made High Water in 63°20′, and in 66°40′ an E. by S. Moon made High Water, which proves that the Tide of Flood proceeds from 66°40′ to the Welcome and Brook Cobham, and not the Tide from the Southward of Carey's Swan's Nest.

Until I see your Journal at large, and your Draught, I cannot

---

[1] Middleton, *Reply*, Appendix, pp. 9–13.

[2] Presumably a duplicate of the letter to Sir Charles Wager of 28 June 1742. See pp. 179–83 above.

[3] This was Middleton's 'Abstract'. See pp. 216–20 above.

[4] For references to the accounts of Foxe and earlier explorers which Dobbs cites in this letter see the footnotes to his Memorial of 1733, pp. 12–22 above.

fix with myself, whether the Lands on your Starbord or East-ward from the Welcome to Cape Hope, were contiguous or broke into Islands; nor do I know whether the great Tide which flowed up Wager River between Cape Dobbs and Whalebone Point came from the Eastward thro' such Broken Lands, or from the North-Eastward from that Strait you passed, where there was a strong Tide before you doubled Cape Hope.

I apprehended from the Abstract sent me, that that Strait lay East and West, on the North of which was Cape Hope to the North-Westward of which you were embayed, and over shot the Tide. I also apprehend that the Mountain you ascended was opposite to the Strait you observed the Tide to come in at, at its West End, and so you saw along the Length of the Strait from End to End, and the farther End was towards Lord Weston's Portland, which according to Fox was in 66°47', and you were then in 66°40' so that the East End of that Strait was to the Northward of Cape Comfort: Whether the Strait you passed going to Cape Hope extended to the Westward of your Course as well as to the Eastward, does not appear from the Abstract you sent me. You also apprehended that the other Strait you saw from the Mountain, thro' which the Tide came, was frozen fast from Side to Side, tho' 6 or 7 Leagues broad; but had it been fast I should imagine it would have obstructed the Tides flowing so rapidly to Wager River and to the Welcome as you observed it.

Upon the Whole, you have ascertain'd that there can be no Passage from the Welcome to 67° – and if there is any to the Northward, it must be attended with more Danger than we apprehended would have been, had it been found at Whalebone Point. But there are two Things, I yet can't easily account for; that is, how the black Whales get to Brook Cobham, if they don't pass and repass by Hudson's Strait, which I think has not been observed by any Journal extant, nor have I heard you mention any seen by you in the Straits, at any Time; the other is from whence that Tide can come which flows from Cape Hope to the Welcome, since a W. by S. Moon made high Water there, and a W. by N. at the Welcome. For if Bylot's and Baffin's Account be true, that a S.S.E.Moon makes high Water at the Northwest End of Hudson's Strait, and a S. by E. moon at Cape Comfort, how could that Tide if it entred the Strait you observed from the Mountain, to the Northward of Cape Comfort, and was but 20

Leagues long, be eight Points longer in making high Water, where you were embay'd, where a W. by S. Moon made high Water: This makes it a Doubt to me, whether it could be from that Tide.

This would make me incline to think if it be from any easterly Tide, it should be from that in Cumberland Inlet, where at Cumberland Isles, 60 Leagues from the Entrance, in about 66° – it flowed four or five Fathoms by Davis's Account, and he said a S.W. by W. Moon made high Water, but it was there check'd by another Tide which came from the South-west. But to this, there is another Difficulty from Fox, who found Lord Weston's Portland in 66°47', which must have been betwixt your new Strait which was in that Latitude and Cumberland Isles; and he says the South-eastern Tide followed him so far from Hudson's Strait.

These Difficulties I should be glad to have your Opinion upon; and whether you think we ought to discredit their Accounts here, as well as at the Welcome, tho' they had more Time here to make regular Observations; or whether, as a great deal of what you pass'd must have been Islands or broken Lands, there might not have been some Passages through these Straits, North and South, as at Cape Hope; where you pass'd the Strait from whence that Tide might flow from the North-Westward; and those Headlands being to the North-Eastward of you, the Tide would return to you from the Eastward. For I observe from Baffin, that the Lands to the Westward of this Bay, are very far to the North-Eastward of the Strait and Bay in which you were; so that there was still room for a Passage betwixt 67° and 72°.

From the great Quantity of Ice you met at the Welcome which was not mentioned by Button, Fox or Scroggs, I should be glad to know whether you think it has usually been there, or whether these two last Years severe Frost has not occasioned a more than usual Quantity; for I apprehend the Frost came on at Churchill, last year, in September, sooner than it usually happens, and was also longer clearing out of the River, nor do I think the Ice you met with near Churchill in August, 1741, has been usually there but after very severe Winters.

When you have Leisure, I shall be glad of your private Thoughts upon these Points, which I hope to have by the Time

I get your Draught and Journal, and if there be sufficient Reasons to put an End to any farther Attempt, as I am afraid there is, then I shall consider whether to make an Attempt to open the Trade to the Bay by dissolving the Company, and making Settlements upon the River of Nelson, Moose and Albany to the South Westward, where the Clime will be more temperate, and by that Means not only deprive the French of all the Southern and Western Trade of the Bay, but also push our Discoveries thro' that Western Continent, and enlarge our Trade and Power there.[1] If you think this a reasonable Scheme and beneficial for England, and will enter into it, I have been preparing some Materials for that Purpose, by a Description of those Countries and Natures of the Climates from the Journals you gave me, and the French and other Accounts I have met with,[2] and shall want any further Informations you can give me of the Trade and Observations of the Country, to shew the Benefit must accrue to England upon Opening the Trade and settling the Country.

Had there been any Hopes in prosecuting our first Scheme I should have met you in London this Winter, but unless other Business calls me, I believe I shan't go this Season, and by another Year I hope the European War will be brought to a Crisis, and then Time may be spared to look into a farther Improvement of our Trade and Settlements.

I wish you Health and Prosperity in all your Undertakings, and am with great Esteem,

> Dear SIR,
> Yours most obedient
> Humble Servant
> Arthur Dobbs.

Lisburn, October 20, 1742.

---

[1] In a duplicate letter of 19 November 1742 with (in places) different wording, the equivalent passage reads: 'I think the only safe way now, is by the Rivers of Nelson, or Churchill, by going up to their End, from thence descending such Rivers as fall from thence into the Western Ocean. This can only be done by laying open the Trade, and dissolving the Company for so far, and then making proper Settlements higher up upon these Rivers to the south-westward in a more temperate Climate....' Middleton, *Vindication*, p. 122.

[2] These 'Materials' were published by Dobbs in 1744 as *An Account of the Countries adjoining to Hudson's Bay, In the North-West Part of America.*

2. Captain Middleton to Arthur Dobbs. 27 November 1742.[1]

I had the Fortune of yours, of the 20 *ult.* which happened to lie some Days at my former Habitation, before it was forwarded to me; and I shall transmit you the Chart, together with the Journal, and other Observations, by the first convenient Opportunity. In the mean time, I shall give you the best Satisfaction I am able, with relation to the Difficulties that have occur'd to you. And first, it is to be noted, that all the Land along the east Side of the Welcome, from 64° of Latitude to the Frozen Straits, is one continued level Land, somewhat like Dungeness, low and shingly. The great Tides you mention, which flow up the River Wager, and off Cape Dobbs, come all from the Frozen Straits, E.b.N. by Compass, according to the Course of the new Strait, that we passed between Cape Dobbs and Cape Hope, the mean Variation between the said Capes 40° westerly, and makes the true Course of this Strait nearest N.40° easterly; the said Strait ends to the westward of Cape Hope, in a Bay 20 Leagues deep,[2] and 15 Leagues broad, which lies W.N.W. by the true Bearings; and we carefully surrounded it, sailing up to the very Bottom within 2 or 3 Leagues, and found no Appearance of a Passage for either Tide or Vessels. All the way I sail'd from Cape Hope, quite down to the Bottom of this Bay, I tried the Tide; and all round I found neither Ebb nor Flood, which must have appeared had there been any. The Land was all very high and bold, ascending into the Country to a vast Height without any Breaks; so that had there been a Passage here we could not have missed of it.

With regard to the Tide, which you think would have been obstructed from flowing so rapidly to Wager River, if the Strait was froze fast from Side to Side.

I need only observe to you, that at Churchill, all the Winter, the Tide ebbs and flows up the River in the same manner as if there was no Ice, being lifted every Tide of Flood from 12 to 18 Feet, all except what is fast to the Ground, and falls again upon the Ebb, though 8 or 9 Feet thick. Now close to the north End of

---

[1] Middleton, *Vindication*, pp. 123–6.
[2] Repulse Bay.

the Frozen Straits, is 100 Fathoms of Water or more, and probably that Depth may continue the whole Length; and then there is Passage free for the Flood and Ebb to pass without lifting; but I observed this Ice was all cracked round the Shores, and on the Island at Churchill.

You seem to be at a loss how to account for the black Whales getting to Brook Cobham, if they do not pass and repass by Hudson's Straits: Now, 'tis true, I never saw any above 20 Leagues up Hudson's Straits; but I have traded with Indians off Nottingham and Diggs, for Whalebone just fresh taken; for my own part, I cannot think these Whales come round Cary's Swan's-Nest, but thro' the Frozen Straits under the Ice, for we saw many of them in Wager River, and in 63° Latitude, and these may not come through Hudson's Straits, but to the northward, as all the north Side of Hudson's Straits appear to be broken Land and Islands; and Cumberland Bay, Baffin's Bay, and Straits Davis may have a Communication with this new Frozen Straits, and Whales, &c. may come from thence.

It is hardly possible to account for the Difficulties about the Tides; for though it flows E.S.E. at Resolution, and S.b.E. at Cape Diggs, which makes five Points in running 130 Leagues; yet it is but one Point in going down to Albany and Moose River, for there it flows south, and the Distance 250 Leagues.

So from Humber to Cromer, on the Lincolnshire Coast (as I mentioned formerly) is but 14 Leagues, and at one Place it flows W.b.S. at the other N.W. Likewise from the Frozen Straits to Churchill is but two Points difference, or one Hour and half of time, in the Distance of 200 Leagues; so that I think no Rule can be fixed, where Tides flow into deep Bays, obstructed by Islands or Counter Tides.

The Ice I met within the Welcome, was most of it to the northward of all the Parts before discover'd; so that none who went before me could have seen it; for most of it lay to the north of Whalebone-Point; and every Year is not alike, with respect to the Wind bringing it to the southward; and it is entirely directed by the Winds here, as well as in all other Parts of the Bay. In our way to Churchill, there was less Ice than usually happens; and it was also sooner clear in the Spring, by 15 Days than common.

Undoubtedly there is no Hope of a Passage to encourage any further Trial between Churchill and so far as we have gone; and if there be any further to the northward, it must be impossible for the Ice, and the Narrowness of any such Outlet, in 67° or 68° of Latitude, it cannot be clear of Ice one Week in a Year, and many Years, as I apprehend, not clear at all.

In any other Attempts, I shall be glad to give you all the Assistance I can, and furnish you with any other Informations that you may think needful to promote your Design; but I hope never to venture myself that way again.

My Friends being out of the Admiralty,[1] I find there will be a great deal of Difficulty to get any thing done for me in the Navy at present; or to procure any other Recompence for my Loss these two Summers in leaving the Hudson's-Bay Service, where I should have £1400 in the Time I have acquired but £160 in the Government's. I remain, with great Sincerity and Respect,

SIR,   Your most obedient humble Servant,
                                   CHRISTOPHER MIDDLETON

P.S. The Eskimaux, and the Northern Indians I had with me, were utter Strangers to each other, in Manners and Language; neither could I make these Eskimaux understand me by the Vocabulary I had of the Language of those in Hudson's Straits.[2]

3. Arthur Dobbs to Captain Middleton. 14 December 1742.[3]

DEAR SIR,

I have your last Favour of the 27th of October, in Answer to the Difficulties I stated, which you have fully answered; so that I am fully convinced there can be no Passage N.W. by Sea, as we seemed to have had Reason to expect; and therefore it would be very wrong to think of attempting it for the future. But I am still of Opinion, that the Publick may have a great Advantage by the Hudson's Bay Trade; if it be laid open, and the Country settled higher up upon these great Rivers, which run into the Bay, by

---

[1] Sir Charles Wager resigned in March 1742, and a new Admiralty Board was appointed.
[2] Not only was the land-based culture of the Caribou Inuit of the west coast of Hudson Bay different from that of the Sadlirmiut of Southampton Island and the western end of Hudson Strait, but each 'probably formed...a fairly discrete dialect community'. C. S. Beals, ed., *Science, History and Hudson Bay*, Ottawa, 1968, I, p. 154.
[3] Middleton, *Vindication*, pp. 126–8.

Moose, Albany, the Severn, the Nelson River; and these Settlements, as the Rivers come from great Lakes to the South-westward of the Bay, would be in a much more temperate Climate, than at the Mouths of the Rivers, among the Swamps, where they and the Bay continue a much longer Time frozen, than further into the Country; so that whoever would settle higher up, might have very comfortable and beneficial Settlements, and not only secure all the Country and Trade Westward of Moose River from the French of Canada, but also by making a Settlement near the Lake Errie, Westward of Pennsilvania, above the great Fall of Niagara, secure all the Navigation of the Lakes, and cut off their Communication with the Mississippi, and also secure a great deal of the Trade to the North Eastward of these Lakes, to Rupert's River, and the East Main. To shew this to more Advantage, I should want a better Description of the Rivers and Lakes to the Westward of the Bay: I have extracted from Monsieur Jeremie,[1] all the Knowledge the French acquired, whilst they possessed Fort Bourbon upon Nelson River, who was himself some hundred Leagues up among the great Lakes which fall into Nelson River, which are in a temperate Climate, and run thro' rich Countries. Now if you concur in this Scheme, we might, by joining in this Scheme, and adding what further you have observed, or have collected from such of the Company Factors or Servants, who may have been curious to search into these Rivers, give a much greater Light in the Description of those Countries and Rivers, as well as Charts of the Bay, and Account of the several Climates, as may fully convince the Publick of the Benefit to be made of these Countries, by opening the Trade, and settling upon the Rivers. I have already sketched out from what I have read, and the Journals you gave me from Albany,[2] and the Nature of their Trade, what may shew the Advantage may be made of that Trade, but it will be much more compleat, from what you are capable to furnish; and

---

[1] Nicolas Jérémie spent many years in Hudson Bay on French service between 1694 and 1715, the last six as governor of Fort Bourbon (York Factory). His 'Relation du Détroit et de la Baie d'Hudson' was first published in 1720, but Dobbs probably used the second edition which appeared in *Recueil de voyages au Nord*, III, Amsterdam, 1732.

[2] Abstracts of the Albany Factory journals for 1729–31 are contained in Dobbs, *Account of Hudson's Bay*, pp. 12–13. Middleton was at Albany in 1730 and 1731 on his yearly supply voyages to the Bay.

if you have no Thoughts of publishing something of this Nature from yourself, I shall be glad of your joining with me in this Attempt. I know Lord Carteret,[1] Winchelsea,[2] and several others, who will support it, if a proper Plan be laid before them; and probably, by the Heads of these Rivers we might gain a Communication with the Nations upon the Western Sea, which may be of Advantage, tho' nothing so great, as if the Discovery had been made by Sea.

I shall be glad to have your Thoughts upon this, and what Materials you think you could furnish towards it; and if we can prepare a reasonable Plan, I shall go over and push it with all my Friends.

I have a Letter from Mr. Samuel Smith Yesterday, that he has forwarded to me your last Journal, and that you will send me your Draught as soon as you have got it copied, for which I am very much obliged to you.

I should be very glad to hear that you were employed in some way satisfactory to you by the Publick, which you have so just a Right to, after having quitted the Company's Service in order to serve the Publick; and wish it were in my Power to contribute to it, I should do it with great Pleasure, and would go over upon that very Account, if it could be of Advantage: In the mean Time, I wish you all Happiness, and hope to hear from you, being with great Esteem,

Dear Sir, Your most Obliged, and
Obedient humble Servant,
Dublin, December 14, 1742. A———D———.

4. Anonymous Letters to Arthur Dobbs. 2 January 1742 (OS) and n.d.[3]

The anonymous Letter sent to me from London, which gave me the first Hint of the Captain's Roguery.

---

[1] John Carteret, 2nd Lord Carteret and 2nd Earl Granville: Secretary of State for the Northern Department, 1742–44.
[2] Daniel Finch, 8th Earl of Winchilsea and 3rd Earl of Nottingham: First Lord of the Admiralty, 1742–4.
[3] Arthur Dobbs, *Remarks upon Capt. Middleton's Defence*, London, 1744, pp. 142–4.

259

SIR,

This Script is only to open your Eyes, which have been sealed or closed with too much (we can't say Cunning) Artifice, so that they have not been able to discover our Discoverer's Pranks.

All Nature cries aloud there is a Passage, and we are sure there is one from Hudson's Bay to Japan. Send a Letter directed to Messrs. Brook and Cobham,[1] who are Gentlemen that have been the Voyage, and cannot bear so glorious an Attempt should die under the Hands of mercenary Wretches, and they will give you such pungent Reasons as perhaps will awake all your Industry. They desire it may be kept secret so long as they shall think fit. They are willing to venture their Lives, their Fortunes, their All, in another Attempt; and they are no inconsiderable Persons, but such as have had it much at Heart ever since they saw the Rapidity of the Tides in the Welcome. The frozen Streights is all Chimera, and every Thing you have ever yet read or seen concerning that Part of our Voyage. We shall send you some unanswerable Queries.

Direct for us at the Chapter Coffee House, St Paul's Church-yard.

January 2, 1742–3.

This I answered upon receiving it, telling them if it were genuine, and they sent over proper Queries, I would go strait over and assist them, and push it forward with all the Interest I could make. To which I had the following Answer:

SIR,

It was with no little Pleasure we received your Letter, and you may depend upon our utmost Assistance towards the Discovery of the so-long-desir'd Passage; but must beg leave to acquaint you, it is with no mercenary Views we have engag'd so far as to send you a Letter, you may be assured that nothing shall deter us from doing public Justice, and only beg the Favour you would suffer us to conceal our Names a little longer. We hope to see

---

[1] Soon to be revealed as Edward Thompson, surgeon of the *Furnace*, and John Wigate, Middleton's clerk on the voyage. It seems likely that Middleton and Wigate had quarrelled after the return of the expedition, for the Admiralty records show that as late as July 1743 Wigate had received no pay for the voyage because Middleton refused to grant him the necessary certificate. See Adm 2/480, pp. 55, 171.

you Face to Face; and perhaps may not be quite unacquainted to you, tho' we have been at Sea in no ungenteel Posts before this Expedition we are speaking of. Our Queries are not so well digested as we will have them; and therefore beg you will please to dispense longer with them and us; yet as a Specimen of what we shall and will do. Query, Why did not our Discoverer give all the Encouragement possible to the Northern Indians he employed, and why he used them as Slaves?

Q. Whether, if he had taken their Advice, he would not have made a short Passage to, &c. before he saw Wager River (or most justly a Streight, the Tide running so rapid) before he was embay'd in the Ice.

Q. Whether he did not haul out of the Tide, to prevent our driving into the desir'd Passage?

Q. If he did not sacrifice the Indians, lest they should tell Tales, being pretty forward in the English Language?

The next or following Post shall bring you Queries *ab origine ad finem.* We are, ingenuously, honoured Sir, &c.

Messrs. Brook and Cobham.

P.S. Direct for us as before. Fox was an honest man.

5. Captain Middleton to Arthur Dobbs. 18 January 1742 (OS). [1]

SIR,
I was duly favoured with yours of the 14th of December; and am sorry that I could not return my Answer sooner, but the ill State of Health that I labour under, prevented me in this as well as many other of my Affairs.

It gives me much Satisfaction to find, that you approve of the Solutions I sent, in regard to the Difficulties you proposed, and that you are convinced I have done all that was necessary to put the Impassability thro' those Seas to the Westward out of Question; in such manner as to render any Attempt needless for the future; but on the contrary, I should have been infinitely pleased, had our Expedition succeeded according to the Reasonableness of your Expectation.

I have seriously considered your Proposition of laying open

---

[1] Middleton, *Vindication*, pp. 128–31.

the Hudson's Bay Trade, and settling the Country higher up, upon those great Rivers which runs into the Bay; and tho' I may agree with you in the great Advantage the Publick would reap from such a Settlement, (could it be made) in the Obstruction it would give to the French, both as to their Trade, and the cutting off the Communication with the Mississippi, yet I must declare my Opinion, that it is altogether impracticable upon many Accounts; for I can't see where we could find People enough that would be willing, or able to undergo the Fatigue of travelling those frozen Climates, or what Encouragements would be sufficient to make them attempt it, with such dangerous Enemies on every Side; no Europeans could undergo such Hardships as those French that intercept the English Trade, who are inured to it, and are called by us Wood-Runners (or Coureurs de Bois) for they indure Fatigues just the same as the native Indians, with whom they have been mixed and intermarried for two, three, or more Generations.

As to the Rivers you mention, none of them are navigable with any thing but Canoes, so small, that they carry but two Men, and they are forced to make use of Land Carriages near the fourth Part of the Way, by reason of Water-falls during that little Summer they enjoy.

Out of 120 Men and Officers the Company have in the Bay, not five are capable of venturing in one of those Canoes, they are so apt to overturn and drown them. Many of our People have been twenty years and upwards there, and yet are not dextrous enough to manage a Canoe; so there would be no transporting People that way.[1]

Should there happen a French War, the best Step we could take towards rooting them out of America, would be, in the first Place, to take Canada....

This is the principal Matter that I can think of at present; had not my indisposition prevented me, I should, before this Time, have drawn up some further Account of our Voyage, but I have nothing material worth imparting to you further, except a Chart of the whole Bay and the Straits, which will be engraved in a

---

[1] The problems outlined in these three paragraphs explain why it was not until the 1770s that the Hudson's Bay Company was finally forced to move inland to meet the competition of its Montreal rivals.

little Time,[1] for you already have my Journals and Observations, as well as the Accounts of those that attempted the Discovery before me.

I am very much obliged to you for your kind Wishes, and all the Favours you have conferred on me, and am as yet quite uncertain as to what their Lordships[2] intend to do for me; they treat me with great Respect, and such as I have the Honour to know, to wit, my Lord Winchelsea, Lord Baltimore, and Admiral Cavendish, have all promised me their Favours. I am,

SIR,   Yours most obedient
January 1742–3   humble Servant
          CHRISTOPHER MIDDLETON

6. Arthur Dobbs to Captain Middleton. 22 January 1742 (OS).[3]

DEAR SIR,   Lisburn, January 22, 1742–3
In my last to Samuel Smith, I inclosed one for Lord Carteret,[4] open for your Perusal, upon our Scheme of opening a Trade to the Bay, to which I refer you; and in Sam's Letter hinted at what I discovered from your Journal at large; that you have made a much greater Progress in the Discovery of the Passage, than you imagined when there; and that from the Lights I have got from your Journal, I can almost prove that you were in the Passage, and that Wager River is properly Wager Strait, and not a fresh Water River; and that the Way you enter'd it was one, tho' not the greatest and easiest way into the Strait: I only want your Chart of the whole new discovered Coast, to establish or contradict my Judgment of it, which I am informed is come to Dublin, but not yet sent to me. However, I can't delay imparting my present Thoughts of it, and my Reasons from your Journal, to shew you were in the Strait, but not in a fresh River; and that the chief Cause of your taking it for a River was from the quantity of Ice, the straitness of the Tide, and its following you from the Eastward, and not meeting the Flood from the Westward, which

[1] Published as a 'Chart of Hudson's Bay and Straits, Baffin's Bay, Strait Davis and Labrador Coast', London, 1743. See pp. 246–7.
[2] That is, the Lords Commissioners of the Admiralty.
[3] Middleton, *Vindication*, pp. 131–5.
[4] This letter has not been found.

was one of the greatest Proofs we went upon, before you left us. Now this last Objection is easily answered; that had the Ocean flowed in near Whalebone Point, as we at first expected, we must then have expected to have thereabouts met the Tide of Flood from the Westward; but since we find the Communication is by a Strait, or Passages thro' Islands, and broken Lands, as in the Magellanick Straits; there the Tide continues to rise, until it meets the Tide from the other Ocean, and the Flood is not expected to meet us until we have at least got thro' half the Length of the Strait; and if you will look into Narborough's Account of the Magellanick Straits,[1] you will find that a parallel Instance. Those Straits are no where above four Leagues wide, in most places not above two Leagues, and in the narrow, at the East Entrance, not above a League wide; and yet he went about fifty leagues into the Straits, before he met the Western Tide. Now you have full stronger Reasons for Wager's River being a Strait; it was but six or seven Miles wide at the Entrance on the East Side, and but from 16 to 44 Fathom deep; as you went up, it increased to four, five, six, and seven Leagues wide; Deer Sound, seven Miles wide, goes off from it, and probably others not mentioned in the Journal; since the Lieutenant,[2] when he was last up 12 Leagues above it, says, he tried every other Inlet, to try if he could meet a contrary Tide, or other Passage out, and the Depth increased to 70 and 80 Fathoms; your mentioning also the Height and Cragginess of the Coast, and not mentioning their being covered with Snow, tho' you mention that Brook Cobham was,[3] makes me conclude that they were not covered with Snow; and there being neither Trees nor Grass still confirms me, that the whole was a Strait of salt Water, and that you were not come into fresh Water; but the Number of Whales and Fish, seen as high as he went, and none being seen below, nor where the Ships lay, in Savage Cove and Sound, is a Demonstration to me, not only that it was salt Water, but also that they came in from the westward, and that you would have found less

---

[1] Narborough's journal of his voyage of 1669–71 was printed in *An Account of Several Late Voyages & Discoveries to the South and North, Towards the Streights of Magellan, the South Seas...by Sir John Narborough, Captain Jasmen Tasman, Captain John Wood*, London, 1694.
[2] John Rankin.
[3] See p. 186 above.

Ice the higher you went; because the Whales could not have come there, without a Passage tolerably free from Ice, otherwise they would have come as far as where your Ships lay, but did not because of the Ice; and that must be the Reason why you did not see them, when you went up to Deer Sound, because the Ice was not then broke up where you were, as it was afterwards when the Lieutenant went up, and probably was much sooner up to the westward; from the Whales also, which you saw in the Bay or Inlet between 63° and 64°, and those seen by Fox in the same Place, and by Scroggs in 64°8', and towards Whalebone-Point, where they had no Ice, tho' you met a great deal there; I conclude, there has been more Ice thrown in there this Year, than usually is; and that all that Coast is a broken Coast with Islands, and Inlets, as Cape Fullerton was, as mentioned by Scroggs; and consequently conclude, that the Whales came into that Corner of the Bay, from the Upper End of that Strait you were in; and that you happened into the most northerly and narrow Entrance, into that Strait, and consequently most pester'd with Ice, and that the most easy and largest Inlet is to the southward of Whalebone-Point, betwixt that and the Head Land near Brook Cobham in 63°20'.

My Reasoning upon your Journal I would have you consider of; for I realy think you have prov'd the Passage, tho' you were not at once able to perfect it ...... what is only necessary to fix or alter my Judgment, would be an Account of the Lieutenant's and Master's Observations, the last time they went up the Strait;[1] what Depths they had upon sounding, what Breadth the Channel continued, which Way it was directed, what Sound went off it on either Side; a great deal depends on their Recollection of these things, as well as whether they met with more or less Ice, whether Snow upon the Land or not, for as to the Tides following them in a Strait is no Objection.

If their Accounts confirm the others I have taken from the Journal, I think I may congratulate you upon your having found the so-much-wish'd-for Passage; and if it be one, am convinc'd the more southerly Entrance, thro' which the Whales come through into the Bay, will be free from Ice. ...... I beg to have your Sentiments upon this, as soon as you can consider it, and

---

[1] See the report of John Rankin and Robert Wilson, 1 Aug 1742, pp. 203–4 above.

have an Answer from your Officers, for the Presumption will be a great Inducement to open the Trade to the Bay; and in a further Discovery, there needs no Wintering in the Bay, only getting there in the Middle of July, and pushing as far in the Strait as can be done in the Month of August, and then returning in September home, which is better than wintering at Churchill, until the Passage through leads them to a warmer Climate on the other Side.

I shall add no more, but that I am with great Esteem,
   DEAR SIR,
    Your most obedient humble Servant,
      A——— D———.

7. Captain Middleton to Arthur Dobbs. 5 February 1742 (OS).[1]

SIR,

I received yours of the 22d of January, and saw the Letter you inclosed in Mr. Smith's to the Lord C[arteret] concerning opening the Trade to the Bay.

You say I have made a much greater Progress in the Discovery of a Passage, than I imagined when there, and that from the Light you have got from my Journal, you can almost prove that I was in the Passage, and that Wager River is properly Wager Strait, and not a fresh Water River; and that the Way I entered it was one, tho' not the greatest and easiest Way into the Streight.

You also observe, that if there is a Communication between the Bay and the Western American Ocean, or Passage thro' Islands or broken Lands, as in the Magellanic Streight, the Tide will continue to rise until we get half Way through, and then meet the Tide of the other Ocean. This I thought of when there, made several Trials, and ordered my Officers to do the same, not only near Deer Sound, but in their Progress up the River as far as they went, and to take Notice of the Flux of the Tides, their Direction and Height, as you'll find inclosed here. Now as by mine and their Observations, it flowed at Savage Sound fifteen Feet, and the same Day but ten Foot at Deer Sound, and fifteen Leagues above Deer Sound, on the W.Side, but six Feet.

---

[1] Dobbs, *Remarks*, pp. 135–8.

The Tides kept their regular Course as high up as I was myself, which was five Leagues above Deer Sound, about seven Hours Ebb and five Hours Flood, twenty Leagues up; whereas, if there had been a Tide form the Westward to have met this, it must have raised the Tide higher, the farther we went up, as it does in Narborough's Account of the beforementioned Streight; but the Flood would not have run above two Hours, as he found it there. All these Observations confirmed me, that it could not be a Streight, as you seem to think.

The Whales we saw in the River Wager certainly come in at the Mouth of that River, where the Ships entered at; for we saw several in the Welcome, and some off from Cape Dobbs, after we came out, and before we went in. The high Land and deep Water gave me great Hopes before I try'd the abovementioned Tides.

Brook Cobham was covered with Snow when we went out, but in our Return Home there was none upon it. The Snow on the Land in the River Wager was much wasted before we got out of it, especially upon the Tops of the Mountains; but in the valleys it lay very thick, and froze so hard as to be able to bear Waggons and Horses.

As to any Passage or broken Lands between the River Wager and 62°40′ I am certain that I searched that Coast very narrowly, and stood into every Bay all along so near, that the Indians I had on Board knew all the Coast, and would have had me to set them on Shore at Cape Fullerton, for they knew their Way to Churchill, and had that Way travelled several Times in the Summer, which they could not have done had it consisted of Islands or Rivers; for they have no Canoes, neither is there any Wood to raft them over as the Indians do, to the Southward.

The Copy of the Lieutenant and Master's Report I have here inclosed,[1] and what is wanting in their Relation I shall mention here. The River, five Leagues above Deer Sound, is eight or ten Leagues broad; the Channel is seventy or eighty Fathoms deep in the Middle, and lieth near N.W. by the true Chart, as far as they went up, and met with as much Ice or more than we did below where the Ships lay. I went several Times up the River myself, but all was so choak'd with Ice, that I could but once get

---

[1] See pp. 203–4 above.

over to the West Shore; so that it is my Opinion, that this River cannot be above one Week or two at most clear of Ice in a Year, and many Years not clear at all.

There must be Land to the Westward, and a very great Tract of Land, from the Reasons I mentioned in the Observations of the Effects of Cold. Whilst the Wind blows from the Northwest Quarter the Air is continually frozen, by the Winds passing over Mountains perpetually covered with Snow. The Land from the Water-side ascends gradually up into the Country, and is very high, as I saw from off some very high Mountains above Deer Sound.

This is all I have Time to think upon at present, but I should be heartily glad you could dissolve the Company, for they have used me and all my Men who were with me very ill; and those who voluntarily entered with me at Churchill, they refuse to pay their Wages due;[1] neither can I get any money for my Servant, whom I formerly put in their Service. There are many other Things which have been very fatiguing to me, and no doubt will be tiresome to you, therefore beg leave you will conclude me to be, as I really am, with great Respect, Sir,

London, Feb.5, 1742–3.
Your most obedient,
Humble Servant,
Christ. Middleton.

8. Lieutenant Rankin to Captain Middleton. 12 February 1742 (OS).[2]

Portsmouth at Long Reach

I Received yours the last Night which did not a little surprize me that My Lord Winchelsea suspected that I was Drunk when I took my Leave of him. I do assure you that I had Drink no More then the Share of one bottle of fine Eall [Ale?] between three of

---

[1] An entry of 5 November 1742 in the minute book of the London Committee has more information upon this. 'John Morgan and John Armount, two of the Sailors that Entred on Board Capt Middleton at Churchill River attended the Committee for the Wages due to them. The Committee looked into their Several Contracts and find that as they had left the Companys Service before their Contracts were Expired their Wages were forfeited besides the Penalties therein mentioned of £10 and £20.' HBC A 1/35, p. 331.

[2] Adm 1/2099; printed in Middleton, *Vindication*, p. 155.

ws at the Duke of Portlands,[1] where I Dinned and two Glas of wine after Dinning, then I went to wat upon my Lord and take my Leave of him and to give the Duke of Portlands Service to him.

I am Dear Sr Infinitely obliged to you for the great Honour you have been pleassed to Do Me, in giving me a good Carrectir to my Lord, and Sr Jacob Ackworth, I shall for Ever Think My Self bound to pray for your good Health, and Prosperity, If ever it should be in my pour to serve you by Night or Day, I shall allways Think my Self in Duty bound to Do it....

9. Authenticity of Captain Middleton's Journal. 19 April 1743.[2]

This is to Certifie the Right Honble. the Lords Commissioners for executing the Office of Lord high Admiral of Great Brittain & Ireland &c.

That this Journal is an authentick Copy of what was kept on Board the Furnace by Capt. Middleton on the late Discovery which was taken by me from the Original as Witness my hand.

James Smith.

Who was sent along with the above said Capt. Middleton as an assistant Clerk by my Friend Arthur Dobbs Esqr.

We whose names are undermention'd have carefully examined & peruz'd this Journal, & testify it to be a true Coppy from the Original Logbook kept on Board his Majestys Sloop Furnace by all the Officers on Board.[3]

Jon. Rankin

Robt. Wilson

Witness our hands this 19th of Aprill 1743.

[1] William Bentinck, 2nd Duke of Portland, a Whig grandee who held no office, and whose main claim to fame seems to have been that he was thought 'to be the handsomest man in England'. *The Complete Peerage*, London, 1945, X, p. 593.

[2] This certificate is on the fly-leaf of the copy of Middleton's journal in the Public Record Office, Adm 51/379, pt I, f.1.

[3] No trace of this 'Original Logbook' remains. There is nothing particularly surprising about this, since such logs were often in poor condition after daily entries during a voyage, and once a neat copy had been made were often disposed of. Middleton wrote later that 'Wygate finished the Copy of my Journal at Woolwich, and Mr. Landrick and Smith, two of Mr. Dobbs's recommending, wrote from this very Journal three others for Mr. Dobbs, the Admiralty, and Navy; which they finished in three Weeks time, after our coming to Town'. *Rejoinder*, p. 105.

10. Minutes of Board of Admiralty. 30 April 1743.[1]

Resolved that the late Lieutenant, Master, Surgeon, and Clerk of the Furnace Sloop be directed to attend the Board on Monday morning next.

11. Minutes of Board of Admiralty. 2 May 1743.[2]

Mr Arthur Dobbs, attending, was called in, and Mr. John Rankin late Lieutenant of the Furnace Sloop was called in and Mr Dobbs queries[3] were read to him to which he gave in but when the whole was gone through the Queries were delivered to him with Directions to deliver an Answer thereto in writing, he being withdrawn Robert Wilson the Master was called in and the same Proceedings put with him as with the Lieutenant and he being retired Edward Thompson the Surgeon, and John Wygate Captains Clerk were called, and the same queries read to them, and then copies delivered to them to give in their answers in writing.

12. William Moor to Captain Middleton. April, May 1743 (extracts).[4]

27 April 1743

What either the Doctor, Thompson, or Wygate, can say will go for nothing, as for the other [Lieut. Rankin], he is an old Woman, and Mr. Dobbs is a Man of finer Sense than to hear his Cock-and-Bull Story.

13 May 1743

I am not a little surprized to hear that the Doctor and Wygate have taken Oath, that it is their Opinion, that there is a Passage thro' the River Wager, as I understand by my Brother's telling of

---

[1] Adm 3/479, 30 Apr 1743.
[2] Ibid., 2 May 1743.
[3] Dobbs's 'queries' are printed in Middleton, *Vindication*, pp. 156–92.
[4] Christopher Middleton, *A Rejoinder to Mr. Dobbs's Reply to Captain Middleton*, London, 1745, pp. 149–50.

me, not that I have yet seen his Letter, only hearing that they intend to make what Disturbance they can imagine.

13. Thomas Corbett to Captain Middleton. 23 May 1743.[1]

Mr Arthur Dobbs having laid before my Lords Comrs of the Admiralty, Objections to your Conduct in your late Voyage in the Furnace Sloop, together with the Discovery Pink, in order to find out a North West Passage; and having proposed several Queries, relating to your Proceedings in that Voyage, to which the late Lieutenant, Master, Surgeon, and Clerk, of the Furnace Sloop, have given Answers;[2] I am commanded by my Lords Commrs of the Admiralty to send you Copies of the said Objections, Queries, and Answers, and am to acquaint you, that the Publick having been at great Expence in fitting and sending out the said Sloop and Pink, in order to make the aforementioned Discovery, which would be of great Publick Utility, their Lordships think it a matter of a very serious Nature, and that they ought to be thoroughly satisfied that the Person entrusted with the Execution of such a Design has strictly performed his Duty therein; and therefore they expect, that you give a very particular and clear Answer to the several Points of Misconduct, with which you are charged, by the aforesaid Papers.

14. Captain Middleton to Thomas Corbett. [May 1743][3]

I have their Lordships Commands signified by your Letter, with the several Papers inclosed therein, containing Objections to my Conduct in my late Voyage in the Furnace Sloop, and Discovery Pink. As it is their Lordships Pleasure, I should answer each Particular in a distinct Manner, I humbly pray their Indulgence, that I may have Time to make my Replies thereto; not doubting, but I shall make such sufficient Answers as will be entirely to

---

[1] Adm 2/479, pp. 320–1; printed in Middleton, *Vindication*, pp. 1–2.
[2] Contained in Adm 3/47, 23 May 1743; printed in Middleton, *Vindication*, pp. 156–92. Some of the more important points from this evidence have been incorporated into the footnotes to Document 15 below.
[3] Middleton, *Vindication*, p. 2.

their Lordships Satisfaction; and prove myself an honest Man, and a faithful Officer and Subject to the King.

15. Captain Middleton to Admiralty Board. [July 1743][1]

As I was not in the least conscious to myself of any Misconduct during my Voyage to Hudson's-Bay, it gave me great Surprize and Concern to hear that Mr. D—— had made a most ungenerous Attempt to ruin my Character and Reputation, and deprive me of your Lordships Favour and Esteem: In both which Respects I might have been a great Sufferer, if your Lordships had not been pleased to order me a Copy of his Accusations. I therefore think myself obliged to return your Lordships my very humble Thanks for allowing me an Opportunity of making a proper and just Defence.

According to your Lordships Commands, I have drawn up full and particular Answers to all that Gentleman's Objections and Remarks; submitting the same to your Lordships candid and impartial Examination; being well assur'd I have therein paid the strictest Regard to Truth, and supported the whole with strong Evidence of Facts, from the Logg-Books and Journals, as also from the Instructions, Councils, Reports, Affidavits, &c. annex'd in an Appendix; as must, I humbly hope, give entire Satisfaction to your Lordships, in every Point alledg'd against me, and entice me to your Countenance and Protection.

Mr. D—— has cast his Reflexions together, in so confus'd and incoherent a Manner, without Order or Method, and so frequently repeated the same things, that I was for some time at a loss how I might make my Answers clear and distinct, as your Lordships had required. At length I perceiv'd I had no other way but to answer him Paragraph by Paragraph; and wherever I met with Repetitions, to refer back to the Answers already given....

[1] Ibid., pp. 3–4.

OBJECTIONS of Mr. Arthur Dobbs to the Conduct of Capt. Christopher Middleton, in a late Voyage for a Discovery of a North-west Passage: Together with Capt. Christopher Middleton's Defence of his Conduct, in Answer to the Objections of Mr. Arthur Dobbs.[1]

It appears that he found a strict Tide at the Headland,[2] *N.E. of Brook Cobham, and that the Tide sometimes rose there 22 Feet, and that many Whales*[3] *were seen there close in upon Shore, but none seen but in that Place and in Wager River by him, and in the same Bay by Fox, and between Cape Fullerton and Whalebone Point by Scroggs.*

What Mr. Dobbs means by a strict Tide, I cannot guess. Being outward Bound in Lat. 63°20' No. 9 or 10 Leagues to the Eastward of Brook Cobham, I met with a Tide off the Head-land, which run but two Miles an Hour, from the N.E.b E. one Day before the Full-Moon: This is no more than what we find all along that Coast; as also between Churchill and York Fort, near the Full and Change: And also, when it blows hard with a Wind northerly, we frequently experience the Tide to rise as high as 20 or 22 Feet. Twenty Years Observations along these Coasts, have confirm'd me in this, and all who have been duly acquainted with them know it well. Our Journals do not mention any Whales, Seals, or Sea-Horses, to have been seen nearer Brook Cobham, than off the Head-land, which is 10 Leagues from it, nor did we see any near that Coast besides there.

But no black Whales seen at any other time in any other Part of the Bay, or in Hudson's Straits, by any Ships who have been in the Bay, either upon Trade, or upon making Discovery.

I have almost every Voyage seen Whales 50 or 60 Leagues up in Hudson's Straits, and have frequently traded for fresh Bone in all Parts of the Straits and Bays, particularly about the Upper Salvages, Salisbury, and Nottingham in the Straits; the Sleepers,

---

[1] The long document which follows was received by the Admiralty Board on 20 July 1743, and is now in Adm 1/2099. It was printed by Middleton in his *Vindication*, pp. 14–65, where Dobbs's objections, queries and criticisms were shown in italic type. This arrangement has been followed below, with printers' errors tacitly corrected.

[2] Baker Foreland.

[3] The references here and later to 'whales' or 'black whales' are to Bowhead Whales (*Balaena mysticetus*).

Baker's Dozens, and as far down as Belcher's Islands, in Lat. 56°
in the Bay, the Company allowing us 25 per cent. neat Profit
upon all such Trade. That this can be no other than the Bone of
Whales actually taken in these Parts, is evident beyond Dispute,
to all who know, that in 10 or 12 Days after a Whale is dead, the
Bone drops off of itself from his Mouth; for it is impossible the
dead Fish should drive 180 Leagues in that Time, since no Ship,
even under her main Course, or at Hull, has ever been known by
the greatest Storm to drive above two Miles, or two Miles and an
Half an Hour: But it is well known, that a very small Part only of
a dead Whale's Body emerges above the Surface of the Water;
well then may it be admitted, that it would require at least 3
Months, in the most favourable Circumstances, for such Fish to
drive from Wager River or Brook Cobham, to any of the before-
mention'd Parts, or to Rupert River, where a dead Whale was
found about 3 Years since, with the Bone all in its Mouth; a sure
Proof that it had lately liv'd therebouts. It is not reasonable to
conclude, that there are no Whales in Hudson's Bay, because we
have never seen any. It should be considered, that in our Track
we always keep at a great Distance from the Shore, at a time of
the Year when the Whales keep in the Bays and great Inlets.
This is the Reason why all those Indians that drink Train-Oil,
and feed on Blubber, choose to inhabit the East Main, as I have
been assured by one of them who lived with me three Years.[1]

*That Wager River is a Strait and no fresh River, is evident from its
Increase and Depth, from the Entrance on the East-side, to the South-
westward and North-westward, and also the Heighth of the Lands, and
there being no Shrubs nor Timber on any of the Lands, tho' always found
in the same, or more northerly Latitudes, upon fresh Water Rivers.*
That Wager River was no Strait, but a fresh Water River,[2] I
collected from the following Particulars. 1st, from the Floods
coming in at its Mouth from the Eastward. 2dly, From its flowing
18 Feet at the Entrance, but 13 at Deer Sound, and at the highest
the Boat went, no more than 5 or 6 Feet. 3dly, From the Water's
being almost fresh in the Mid-Channel above Deer Sound, so
that the Men chose to drink it alongside the Boat, when myself

---

[1] This was 'Charles', who had died in 1741. See p. 81 n. 4 above.
[2] To be precise, an inlet with a small river flowing into its head.

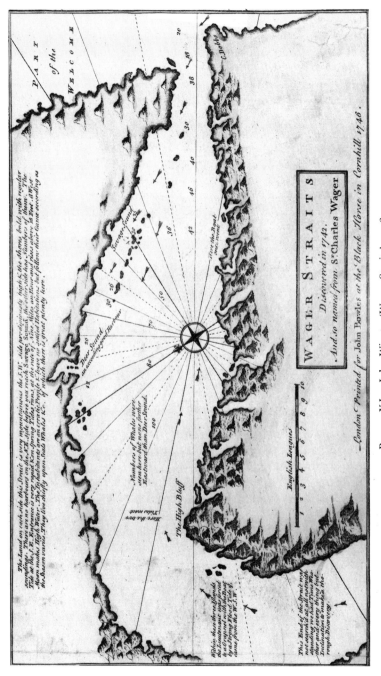

PLATE XI. John Wigate: 'Wager Straits', 1746
(British Library)

275

was present. 4thly, From the Water-falls being so strong, as to force the Boat to come to a Grapnel, being unable to proceed higher up.

The East Entrance of Wager River was only 7 Miles wide, and from 14 to 44 Fathoms in the Mid-Channel, as they sailed in, with a rapid Tide, which run from 6 to 9 Miles in an Hour, but farther up Westward, even from 20 Leagues to 30 Northwest, it increased to 8 and 10 Leagues wide; and so as to have no Ground with a Line of 68 Fathoms.
It is a fallacious Way of arguing Wager River to be a Strait from its Increase and Depth of Water. In several Parts of the Norway and Swedish Coasts, there are large Rivers which the Natives call Fewrs, not above 10 or 12 Fathom at the Entrance, and yet they discover no Ground within, with many hundred Fathoms of Line. It is indeed not difficult, tho' it would be too tedious, to account for all such Rivers enlarging their Capacities, both in Breadth and Depth.

The Land I saw here was as high to the full, as any I met with about the River Wager: As for the want of Trees and Shrubs, those who have travelled from Churchill N.W. as far as the Arctic Circle, by Land, as Norton[1] and many others, all agree, that after they had past the Lat. of 61° they never saw the least Tree or Shrub, tho' they went 2 or 300 Miles within Land, amongst Lakes and Rivers of fresh Waters.

At 20 Leagues from the Entrance, it was full of black Whales, Seals, and Sea-Horses, when there were no Whales seen below, or without the River.
I saw myself only two small Whales, neither of them of the Whalebone kind, in Wager River, these were at Deer Sound, where the Lieutenant and Master saw others of the black kind, but none were seen above it; these, they were of Opinion, came by some Inlet on the East-side the River.[2] Mr. Dobbs says, that the River, at 20 Leagues from the Entrance, was full of black

---

[1] Probably a reference to Richard Norton's journey of 1717, when as a young lad he accompanied a band of Chipewyan Indians north from Churchill River for an unknown distance (but certainly not as far as the Arctic Circle). See *DCB*, III, p. 489.
[2] True of the master, Robert Wilson; but Lieut. Rankin thought the whales in the Wager came 'through the Channels bounded by the broken Lands on the West Side.' Middleton, *Vindication*, p. 161.

Whales, Seals, and Sea-horses. None ever saw Whales above Deer
Sound, which yet is but 15 Leagues higher than the Entrance.
But how comes it that none of these were seen yet higher up,
nearer his pretended Passage into the Western Ocean, where it
was clear of Ice, if they came in that Way; whereas myself and
others saw three at our coming out of the River? After all, if the
Whales came not in from the Eastward, why should there be
such Abundance of Eskimaux about Savage Sound, but eight
Leagues within the River's Mouth, with Store-houses of Blubber
and Fin, and none to be seen elsewhere on the Coasts of this
River? Whereas, did they come in higher from the Westward,
the Inland whereof these Indians chiefly inhabit, we should
certainly have found them and their Store-houses that way, and
not down the River 60 Miles from their Homes. As for Mr.
Dobbs's Seals and Sea-horses in the River Wager, I take them to
be all his own; I never saw any there myself, nor have I heard
that of my People ever did.

——*All broken Land at the Northwest End, with a great Collection of
Waters full of Islands, the Lands on the Sides as high as the lands at the
Cape of Good-Hope, and a large Opening on the Southwest Side,*
The Lieutenant and Master say indeed in their Report,[1] that
they saw, far to the Northward, a large Collection of Waters,
with mountainous Land on the Sides; and on the West-side bluff
Points, and broken Land: But then they take Notice also of a
great Run or Fall of Water on this Side the said Collection of
Waters, which doubtless must have rendered any Progress upwards impracticable; and affords a strong Argument against any
Communication between Wager River and the Western American Ocean. If it be worth while to form any probable Conjec-
tures about such large Collections of Waters, I wou'd say, 'tis
likely they are no other than a kind of Lakes of melted Snows
from the Mountains; for several such we saw every where between the Hills, in the Valleys, where we were ashore on Mountains about Cape Frigid, and above Deer Sound; as also on the
S.W.Side of the River Wager, where I was myself the Day before
we left that River.

[1] See p. 204 above.

————*which was never attempted nor look'd into,*————

tho' Mr. Dobbs is pleased to say, that this Side was never so much as look'd into at all. The Truth is, we had made several unsuccessful Attempts to land there, but never could for Ice, before that Day.

————*nor none of the Bays nor broken Lands betwixt Whale Cove and Cape Dobbs, the South Cape of Wager River, were searched into at all,*————

At our Return from Cape Frigid to Brook Cobham, we searched exactly all the West-shore, as near as the Islands and Rocks permitted us with Safety; and saw all the Main-land and Bottom of the Bays, as is explained at large in our Logg Book, shewing the Course and Distance sailed every Hour, in hauling off or on, to deepen and shoalden the Water, which the Journal expresses less particularly; especially from Whalebone Point to Brook Cobham homewards: The rest of the Way Northward we had traversed outward bound. We had very little hazy Weather, except in the Night, and then we lay by till Day-light, and hauled in as near the Shore as we durst. It was not possible to miss any Inlets where there could be any Hopes of a Passage. Off Cape Fullerton, we met with Rocks and broken Ground 5 Leagues distant, which obliged us to haul farther off to deepen our Water, and lay too for moderate clear Weather, between the two Shores. But when it cleared up, we stood in N. and N.b.W. into 40 odd Fathoms; if we came within that Depth, we fell into broken Ground, sudden Shoaldings, Riplings, and Overfalls. But between Lat. 64° and 63°, we had better Soundings, and could come nearer the Land, tho' at Night we were obliged to keep a League or two further out,[1] and drive, as per Logg Book, and stand in Shore in the Day: We never, but once, were above 4 or 5 Leagues off Shore, and that was towards Morning, in Expectance of Day-light; in most other Places not above 2 or 3 Leagues from the Land, and in 9 Fathoms Water off the Head-land in Lat.63°20'. All the North-side of the Welcome is high Land, and as far as Brook Cobham, appears very near at 4 or 5 Leagues Distance. Fox's Account of this Coast, and its Tides, may be met with in a Book printed at London in 1635, entitled *North-west Fox, or Fox from the North-west Passage.*

---

[1] So missing the entrance of Chesterfield Inlet.

——tho' the chief Places pointed at by Fox and Scroggs for a Passage; they having mention'd them to be all broken Lands and Islands, where many Whales were seen, where were high Tides from 4 to 5 Fathoms, —— Scroggs's Account is in the Possession of the Hudson's Bay Company. I have carefully perused both that and Fox's many Years since. They are so profoundly unintelligible, that one may venture to say, no uninspired Person can make any Thing of them.

——but no Stop made there by Capt. Middleton, nor his Boats ever once sent on Shore, to try the Tides, or search after Inlets or Straits, tho' he had very fine Weather all the Voyage; and tho' at a Council, they had agreed to search that Coast; great Part of it being past in the Night, and having not been at any Time nearer the Islands or Head-lands than 5 or 6 Leagues,—— The Reason I did not send the Boat on Shore to try the Tides, was too melancholy a one to be easily forgotten; the greatest Part of our Men were not only sick, but had also lost the Use of their Limbs; so that if I had mann'd the Boat, the remaining Hands would have been insufficient to have work'd the Ship, or handled the Sails. The Truth of what I say will scarce be call'd in question, when it is known how many of the poor Creatures I was obliged to leave at the Orkneys, and how many of them since we came home, have been, and still are soliciting for Smart Tickets,[1] most of which will, I fear, be for ever unserviceable to their Country and to themselves. If I had not impressed 8 or 9 Men at the Orkneys, as I then wrote to my Lords Commissioners of the Admiralty, I could not possibly have brought the Ship home, having not above 3 Men and 4 Officers who did Duty, that were able to come on Deck.[2]

---

[1] In order to be able to apply for a pension.

[2] The replies sent to the Admiralty in May 1743 show a direct conflict of evidence on this point. Wilson supported Middleton's contention on the state of the crew. Off Brook Cobham, he recalled, 'The ship lay in a dangerous Roadstead, if the Wind came on the Shore or thick Weather; so that the Boat could not find the Ship. We durst not let go one of our Bower Anchors, having but two left; and the Men, when our Boat was from the Ship, could not get it up again, if it had blown so as to make a Sea; for they grew worse every day, and we had not above six in both Watches, besides three or four Officers, that could go up to hand or reef.' Ibid., pp. 181–2. Thompson, on the other hand, insisted that 'out of fifty-three Men and Boys, we brought out from Churchill, we had but eight that were uncapable of doing their Duty, as I am very well assured from my sick Book, so never wanted a Boat's Crew upon any Emergency; and when the Master gave an Account of the Tide at Marble Island rising twenty-two Feet, and was desirous of going a-shore again, to be more fully satisfied, the Captain told him, he should be damn'd before he went a-shore again.' Ibid., p. 182.

But to return to the Tides; they were so far from being neglected by me, that I tried them frequently, and almost every Hour, as also the Currents, which I could do as well on board, or in a Boat near the Ship in the Channel, and much better than within Head-lands or near Islands, which, by forming Eddies, produce a Confusion and Irregularity in them, to which Cause is undoubtedly owing to the gross Inconsistencies which abound in Fox, Mr. Dobbs's favourite Oracle. My Instructions ordered me to observe the Height, Course, and Direction of the Tides; but to observe them almost every Hour in all Places, as I did here, would not only have been quite incompatible with our ever returning home again, tho' I had tried but 20 Leagues of Coast, in such high Latitudes, where what is called Summer is so quickly over; but it would also have been altogether unnecessary. For wherever I judged it proper to examine, I never fail'd to do it, as at Churchill, Whale Cove in Lat. 62°20′, Wager River, and the Frozen Straits; and having the exact Course and Height of the Tides from my own Experience, at these Places, as also in all Parts of Hudson's Bay, I could not mistake the Floods for the Ebbs afterwards, by observing the Slacks, as Mr. Dobbs, an utter Stranger to such Matters, has attempted to insinuate.

——*the Ships having quit the Discovery in the Beginning of August,*
——

The Discovery was not quitted before the 15th of August, when we left Brook Cobham. This Month is confessedly the fittest of all the Year, and the only one too, for making and perfecting Discoveries in these Parts; the Seas being then tolerably clear of Ice in some Years; for in others, there is no passing at all to the Northward of Lat. 64°. If I had staid longer than I did, how could I have expected to pass Hudson's Straits, who well remember the Fate of one of our homeward bound Ships, which was lock'd up in Ice near Mansfield Island in the Middle of September, where she lay confin'd three Weeks, and had her whole Crew almost frozen to Death. We usually pass the Straits homewards the latter End of August, or the Beginning of September at farthest, and even then our Sails and Rigging are frozen to such a degree, that if a Topsail be handed, we are two or three Days before we can get any Part of it set; but that Fresh-water-gentleman could ever imagine this in an easy Chair!

Since Mr. Dobbs is here again reiterating his Complaints of my Neglect of the Coast between Whale Cove and Cape Dobbs, I must observe, that tho' I did examine it carefully all along, as I have already set forth, yet was I no ways directed by my Instructions to do so.——Let me add, that southward of Latitude 65°, a Passage has been sought carefully and for no purpose for this hundred Years and more. For Button, Fox, and many others since, have kept along Shore by Sea as far as 65°, and others still higher within Land; which is sufficient to put this Point quite out of Dispute.

——*When almost all the Ice was dissolved in Wager River, and none to obstruct them to the southward of that River, that Month being the best Month in the Year to perfect the Discovery. The only pretended Reasons given by Capt. Middleton why he took Wager Strait for a River, were these; That the Tide flow'd into the Strait from the N.E. that it was full of Ice as far as the Ships went up, and somewhat higher, and therefore he took the Ice to be breaking up, as he went in; and that at a Point, near which they apprehended there was a Current or fresh Stream two Leagues from them, they apprehended the Water was brackish.*

The first was no Reason; for if it was a Strait, the Tide of Flood must follow them westward, until they met the contrary Tide, and as probably they had not got half Way through, the Flood must necessarily follow them from the eastwards.

The second Reason why the Ice was but breaking up when they entered the River must be also false; for none can imagine, that Whales in great Numbers should lye up the River under the Ice not broke up; it appears also that there was much less Ice above than below. Nor can the third be a Reason, because the Water near a Stream they apprehended to be a fresh Current should be brackish, tho' that is controverted; since there were great Openings into the River besides that Stream that they never tried, and no doubt the dissolving of the Snow from the Lands, as well as Ice, might lessen the Saltness of the Water at that Season in narrow Inlets.

Mr. Dobbs having brought me back to Wager River, I must attend him there again. None of our Journals say, that the Ice was but just breaking up in the main River. At the time the Lieutenant went up to Deer-Sound, it was not indeed broke up in the Inlets and Bays, as his Report testifies, but did break whilst he was there; yet assuredly it had been cleared away at the upper

Part of the River some Time. If the River itself had not been broken up, we could not have got our Ships into it: But it is well known, that in all frozen Countries, the upper Ice of the Rivers is blown up and first of all gives way, from the Freshes produced by melted Snow, which also hurries the Ice downwards in Concurrence with the Stream, and out of the River's Mouth into the Bay or Ocean.

And now I am speaking of melted Snow, I cannot avoid remarking the Weakness of this Gentleman's Conjecture, that these Dissolutions should so far take off the natural saline Quality of this imaginary Sea-water, in so wide and deep a Bason, as to render it but barely brackish; when it may be made appear, by an easy Computation, that such Addition can never amount to a thousandth Part of the total Content of the Water, and therefore must be altogether incapable of producing any sensible Alteration in its Taste.

————*Another Reason he also alledged why it was a River was, that the Height of the Tide diminished the farther westward he went, as from 13 Feet, where the Ships lay, to 10 Feet at Dear-Sound, 10 Leagues higher, and to 6 Feet at the furthest Bluff Point the Boats were at; however this last was only computative, having not had time to make a full Trial; but this, if true, can be no Reason; for it proves just the same in Magellan Straits; by Narborough's Account the Tide on the east Side rises 4 Fathoms, within the second Narrow 10 Feet, and in the Middle, where the other Tide meets it, it rises but 8 or 9 Feet.*

To make out this rapid Tide in Wager River, and to account for the Whales being there, and coming in by the Way the Ships entered, he alledges there was a great Tide flowed through a frozen Strait north eastward of Wager River, from Hudson's Strait by Cape Comfort, which was 18 to 20 Leagues long, from 4 to 7 wide, but filled with Islands, and fast froze from Side to Side, under which these Whales must have passed, and the Tide which filled not only the great Bay, above Cape Hope and Wager River, but also the whole Welcome, as far as the Point near Brook Cobham, where he supposes the southern Tide met it, and raised the great Tide there.

I do believe that my Conclusion, drawn from the lessening of the Rise of the Tide in ascending Wager River, will appear just to all who have been much experienced in such Affairs; yet I own, that the Instance of the Tides in the Strait of Magellan, which Mr. Dobbs brings from Sir John Narborough, admitting that they were duly observ'd, is an Exception to this general Rule, and has often been remark'd as the only known one of the kind. However, no one who has passed that Strait, takes the least Notice of any Brackishness or Freshness of the Water; tho' they all remark the Abundance of Trees on its Coasts. In a word, the several Phenomena and Properties of the River Wager do universally agree with those of all other Rivers where the Tide flows, in the known World.

In Answer to this it appears, that no Whales were seen near that Strait nor Bay above Cape Hope, nor any where near Wager River, at the east End, nor in the Welcome, until near Brook Cobham, and consequently the Presumption is strong, that the Whales never come in that Way. There are also strong Reasons to shew, that no Tide from Cape Frigid could cause the Tide in the River Wager———

It is true, as Mr. Dobbs observes, that our People saw no Whales during our short Stay at the frigid Strait, or in Repulse Bay above Cape Hope, tho' there might be great Numbers in shore which escaped our View, as those certainly would which I have said we saw off the Head Land in Latitude 63°20', if we had not been within five or six Miles of the Shore, and the abundance of Sea-horses and Seals which appeared every where thereabouts, is no small Indication that those Parts are not without Whales, since they are seldom seen in Numbers, but where Whales also come. I have already contradicted his Assertion, that none were seen near the east end of Wager River, by instancing three myself and others saw there.

———and that it is highly probable, that there is no such Strait, and that it is only in Imagination, or calculated to serve that particular Purpose. For from the Observations he made in Wager River, where he stayed three Weeks, he could ascertain the Time of Tide at High-water, where the Ships lay in Savage Sound, which was fixed to a west-and-by-north Moon, making High-water.

He might as well have said, 'Tis likely Hudson's Straits is an imaginary one, as that, 'tis probable there is no such Place as the Frigid Straits. When I was on Shore at Cape Frigid, I sent the Carpenter and Gunner to the Top of the highest Mountain there, from whence they could overlook and take a distinct View of all the Straits to the southward, and the Land, Islands, and Bays all round. At their Return, I strictly examined them as to the Particulars they saw; whether they were positively sure that the low Beach joined to the Land we stood upon? They assured me it did; that we were on no Island cut off from the Beach; and that the Frozen Straits, of which they delivered me a Plan next Morning on board,[1] was at least twelve Leagues wide from the east to the west Side; and not less than four or five Leagues over at the Mouth or narrowest Part. I could indeed see every thing very well from my own Station, except to the southward towards Cape Comfort, and the high Land that way; so that I was satisfied the Frozen Strait did not surround the Land we were upon: Besides had it been so, we could not have had a Tide so strong as four Miles an Hour, which had like to have halled the Ship into it. When I went on Shore we stood in within two Leagues of it, and were oblig'd, tho' the Wind blew a fresh Gale off the Mouth or Entrance of the Strait, to stand from it, thereby to prevent our being halled in among the Ice on the Ebb, and set off from it on the Flood. I left the Ship between nine and ten in the Morning, and got ashore by eleven, when I found the Water had fallen five or six Feet by the Shore, and noted it in my Memorandum Book. At my Return to the Boat at half an hour past 4 in the Afternoon, those who kept the Boat acquainted me, that it had flowed four Feet, and I presently measured what Height it had to flow to the Marks of the last Tide, by a Pole set up at the Water's Side, and found that a Level continued from the said Marks to the Pole made twelve Feet, which added to the four Feet the Men had observed, made in all sixteen Feet for the whole Rise of the Tide; though by some Marks of Sea-weeds, &c. on the Shore, it appeared to have flowed, upon extraordinary Circumstances, eight or ten Feet more. From the ebbing Water when I landed, I concluded the Time of High-water that Evening would between 8 and 9 o'Clock, it being almost four Days after the full Moon, and consequently a W. or W.b.S.Moon made High-water, and not a N.W.b.N.Moon, as Mr. Dobbs, the better to suit his purpose, would have it.

---

[1] This plan or map by the gunner, George Axx, is reproduced in Middleton, *Forgery Detected*, London, 1745, p. 5.

He tried the Tide when he was on shore at Cape Frigid, where he supposed the Frozen Strait, on Sunday the eighth of August, and found it Low-water at seven at Night, just at Sun-set as he affirms; the Moon was at full the fifth at six in the Morning in London; so allowing for the Difference of Longitude, it was then three Days and eighteen Hours after the Full; so that taking three Hours for the Difference of the Tide in that time, it was Low-water at full Moon, at four in the Evening, which was a S.W.b.W. Moon that made Low-water, consequently a N.W.b.N. Moon made High-water there, which was four Points or three Hours later than the Tide in Wager River, and consequently could not be caused by that Tide.

I must here however do Mr. Dobbs the Justice to confess, that when he ask'd me at my Lodgings, the only time he was pleased to call since my Return, how it flowed there on Sunday the eighth of August; having not my Memorandum Book at hand, I answered him, That to the best of my Memory, it was High-water just at Sun-set, about seven a'clock: whereas I should have said a little after eight, the Sun setting at that time; and if, as he relates, I said Low-water, that was an inadvertent Blunder, for which I ask his Pardon.

He also found at Brook Cobham, that a West or W.b.N. Moon made High-water there, and therefore that Tide could not flow from Cape Frigid, as he alledges from his Journal.

But to return to the Tides: Those who were on board perceived no Tide, either of Ebb or Flood between the low Beach and Cape Frigid, whilst they were driving and working to wait for the Boat; whereas if the Land of that Cape had been an Island cut off from the low Beach, the strong Tide would have come round it. But I lying off the Bay formed by the low Beach and Cape Frigid, several Hours after my returning on board, found no Appearance of any Tide that Way.

After all, were I to grant him his Tide at Cape Frigid, how much could that avail him? It is not possible to account for all the Anomalies and Peculiarities of Tides, without an accurate Knowledge of the almost infinite Causes and Circumstances to which they may be owing; as I wrote to him in November last. Though it flows E.S.E. at Resolution, and S.b.E. at Cape Diggs, making five Points in running 130 Leagues, yet it amounts but to a single Point in going down to Albany and Moose River; for there it flows S. and the Distance is 250 Leagues. Again, from Humber to Cromer, on the Lincolnshire Coast, is but 14 Leagues; yet at the former it flows W.b.S. and at the latter N.W. Likewise at the Orkneys it flows S.S.E. and the very same at Orfordness. I could bring hundreds of other Instances from my own Experience; so that where Tides flow into deep Bays, and are obstructed by Islands, or counter Tides, no Rules can be fix'd.

The late learned Dr. Halley, in his excellent Illustration of Sir Isaac Newton's Theory of the Tides, has set this Matter in a very just Light. And because he was not only well versed in the Philosophy of the Ocean, but also a most expert Seaman, I shall not scruple to transcribe his Words.

Speaking of the Phenomena of the Tides, according to the pure Laws of Gravity, he says, 'All these things would regularly come to pass, if the whole Earth were covered with Sea very deep: But by reason of the Shoalness of some Places, and the Narrowness of the Straits thro' which the Tides are in many Cases propagated, there arises a great Diversity in the Effect, not to be accounted for without an exact Knowledge of the Circumstances of the Places; as of the Position of the Land, and the Breadth and Depth of the Channels, by which the Tide flows: For a very slow and imperceptible Motion of the whole Body of the Water, where it is, for example, two Miles deep, will suffice to raise its Surface ten or twelve Feet in a Tide's time; whereas if the same Quantity of Water were to be convey'd upon a Channel of forty Fathoms deep, it would require a very great Stream to effect it in so large Inlets as are the Channels of England, or the German Ocean, &c.' *Philosophical Transactions*. No. 226.[1]

It appears also that on the sixth of July, as he was standing off and on a Head Land in about 63°20' at five in the Morning, he lower'd the Boat to try the Current, and found it set N.N.E. two Knots two Fathoms, it being then full Moon, and a W.or W.b.N. Moon making High-water there and at Brook Cobham, and it being then a W.b.S.Moon, it was then flowing Water, and the Current setting slowly N.N.E. the Flood must have come from the S.W. and not from the N.E.b.N. as he afterwards

---

[1] A particular thrust at Dobbs, since he had cited Halley with approval in his earlier Memorial. See p. 18 above.

pretends, and consequently a Tide might have come from the south-westward from some Inlet,——

For want of Experience in the Nature of Tides and their Course, and a strong Desire of bringing the Flood out of some Suppositious Inlet on the western Coast, he criticizes my Observation of July 6, endeavouring to invert the true Course. Here as usual, he keeps up strictly to Rule and Theory. But those who have been much in Practice will inform him, that upon all Coasts where the Tides flow, they are frequently found to vary their Course a full Hour and sometimes an Hour and half, just as they happen to be accelerated or retarded by conspiring or adverse Winds; I do not mean blowing on the Coast where the Observation is made, but at a remote Distance: These, I say, do produce various Irregularities in their Height and Length of flowing, in one and the same Place, and under the very same lunar Circumstances. I have known, for instance, that in the River Thames it has outrun its Course two Hours, and ebb'd and flow'd two or three times in one Tide, and all from Winds. I must observe, that Mr. Dobbs in this Remark had no less than twice miscopied my Log-Book, setting down two Knots two Fathoms, for two Fathoms only, and five instead of six o'Clock.

——it being the same Place where he afterwards saw the Whales. It appears also, that he sent the Lieutenant and Master in the Boat, when he was in Wager River, to look out for a Cove or Place of Safety for the Ships, in case they could not get out in one Tide, lest they should be carried up again by the Rapidity of the Tide, upon the Return of the Flood, it running at the Rate of 6 to 9 Miles in an Hour,——

He closes his Remark with another Touch upon the Whales, his constant Pilots; I presume I have said enough upon this Point already....

——the Boat was carried out along with the Ice, by the great Current of the Ebb, directly by the South-west Shore, S.E. towards Cape Dobbs, and at the Turn of the Tide at low Water, they got out of the Stream into the Eddy Tide, on the N. Shore, and so came up again with the Flood.

He hath misrepresented the Affair of the Boat's being carried out of Wager River by the Current of the Ebb. She was carried S.E.b.S. as the Tide sets, along the South Shore, 4 or 5 Leagues, and no more; and then she came into the Eddy, occasioned by the Ebb from the W.b.S. round Cape Dobbs. I tried the Current of the Ebb a Day before the Full Moon, and found it to run 5 Knots and no more. Mr. Dobbs speaks of 9 Knots. I know of no such Current in the World. London Bridge scarce runs so much.

It appears also upon the Ships going out of the River, that to prevent their being forced back again by the Return of the Tide of Flood, they made their Course as far as they could towards the North-east, to be out of the Current of the Tide of Flood, which must be an Evidence that the Tide of Flood came from the South-westward, round Cape Dobbs to the River Wager; for had it come from the North-east, by the supposed frozen Strait, they must, by standing that Course, be directly in the Way of the Tide of Flood to carry them back again into the River,——

On the 4th of August, at 6 o'Clock in the Evening, we came down the River Wager as far as the lower Islands. The Water had then ebbed one Foot, as all our Journals and Logg Books mention. By eight it was calm, and being then just out of the River's Mouth, we made all the Way we could, the Boats towing the Ship, which was also rowed with Oars, whilst we had the Ebb Tide helping us, which set out Eastward between the two Lands which form the Entrance of the River. By 12 we were got 4 Leagues out of the River, as also, out of the Indraught of the River's Tide, the Calm continuing these last 4 Hours, and the Flood Tide just coming from the Eastward at 1, did not run above 2 Knots; for the Indraught of the Tide of Rivers has very little Effect, at the Distance of 3 or 4 Leagues. From 12 to 2 we had a small Breeze at S. and stood E.S.E. 5 Miles; and from 2 to 4 E. 3 Miles: At 6 it was almost calm.

——and to have avoided that, they ought to have kept their Course towards Cape Dobbs, that the Tide of Flood might have carried them to the Southward. The Captain, Clerk, Carpenter, and Gunner, went on Shore at Cape Frigid to view the Land and supposed frozen Strait; the Carpenter and Gunner went to a Hill a Mile and half further than the Captain and Clerk, and upon their Return, as the Clerk affirms, they said the Hill they were upon was an Island, but the low beachy Land to southward of them was joined to the Eastern and Northern Land, which joined the West Land, and formed the Bay above Cape Hope, and that there was no frozen Strait to South-eastward of them, as the Captain has

*laid down in his Journal, and consequently no Tide could flow through
it from the N.W. of Hudson's Strait by Cape Comfort.*

Now this Gentleman is of Opinion we ought to have gone
towards Cape Dobbs, quite back again: How then could we have
avoided being forced ashore among all the Ice that lay off the
Cape, or again into the River? When we could lay only W.S.W.
and S.W. on the other Tack, the Wind being South and S.S.E.
and the Flood coming strong from the E. and E.b.N. This surely
had been a fine Way of meeting the Flood, and keeping to my
Instructions.

What I have said before[1] I believe may be fully sufficient to
evince the Reality of the Frozen Strait; yet I will add, that if,
according to Mr. Dobbs, there be no such Strait, whence should
the strong Tide of 4 Miles an Hour, which we met with there,
come, and which the Lieutenant observed to force the Ships very
rapidly to the North-eastward, in lying to about 10 o'Clock in the
Morning, as the Clerk affirms? who adds, that it must be a Flood
Tide, tho' we afterwards found by the Shore that it was an Ebb,
and that it had flowed near 8 in the Morning, as I have mentioned before. This is the Effect of Ignorance, or something
worse.

Mr. Dobbs is for denying a Passage to the Tides, by stopping
up the Straits with Islands, which is somewhat like stopping up
the Thames with London Bridge; for tho' our Journals mention
the narrowest Part to be but 4 or 5 Leagues wide, yet that is by
no means to be understood of the Distance from Main to Main,
but between Islands and Islands which lye off from the Shores.
The Main-lands, which include this Strait, are very high, and
therefore may be 3 or 4 Leagues more asunder than by our
Guess; for determining the Distance of Lands at Sea is no other
than guessing; however, I am sure the Interstices between the
Islands, where narrowest, are 4 or 5 Leagues, and may be more.

———*There being no Tide or Current in the Bay beyond Cape Hope, is a
further Reason that the Tide did not flow in that Way, for that Bay
would have been directly in the way of the Tide; but if the Tide of Flood
came from the South-west, it was a very good Reason why there was no
Tide or Current there, it having no further to flow that Way. Nor can it*

[1] P. 284 above.

be presum'd that so rapid a Tide, and so great a Quantity of Water should flow through so narrow a Strait, which in some Places was not 4 Leagues wide, and almost filled with the Islands, so that the Water, considering the Islands within it, was not 2 Leagues wide, so as to fill the Bay above Cape Hope, Wager River, which was 8 or 10 Leagues wide, and all the Welcome——

That there is no Tide or Current in Repulse Bay, is no Reason why the Tide did not flow in at the Frozen Strait. The Tide did point directly to the Bay; but it is a well-known Property of the Tides, that in Bays, where the Current of the Tide has no Outlet, it will swell by the Shore, but retain at the same Time such a Stagnation, as gives the same Resistence to the Current, as the Shores themselves give; and for this Reason no Tides are ever discerned in Bays. Even in the River Thames, the Watermen and all Craft are known to keep on from Point to Point, as the Tide sets, to keep in the Stream of it. Now this Gentleman would have it, that Wager River, where the Strait is but 7 Miles wide, bids fairer for filling the Welcome, and all these Bays, than the Frozen Strait, of as many Leagues, which is much nearer the Eastern Ocean.

——as far as the Point near Brook Cobham, where the Captain owns there was a rapid Tide, and alledges the southern Tide met the other there, altho' it appears that the Eastern Tide was lost in the Bay, and could not raise a high Tide there, it being also agreed, that a North-westerly Wind at Churchill, raises a higher Tide at Neap, than an easterly Wind does at Spring Tides, all these confirm that a westerly Tide must occasion so great Tides in that Part of the Bay——

Near Brook Cobham, I own, the Tide ran two Knots and no more at a Full Moon; and I have found it run the same or more Knots between Churchill and York Fort; and upon trying the Tide about 8 in the Morning between Wager River and Cape Hope, we found the Ebb 4 or 5 Miles an Hour, in such Eddies and Whirlings, that the Ships could hardly steer. The Ebb set E.b.S. by Compass: The first Trial, in bringing up the Boat, the Master lost one of our small Graplings, the Strength of the Ebb breaking a new twelve Thread Rope. He came on board again and got another, and upon the second Trial found it 4 Knots. We made no less than twenty Trials in going forwards and backwards between Wager River and Cape Frigid, but found it no where half so strong as in the Narrow of the New Strait, except at Cape Frigid and the Mouth of Wager River. I observed the last Time I was at Churchill, and had it confirmed by Officers who had been there and at Fort York above 15 Years, that a North, and a North-east Wind, made a higher Neap Tide, than a South, or South-west Wind did a Spring Tide, which is a Confirmation that the Tide comes through the Frozen Strait from Baffin's Bay, &c.

———*and since no Whales were ever seen in any other Part of the Bay, or in Hudson's Streights, but near the East-entrance, as they pass up to Davis's Straits, and that all true black Whales go in the Winter to warm Latitudes: all these Things considered, is almost a Demonstration that these Whales come from the Western Ocean, and that the rapid Tides near the Welcome, proceed from the same. The Captain, to evade the Force of this Argument about the Whales, says, that tho' he never saw any Whales in the Strait or Bay, he has however, got Whale-fin lately taken from the Indians, on the East Main, and therefore Whales must have been there. To this I answer, that since the Eskimaux Indians kill Whales on the North-west Side of the Bay, where the Company trade with them for Fin and Oil, the Presumption is, that some who have been wounded by them, have got away, and died, and by the North-westerly Winds have been driven to the East Main; and there the Fin was got by the Natives———.*

Here again he is drawing Conclusions from the Whales, which he will needs have to come out of the Western Ocean, as well as the Tides; tho', as to the latter, all Journals contradict him. He insists also, that all the Bone which is traded from the Natives near the East Main, must be of Fishes which died of Wounds they received near the West Main, and are driven this Way by North-west Winds. But I have observed before,[1] that the Fin drops out of their Mouths in 10 or 12 Days after they are dead, and that it would take up more than a Year to drive them so great a Distance; to which may be added, that Hudson's Bay is not clear of Ice two Months in twelve.

At Whale Cove it flows W.N.W. at Brook Cobham W. or W.b.N. at River Wager W. The Flood Tide comes the Course of

---

[1] P. 274 above.

the Welcome from the Eastward in all these Places, which may be proved from our Journal.

If there were any Passage between Churchill and Whalebone Point, near Lat. 65°, it would have been long enough ago found out, by one or another of all those who have been that Way; some of them several Years together; as Sir Thomas Button and Fox; Governor Kelsey, three or four Voyages, the last in my Memory; Napper, Handcock, Governor Knight, Vaughan, and Scroggs; who went to trade and make Discoveries in all the Bays, Coves, and Creeks along Shore, several of whom harboured every Night; and Governor Kelsey exchanged two of his own Indians for two Esquimaux, kept them at Fort York a whole Year, learned them some English, and then returned them to their Friends. Afterwards, as he went along that Coast, he saw and spoke with them several Times, but could get no Intelligence from them which afforded him the least Probability of a Passage.[1] Of this I furnished Mr. Dobbs with the most exact and particular Account I was able to give him several Years ago: But no Matters of Fact have Power to convince him; and his Scheme rests entirely upon Presumptions, which all Observations and Experience directly contradict. I have perused all the Company's Journals about this Discovery, as well as all others I was able to procure, whether in Print or Manuscript, from the Year 1615 down to the present Time. My Inclination has led me that Way this many Years, as much or more than his, or almost any Man's living, as all my Acquaintance, and himself too, know very well. I winter'd at Churchill for this purpose in 1721, and made all possible Enquiry then, as well as the last Year, among all the Indians and English who had travelled Inland to the northward; and I am thoroughly satisfied that any further Search must be fruitless, either by Sea or Land. Nor does it appear, that Mr. Dobbs himself so much as dream'd of any such thing before I last went out; else why was he not careful to have it inserted among my Instructions; whereas instead thereof I was strictly ordered to begin at Whalebone-Point, and search to the northward, still meeting the Tide of Flood, whether it should come from the eastward or westward.

---

[1] This was presumably on Kelsey's voyage north from York in 1721.

As a further Confirmation of a Strait or Passage near the Welcom, the northern Indians who came to Churchill, as well as those who were on board Scroggs, and those lately on board Capt. Middleton, said, there was a large Copper-mine upon a Strait northward of their Country which went westward, that they could conduct a Sloop to lay her Side to it, and take it on board, and traced the Coast upon a Deer-skin to be near the Welcome; and the Indians with Scroggs offer'd to go on Shore near Cape Fullerton, saying they were near it, and within three or four Days Journey of their own Country, but he could not part with them.

All the Indians I have ever convers'd with, who were at the Copper-mine, agree in this; That they were two Summers going thither, pointing towards the north-west and Sun-setting, when at Churchill; and that where this Mine is, the Sun, at a certain Season of the Year, keeps running round the Horizon several times together, without setting. Now we know from the Principles of Cosmography, that this cannot be true of any Place, whose Latitude is less than 67 or 68 Degrees, even allowing for the Effects of Refraction: And if the Credibility of the Testimony of these simple Indians be called in question, I can mention that of Mr. Norton, who was Governor at Churchill above twenty Years, and had travelled almost a Year north-westward by Land with this Country Indians. This Gentleman has often affirmed the same thing of the Sun; and that in his whole Journey he met with no Salt River, nor Tree, nor Shrub, but only Moss; and that he and his Retinue were reduced to such Extremity as to eat Moss several Days; having nothing else that could serve them for Sustenance but their Leather Breeches, which they eat up also. Now it will appear, from a just trigometrical Computation, that Churchill being in Latitude 59°, and the Mine in Latitude 67°, and the Bearing N.W. the Difference of Longitude between Churchill and the Mine is 17°45′. But Wager River's Entrance being in Latitude 65°20′, and 10 Degrees of Longitude east of Churchill, the Difference of Longitude between the Mouth of the River and the Mine is 27°45′, and their Distance in the Arch of a great Circle, or their nearest Distance, no less than 700 Miles.[1] From what I have here made out

---

[1] In general terms Middleton's assertions here were to be confirmed by Samuel Hearne's journey to the Coppermine River in 1771. Hearne located the mouth of the river in lat. 71°54′N, almost four degrees too far north.

concerning this Mine, and the Way to it, upon the Report of the Indians and of Governor Norton, it follows, even to Demonstration,

1st. That neither Wager River, nor any other River or Sea does extend so far westward, from any Part of Hudson's-Bay in less than Latitude 65°, as to cross the Rout that lies between Wager River and the Mine. And,

2dly. That if there be any Passage at all, it must run up so high northward, as to cross the Parallel of 67° on the east Side of the Mine, and consequently must be frozen up, and absolutely unnavigable the whole Year.

But, after all, a Passage is Mr. Dobbs's Philosopher's Stone, and must be sought for till found. If you miss at Brook Cobham and Wager River the next Bout, then try Nelson and Churchill Rivers. (See his Letter of November 19).[1]

With all my heart, say I, for my own sake! provided Mr. Dobbs himself accompanies the Expedition, to see there be no Neglect or Concealment: And in his Voyage it may not be amiss for him to consider the following Particulars.

Hudson's Strait is fourteen Leagues wide at the Entrance; forty Leagues up it is thirty Leagues over; and the nearest Distance between Cape Walsingham and Nottingham Isle is twelve Leagues; the whole Length being about 130 Leagues. Many Years we cannot pass the Strait outward-bound before the latter End of August, and then with incredible Fatigue, and perpetual Danger of losing Lives and Ships. Two out of three were lost within these sixteen Years.[2] After passing the Strait, there is still the Bay to cross, in which I was detained no less than six Weeks in Ice, the last Voyage I undertook for the Company.[3] I never was able to arrive at the Factory above five or six times before the 20th of August, in three and twenty Voyages I have made thither: And it is a standing Order not to attempt to come back the same Year, unless we can sail from the Forts by the tenth of September. Till a little above twenty Years ago, a Voyage was seldom made without Wintering.

Now supposing there were another Strait on the western

---

[1] P. 254 n. 1 above.

[2] The *Mary* in 1727 and the *Hudson's Bay* in 1736, both commanded by William Coats.

[3] See p. 67 above.

Coast of Hudson's Bay, or between Latitude 61° and 63°, and that this Strait were about as long and wide as that.

In the first place, there could be no entering it before the latter End of August for Ice, whether from England or your Wintering-place in the Bay: For though we got out at Churchill River by the first Day of July last Year, yet the like has not been known these twenty Years, by a Fortnight at least. But notwithstanding so favourable a Winter, and early a Spring, had we not work'd Night and Day Tides, from the Beginning of April to the Middle of June with infinite Labour in cutting out our Ships, which were bedded twenty-three Feet in the Ice and hard frozen Snow, as may be seen in the Journals, we should not have got out so soon by a Month. After all, this was of no Service in forwarding us; for being got into the Bay, we found all the Shores lined with Ice with many Leagues, so that no Opening could be entered; and the great Rivers and Straits, beyond 61 Degrees, are full of it until the Middle or latter End of August, and many Years not clear at all. I have been fast myself in Hudson's Straits for some Days in September, till a north-west Wind happened to set me and the Ice a going together. Of all the Sloops in my time which the Company have sent almost every Year along the Coast towards the Welcome, either upon Trade or Discovery, none but Scroggs could ever get beyond Latitude 64° for Ice; and since the Year 1718 they have lost two Sloops and a Ship that Way. Many of them could not get beyond 62°20′. Now all this well weigh'd, what Chance have Ships for passing such a Strait as we have supposed?

But grant there was no Ice to prevent a Ship's passing about the latter End of August, yet at that Season the Winter begins to set in here, with hard Gales and such Quantities of drifting Snow, that it was out of all human Power to handle a Sail, or keep the Deck.

The Lieutenant, when he was on Shore near Deer Sound in Wager River, set an Opening by his Compass S.W. of him, on the west Side of a Strait betwixt a high bluff Point, and a lower Point. This Inlet was opposite to the Place where the most Whales were seen, and was never enquired into or proceeded upon by the Captain, although acquainted with it, nor the Opening among the Islands to the north-westward, beyond the Place the Lieutenant went to, although the Lieutenant and

Master, under their Hands, reported they believed there was another Way into the Sea, than the Way the Ships entered, by which the Whales came there, and found little or no Ice to obstruct their going farther, there being much less Ice to the westward, than was at the Mouth of the River.
I have the Lieutenant's Paper about this Bluff Point still in my Possession, and a very odd one I think it is, at least far beyond my Comprehension; however I beg leave to submit it to the Opinion of my Lords Commissioners, as it is a Sample of his other Reports.[1] 'Tis hard to conceive how on the Bearings he mentions, any Object could be seen, except on the east Shore, being that whereon he stood; for the River lies nearly north and south by Compass: Mr. Dobbs says it was opposite to the Place where most of the Whales were seen; which should be somewhere against Deer Sound; but I could distinguish nothing thereabouts, which in the least answered the Description.

The Lieutenant and Master in the Report delivered me,[2] signed with their own Hands, say, That they believe there is another Way into the Sea, besides that which our Ships came in, at somewhere on the east Side; and that they imagine the Whales came through this Passage. Indeed they were sent up on purpose to search for such a Passage, and to meet the Flood, for fear we should not have the River's Mouth clear of Ice before the Winter set in upon us, and so all perish there. For after I had, for the Reasons before recited, given up all Hopes of a Passage through this River, I must confess I would have parted with all I had in the World to have been out of it again.

The Captain, before he went on the Voyage, was offer'd by some of the Directors of the Company £5000 to return to their Service, and not go the Voyage; or to go search for the Passage in Davis's Straits, or in any other Place but where he was directed: To which he answered, He might take their Money and be of no Service to them; for the Gentleman who had projected the Voyage, had it so much at heart, that if he did not go, he would get somebody else to go; but before he had done with it, he hoped to go in a Coach and Six: To which one of them answer'd, He hoped to see him at the Devil first,——
I deny, my Lords, that any of the Directors, either by themselves

---

[1] Rankin's paper of 15 July 1742 is printed in Middleton, *Vindication*, pp. 151–3.
[2] See pp. 203–4 above.

or others, offer'd me five thousand pounds, or even one shilling, to return to their Service, and not go the Voyage; or to go search for the Passage in Davis's Straits, or in any other Place but where I was directed: And granting such an Offer was made, Mr. Dobbs acquits me of any Crime by the Answer, he says, I made (or rather, that he in this place is so kind to make for me) viz. 'That I might take their Money and be of no Service to them; for the Gentleman who projected the Voyage, had it so much at heart, that if I did not go, he would get somebody else to go.' What follows, about my Hopes to ride in a Coach and Six, and Somebody's wishing me at the Devil, is such idle Trumpery, that I cannot induce myself to imagine your Lordships believe it deserves a serious Answer; and I am surpriz'd the Projector himself should think so.

———*They afterwards, by Sir Bibye Lake their Governor, promised him two Years salary, at £120 per Ann, not to do any thing to prejudice or obstruct their Trade, which he says was only upon Account of preventing his Crew's trading in the Bay*———.
Again, had I through Vanity, or any other Motive, been so foolish and wicked to assert I was offer'd £5000 to quit the King's Service; yet I presume your Lordships will not apprehend my Refusal of so large a Bribe redounds to my Disreputation: Besides, such a Refusal makes it senseless and absurd to suppose, that I should accept of so paltry a Consideration as two Years Salary, at £120 per Annum, to neglect my Duty in prosecuting the Discovery; when the very same Persons, at the same time, were offering me £5000 to return to a very beneficial Employment.

I readily grant, that the Governor and Directors of the Company recommended the Protection of their Trade to me. In them it was a very natural and reasonable Request; and, for my part, I esteem'd it the Duty of my Station to maintain them as far as I had Power and Authority, in the Rights and Privileges which were granted them by one of his Majesty's Royal Predecessors. Besides, when they had been so generous to allow me to winter at one of their Factories, it would have been a mean and base Return for their Hospitality, as well as the highest Ingratitude, to rob and plunder them, either by trading with the Natives myself, or suffering others under me to trade

with them; though I freely confess great Advantages might
have accrued by it.

*——so that 'tis plain Rewards or Bribes were offer'd to him, to prevent
his perfecting the Discovery, and every Omission or Neglect laid open to
be suspected.*
Mr. Dobbs concludes this Paragraph with asserting, that "Tis
plain Rewards or Bribes were offered him, to prevent his perfecting the Discovery'. What then? Does he not make it also as
plain that I refused Bribes, if any were offered? But how comes
it to be so plain that they were offer'd? Neither the Lieutenant,
Surgeon, nor Clerk charge me with any Bribes; and will your
Lordships think a bare Assertion, from one that appears now to
be my Enemy, a sufficient Proof? I hope not.

The Truth is, Mr. Dobbs's large Professions of Sincerity and
Friendship, once induc'd me to place great Confidence in him,
and unbosom myself freely to him; and 'tis possible, I might tell
him several members of the Company were desirous to have me
continue in their Service; and that as I had faithfully discharged
the Trust they had reposed in me for twenty Years together,
they expressed such Dissatisfaction of my quitting their Employment, that I should not doubt of obtaining of them very advantageous Terms, in case I should be inclined to treat with them
about returning to their Service.

*He also in the hearing of his Officers at Churchill, told the Governor and
Officers of the Company there, that he would be a better Friend to the
Company than they expected; for he would be able to make the Voyage
without any Man on board, being the Wiser, whether there was a
Passage or not——.*
I do remember, that being once with the Governor and some
Officers of the Company, they jeeringly said, we were to be
regarded as a kind of Enemies; and that I answered, Perhaps
they might find me a better Friend than they imagined, or to
that purpose; meaning thereby, not only the Power my Instructions gave me to protect their Trade, and which they understood
well enough; but something else also, which they could not so
easily comprehend. To explain myself to your Lordships, the
Agents of a certain Gentleman had, without my Knowledge or

Consent, shipped on board the Discovery, as many Goods, to be disposed of to the Indians, as would have gained them many hundreds of Pounds. This I discovered at the Orkneys, and was resolved, as I was in Duty bound, not to suffer any body on board to trade with the least part of them.[1]

The Words I am charged with in the latter Part of his Accusation were spoken to my own People on board, as a Reproach to their Ignorance and Stupidity, and their Aversion to be instructed; and I most solemnly declare it, not in the hearing of any one that belonged to the Company, to the utmost of my Remembrance. Besides the Lieutenant and the two Masters, there was not a Person in either Ship skilled enough in Sea-affairs, to have so much as guess'd in what Part of the World he was, without being told.

Here are now two Expressions of mine, utter'd at different Times, in different Places, and to different Persons, and to quite different Purposes, most ingenuously coupled together by the single Particle for, and so wrought up into one terrible Charge against me!

I humbly submit to your Lordships Candour whether, if I had really thought fit to have given the Governor such kind of Assurances, as this Gentleman pretends, it is likely I should have been infatuated to such a degree as to do it in so publick a Manner, and before such Witnesses?

————and in consequence of this Declaration took care, that nothing should be mentioned in the Log-book but what he saw and directed; and said, He would break up all their Boxes who kept Journals, and take their Books and Papers from them————

As there was no such Declaration, there could be no Consequence. The Lieutenant disowns any such Orders of mine about Entries, and I am afraid the Log-book will be thought rather to abound, than to be defective in Particulars. The Charge of taking away Journals, Papers, &c. is absolutely false.

[1] Although Samuel Smith wrote to Middleton on 27 May 1741 (see p. 93 above), explaining the trade goods, Middleton later insisted that he had not seen the letter until he was at the Orkneys, where he decided 'that such things are not allowed in the King's Service'. See Middleton, *Reply*, pp. 78–9.

See Lieutenant's and Master's Answer to Qu.20[1] and the Affidavits.

He also, when he was in Wager River, discountenanced and discouraged any who said it was a Strait and not a River, and that there was a Likelihood of there being a Passage that Way——

I never discountenanced, but, on the contrary, encouraged every one to speak and report according to his Judgment with Freedom; unless giving such Reasons against a Passage as I have laid down before, pag. 2. are to be look'd upon as discouraging; and further I refer to the Lieutenant's Answer to Query 20, and to the several Affidavits of Towns, Von Sobriek, Grant, Cooper.[2]

——*and during the whole Voyage kept all on board him as much in the Dark as he could. If then the Captain had not an Inclination to suppress the Discovery, or at least to conceal it so far, as to make it answer his Purpose with the Company, in order to procure a Reward from them for concealing it; they fearing upon a Discovery of the Passage's being made, that their Right to the Monopoly they at present enjoy might be enquired into, and their Trade laid open; how came he to discourage any on board from making any Enquiry about the Discovery?*——

It has ever been my Endeavours (and was so this Voyage especially) to instruct such as I have found ignorant, and to improve such as had already made some Proficiency, whether in the Navigating Part, taking Observations of all kinds, or computing from them when made. For the Truth of this, I appeal to all the Judges of such Matters who have known me for above these twenty Years together; and I have the Satisfaction to find it acknowledged to your Lordships by the Master, in his Answer to Query 5,[3] and 20;

---

[1] Where Rankin responded: 'I can't say that the Captain discouraged or discountenanced me in making any Discovery, tho' some of the Officers of the Ship are of another Opinion; nor did I ever hear the Captain threaten to take their Books and Papers from them, or give Orders that nothing should be entered in the Logg Book which should give any Hopes of a Passage.' Middleton, *Vindication*, p. 191.

[2] Printed ibid., pp. 141–7.

[3] Where Wilson wrote that Middleton 'never hindered any body from keeping what Account they would, and would always readily instruct any Officer that would ask him, in observing the Latitude, Variation, or any other curious Matter, and shewed several how to keep Journals that had never been at Sea before, and preferred them in the Voyage according to their Merit, tho' he had never seen them before.' Ibid., p. 163.

I further refer to the several Affidavits...and as for what he surmises in relation to the Company, I shall give a full Answer to that by and by.

——and when they apprehended from the Number of Whales at the west End of Wager River,——
A meer Fiction. Before, he says, at twenty Leagues from the Entrance it was full of Whales. To which I answered, That none were seen above Deer Sound, which is but fifteen Leagues within the River. Now he has brought them quite up to the west End, thirty or forty Leagues, though we never saw one there, nor does any Report or Journal make the least mention of any such thing.

——from the Depth of the Water, Breadth of the Strait, Heighth of the Coast, and Rapidity of the Stream, that there was a Prospect of a Passage.
Answered and confuted in Page 16 and 17.

——How came he to say that they were double tongued Rascals,——
I deny that I ever used any such Expression, and should be glad to know whence he had his Intelligence.

——and that he would cane the Lieutenant, broomstick the Master, and lash all the others, for taking upon them to dispute it,——[1]
The Lieutenant in his Answers to Queries 5 and 20, disavows his Knowledge of any such Threatenings; so does the Master, and disbelieves them also in his Answer to Query 5; and the Men swear the same in all their Affidavits. The very Authors of this Forgery have thought it proper to grant, in their Answers to Query 5, that nobody heard any Thing of Threatening but themselves, and I desire to leave it to the Opinion of your Lordships, how far they deserve to be credited.

——And when he, upon Account of their Clamour was under a Necessity of sending up the Lieutenant and Master in a six oar'd Boat, to make

---

[1] These accusations had been levelled by Thompson and Wigate, ibid., pp. 163–4.

further Observations of the Tides, and to know whether the Whales came into the River any other Way,——

I am not conscious that I acted in any respect, so as to give Occasion to Clamour, nor was I sensible of any. My whole Intention of sending the Boat up this last Time, was to try if there could be found any Outlet into the Welcome, besides that wherein we entered. Many Years Experience of the sad and sudden Effects of Cold in this Country, persuaded me that this could be no unreasonable Step towards preserving his Majesty's Ships and Subjects committed to my Care, in case Winter should set in before we could be able to repass the Mouth of the River, at that Time much clogged with Ice; and that this was my principal Motive, will, I humbly presume, appear unquestionable to your Lordships, both from my Order of July 27th to the Lieutenant and Master and from their Report of August 1 at their Return.

——*Why did he limit them to go no further up than he himself had been before, and to come back with the utmost Dispatch that the Nature of the Service would allow of*——

They were not so limited as he alledges. It was a Blunder of my Clerk's to write, as far as Deer Sound in the Order; and I not only told him so at the going off of the Boat; but likewise verbally gave the Lieutenant leave, as himself and the Master both acknowledge in their Answer to Query 3[1] to proceed up as far as he could conveniently, without retarding the Ships from sailing out of the River, because I intended to sail in a few Days: For I own, that for the Reasons mentioned just now, I was much more intent on getting out of the River, than on further prosecuting the Discovery of a Passage within it; even tho' I had entertained the strongest Presumption that there might be one; whereas I had very cogent Inducements to think there was none; and besides; to have sought one against an Ebb, would have been going contrary to my Instructions.

——*And when they exceeded his Orders by about 15 Leagues, and then*

---

[1] Rankin's evidence is crucial on this point as he acknowledged that Middleton 'Verbally consented that I might run up the River or Strait, as far as I could conveniently do, without retarding the Ships from sailing out of the River....' Ibid., p. 159.

reported, that from thence they saw a large Collection of Waters North of them, with many Islands and high bluff Points, with broken Lands on the West Side, as well as on the East, and that they saw a great many black Whales, and did believe there was another Way into the Sea, besides that the Ship came in at, why did he only, from a Bottle of Water's being brackish (which is also disputed) which was taken up near an Inlet where they apprehended there was a fresh Stream, sail directly out of the River, and quit the Discovery on the 4th of August, the only Month in which the Discovery could be best attempted,——

Here he would insinuate again, that Whales were seen 15 Leagues above Deer Sound, whereas the Report sets forth, that it was at Deer Sound on their Return, and no where else that they saw them in that River. The Passage into the Sea, if any, the same Report says they did believe was somewhere on the East Side the River, and not Northward or Westward, as he seems here to pretend: It no where appears that a Bottle of Water was taken up near a fresh Inlet; the Master, in his Answer to Query 1, says, that the Water was positively fresher and fresher as they went higher, and the Affidavits of Towns, Von Sobriek and Grant all set forth expressly, that from 4 Leagues above Deer Sound, to the utmost Heighth the Boat went, the Water, even in the Mid-channel of the River, was but barely brackish, and that the Men all drank of it alongside, instead of Beer. The rest is answered already.

——and leave these Openings, which were then free from Ice, which led towards the South-west, West, and North-west undiscovered?——

If these Openings were left undiscovered, how came he to apprehend there were any such? But not to insist on his Hibernicisms, or other Improprieties of Language, the Lieutenant says in his Report of July 25, that he saw several Openings or Coves on the South Side of the River, but that he could not get near them for Ice.[1] I have said before, that we had made several Attempts to land on the South-west Side, but never could succeed for Ice, till the Day before we left the River, when I landed there myself. I will add here, that when I was myself up with the Boat 4 Leagues above Deer Sound, I also attempted to land on that Side, but could get no further than half Way over.

---

[1] See p. 200 above.

———*and pretend to look for the Passage North-eastward, and after-wards South-eastwards, by his imaginary frozen Strait.*

My Instructions ordered me always to direct my Course so as to meet the Tide of the Flood. I did so here till I could do it no farther, finding my self inclosed in Ice, and embayed by Land. I have proved the Reality of the Frozen Strait in Pages 28 and 35.

———*How came he afterwards, when it was resolved in Council to try the West-side of the Welcome from Cape Dobbs to Brook Cobham, where he had met with a rapid Tide going Northward, and where Fox, Norton, and Scroggs had said there were broken Lands and Inlets, where great Numbers of Whales had been seen, and Norton had assured him that from a Mountain he saw an open Sea leading to the Southward of the West from Whalebone Point: I say, how came he in good Weather, and with easterly Winds, to keep 5 or 6 Leagues to the Eastward of those Head-lands, and to pass from Cape Dobbs to Cape Fullerton in the Night, and afterwards slightly to coast along the Bay to Southward of Cape Fullerton, without any Stop but by lying by in the Night, altho' he saw many Whales as he passed along, never once trying the Heighth or Direction of the Tide, or sending in his Boats to look for any Inlet———.*

That we pass'd from Cape Dobbs to Cape Fullerton in the Afternoon before Sunset, will appear from our Journals, and more particularly from our Logg Books. To his Repetitions of Fox's, Norton's, and Scroggs's Authorities, I would answer, by asking if he thinks we have not confuted their 4 and 5 Fathom Tides by our three Weeks Observations upon the Tides in Wager River? And if he cares not to credit me in this Matter, let him consult his Friend the Lieutenant's Journal. Scroggs, for his Part, asserted at his Return, that there was no going much further than the Whalebone Point, which was his ne ultra, for a Bar of Rocks; tho' we went 60 Leagues beyond it; and 5 Fathom Ebb, we found near the same Place, to be no more than 16 or 18 Feet. What Norton, or, I rightly remember, his Carpenter, advanced about seeing from a high Land within Whalebone Point, an open Sea that stretched away southward of the West, was, in all Probability, either the River Wager, or else some such large fresh Water Lakes, as myself, the Lieutenant, and those that were with us, saw from the Mountains every where about Deer Sound, and likewise on the South Shore of Wager River, the Day I was there, and about Cape Frigid, and in short, wherever we landed in these northern Parts. That it could be no Sea stretching far Westward, has been already made appear from the Account given of the same Norton's and the Indian's Land Voyage, Page 41.[1] The rest has been answered, and I further refer to our Journals, to the Master's Answer to Query 13, and to the several Affidavits of Towns, Von Sobriek, and Grant.

———*notwithstanding the Presumptions that the Whales came only from the Westward;*———
———Answered and contradicted before and disbelieved by the Lieutenant and Master in their Report of August 1.

———*From the Accounts of Fox, Norton, and Scroggs, of its being a broken Land with Inlets*———.
———The Invalidity of their Authorities were shewn just now ———.

———*and the Indians who had informed them, that there was a fine Copper Mine on an Arm of the Sea thereabouts, where they could bring a Vessel to lay her Side to the Place*———.
———Answered.

———*How could he neglect this without some Design, after a Consultation held and agreed to for to search that Coast; the Tides there, by Scroggs, and Fox's Accounts, being very rapid, and high Tides rising from 4 to 5 Fathoms by their Accounts, and yet these Coasts and these Tides never attempted to be known by him; and thus that whole Coast, where the chiefest Presumption was of a Passage, from all former Accounts, as well as the present, was never searched, but only sailed along en passant, with this only Remark in the Journal, 'that he saw the Land from Cape Hope to Brook Cobham, and knew it to be a Mainland', tho' by his Journal he pass'd great Part in the Night, and was at nearest 5 or 6 Leagues from the Head-land to the Eastward; and at the same time owns, there were deep Bays, and many Islands in those Bays.*
Repetitions again repeated, tho' answered again and again; so often, indeed, that I am really ashamed to trouble your Lordships any more, with References to the Answers.

---

[1] Here, p. 293 above.

Why did not the Captain in sailing Northward from Churchill, when he came up with the Head-land in 63°20', off which he had deep Water and strong Tides, and very easy Weather, as he had the whole Voyage, why did he not then, I say, send the Boat ashore to try the Heighth as also the Direction of the Tide, and so try whether there any Openings or Inlets in the Land? For since his getting to 63°55', he saw much Ice on Shore to Northward, he could lose no Time in making a thorough Search there, until the Ice was diminished in the Welcome, that Bay being the principal Place where Fox had discovered so many Whales, and found such high Tides as from 18 to 24 Foot——.

Because, as I have said before, my Instructions directed me, after I came to Carey's Swan's Nest, to steer Northwesterly, so as to fall in with the North-west Land, at Sir Thomas Roe's Welcome, or *ne ultra*, near the Latitude of 65 Degrees North. This Mr. Dobbs knew full well, at a Time when he never had a single Thought that the Coast he here speaks so much of, was worth examining; otherwise surely he would have taken Care that my Instructions should not have been defective in this Point. He is resolved, I find, to ring Changes on Fox, Tides, and Whales in my Ears, without Mercy. Really, my Lords, I can say no more about them than I have said already.

——It was also already observed, that he mistook the Tide of Flood there for the Ebb on Tuesday the 6th of July, at Full Moon; so that he was not so very accurate in observing the Tides as he ought to have been——.
This has been fully answered, and undeniably confuted.

——And a thorough Discovery there at that Time had been safer, as well as more satisfactory, than putting into the Ice to the Northward, until it was more dissolved.
But would it have been consistent with my own Safety to have departed from my Instructions, in quest of a Passage on that Coast, where also it had been given over for so many Years, and after so many Attempts?

Why did he, when the Tide carried him with such Rapidity into the River Wager, get out of the Way of the Tide, to the North-east, instead of the South-west, which was the Side he ought to have endeavoured to discover, and not the North-east Side, unless he apprehended he might discover too much, by going higher up with the Tide; for in case he found

Inlets on the South-west Side, he could not then conceal the Passage from his Officers and Crew———.

When we first entered Wager River, and indeed during the whole three Weeks we were there, as I have said before, we found it impracticable to come near the South-west Shore, except once with the Boat; and were glad at any Rate to get the Ships into some safe Roadstead, as may be seen in our Journals, 13th 14th and 15th of July. The Pink was in the most imminent Danger, being driven up and down by three successive Tides, and several Times carried so close upon Islands, that the Men might have jump'd on Shore, as the Master's and Mate's Journals express more particularly: Nor was the Furnace's Condition much better; for all Hands were forced to be employed in steering her, and fending off the Ice two or three Tides together, whilst she lay at Anchor.

Why did he prevent the Lieutenant's taking along with him from Churchill, one of the Factory's Men, who perfectly understood the Northern Indian Language, who would have been of great Use upon the Discovery, when the Lieutenant told him, he would take all the Blame, in case any Complaint was made of it, since it was for the Good of the Service.

I find the Master has given a very pertinent Answer to this, in his Answer to Query 16.[1] For my own Part, I say, that near two Months before the Northern Indians came down, I did, in the Lieutenant's Hearing, express a Desire of obtaining this Person of the Company, in case none should come that Year, for they sometimes miss. But they arriving at their usual Time, I could only importune the Governor to prevail on two of them, who best knew the Country, and could speak the Language of several Nations, to go along with us; together with a third Indian of their own, who could converse with those others very intelligibly, having travelled with them two Winters, and understood English very well besides. To procure this Favour, I found it requisite to

---

[1] Wilson wrote: 'I do not remember that the Lieutenant did press the Captain to take another Man; but if he did so, in my Opinion, the Captain did much better in getting two northern Indians, that pretended to know the Country, and speak the Languages of several Nations; and also a third Indian from the Factory, who could converse with these two northern Indians, he having travelled with them several Winters before, and understood English besides.' Ibid., p. 185.

make the Governor very considerable Presents, who exacted also a strict Promise from me, that I would return the two Northern Indians ashore, somewhere about Whale Cove or Brook Cobham, laden with Goods, and furnish'd with Arms for their Defence. As for the other Indian, whom I had known from a Boy, I had leave both from the Governor and his Parents to bring him home to England, if I thought fit; which I did, and he soon after died of the Small-pox.[1] Now, had I permitted the Lieutenant to have impressed that other Man, or had otherwise attempted to take him away by Force, I should have acted contrary to my Instructions, which required me expressly, not to give any Disturbance to the Ships or Sloops of the Hudson's Bay Company; for that Man was Linguist to one of their Sloops for the Northern Trade: Besides, I could not have promised myself any Service from one thus compulsively dragged away against his Inclination.

Query, Whether the Northern Indians on board him did not point out to go into the Western Shore, between 62° and 64° Degrees, before he was inclosed in the Ice, which was a strong Presumption that there was an Inlet thereabouts?———
I absolutely deny the Truth of what is insinuated in this Query.

Why did he, when the Indians who were beginning to understand and speak the English Language, were desirous of coming to England, put them ashore against their Inclinations, in a very indifferent Boat, on an Island some Leagues from the Main, at a great Distance from their Country, unless to prevent their giving an Account of what they knew in relation to that Country and Strait, in case they came to speak the English Tongue?
They expressed no Desire of seeing England that I know of; and if they had, what would have excused me to the Governor, or to myself, for bringing them hither; when, as I had observed just now, I had so solemnly engaged to land them somewhere about Whale-Cove, or Brook Cobham. The rest is contradicted by the

---

[1] This was 'Scooth'. See p. 219 above.

Master's Answer to Query 18, and by the several Affidavits of Towns, Grant, and Cooper.[1]

Why did he, when employed by the Government in so useful a Discovery, after having been offered £5000 from the Company to quit the King's Service, or to search for the Passage in Davis's Straits, or any other Place, where it was unlikely to find it, enter into an Agreement, or at least accept of an Offer made by Sir Bibye Lake their Governor, of giving him two Years Salary, not to do any thing to interfere with their Trade, and upon this gave an Order, under severe Penalties, that none of his Crew should have the least Intercourse or Trade with the Natives; and whether upon doing this, and concealing the Passage, he might not have had greater Expectation from the Company; and whether, upon his Return, his sending Letters immediately to the Company, and desiring that none of his People should communicate any thing about the Voyage or Discovery for some time, and even to conceal all material Articles from the Gentleman who projected the Voyage, until he forced it out of him from the Observations from his Journal, after keeping it from him for three Months, and by repeated Letters, assuring him, the whole was impracticable, whether this, I say, did not look like a Design to make his own Terms with the Company, before he would publish his Journal; for if all he had in view was only the two Years Salary, not to damnify their Trade, and this had only a Reference to his Crews not trading with the Natives, the revealing what he knew concerning the Passage and Voyage, would have been of no Detriment to him with the Company.

This last Paragraph contains a Repetition, after his usual manner, of sundry Matters which he had dwelt long enough upon before; particularly Complaints of my being offered £5000 from the Company to quit the King's Service, or at least of accepting

---

[1] There is, once again, a direct conflict of evidence over this episode. Wilson wrote that one of the Northern Indians seemed 'somewhat dejected' at departing the ship, but that their boat was in good condition and that 'They knew their Way home very well, as they told us, and were sufficiently fortified against all the Men in the Country, having Firearms well stocked with Ammunition, and more of every Thing than they could well carry.' Thompson painted a very different picture, of the Indians being given 'an old leaky boat' which they did not know how to handle. So great was their fear of the Eskimos, he wrote, that 'they were actually forced over the Ship side into the Boat, and towed ashore upon Marble Island...and there left.' Ibid., pp. 188–9. Moor's journal entry for 15 August 1742 is of interest: 'Sent the two Northn. Indians and gave them our Yaul and everything else, that any of the two Ships Companys, cou'd think wou'd be of any Service to them.' Adm 51/290, pt IX.

two Years Salary, not to do any thing to interfere with their Trade; all which I have fully answered before, and I hope to your Lordships Satisfaction. But now the Snake in the Grass begins to shew himself; for he sums up all with this grand Complaint, that Upon this I gave an Order, under severe Penalties, that none of my Crew should have the least Intercourse, or trade with the Natives. My Lords, I have already said, I was bound in Duty and Gratitude to do this, whether the Company rewarded me or not. Permit me here, my Lords, to recriminate in my Turn, and observe that by this means the Gentleman who projected the Voyage, as he affects to stile himself, as well as his Agents on board, met with no small Disappointment. Had I allow'd them Liberty to infringe the Company's Rights, and make such Depredations for their private Benefit, as they seem'd to intend, I am persuaded I should have heard none of these Complaints so often reiterated; nothing of my Friendship to the Company; of Rewards and Bribes from the Company; of endeavouring to make my own Terms with the Company; of great Expectations from the Company; all of which are Allegations newly trump'd up, and manifestly the Effects of Spleen and Disappointment. Does not this shew, that the Projector of the Voyage had the Advantages of a clandestine Trade as much or more at heart, than the publick Utility of a Discovery? Whence otherwise should arise his Endeavours to stigmatize the Company, and dissolve their Charter? Whence his unwearied Application to prejudice my unblemish'd Character with your Lordships, or the Publick? Whence his Project of a new Settlement, and a further Prosecution of the Discovery, but to intrust it with such as should not baulk his Expectation in other Matters?

16. James Isham to Captain Middleton. Churchill River, 6 August 1743.[1]

SIR,

I Received yours with Pleasure,[2] and am sorry to hear those two base Men shou'd offer such Violence. Yes, was I in England I

---

[1] Middleton, *Reply*, p. 14.

[2] Middleton's letter, which has not survived, must have been sent to Isham on the Company ship bound for Churchill that spring, just as the proceedings against Middleton were taking shape.

cou'd take my Oath that those two Men, Wygate and Thompson, were us'd by you, while here, better than any Men belonging to you, and never shou'd have thought they wou'd avouch such false and abominable Scandal; and I do not doubt but you may clear all Objections they may lay to your Charge where God and Truth is on your Side. One northern Indian return'd, but cou'd give no Account of the other saying he was not put a Shore with him, by which I imagine he killed his Consort.[1] He cou'd give no Account of any Rivers, &c. going directly Inland as soon as a Shore. I hope you'll continue your Health: As for my part I have sent to return Home, but doubt shall not enjoy that Happiness, having been sixty Days this Winter not able to go out of the Room by the Lameness in my Thigh, and a Fever that remains very violent.[2] Poor Trade. Pray my Service to all Friends, hoping you'll accept the same, and I conclude

Your Well-wisher and
Humble Servant,
J. Isham.

17. Arthur Dobbs to Judge Ward, 21 February 1743 (OS).[3]

These affairs at present stop all my Schemes tho' I shan't give them up this fortnight, by which Time I hope things will blow over or come to a crisis[4] that I may know how to act, proceed or delay. My 2d Book[5] is now publishd which I have dedicated and presented to his Majesty and have distributed them among all our Grandees, and I have the Satisfaction that all who have lookd into them approve of what I am doing, and believe there

---

[1] Probably killed for his trade goods, Isham told the Company. HBC A 11/13, f. 81. The next year Isham wrote again to Middleton telling him that both Indians had survived. Middleton, *Forgery Detected*, pp. 32–3.

[2] Isham was confined to the fort from 23 December 1742 to 1 February 1743. It was, he entered in the factory journal, 'a Dismal House for a Sick man, by the Continual Smoak Occasioned by the Chimneys'; but it seems to have been during this time that he set down on paper his 'Observations on Hudsons Bay'. See Rich and Johnson, *Isham's Observations*, p. 319.

[3] Ward Papers: D 2092/1/6/65.

[4] Almost certainly a reference to the imminence of war with France. Within days of this letter an invasion scare swept the country with the appearance of the Brest fleet off Dungeness, and in March the two countries declared war.

[5] *An Account of the Countries adjoining to Hudson's Bay.*

is a Passage and the Company are faulty and M——n a Rogue. I have sent a Parcell of my Remarks upon M——ns defence[1] in the ship gone for Dublin in which is one for you, and I have sent by Cornet Adams who goes in a day or two for Ireland my 2d Book for you which may perhaps overtake you before you go Circuit, wherein the Passage will appear in a stronger light than what you have yet seen.

18. Petition of Captain Middleton to the Lords Commissioners of the Admiralty [January 1745].[2]

That Your Petitioner being sent to search out a North West Passage to the Western American Ocean, he proceeded on, and in the said Voyage, according to his Instructions, but finding, by Experience the Hopes of such a Passage vain, after having lost a Number of his Men, by the Severity of the Climate, and many more being disabled and incapable of doing their Duty, he returned and gave an Account to this honbl Board of his Proceedings.

That soon after, your Petitioner was taxed with Misconduct, and several Witnesses were examined before this Honble Board with Relation to the said Voyage, and their Lordships were of Opinion that the Accuser had not made Good any One Article of his Charge.

That Notwithstanding such their Lordships' Opinion the Accuser attack'd your Petitioner in a printed Pamphlet to which he reply'd, and was permitted by this honble Board to dedicate the said Reply to their Lordships; to which he begged Leave to referr.[3]

That his Antagonist, imposed upon by too great a Confidence in his Informers, had suggested to the Publick many Falsities of a heinous Nature, and to support his Charge of your Petitioner's Misconduct, had publish'd a downright Forgery, tho' possibly Ignorant of it's being such.

---

[1] Clearly, Dobbs's *Remarks upon Capt. Middleton's Defence*, London, 1744.

[2] Adm 1/2099: undated, but received 3 Jan 1744 (OS).

[3] All this was undoubtedly true, but the fact remained that despite the wartime shortage of capable officers, Middleton had not been employed since his return from Hudson Bay in 1742. Only in June 1745 was he offered a command once more, of the *Shark* sloop.

That this Paper War has cost Your Petitioner upwards of Two hundred Pounds to defend his Character.

That he is informed, notwithstanding all he has written in his Own Defence; Notwithstanding he has exposed the unfair Methods pursued to ruin him, that his Antagonist is preparing afresh to attack his Reputation,[1] the Defence of which he will never abandon tho' to the undoing his Family.

Wherefore

To prevent this Misfortune and as he was sent out at the Expence of the Public, that it may receive Satisfaction with regard to the said Voyage.

Your Petitioner humbly prays that he may be brought to a Tryal; that his Conduct during the said Voyage, may be examin'd into before Your Lordships, or before such competent Judges as your Lordships shall think fit to appoint; and on such examination be either punished with Infamy, or honourably acquitted, and recompenced the Loss he has sustained in quitting an Employ of Eight hundred a Year, by which he has not only entirely lost that Business but upwards of Three Thousand Pounds, to enter into the Service of his Country.

19. Arthur Dobbs to Thomas Corbett, 11 January 1744 (OS).[2]

I have your Favour of the 8th acquainting me that the Lords Commissioners of the Admiralty have been petitioned by Captain Christopher Middleton to have his Conduct during his late Voyage to discover the North West Passage enquired into, and Desiring to know if I had any Charge and what to Exhibit and what witnesses I wou'd have to appeal against him.

I must Beg leave to Inform their Lordships that I never intended to prosecute Captain Middleton criminally at my private Expence. If their Lordships wou'd have him prosecuted at the publick Expence, I shall give them all the Aid and Assistance I can in collecting and bringing Evidence before whatever Court Martial they shall please to appoint, and have no Doubt but it

---

[1] A reference to Dobbs's forthcoming *Reply to Capt. Middleton's Answer.*
[2] Adm 1/2099, 11 Jan 1744 (OS). Several words are missing because of a tear in the page; the editors' suggestions are in square brackets.

shall [find] that he hath been Guilty of great Misconduct and Negligence [in not] prosecuting the Discovery, and that he hath misrepresented [Soundings?], Tides, Straits &c. But as their Lordships Intentions [are to] have Justice Equally done to the publick and Captain [Middleton] I must beg leave to Observe, that the Captain pressing for [a Trial] at this critical Time, after having declin'd it near a Year and [nine] Months, only having desired leave of their Lordships of the Admiralty to appeal to the publick in print, is only intended to skreen himself when he knows several material witnesses are absent for George Axx the Gunner is gone in the Aldborough to Carolina, Hodgson the Carpenter is abroad in the Merchants Service, Mr Wigate the late Clerk is under Sailing Orders aboard Captain Innis for the West Indies. Alexander Morrison, John Armount and Abraham Humble, not known where they are, all of whom by my Remarks in print appear to be material Witnesses; Mr Wilson the late Master and John Guy are in the Captains power to be produced or not as it shall serve his purpose, and there are none here that I know of except the Lieut., Surgeon, and Captain Moor late Master of the Discovery pink, who tho' when he was called upon to answer the Queries he cou'd not Justify his Kinsman Captain Middleton yet I apprehend wou'd unwillingly be brought against him as an Evidence in a Criminal prosecution. So that I am persuaded their Lordships wont order the time of Tryal until these Material Witnesses for the Crown or at least a reasonable number of them may be collected and produced. But I shall immediately enquire if any of these or what others can be produced, and shall lose no time in giving the Lordships notice of it.

Since Captain Middleton at his own Request hath appeal'd to the Publick in print, which obliged me to Reply to him, and he hath since Reply'd to my Remarks, and in a Subsequent pamphlet hath attack'd my Character in the grossest manner I believe their Lordships will Indulge me in Answering him, which he is now so solicitous to prevent, by moving for a Tryal to prevent further altercations in print, when he knows I have as full Answers which must Expose him in the press, and as in these several Books is contain'd the full Charges against him and his Defense, when the Court Martial is appointed I hope their Lordships will Referr these several Books and the Reasonings in them to their Consideration, and then let them Examine the several Witnesses how far they support the Charges against him or appear in his Defense, and upon their Report their Lordships be capable of Judging whether his Conduct hath been praise worthy or blamable, and whether the Facts he affirms are true or false.[1]

[1] In the margin of the letter Corbett scribbled a laconic 'nothing done upon'.

BIBLIOGRAPHY

I. MANUSCRIPT SOURCES

I.1. **Public Record Office**

I.1.1. *Admiralty*
The Adm 51/ series contains the journals of Captain Christopher Middleton for the *Furnace* (Adm 51/379, I–III, 1741–2) and William Moor for the *Discovery* (Adm 51/290, X, 1741–2). Middleton's letters from 1741 to 1747 are in Captains' Letters, Adm 1/2099, 2100, 2105. Correspondence, instructions and other papers relating to the expedition and its aftermath are in Adm 2/57 (Orders and Instructions, 1741–2); Adm 2/202 (Lords of Admiralty: Out-Letters, 1740–2); Adm 2/473, 479, 480 (Secretary of the Admiralty: Out-Letters, 1741–3); Adm 3/45, 47 (Admiralty Board Minutes, 1740–44).

I.1.2. *State Papers*
Documents relating to the 1741–2 expedition are in SP Dom.42/81 (1726–42) and SP Dom.43/103 (1741).

I.2. **National Maritime Museum**

ADM L/F/109 is Lieutenant John Rankin's log of the *Furnace* (1741–2). ADM/B/114 (Navy Board Letters, 1741) has correspondence about the preparations for the discovery expedition.

I.3. **Hudson's Bay Company Archives, Provincial Archives of Manitoba**

A 1/35 (Minute Book, 1740–3), A 2/1 (General Court Minute Book, 1690–1741), and A 1/122 (Rough Minute Book, 1731–7) contain the Company's reaction to the Middleton discovery expedition. A 6/5 (Correspondence Book Outwards, 1727–37) and A 6/6 (1737–41) have the annual letters and instructions to the Company posts, and those to Churchill are particularly relevant to Middleton's expedition. A 11/13 (Inward Correspondence from Churchill, 1723–63) contains letters from the factors about the Company discovery expeditions of the period, as well as James Isham's letters about Middleton's expedition and its wintering at Churchill. The Churchill journals are in the B 42/a/ series, in which Isham's journal for 1741–2 (B 42/a/23) is particularly revealing. The York journals (B 239/a/) also have some material on the Company's northern expeditions. E 18/1 contains, inter alia, two copies of the Dobbs memorial of 1733 (for the location of other copies of the memorial see p. 9 n. 1).

I.4. **Public Record Office of Northern Ireland**

D.2092/ contains eighteen letters written by Arthur Dobbs to Judge Michael Ward between 1734 and 1748, most of which refer in frank, sometimes unguarded, terms to his attempts to find a Northwest Passage.

II. PRINTED SOURCES

Anon., *An Account of Several Late Voyages & Discoveries to the South and North, Towards the Streights of Magellan, the South Seas...by Sir John Narborough, Captain Jasmen Tasman, Captain John Wood*, London, 1694.

Barrow, John, ed., *The Geography of Hudson's Bay: Being the Remarks of Captain W. Coats in many voyages to that locality, between the years 1727 and 1751*, London, Hakluyt Society, 1852.

Blake, E. V., ed., *Arctic Experiences: containing Capt. George E. Tyson's Wonderful Drift on the Ice-floe, a History of the Polaris Expedition, the Cruise of the Tigris and Rescue of the Polaris Survivors*, New York, 1874.

Christy, Miller, ed., *The Voyages of Captain Luke Foxe...and Captain*

Thomas James...in search of a north-west passage, in 1631–32, London, Hakluyt Society, 1894.

Clerk of the *California* [T. S. Drage], *An Account of a Voyage for the Discovery of a North-West Passage by Hudson's Streights, to the Western and Southern Ocean of America,* 2 vols, London, 1748–9.

Coxe, Daniel, *An Account of the English Province of Carolana,* London, 1722.

Davies, K. G., and Johnson, A. M., eds, *Letters from Hudson Bay 1703–40,* London, Hudson's Bay Record Society, 1965.

Dobbs, Arthur, *Remarks upon Capt. Middleton's Defence....,* London, 1744.

An Account of the Countries adjoining to Hudson's Bay, In the North-West Part of America, London, 1744.

A Reply to Capt. Middleton's Answer...., London, 1745.

Doughty, A. G. and Martin C., eds, *The Kelsey Papers,* Ottawa, 1929.

Douglas, R. and Wallace, J. N., eds, *Twenty Years of York Factory 1694–1714. Jérémie's Account of Hudson Bay and Strait,* Ottawa, 1926

Ellis, Henry, *A Voyage to Hudson's Bay by the Dobbs Galley and California, In the Years 1746 and 1747, For Discovering a North West Passage,* London, 1748.

Halley, Edmond, 'The True Theory of the Tides, Extracted from that Admired Treatise of Mr Isaac Newton, Intituled, *Philosophiae naturalis principia mathematica*', *Philosophical Transactions,* London, XIX (1697), pp. 445–57.

Hearne, Samuel, *A Journey from Prince of Wales's Fort in Hudson's Bay to the Northern Ocean, Undertaken by order of the Hudson's Bay Company, for the discovery of Copper Mines, a NorthWest Passage &c. In the Years 1769, 1770, 1771, and 1772,* London, 1795.

Kenney, J. F., ed., *The Founding of Churchill Being the Journal of Captain James Knight, Governor-in-Chief in Hudson Bay, from the 14th of July to the 13th of September, 1717,* Toronto, 1932.

Lahontan, Louis Armand de Lom d'Arce, Baron de, *New Voyages to North America,* London, 1703.

Markham, A. H., ed., *The Voyages and Works of John Davis,* London, Hakluyt Society, 1880.

Markham, C. R., ed., *The Voyages of William Baffin*, London, Hakluyt Society, 1881.

Middleton, Christopher, 'New and Exact TABLE Collected from several Observations, taken in four Voyages to *Hudson's Bay*...Shewing the Variation of the *Magnetical Needle*... from the Years 1721, to 1725....', *Philosophical Transactions*, XXXIV, 73–6, London, 1726–7.

'Captain Middleton's Account of the Extraordinary Degrees and Surprizing Effects of COLD in *Hudson's-Bay, North America*....', ibid., XLII, 157–71, London, 1742–3.

A Vindication of the Conduct of Captain Christopher Middleton...., London, 1743.

A Reply to the Remarks of Arthur Dobbs...., London 1744.

Forgery Detected...., London, 1744.

A Reply to Mr. Dobbs's Answer to a Pamphlet, entitled, Forgery Detected, London, 1745.

A Rejoinder to Mr. Dobbs's Reply to Captain Middleton...., London, 1745.

Oldmixon, John, *The British Empire in America*, 2nd edn, 2 vols, London, 1741.

Parry, W. E., *Journal of a Second Voyage for the Discovery of a North-West Passage from the Atlantic to the Pacific*, London, 1824.

Purchas, Samuel, *Hakluytus Posthumus or Purchas His Pilgrimes*, XIV, Hakluyt Society, Glasgow, 1906.

Report from the Committee Appointed to Inquire into the State and Conditions of the Countries Adjoining to Hudson's Bay, and of the Trade carried on there, London, 1749.

Rich, E. E. and Johnson, A. M., eds, *James Isham's Observations on Hudsons Bay, 1743 and Notes and Observations on a Book entitled* A Voyage to Hudsons Bay in the Dobbs Galley, 1749, Champlain Society, Toronto, and Hudson's Bay Record Society, London, 1949.

Robson, Joseph, *An Account of Six Years Residence in Hudson's-Bay, From 1733 to 1736, and 1744 to 1747*, London, 1752.

III. SECONDARY WORKS

Banfield, A. W. F., *The Mammals of Canada*, Toronto, 1974.

Barr, William, 'From Wager Bay to the Hebrides: the Duties of an Eighteenth-Century Bomb Vessel', *The Musk-Ox*, No. 16, 1975, pp. 31–51.

'The Forgotten Explorer, Christopher Middleton and the Northwest Passage', *The Beaver*, 70, 4, 1990, pp. 34–42.

Beals, C. S., ed., *Science, History and Hudson Bay*, 2 vols, Ottawa, 1968.

Clarke, Desmond, *Arthur Dobbs Esquire 1689–1765 Surveyor-General of Ireland, Prospector and Governor of North Carolina*, London, 1958.

Davies, K. G., 'Henry Kelsey', *Dictionary of Candian Biography*, Vol II, 1701 to 1740, Toronto and Quebec, 1969 (hereafter *DCB*, II), pp. 307–15.

Dodge, E. S., 'James Knight', *DCB*, II, pp. 318–20.

Geiger, John and Beattie, Owen, *Dead Silence: The Greatest Mystery in Arctic Discovery*, London, 1993.

Godfrey, W. E., *The Birds of Canada*, Ottawa, 1966.

Goodwin, Peter, *The Bomb Vessel* Granado *1742*, Annapolis, 1989.

Helm, June, ed., *Handbook of North American Indians*, Vol 6, *Subarctic*, Washington, DC, 1981.

Howse, Derek and Sanderson, Michael, *The Sea Chart*, Newton Abbot, 1973.

Jack-Hinton, C., *The Search for the Islands of Solomon, 1567–1830*, Oxford, 1962.

Johnson, Alice M., 'John Fullartine', *DCB*, II, pp. 231–3.

'Richard Norton', *Dictionary of Canadian Biography*, Vol III, 1741 to 1770, Toronto and Quebec, 1974 (hereafter *DCB*, III), pp. 489–90.

May, W. E., *A History of Marine Navigation*, Henley-on-Thames, 1973.

Montgomery, Margaret, 'Does the Bay Freeze?', *The Beaver*, Outfit 282, June 1951, pp. 12–15.

Neatby, L. S., 'James Napper', *DCB*, II, p. 493.

Rich, E. E., *The History of the Hudson's Bay Company 1670–1870*, Hudson's Bay Record Society, London, 1958–9.

'James Isham', *DCB*, III, pp. 301–4.

Ruggles, Richard I., *A Country So Interesting: The Hudson's Bay Company and Two Centuries of Mapping 1670–1870*, Montreal, 1991.

Taylor, E. G. R., *The Mathematical Practitioners of Hanoverian England*, Cambridge, 1966.

Taylor, E. G. R. and Richey, M. W., *The Geometrical Seaman*, Cambridge, 1962.

Tushingham, A. M., 'Observations of Postglacial Uplift at Churchill, Manitoba', *Canadian Journal of Earth Sciences*, 29, 1992, pp. 2418–2425.

Williams, Glyndwr, *The British Search for the Northwest Passage in the Eighteenth Century*, London, 1962.

  'William Coats', *DCB*, III, pp. 127–8.

  'Christopher Middleton', ibid., pp. 446–50.

  'William Moor', ibid., pp. 471–2.

  'John Rankin', ibid., p. 544.

  'John Scroggs', *DCB*, II, p. 604.

  'George Spurrell', *DCB*, III, p. 598.

  'Edward Thompson', ibid., pp. 624–5.

  'John Wigate', ibid., p. 663.

Williams, Glyndwr and Frost, Alan, eds, *Terra Australis to Australia*, Melbourne, 1988.

INDEX

The names of Capes, Indians, Ships are grouped under those headings.
The Roman numerals given immediately after the names of geographical
and other sites refer to the map or maps in the volume where those sites
can be located.

Cibola, 34 n.1
Clerk of the *California*, and the Scroggs voyage, 58 n.1, n.2, 59 n.2, n.3, 60 n.2
'Clerk, the' (of *Furnace*), *see* Wigate, John
clothes, winter, 121, 130 n.3, 133 n.1, 135, 135 n.1, n.2, 136 n.2, 147, 228
Coats Island (**III**), 2, 12 n.7, 101, 114 n.2
Coats, Captain William, 40, 40 n.3, 42 n.4, 45 n.4, 69, 69 n.2, 108, 244, 248
'Company Land', 33 n.1
compass: azimuth, 78, 78 n.6; crown, 79, 79 n.1 *see also* variation, magnetic
Conway, Francis Seymour, 2nd baron, 55, 55 n.4, 56–7, 65
Cooper, Thomas, 300, 309
Copley, Sir Godley, his gold medal awarded to Middleton, 237, 239, 243 n.4
copper, 27, 27 n.2; copper mine, 58–9, 293–4
Coppermine River, 59 n.1, 293
Corbett, Thomas, 76 n.1, 91, 220–21, 271–2, 313–15, 315 n.1
councils, on Middleton expedition, 89, 89 n.1; (31 July 1741), 101, 115, 182; (21 March 1742), 156, 159 n.2; (12 July 1742), 192–3; (8 August 1742), 210–11
'country distemper', 147–9 *see also* pleurisy
Coxon, John, 88 n.1
'Coxton, Captain', 88, 88 n.1 *see* Coxon, John
Cumberland Inlet (Bay, Sound), 25, 253, 256
'Cumberland Isles', 253
current log, *see* tides

Daly Bay, 59 n.2, location of, 213 n.4
Davis Strait, 2, 12, 19, 19 n.1, 47, 179, 233, 256, 296–7
Davis, John, voyage (1586), 19, 253
'declination', *see* variation, magnetic
deer, 59, 150, 197, 197 n.3, 198–9, 199 n.1, 203, 214, 223, 226 *see also* caribou; deer skins, 135, 222, 228
Deer Sound (Douglas Harbour) (**V**), 106, 197, 197 n.2, 199–201, 203–

4, 265–8, 274, 276–7, 281–2, 295–6, 301, 303–4
Deptford, dock, 76, 78 n.2;
Descartes, René, 229
Devonshire, William Cavendish, 4th Duke, 90
Digges Island, *see* Cape Digges,
Dobbs, Arthur, x; his 'Memorial', 1–4, 9–36, 56, 56 n.2, 57, 65–6; different versions, 9 n.1; contacts with Hudson's Bay Company, 4–8, 36–9, 44–7, 73; contacts with Middleton, 6–8, 36–8, 42–4, 47–8, 51–62, 65–8; contacts with Wager, 49–50, 55–6; threat to HBC, 72, 239, 241, 245–8; relationship with Samuel Smith, 93, 93 n.3; cape named after, 192, 217, 223; further correspondence with Middleton: during expedition, 220; after expedition, 251–9, 261–8; campaign against Middleton, 239–45, 270–2; continuing belief in Northwest Passage, 241; correspondence with Admiralty, 240–41, 313–15; his publications against Middleton, 244, 312, 312 n.1, 313, 313 n.1, 314; organises new expedition, 243, 245, 248; his *Account of Hudson's Bay*, 245–6, 254 n.2, 311, 311 n.5; hopes to dissolve Hudson's Bay Company, 254, 254 n.1, 257, 263, 266, 310; his 'Objections' to Middleton's conduct, 273–310; refuses to prosecute Middleton privately, 313–14
Drage, T.S., *see* Clerk of the *California*
ducks, 59, 126, 198, 214
Dutch, explorations in North Pacific, 33 n.1

East Greenland Current, 12 n.4
East Main, the (**IX**), 258
Elton, John, 141 n.2, *see also* quadrant
England, Jonathan, 173 n.5
Eskimo, Eskimaux, Eskemoe *see* Inuit
Eskimo Point (**VII**), 118, 244
Exelby, John, 220 n.3

fish, fishing, at Churchill, 142, 143 n.2, 151, 154, 225–6, 226 n.1, 228
Fisher Strait, 3